THE REFUGE

THE REFUGE
Anchoring the Soul in God

The Collected Works of St Ignatius (Brianchaninov)—Volume 2

by Bishop Ignatius (Brianchaninov)

Translated from the Russian by Nicholas Kotar

Holy Trinity Publications
The Printshop of St Job of Pochaev
Holy Trinity Monastery
Jordanville, New York
2019

Printed with the blessing of His Eminence,
Metropolitan Hilarion First Hierarch
of the Russian Orthodox Church Outside of Russia

The Refuge—Anchoring the Soul in God
© 2019 Holy Trinity Monastery

PRINTSHOP OF
SAINT JOB OF POCHAEV

An imprint of

HOLY TRINITY PUBLICATIONS
Holy Trinity Monastery
Jordanville, New York 13361-0036
www.holytrinitypublications.com

ISBN: 978-0-88465-429-2 (paperback)
ISBN: 978-0-88465-432-2 (Epub)
ISBN: 978-0-88465-433-9 (Mobipocket)

Library of Congress Control Number 2019940251

Series Cover Design: Aubrey Harper—behance.net/aubreyharper
Image: Mikhail Nesterov, The Chapel of St Alexander Nevsky in
Abastumani, oil, 1900. Bashkir State Art Museum.
Scan: Holy Trinity Publications, Jordanville, New York.

Reprinting 2025
All rights reserved.
Printed in the United States of America
Versa Press Inc. 1465 Spring Bay Road, East Peoria, IL, 61611
versapress.com

Contents

Foreword

We are pleased to continue our publication of the first complete English translation of the Collected Works of St Ignatius Brianchaninov. You have in your hand what is the second volume in the Russian original, that we have entitled *The Refuge: Anchoring the Soul in God.*

St Ignatius reminds us that in much of human existence a refuge can be a place of "boredom and emptiness of soul." But when we take the Lord as our refuge even the most simple of habitations can be transformed into a place of inner stillness and peace, where the heart is fully opened to the embrace of God's love. At the heart of this place is prayer, "a refuge of God's great mercy to the human race." Remaining in this refuge of prayer God in His own time will give healing to the sinner and He will lead them to salvation.

Throughout this work St Ignatius weaves together meditations on Scripture (especially the Psalms) and amplifies these with the wisdom of many Christian saints of the first millennium, in particular the ascetical writings of St John of the Ladder, St Macarius the Great, and St Isaac the Syrian. It is an active exhortation for us to reacquire the original nobility with which God fashioned us.

May reading this volume be a source of hope, "an anchor of the soul, both sure and steadfast, and which enters the Presence behind the veil" (Heb 6:19).

Holy Trinity Monastery
Pascha 2019

PART I

CHAPTER I

Blessed Is the Man (Psalm 1)

The God-inspired Psalmist sings "Blessed is the man . . ." striking the resonant strings.

When the noise of the world deafened me, I could not listen to him. Now, in the silence of solitude, I begin to hear the mystical singer. Both his music and his song become clearer to me. It is as if a new sense opens up inside me, an ability to listen and understand him. I sense in his music a fresh feeling, in his words a new meaning—as wondrous as God's wisdom.

Saul! Stop raging! May the evil spirit abandon you for a time! This is what the holy David sings, strumming the sonorous strings.

I call Saul to mind, for my mind is disturbed as was Saul, agitated by thoughts suggested by the prince of this world. It—my mind—was established by God at the beginning of the kingdom of Israel—that is, the creation and redemption of mankind—as a king, a lord of soul and body. By disobeying God, by violating the commandments of God, by breaking union with God, my mind deprived itself of dignity and grace. The powers of the soul and body do not submit to it; it is under the influence of the evil spirits.

Holy David sings and declaims words from heaven. The strain of his psaltery is the music of heaven! The subject of his hymn is the blessedness of man.

Brothers, let us listen to the divine doctrine set forth in this divine hymn. Let us hearken to the words; let us listen to the music by which heaven speaks, cries out to us.

You who seek happiness, who run after pleasures, who thirst for delights! Come and hear the holy song; come and listen to the salvific teaching. How much longer will you rush about, scouring the valleys and mountains, prowling over impassable deserts and wilds? How much longer will you torture yourselves with constant, futile toil, unrewarded by any fruits, any lasting acquisitions? Incline your humble ear, and hear what the Holy Spirit says through the mouth of David concerning human blessedness, toward which all people strive, for which all mankind hungers.

Let everything fall silent around me! Let my very thoughts fall silent within me! Keep silent, my heart! Let reverential attention alone live and act within me! Let holy impressions and thoughts enter the soul, guided by holy attention!

David was a king, and yet he did not say that the throne of kings is the throne of human blessedness.

David was a commander of armies and a hero in battle; from youth to old age he contended with foreigners in bloody carnage. How many battles he fought! How many victories he won! He extended his kingdom from the banks of the Euphrates to the banks of the Jordan. And yet he did not say that human blessedness is found in the glory of the victor and conqueror.

David had all possible earthly consolation, and yet he did not acknowledge any of them to lead to human blessedness.

When David was a young man, when his work was to shepherd the sheep of his father Jesse, suddenly, by the command of God, the prophet Samuel came and anointed the lowly shepherd as the king of the nation of Israel. And yet David did not call the hour of his anointing an hour of blessedness.

David spent his childhood years in a wild desert. There, his muscles began to feel the valor of a warrior's strength. Without weapons, with his hands alone, he flung himself at a lion and a bear, and he choked the life out of them. There, his soul began to be moved, filled with heavenly inspiration. The hands that defeated the lion and the bear wrote the Psalter, strummed the strings, pulled taut and attuned by the action of the Spirit, and outflowed harmonious, pleasing, spiritual, wise music. This music resonated far across times, centuries, and millennia. It was repeated and is repeated by countless voices; it glorified the name of David to all the ends of the earth, in all the ages of Christian history. And yet David did not say that life in the desert, a life full of miraculous works and inspiration, was human blessedness.

"Blessed is the man," in whatever place, in whatever calling, in whatever social status or order he may be, "that hath not walked in the council of the ungodly, nor stood in the way of sinners, and hath not sat in the seat of the scornful" (Ps 1:1).

"Blessed is the man" who keeps himself from sin, who deflects sin away from himself, whatever form it takes, in whatever garment it chooses to appear before him, whether in an iniquitous deed, or a thought that advises lawlessness, or a feeling that brings the pleasure and intoxication of sin.

If a weak woman deflects sin from herself with firm courage, then she is the blessed man praised by David.

The participants of this blessedness, those of spiritual maturity in Christ, include youths and children who have resisted sin. The just God is no respecter of persons.

Blessed is the man whose entire will is in the keeping of God's law (see Ps 1:2). Blessed is the heart that has ripened in the knowledge of God's will, that has seen "that the Lord is good" (Ps 33:9), that has acquired this vision by tasting of the commandments of the Lord, and that has united its will with the will of the Lord. Such a heart is the blessed man. Blessed is the heart that is afire with divine zeal! Blessed is the heart that burns with the insatiable desire to do the will of God! Blessed is the heart that sweetly suffers beyond all endurance with the love of God! Such a heart is the place, home, bridal chamber, and throne of blessedness!

From the early morning, the eagle sits on the tip of a high crag. Its sparking eyes hungrily seek out prey. It rises into the blue sky, swims in the wide expanse on extended wings, and seeks its prey. And when it finds its prey, it becomes an arrow, a lightning bolt as it attacks; then it rises like an arrow again with its prey and disappears. Once the chicks are fed, the eagle again is on watch, either on the cliff or in the sky. Similar to this is the heart that is infected with the wound of incurable love of the commandments of God! In this love is blessedness. The commandments are not merely found in the doing. Within them is hidden, and through them is revealed, spiritual wisdom. The prophet says:

> Through Thy commandments I understood . . . With my whole heart have I sought Thee . . . I ran the way of Thy commandments, when Thou didst enlarge my heart . . . And my study was in Thy commandments, which I greatly loved . . . The Law of Thy lips is better unto me, than thousands of gold and silver . . . Therefore have I loved Thy commandments more than gold and topaz . . . Thy words have I hid within my heart, that I should not sin against Thee . . . I am as glad of Thy words, as one that findeth great spoils . . . Set me on the path of Thy commandments, for therein hath been my desire. (Ps 118:104, 10, 32, 47, 72, 127, 11, 162, 35)

The sun rises; people hurry to work. Each person has his goal, his purpose. Just as every soul has a body, in like manner every human pursuit has a goal and a purpose. One man works and cares to secure perishable treasures; another labors to supply himself with abundant pleasures; yet another seeks earthly, vain glory; finally, another says and thinks that his actions benefit the government and society. But the friend of the Law of God has one goal in all his work and all his endeavors—to please God. The entire world becomes for him a book of the Lord's commandments. He reads this book with his deeds, actions, his very life. The more his heart reads this book, the more it becomes illumined with spiritual wisdom, the more it warms to the path of piety and virtue. It grows fiery wings of faith; it begins to trample underfoot all hostile fear, to fly over any abyss, to dare begin every good deed. Blessed is this heart! Such a heart is the blessed man.

Night comes with its shadows, the pallid sheen of the night lights of the sky. It collects people from the surface of the earth into their tents, their refuges. In these refuges is found only boredom and emptiness of soul. And so they try to drown out their torture with mindless diversions; idleness and perversion of temperament give way to loud amusements, and the vessels of the temple of God—the mind, heart, the body—are used by Belshazzar for vile ends. The slave of the earth, the slave of temporal earthly cares has barely managed to tear himself away from the worries that inundated him during the course of the day, but in the silence of night he prepares for himself new worries for the coming day. His days and his nights—his entire life—are a sacrifice to vanity and corruption.

A humble oil lamp glimmers before the holy icon, faintly illuminating the cell of the ascetic. He also has his work with its constant, all-consuming cares. He brings into his cell his memories of the day; he compares them with the tablets of God's revealed will to man—the Scriptures. He washes away his insufficiencies in action, thought, in the movements of the heart with tears; he heals them with repentance. He begs new powers, new light from heaven to renew and strengthen his labors. Gracious light, supernatural power descends from God into the soul that offers prayer with pain in the heart at the poverty and weakness of humanity, at its tendency to fall. Thus "day unto day uttered speech, and night unto night showeth knowledge" (Ps 18:3). Such a life is constant spiritual progress, an endless acquisition of eternal benefits. This is how the blessed man lives.

And may this man be "like a tree planted by the water-side" (Ps 1:3). Such a tree does not fear the burning rays of the sun, nor does it fear drought. Its roots are always satiated with moisture; they do not wait for the rains. These roots are never malnourished like those of sickly and wilting trees growing in mountainous and desert terrains. The tree that grows on a mountain, exposed to the wind and sun, that rarely drinks the rain of the skies, that seldom freshens itself with dew from heaven, is like a person who is inclined to piety but leads an inattentive, distracted life, a person who cares little or superficially for the study of the Law of God. Sometimes, he is refreshed with the dew of compunction; sometimes, the life-giving rain of repentant tears falls on his desiccated soul; sometimes, his mind and heart are aroused by a striving toward God. But this state is not and cannot be constant or even long-lived. When pious thoughts and feelings are not illumined by the clear and complete knowledge of the will of God, they cannot have any definitiveness, any foundation, and so they do not have strength and life.

He who studies the Law of God day and night is like "a tree planted by the water-side." Cool, fresh water constantly flows over his roots; his mind and heart—for these are the roots of man—constantly plunge into the depths of the Law of God. They drink deeply of the holy Law of God. The pure, full powers of life eternal fill such a man. This water, this power, this life, is the Holy Spirit, abiding in the Holy Scriptures, abiding in the commandments of the Gospel. Whoever constantly plumbs the depths of the Scriptures; whoever studies them with a humble spirit, asking God to illumine him in prayer; whoever aligns all his actions, all the movements of his soul, with the commandments of the Gospel—such a man will become a communicant of the Holy Spirit without fail. The Holy Spirit said of Himself: "I am a part of them that fear Thee, and of them that keep Thy commandments" (Ps 118:63).[1]

The study of God's Law requires patience. This study is the possession of your own soul: "By your patience," commands the Lord, "possess your souls" (Luke 21:19). This is the science of sciences! This is a heavenly science! This is science imparted to man by God! Its paths are separate from the usual paths of human, earthly sciences, sciences that arise from our fallen intellect, from our fallen state. Human sciences puff up and inflate the mind, actualizing and increasing the human ego. But divine science is revealed to a soul that has been prepared, burnished to a shine, wiped clean by self-rejection, deprived of selfish identity by humility, becoming a mirror with no form of its own, capable only of reflecting divine qualities. The divine science is the wisdom of God, the word of God. Jesus ben Sirach speaks of her:

> Wisdom exalts her children and lays hold of those who seek her. Whoever loves her loves life, and those who come to her early in the morning will be filled with gladness. He who holds fast to her will inherit glory, and the Lord blesses every place she enters. Those who serve her will minister to the Holy One, and the Lord loves those who love her. He who obeys her will judge the nations; and he that gives heed to her will live with confidence. (Sir 4:11–15)

This is divine science! This is the wisdom of God! It is the revelation of God! God is contained in it! The only approach to it is through humility. The only approach to it is the rejection of one's own reason. It is unapproachable for human reason, for reason has rejected it; reason has considered it madness. Reason—that brazen, proud enemy of divine science—blasphemously calls it foolishness, because it appeared to mankind on the Cross, and it illumines mankind from the Cross. The way to it is by self-denial. The way to it is by crucifixion. The way to it is by faith. Sirach continues: "If he trusts in her, he will inherit her" (Sir 4:16).

Genuine, God-pleasing faith, devoid of flattery or falsehood, is found in the fulfillment of the commandments of the Gospel, in a strenuous and constant inculcation of the soul to them, in battle with the intellect and with the ungodly emotions and strivings of the heart and body. The intellect, the heart, and the body of fallen man alike are antagonistic to the Law of God. Our fallen reason does not accept the mind of God; the fallen heart opposes the will of God; the very body, having been subject to corruption, still seeks its independent will, which imparted to man only the death-bearing knowledge of good and evil by an experiential fall into sin. Narrow and sorrowful is our path to the wisdom of God! Holy faith leads us to it, trampling upon and destroying the opposition of the intellect, the heart, and the body of the fallen. Here we need patient endurance! "By your patience possess your souls" (Luke 21:19).

Whoever wishes to bear spiritual fruit—let him patiently wage prolonged warfare against sin, so full of various upheavals and troubles. Only he who nourishes the fruit of the Spirit—so holy and gentle!—will see this fruit on the tree of his soul, but only after great and courageous endurance. Let us listen to the wise one again. "At first she will walk with him on disturbing paths and bring fear and dread upon him; and she will torment him with her discipline until she can trust his soul and test him with her ordinances. Then she will come straight back to him, and will gladden him, and reveal her secrets to him" (Sir 4:17–18).

Days, months, years pass, and God's time comes, the "times or seasons which the Father has put in His own authority" (Acts 1:7), and the tree planted by the waterside begins to bear fruit. This fruit is the palpable communion of the Holy Spirit, promised by the Son of God to all who truly believe in Him. Wondrous is this fruit of the Spirit! It transforms the whole man. The Holy Scripture is transferred from the page to the soul; the word of God and the will of God, the Word and the Spirit, are traced by an invisible finger on the tablets of the mind and the heart. What occurs with this person was promised by the Son of God: "'Out of his heart will flow rivers of living water.' But this He spoke concerning the Spirit, whom those believing in Him would receive" (John 7:38–39). This is how the beloved disciple of the Saviour—the confidant of Wisdom and the recipient of her theology—explains the Lord's words.

Even the leaf of such a tree "shall not fall" (Ps 1:3). The leaf, according to the Holy Fathers, is ascetic labors of the body, and these receive their reward— incorruptibility and life—after the renewal, rebirth of the soul by the Holy Spirit. The will of such a person unites with the will of God. He desires only what is pleasing to God; he fulfills only the will of God. This is why he has God as a fellow worker in all his undertakings, and "all whatsoever he doeth, it shall prosper" (Ps 1:3).

No such comparison belongs to the ungodly! The inspired David does not compare them with trees or anything else that has signs of life. He offers another simile for them. "Not so are the ungodly, not so," sings the royal prophet, "but they are like the dust, which the wind scattereth away from the face of the earth" (Ps 1:4). Ungodly ones! You are lifeless dust, raised by a stormy wind—the noisy vanity of the world—from the face of the earth. You spin about in the air; you are carried about by a thick cloud that obscures the sun and the rest of nature.

Do not look at this cloud! Do not believe the delusion of your eyes! For the eyes, this empty dust, this worthless dust appears to be a cloud. Close your eyes for a moment, and the cloud of dust will pass away, borne by a power-ful, instantaneous breath of wind, and it will not damage your eyesight. In a moment, you will open your eyes and see—where is the huge cloud? You will seek its vestiges, but there is no cloud, there is not even a trace of it, and there is not even a sign of its having existed at all.

In a terrifying hymn, David continues to declaim his fateful condemnation of the ungodly. "Therefore the ungodly shall not rise at the judgment, nei-ther the sinners in the council of the righteous" (Ps 1:5). They have no place in the first resurrection that St John described in the Revelation (Ch. 20), that is, the resurrection of the spirit, accomplished during earthly life, when the all-accomplishing Spirit will touch the soul and give it second life. The soul resurrects, vivified for a divine life. Its mind and heart are illumined, becom-ing communicants of spiritual reasoning. "Spiritual reasoning is the sense of eternal life," said the spirit-bearing St Isaac the Syrian.[2] This mind-set is a sign of resurrection. On the other hand, a carnal mind is the invisible death of the soul (see Rom 8:4).

Spiritual reasoning is the activity of the Holy Spirit. It sees the sin, the passion in itself and in others. It sees its own soul and the souls of others. It sees the snares of the prince of the world, and it deposes every thought that seeks to usurp the mind of Christ. It deflects sin from itself in whatever form it approaches, because the spiritual mind is the kingdom, the light of the Holy Spirit in the mind and the heart. The ungodly shall not rise to a spiritual mind-set! Such a mind-set is the counsel only of the righteous, their exclusive inheritance. It is unapproachable, inconceivable for the ungodly and the sinful. It is the vision of God, and only "the pure in heart will see God" (Matt 5:8).

The way of the ungodly is hateful to God. It is so foreign and detestable to Him that the Scriptures describe God as turning away from it, as though He does not know it. On the contrary, the way of the righteous is so pleasing to God that the Scriptures say, "The Lord knoweth the way of the righteous" (Ps 1:6). Truly, He alone knows this way. Blessed are you, O way! You lead me to God! You are hidden in the eternal God! Your beginning is God, and your end is God! You are endless, as God is endless.

The way of the ungodly has a limit, a most bitter end! This end is the edge of a deep, dark abyss, the eternal repository of eternal death. And it will itself perish—this way of the ungodly—forever in this horrifying abyss, after leading all those who walked it to the edge of the abyss and then throwing them in.

"The Lord knoweth the way of the righteous, but the way of the ungodly shall perish" (Ps 1:6). "Blessed is the man that hath not walked in the counsel of the ungodly," who was not swayed by their frame of mind, their mores, their actions, "but his delight is in the Law of the Lord" (Ps 1:1–2).

Thus the heavenly, wondrous singer chants, and the ascetic in the wilderness hearkens to his holy, inspired song.

Nikolo-Babaev Monastery,
1847

CHAPTER 2

Joseph: An Edifying Story
Taken from the Book of Genesis

In the midst of their calamities, the thought of gratitude to God comes miraculously to the righteous ones.[3] It tears their hearts from their sorrows and inner darkness, raising them to God, to the dominion of light and consolation. God always saves those who run to Him with simplicity and faith.

The holy patriarch Jacob was returning from Mesopotamia to the land of Canaan, to the land of his birth, to the inheritance destined for him by God (Gen 32). Suddenly, the news came that irate Esau, his brother, was coming to meet him, and with him were four hundred armed men. While they were still in their youth, Esau had tried to kill Jacob in a fit of jealousy. In order to avoid an early and violent death, Jacob traveled to Mesopotamia. There he lived for twenty years. Time could have healed the heart of Esau, wounded by hatred . . . No, he comes to meet his brother with an armed band. The size of the band, its war-like aspect, betrayed its evil intentions. Time had not healed the hatred inside Esau. As he grew into manhood, so also grew his hatred for his brother.

Jacob grew afraid. He did not know what to do. He decided to divide his property, including his household and numerous flocks, into two groups.

"If furious Esau," he thought, "will cut apart one group, perhaps his anger will be sated, and he will leave the second group alone."

Behind both groups stood the wives and children of Jacob, and behind all of them stood his faithful wife Rachel with her only son, Joseph, the youngest of Jacob's sons.[4] Joseph, as the youngest, took the last place, but this place was also considered safest by the far-seeing love of his father. The eyes of love are keen, and keen also are the eyes of zeal. Having made such arrangements, the righteous one hurries to the usual refuge of the righteous—he hurries to stand before God in reverent prayer. He confesses to God, "Let me be satisfied with all the righteousness and all the truth You have shown Your servant; for I crossed over this Jordan with my staff, and now I have become two companies" (Gen 32:10).

Surrounded on all sides by danger, the righteous one pours his heart out before God, reconciles his accounts with fate, and finds himself completely content, knowing that God, Who had commanded the journey to Mesopotamia and the return from it, did everything according to His promise. "Let me be satisfied with all the righteousness and all the truth You have shown your servant." What profound, sincere humility! Humility alone is worthy to stand before God; it alone is worthy of conversation with God; it is never abandoned by God. God hears it mercifully, pouring forth abundant mercies on the one who prays with humility. According to God's command, the heart of Esau was transformed. Until this moment it blazed with fury; now, unexpectedly, it catches fire with love for Jacob. Esau flings aside his sword and runs into the embrace of his brother, and the two weep in each other's arms (Gen 33:4).

Time passes. Jacob has been in Canaan for a long time. His most beloved wife, Rachel, died giving birth to her second son, Benjamin. Jacob has already suffered much grief from his tempestuous sons, who behaved in the promised land as though they were conquerors. In the area surrounding his tents, near Hebron, they pastured their numerous flocks, and sometimes they would travel far to other, more fruitful pastures. Jacob remained constantly at home, weighed down by years and kept within by his spiritual achievements, which drew the mind and heart of the old man to God. Thus, he came to love solitude in his tent. Such a man has no time or inclination to get involved in life's worries. Always near him was his consolation—his favorite son Joseph, who was beautiful in soul and body. His care for his elderly father and his attention to the profound, holy instruction of his father, who had seen God, were Joseph's entire occupation, his exclusive pleasure. The words of piety fell into his soul like a seed falling into fertile soil and quickly bearing fruit. Holy purity came to shine in Joseph's soul. In a pure heart, God begins to be reflected, like the sun in calm waters. The virtue of Joseph inspired in his brothers not a healthy spiritual rivalry, but envy. Unfortunately, this happens more and more in human society.

The brothers invented and spread an evil rumor about Joseph—what exactly, the Scriptures do not say. However, the sagacious and grace-filled Jacob was not fooled by the cunning fiction, and he continued to love Joseph. As a sign of his exceptional love, he gave him a gift—a coat of many colors.

Vividness and variety of colors were especially valued—and are still valued—among the nomads of the East. Was not this cloak a symbol of the future life of the youth, which would be mottled with many different circumstances? Inspiration encouraged the prescient elder to express his prophecy not by a word, but by a symbol—the cloak of many colors.

From this moment, the strange adventures of Joseph begin. He becomes a prototype—the longest Biblical shadow of our Lord Jesus Christ, and his virtuous life is an example for any pious and virtuous person who is subject to various, strange misfortunes. During all his calamities, he remained constant in piety and virtue. Nowhere is he ever abandoned by God; instead, everywhere he is preserved. Finally, he comes to be wondrously glorified. Let us listen to the curious tale of the miraculous and instructive adventures of the youth who was dressed by his prophet-father in a tunic of many colors.

The brothers of Joseph, seeing that their father loved him more than all his other sons, came to hate him. Every word, every glance made them boil with dark anger. He did not understand the sickness that had seized them; his pure heart saw all of them as equally pure and well intentioned. With complete trust, he revealed his heart to them. This guileless heart was already chosen by God as a vessel for mysterious revelations. The grace of the Holy Spirit, because of the young age of Joseph, began to reveal its presence and activity in remarkable dreams. A mysterious hand vividly drew strange dreams in the youthful imagination of Joseph. He was then seventeen years old.

With complete candor, not suspecting any evil, he told his brothers of his dream. Apparently, the dream left a vivid impression in the soul of the young man, which needed to be explained. He wanted to hear this explanation from the lips of his older brothers. "Thus he said to them, 'Hear this dream I dreamed: there we were, binding sheaves in the field. Then behold, my sheaf arose and also stood upright; and indeed your sheaves stood all around and bowed down to my sheaf.' So his brothers said to him, 'Shall you indeed reign over us? Or shall you indeed have dominion over us?'" (Gen 37:5–8). They hated him twice as much for his grace-inspired dream and for the holy, innocent candor that they had misinterpreted and perverted to the wounding of their own souls.

Then Joseph saw another dream. With childlike innocence, as though in justification of the first dream and to prove that these wondrous dreams came to him unwillingly, independently of his own will, Joseph once again described his dream to his father and brothers. "Look, I have dreamed another dream. And this time, the sun, the moon, and the eleven stars bowed down to me"

(Gen 37:9). When his father heard him, he rebuked Joseph. "What is this dream you have dreamed? Shall your mother and I and your brothers indeed come and bow down on the ground before you?" (Gen 37:10). The experienced and spiritually wise father stopped his son, not because he believed the dream to be idle reverie or Joseph's own prideful invention, but to protect the young soul from falling prey to arrogance. At the same time, it was a stern rebuke intended to dampen the envy and hatred of his brothers.

Christian ascetic teachers command us not to pay any attention to revelations that come to us by means of the soul's or body's senses. They command us to preserve a discerning coolness in the midst of any such supernatural phenomena, a salvific discretion.[5] Sometimes dreams do come from God, as we see from the dreams of Joseph, but the state of one who sees dreams and visions is very dangerous, very near to self-deception. To see our sins: that is the safest kind of vision! "A contrite and humble heart God shall not despise." (Ps 50:19 LXX)—this is a beneficial state, devoid of any self-delusion, a state that God blesses! Discernment that is capable of understanding, parsing, and explaining visions is inherent only in those who have already labored long in spiritual asceticism. It is acquired only after a long time and is a gift of God. The holy Jacob had this gift. He stopped his son from telling more prophetic dreams, but he himself (the Scripture witnesses) pondered his son's words in his mind, because these words had the imprint of the Spirit. But the brothers of Joseph were differently affected by the new dream. It only increased their hatred and envy.

Once, they led their flocks to Sechem. Jacob said to Joseph, "Your brothers are in Sechem; I want to send you to them."

Joseph answered, "I am ready to go."

"Go," continued Jacob, "see if your brothers are well, if our sheep are well. Then come back and tell me."

Sometimes people part very easily. When parting, it is as if they do not part. Saying goodbye, it is almost as though they say nothing at all. But this frivolous parting is often a final parting; often a prolonged, sorrowful separation follows it. The old man did not know that by sending Joseph away, he was parting from his beloved son for a long, long time. Could he imagine that by sending Joseph to his brothers, he was sending him to his killers? He knew their hatred, but could he have imagined that the brotherly hatred had increased to a conspiracy, to a decision to commit fratricide? The elder's lack of malice was a virtue of experience, not Joseph's childish lack of malice. Joseph walked straight up to the knife, like a lamb. The wise Jacob, despite his great spiritual growth, despite extensive experience gathered during a long and arduous life, could still not imagine that his passionate sons were capable of the terrifying crime of fratricide.

To avoid thinking evil of one's fellows is inherent to holiness; holiness considers the most obvious criminals as less evil than they are in actual fact. We have seen many holy people who are not fooled by obvious sin but are instead fooled by their great love and trust for their fellow man.

Elder! You are parting with your beloved son Joseph for a very long time! You have the gifts of prescience and prophecy; but in this instance God, Who inconceivably arranges the fates of all men, veiled the future from your gaze with an opaque shroud. You sent Joseph away for a few days, but you will only see him after many sorrowful years. And he will see the land of Canaan—the land where your tent stands—only when the days of your burial will come, and even then only for the short days of your funeral! His bones will be brought back here; with him will return his numerous issue, and with an armed hand they will come to rule the inheritance of their forefather, the once-young Joseph.

Joseph left his father's home in Hebron and came to Sechem. His brothers had already left that place. He did not know where to find them, and so he began to search and ask for them. Unexpectedly, he met a stranger who asked Joseph whom he sought. Joseph answered, "I seek my brothers; tell me, if you know, where they went with their flocks?"

The stranger answered, "They departed from here. I heard that they discussed among themselves: 'Let us go Dothan.'" Directed by the words of this person, whom fate seems to have brought to Joseph on purpose to direct him to his destiny, the young man begins to once again seek his brothers—the sacrificial victim seeks his sacrificers—and finds them in Dothan. They recognize him from a distance and immediately begin to conspire to kill him. Horrible words are uttered in this fraternal assembly: "Look, the dreamer is coming. Let us kill him and say that he was eaten by a predatory animal. Let us see then what will happen with his dreams!" After the horrifying words, arms are raised in preparation to do the crime.

However, Reuben, the eldest son of Jacob, "delivered him out of their hands" (Gen 37:21). He said, "Let us not kill him with our own hands! Drop him into one of the pits here, but do not raise your hands against him!" For the softened Reuben thought to return the favored son to his father. They took off Joseph's coat of many colors and threw him into a deep, dry well. A living man was cast into a terrible grave. Joseph is in the pit, in the very jaws of death! . . .

O holy youth, such an experience begins your spiritual expertise! How wondrous is the strength of your soul that endured such cruel sorrow! Firmness in sorrows is given by a blameless, spotless conscience. Teach us also to seek your purity and firmness, these great buttresses for the heart during life's misfortunes.

Joseph is in the pit. What do the brothers do? They sit to eat! What horribly ripened hatred! When a passion ripens in the soul, the soul no longer senses its fatal sickness. It is more horrible to be a heart in the depth of such evil than a body, with an angelic spirit, in a deep pit. The sons of Jacob committed a crime as though they were doing their duty: so habitual had hatred for their brother become that as the Scriptures say, "they then sat down to eat a meal" (Gen 37:25).

Of course, there could be nothing good in the taking of such repast. The meal was unruly. Can murderers dine in any other manner? Loud laughter interrupted horrible silences; that was the laughter of a soul that had thrown off itself the clothing of shame. This soul found pleasure and satiety in the doing of the evil. Occasionally hellish words would erupt, as though from the depths of the earth, from hearts that had decided to commit fratricide. Dark and bestial were the faces of the diners. Their vision and their hearing were morbid, wildly wandering all over. Wisdom had no more control here. What wisdom? When the passions overcome a person, then the mind, deprived of lordship, serves as an obsequious and resourceful slave of the passions for the gratification of their evil, capricious, and criminal desires.

The sons of Jacob hold feast over a grave with a living corpse, and so their gaze wanders hither and thither. Unexpectedly, they notice a group of travelers. These were Ishmaelites, merchants. They came from Gilead and were traveling to Egypt. Their camels were abundantly laden with spices, balm, and myrrh—these were intended for sale in Egypt. A voice was heard among the rabid diners: "What profit is there if we kill our brother and conceal his blood? Come and let us sell him to the Ishmaelites, but let not our hand be upon him; for he is our brother and our flesh" (Gen 37:26–27). This was the voice of Judah, the fourth son of Jacob; Judah offered the sale of their brother-saint. Many centuries will pass, another Judas will appear, and he will say about another righteous one, the very God-Man Himself: "What are you willing to give to me if I deliver Him to you?" (Matt 26:15).

The gold coins jingle . . . Joseph is taken from the well and quickly sold to the Arabs. Not a single haggling word about price or the prisoner is uttered on either side. The Scriptures would not have remained silent about such words if they had been said. The Scriptures in this tale relate even words that are only somewhat worth listening to. The gold coins jingle . . . there were twenty of them. How similar is this sound to the jingle of thirty pieces of silver! . . . O blessed youth, sold for twenty gold coins! You have become a worthy prototype of the One Who was sold for thirty pieces of silver.

Reuben was not present at the iniquitous meal where the crime was celebrated. Neither was he a member of the conspiracy to murder Joseph. Secretly, he comes to the pit and calls to the buried one. There is no answer. Again, he calls, and again—no answer! In despair, he tears his clothes, runs to his brothers, and says to them, "The lad is not there; and I, where shall I go?" In answer, the coins jingle. There were twenty coins—two for each. The nine brothers who were present at the sale did not forget the tenth who was absent.

In the meantime, the sons of Jacob concocted a plan to hide their crime from their father. They killed a goat kid and covered Joseph's cloak in its blood. Then they sent it to their father with a harsh question: "We found this; do you recognize it as your son's or not?" He recognized it and said, "This is the clothing of my son; has a wild animal eaten him? A wild animal has seized Joseph!" Jacob tore his clothes, put on sackcloth, and bewailed his son for many days. His sons and daughters gathered to him; they consoled the old man. But he would not be comforted, saying, "I will go with groaning down to hell to see my son." For a long time, he repeated these words and wept.

The Ishmaelites brought Joseph to Egypt (Gen 39) and sold him to Potiphar, a nobleman of Pharaoh's court ("Pharaoh" was the title of the king of Egypt), and the leader of the royal bodyguards. The Lord was with Joseph, mysteriously watching over him, helping him. Soon Potiphar noticed that his slave was blessed by heaven, and he came to love him dearly. Soon, Potiphar gave Joseph the management of his entire household and estates. The Lord, for the sake of Joseph, gave prosperity to the Egyptian. The grace of God poured over his entire estate, his house and his fields. Potiphar trusted Joseph completely. He did not even oversee anything; he left everything to Joseph.

Joseph was a stately youth, of great physical beauty. His beauty attracted the gaze of Potiphar's wife. Lust seized her—openly, directly, she declared her passion to the young man. The youth did not agree to lie with her. He exhorted the woman, who was on fire with mad and iniquitous desire, saying, "My lord has so come to trust me and so depends on me that he does not even know what is going on in his own house. He has delivered all his goods into my hands without requiring an account of me. There is no one higher in his household than I; everything is administered by me, save for you, his wife. How can I do as you ask? How can I sin before my God?"

The sinful woman does not listen to the wise words of the son of Jacob. The passion that has mastered her says something else to her. She hears only the voice of lust; the words of Joseph fly into one ear and out the other, empty noises without meaning or significance. From time to time, the wife repeats her proposition, always with the same brazen impudence.

One time, Joseph was working in the house, as was his duty. As it happened, there was no one in the house except for the mistress. She grabbed the clothes he was wearing, begging, demanding that her desire be fulfilled immediately. Joseph tore himself away from her and escaped, but his outer clothing remained in the hands of the Egyptian woman. Her unfulfilled sinful passion immediately transformed into demented hatred. The one who only a moment before sought the pleasures of a beautiful body now frantically thirsts for his blood.

The maddened Egyptian woman wails; with a loud shriek and cry, she calls all the servants. They come. "Look," she says to them, "this young Hebrew was brought into our house to mock us! He came to me . . . he said to me . . . I screamed loudly . . . Afraid of my screaming, he ran away from me . . . here is his clothing in my hand!" She kept the clothing until Potiphar's return.

A second time has clothing become a silent false witness against Joseph. When the nobleman returned, his wife told him what had happened. She said pitifully and quietly, "The young Hebrew—whom you brought into our house to dishonor us!—came to me and offered me to sin with him. When I screamed loudly, he ran away, leaving behind his outer clothing."

Hearing the ring of truthfulness in the account, in which a cold and precise narrative cleverly hid a horribly tormented soul and hellish slander, seeing in the hands of his wife the seemingly incontrovertible proof of the incident—the clothes of Joseph—Potiphar became exceedingly angry. He decided that questioning and juridical proceedings were excessive, unnecessary, since the crime of his slave was obvious. He commanded that Joseph be cast into the prison for political prisoners.

The Lord, Who chose Joseph from the days of his childhood; the Lord, Who helped him in slavery in the house of Potiphar—He did not abandon Joseph in prison. The chief prison keeper came to like him; eventually, he entrusted the entire prison and all the imprisoned to Joseph's care. Like Potiphar, he put all his trust in Joseph. After some time had passed, two of Pharaoh's servants—the chief cupbearer and the chief baker—committed offenses before their king.

Enraged Pharaoh imprisoned them in the same prison that still held Joseph. The keeper of the prison entrusted their care to Joseph. After spending several days in prison, they each had a dream on the same night. In the morning, Joseph came to them and noticed that both were disturbed. He asked them, "Why do you look so sad?" They answered, "Each of us has seen a dream, but there is no one here to interpret them." Joseph said, "Is it not God Who gives the gift of interpretation of those dreams that He sends? Tell me your dreams."

From these words of Joseph, we see his spiritual advancement, the fruit of his trials. When he saw dreams in childhood, he only sensed that they had meaning, and he retold them to his father and brothers, seeking their interpretation, not daring to interpret them himself. Now, no sooner does he hear that the prisoners saw dreams than he already hopes to find the resolution of the cryptic dreams through God, to Whom he had drawn near, with Whom he had become intimate through his sorrows, faith, purity, and prayer. Dreams had led him to the crucible of sorrows; dreams will now lead him out of that crucible, into which the providence of God usually casts people called by Him to great deeds.

The chief cupbearer began his account: "It seemed to me that before me was a vineyard; in the vineyard I saw three branches that had blossomed first into flowers, then into rich clusters of grapes. The cup of Pharaoh was in my hand. I took the grapes, pressed them into Pharaoh's cup, and gave it to Pharaoh."

Joseph answered, "Here is the meaning of this dream. Three branches are three days. In three days, Pharaoh will remember you and reinstate you as chief cupbearer. You will bring Pharaoh the cup as before. When that time comes, remember me in your good fortune. Show me mercy: tell Pharaoh about me and take me from these dark walls. I have been stolen from the lands of the Hebrews and have done nothing criminal, and still I have been cast into this terrible prison."

When the chief baker heard this interpretation, he also told Joseph his dream. "I also saw a dream. It seemed to me that I held three baskets of bread on my head. In the top basket were all kinds of baked goods preferred by the Pharaoh. Suddenly, birds flew down and began to eat the baked goods."

Joseph answered, "This is the meaning of your dream. Three baskets are three days. In three days, Pharaoh will take off your head. Your corpse will hang on a tree, and the birds of the sky will eat your body."

Three days passed, and it was Pharaoh's birthday. He gave a feast for the members of his court, and in conversation with them he remembered the two prisoners. He reinstated the chief cupbearer to his previous position, but he commanded that the chief baker be executed, just as Joseph had foretold. But the chief cupbearer forgot about Joseph. The righteous one still needed to languish in prison for a time! He still needed solitude and darkness, so that his soul would plunge even deeper into prayer, so that he would come even closer to God, so that his soul would become even brighter with spiritual knowledge.

Two more years passed. Pharaoh saw a dream (Gen 41). It seemed to him that he stood by a river. Out of the water seven cows walked out—fat, beautiful—and began to pasture by the bank. After them, seven more cows walked out of the water—thin, ugly—and they also began to pasture next to the other cows by the river. Suddenly, the thin cows devoured the fat ones, and it was impossible to see that the fat cows were inside them, for they remained as thin as before. Pharaoh woke up.

Again he fell asleep and saw a different dream. It seemed to him that seven heads of grain, filled with ripe berries, grew from a single stalk. After them, another seven heads grew, but these were thin, as though desiccated by heat and wind. These seven thin heads swallowed the seven ripe heads. Pharaoh woke up, and his heart was disturbed.

With the coming of morning, he ordered that all the learned and wise men of Egypt come to him to hear his dream. But they could not interpret the dreams that brought the Pharaoh into such a state of brooding and confusion. Then the chief cupbearer said to Pharaoh, "Now I remember my sin! When you, O king, was angered with your slaves, with me and the chief baker, you ordered us to be locked away in the prison that is adjacent to the house of the chief bodyguard. Each of us, in the same night, saw a dream. There was a young Hebrew there, the slave of the chief bodyguard. We told him our dreams, and he interpreted them. He foretold that I would be reinstated, and that my companion would be executed. And that is what happened to both of us."

Pharaoh sent for Joseph and commanded that he be brought before him. Joseph was taken from the prison; he was released by the hand of God. According to the custom of that country, his hair was cut and his clothing was changed. Then he stood before the face of Pharaoh. The king of Egypt told him his dreams and complained that his wise men could not interpret them. "I heard it of you," said Pharaoh to Joseph, "that you interpret dreams."

Joseph answered, "Without God, Pharaoh will not receive a satisfactory answer." Unwillingly, Joseph discovers his spiritual state! He confesses the evident, miraculous, fundamental divine action, the action of the Holy Spirit that does not depend on man, but that visits man by the will of the Most High and reveals many secrets to man. This invisible communion with God, this action of grace—this is what Joseph sensed in his soul. His constancy in virtue in the midst of misfortunes and sufferings raised him to a great level of spiritual achievement—or rather, it was the grace of the Holy Spirit that constantly overshadows the virtuous, and especially innocent, sufferers.

"Both of your dreams," he said to Pharaoh,

> have the same meaning. Your dreams are one dream. The seven fat cows symbolize seven fruitful harvests; the seven ripe heads of grain symbolize the same. The seven thin cows and the seven desiccated heads of grain indicate seven years of famine. God shows Pharaoh that which He intends to accomplish. Seven years will come, and during their time Egypt will have plentiful harvest. Then another seven years will come, and their dearth will make people forget the bounty of the first seven years. Famine will strike and ruin the land. The very traces of the preceding bounty will be wiped out by the seven years of dearth, because the famine will be very severe. Twice this dream occurred to Pharaoh—that is a confirmation of God's word and a sign that God will hurry to bring His intention into action. O King! Choose for yourself a wise man and entrust the land of Egypt to him. Let him collect one fifth of every harvest for the next seven fruitful years; the collected grain must remain under Pharaoh's management and be kept in the cities. Thus, Egypt will have stores of grain for the seven years of failed harvests, and the people will not perish from hunger.

Joseph's words were pleasing to Pharaoh and his court. Pharaoh said to them, "Where else will we find a person who will be so filled with the Spirit of God as this man?" Then, turning to Joseph, he said to him, "God reveals secrets to you, and so there is no other person who compares with you in wisdom and good sense. Be the head of my household; let all my people obey you! Only in kingship will I be greater than you. I place you over the entire land of Egypt."

Pharaoh took his ring from his finger and placed it on the hand of Joseph, dressed him in the royal purple, placed a golden chain around his neck, and commanded that he be the second in Pharaoh's chariot. In this chariot, the new nobleman was borne throughout the city; before the chariot walked a herald, proclaiming the power and rank of Joseph. At that time, Joseph had just turned thirty years old.

Pharaoh married his new favorite to Senath, the daughter of the priest of the sun, and renamed him Zaphnath-Paaneah. What did this name mean? It means "saviour of the world."[6] Thus Joseph became a foreshadowing of the

God-Man Who would come into the world to save the fallen and lost human race. He foreshadowed Him when he was sold by his brothers to the foreigners. He foreshadowed His burial by his imprisonment. By his sudden exaltation and glorification, he foreshadowed the glory of Christ's resurrection. The daughter of the priest of On, who married Joseph, was a prototype of the Church of Christ, the Church of former pagans. The salvation of the Egyptians from death foreshadowed the salvation of mankind from eternal death. The giver of earthly bread was a prototype of the One Who was both the "living bread which came down from heaven" (John 6:51) and the giver of this Heavenly Bread. From the midst of these mysterious Old Testament prototypes, the consoling name, "Saviour of the world," was heard for the first time. Wondrous was the providence of God that foretold the great work of God, the redemption of mankind, in the shadows of Biblical prophecy. How long ago did these shadows begin to appear! How vividly did they describe the truth! How mysterious were they for their contemporaries! How evident and obvious did they become, when God revealed to mankind the proper interpretation of the Scriptures that He had inspired!

Joseph proceeded to fulfill the duties to which God Himself had called him through the hand of the ruler of Egypt. He undertook a journey through all of Egypt and, having seen the country, made the necessary arrangements. For seven years, the land gave plentiful harvest. During these seven years, Joseph collected reserves of grain. These were kept in the cities under strict oversight and guarded in large granaries. He collected an uncounted amount of wheat. It lay in the granaries like mountains of sand. During these fruitful years, Asenath gave birth to two sons. Joseph named the firstborn Manasseh. By naming him thus, he inserted a profound thought into the name of his eldest son: "thus did God arrange my life, so that I would forget my sufferings." The second he called Ephraim, connecting another profound and pious thought with this name: "God has made me fruitful in the land of my humiliation." These are the meanings of the Jewish names of his two sons.[7]

Seven years of bounty passed, as does everything subject to time, and the years of famine approached. As Joseph foretold, famine began to rage over the entire land. The people of Egypt cried out to Pharaoh, begging for bread. Pharaoh answered his subjects: "Go to Joseph and do everything that he tells you." Joseph opened the reserve granaries and began to sell bread to the Egyptians. The famine spread out over the entire face of the earth. The inhabitants of neighboring countries heard that bread was being sold in Egypt, and, oppressed by hunger, they began to travel to Egypt to buy grain.

The wise, prudent ruler had saved grain in amounts that would feed not only Egypt but would also attract the money of other nations into the coffers of the Egyptian kingdom.

Among the other lands that were downtrodden by hunger was the land of Canaan. The family of the holy patriarch Jacob also suffered from a lack of food. The rumor that bread was being sold in Egypt reached the ears of the elder (see Gen 42). He said to his sons, "I heard that there is wheat in Egypt. You did not pay attention to this? Go there and buy some bread to sustain us. Otherwise, we will die of hunger." Submitting to the will of their father, ten of Joseph's brothers traveled to Egypt to buy bread. Jacob did not release Benjamin with his brothers, saying, "Lest something evil happen to him along the way."

Having arrived in Egypt, the sons of Jacob came with the other buyers to the place where the bread was sold. Joseph himself was selling the bread. When his brothers stood before him, he immediately recognized them. However, they had not the slightest suspicion that they stood before the brother they had sold into slavery for twenty gold coins. After all, how could they have recognized him?

When they parted with him, he was barely seventeen years old. Now he was closer to forty. Changed by the years, he was no less changed by the majesty and brilliance of his rank, the first lord in the kingdom of Egypt, which at that time was the greatest civilization in the world, with the best education, military power, and internal organization. Having approached Joseph, his brothers bowed low, touching their heads to the ground. Joseph remembered his youthful dreams . . .

Wise, virtuous Joseph! He decided to delay revealing himself to his brothers to another time. What self-control this great soul had! Was not Joseph's heart consumed with the desire to immediately give the joyful news to his elderly, holy parent, who sorrowed greatly, knowing nothing about Joseph's fate for the last twenty years, considering him lost irretrievably? But he did not listen to the appeal of his merciful, loving heart and chose a manner of action that was absolutely necessary for his brothers' benefit, as well as his own.

Joseph knew the crude, unrestrained manners of these people; these were half-wild shepherds who had grown up on pastures, who had spent their entire lives with cattle, used to expansive, boisterous freedom under the open skies and in unpopulated wildernesses. They did not know how to govern their own passions; they knew no limits to their self-will; they were insubordinate to their father, even insulting him in various ways; whatever desire they had, no matter how sinful, they always fulfilled it; their hands were more than once red with the blood of the innocent. This is how the Scriptures describe the sons of Jacob. They needed a lesson. For their own benefit, they needed to be acquainted with submissiveness, with proper behavior. Their cruel souls, habituated to disdain their own consciences and the fear of God, could not be shaken in any other way and could not have been forced to their senses and to self-awareness, except by the pain of mortal fear.

Foreseeing the duration of the famine, Joseph also foresaw the necessity of Jacob's family's eventual relocation from Palestine to Egypt. Is this not why he accused his brothers, upon their very first arrival in Egypt, of being spies? If his brothers had brought their unbridled natures, their rowdiness, to their new home, they would have quickly incurred the wrath of the Egyptians. The prosperity of the family of Jacob would quickly have been reduced to nothing, as would the rank of Joseph himself. His family and he himself would have been subjected to the worst misfortunes. That which he had acquired thanks to his lengthy sufferings must be protected, preserved by wise action.

Joseph treated his brothers with disdain and severity, like a strict master. "Where are you from?" he asked them. They answered, "From the land of Canaan; we have come to buy bread." He protested, "You are spies; you have come to investigate our country!" They answered, "No, lord! We are your servants, and we have come to buy bread. All of us are brothers, the sons of one father. We have come in peace; your servants are not spies." Joseph continued, "No, no. You have come to spy out our lands!" They answered, "We are twelve brothers. Your servants are from the land of Canaan. The least of us has remained with his father, and one of us is no longer living." Joseph said, "Your words are false. I speak truth when I call you spies. I swear by the inviolability of Pharaoh that you will not leave here unless your youngest brother comes to me. This will be your only way of justifying yourselves. Let one of you go and bring back your brother. You will remain here under guard, until it becomes clear that your words are true, or not. If your words turn out to be false . . . I swear by the inviolability of Pharaoh, you are spies!" With these words, he put them under guard.

Three days passed. On the third day, he called them to himself and said, "I am one of those who fears God. This is how you must act. If you come in peace, then go, take the wheat that you have bought, but one of you must remain here as a hostage. The next time you come, you will bring me your brother; by this, you will prove the truthfulness of your words. If you do not bring your youngest brother, then you will no longer see my face!"

All this Joseph said to his brothers through an interpreter. He did not yet dismiss them at this point, and while he began to speak with other buyers, the sons of Jacob began to speak to each other quietly in their native tongue. Could they have guessed that this severe Egyptian lord could understand them? But he was listening to every word with intense concentration; his soul—so full of holy love, acting in holy, salvific wisdom—caught every word. "Truly," said the sons of Jacob to each other, "our sin pursues us, of which we are guilty before our brother Joseph. We disdained his profound sorrow; we did not listen to him when he begged us; and for his sake now we are being punished!"

Reuben said to the other, "Did I not tell you not to touch the youth? You did not listen to me; and now, his blood cries out to heaven!" The words of his brothers pierced the sensitive heart of Joseph. He had to leave them for a moment and console the heaviness of his heart with streams of tears. Then he came to them again, chose Simeon from among them, and ordered that he be bound before their eyes. In the wise actions of Joseph, everything had its reason. Scripture remains silent concerning the reason why the wild and savage Simeon's fate was bondage, but the same Scripture makes it obvious that he needed the severest lesson. All ten brothers were guilty of heavy sins, but Simeon sullied himself with the horrifying murder of the Shechemites, an act that brought severe danger on the entire family of the holy patriarch, from which they were delivered only by an extraordinary intercession of providence. And was it not his hand that was raised for another murder, more terrible and criminal? Joseph gave the secret command to fill the bags of his brothers with wheat and to return the money they had paid into each bag, and even to give them extra money for the return journey. Evidently, every one of them had separately paid for his bag of wheat—this habit is one of those that illuminate for us the distant customs of Biblical antiquity.

Having packed the donkeys with bags of wheat, the sons of Jacob began their return journey. At the first stop, one of them, intending to feed his donkey, took off the bag from his back. Somehow, it became untied, and he saw his bundle of money lying at the top of the bag of wheat. He called to his brothers: "My money has been returned to me . . . Look, here it is in my bag!" Their hearts were horrified; they were disturbed and said to one another, "What is God doing with us?"

Having arrived in the land of Canaan, to their father, they recounted everything that had occurred with them and said,

> A lord of that land treated us severely and even imprisoned us for a night, as though we were spies. We said to him, "No, lord, we are not spies. We have come in peace. We are twelve brothers, sons of one father. One of us is no

more, and the youngest remained with his father, in the land of Canaan." But the lord of that land answered us, "This will be the proof of your trust-worthiness—one of you will remain with me as a hostage; you will take your bought wheat and go, but you must bring your youngest brother to me. By this I will know that you are not spies, but peaceful men, and then I will return your brother, who now remains as a hostage, and you will then have the right to trade freely in the land of Egypt."

When they poured the wheat out of their bags, each one of them found the bundle of money with which he had paid for the wheat. Seeing their money returned to them, they were afraid. Their father also was afraid. "You," he said to them, "have made me completely childless! Joseph is no more; Simeon is no more; and now you want to take Benjamin from me? Because of you all these troubles have fallen on my head." Reuben answered him, "You may kill both my sons if I do not bring Benjamin back to you." But the elder answered, "My son will not go with you! His brother died; he alone remains. If anything evil were to befall him on the road, then you will send me sorrowfully in my old age into hell."

But the famine worsened and grew more severe, completely overcoming the earth (Gen 43). There was no more wheat in the house of Jacob, and the elder said to his sons, "Go again to Egypt and buy us some bread." Judah answered him, "The lord of that land told us, confirming his words with an oath, that we will not see his face if we do not bring our youngest brother with us." Jacob said, "Why did you do this evil deed? Why did you tell that man that you have a brother?" They answered, "The lord asked us severe and detailed questions. He asked, 'Does your father yet live? Do you have any other broth-ers?' We answered his questions. How could we know that he would say, 'Bring me your brother'?"

Then Judah tried to persuade his father, "Send the boy with me; we will go, buy bread to feed you and ourselves, lest we die of hunger. I will take responsi-bility for Benjamin; my hand will be called to account for him. If I do not bring him back and present him to you, let your anger be on my head for the rest of my life. If we had not lingered so long, we could have traveled to Egypt and back twice already." His father answered, "If that is so, do the following. Take some of our local goods and give them to the lord as a gift. Take some balm, honey, spices, myrrh, and some nuts. Take twice the money, so that you can return that which you found in your bags. Perhaps they were placed there by some misunderstanding. And take your brother. Gather your things and go.

May my God incline that lord to mercy, so that he may release Simeon and Benjamin. Or I will be left completely childless!"

The sons of Jacob took gifts and twice the money and traveled to Egypt. Having arrived, they presented themselves to Joseph. Joseph saw Benjamin, the only brother with whom he shared a mother, and his soul was troubled. He called the steward of his house and said to him, "Lead these men to my home and prepare a good meal for them. At midday they will dine with me." The steward did as Joseph commanded and led his brothers into his house. Seeing that they were being led into Joseph's house, they said to each other, "They are taking us there because of the money that we found in our bags, so that they may slander us and accuse us, enslave us and take our donkeys." Therefore, before they stepped into the house, at the gates, they stopped the steward and said to him, "We beg you, listen to us. When we came the first time to buy bread, and after we took back our bags on our return journey, we untied them at the first stop, and suddenly our own money appeared in those bags. This same money we have returned in full. And to buy new bread we have brought more money. We do not know who returned the silver into our bags the first time."

The steward answered, "Be calm and do not fear anything. Your God, the God of your fathers, returned the money into your bags. As for the money that you paid the first time, it is written down in my accounts as fully paid." He then brought Simeon to them. Then he brought them water, and their feet were washed, and their donkeys were fed. The brothers laid out their gifts and prepared them for the arrival of Joseph at midday.

When Joseph returned to his house, his brothers brought him the gifts and again bowed their heads to the ground before him. He asked them, "Are you in good health? Is the elder, your father, of whom you spoke to me, in good health also? Is he still alive?" They answered, "Our father lives still and is in good health." "Blessed is that man before God!" said Joseph. They again bowed deeply before him. Finding Benjamin among them, Joseph asked, "Is this your youngest brother whom you promised to bring to me?" When they answered positively he said, "May God bless you, my child!" Again Joseph was troubled; his heart began to beat fiercely; tears sprung from his eyes. Quickly he retired to his bedroom; there he had his fill of tears. Then he washed his face, came out to his brothers and, holding himself in check, said, "Lay out the meal."

The sons of Jacob were served separately from the other Egyptians who came to dine with Joseph that day. The Egyptians, according to the Scriptures, could not eat at the same table as the Hebrews; they, according to their faith, disdained the company of shepherds. So the sons of Jacob were placed directly opposite Joseph, in order of age. They were surprised to see themselves being seated according to their respective ages. They were given food, each person a separate portion. Joseph himself served them, but he served Benjamin a larger portion than the rest of his brothers. Wine was also brought out. The hearts of the sons of Jacob were relieved at this luxurious and gracious meal. Since they were not used to limiting themselves in anything, the shepherds of the wilderness ate until they were satisfied and drank much. This meal foreshadowed the spiritual supper of Christ the Saviour, offered to Christians at the Divine Liturgy. The Lord willed to become our brother; He acquired lordship over the world—the mystical Egypt—and for His brothers, burdened by the yoke of sin, He "hast prepared a table before me . . . and Thy cup that inebriateth me" (Ps 22:5), His all-holy Body and most pure Blood. Christians who commune of this divine food forget the sorrows that weighted them down during their wandering in Egypt, the foreign land, the land of exile. This land, filled with bitterness and misfortune, both visible and invisible, is the earthly life.

In the meantime, Joseph gave a secret command to his servants (see Gen 44): "Fill the bags of these men with wheat, as much as possible, so that they can barely carry them off. Put each man's money into the bag atop the wheat. As for the bag of the youngest, in addition to his money, put in my own silver cup." All this was done as Joseph commanded.

The morning came. The sons of Jacob embarked on their journey with their donkeys laden with bread. When they had left the city and were still not far away, Joseph said to his steward, "Go quickly in pursuit of those men, find them, and say to them, 'What is this? Why have you answered evil for good? Why have you stolen my silver cup? Is this not the cup from which my lord drinks? He uses it also for his divination.'" The steward, having reached them, repeated the words commanded by Joseph. They answered, "In vain does your master speak thus! No, your servants have not done this. Here is the money that we found in our bags and brought back from the land of Canaan, and so why should we steal silver and gold from the house of your master? If you find it, let him who stole the cup be put to death, and we will give ourselves into slavery to your master."

The steward answered, "Let it be according to your word. Whoever has stolen the cup will become the slave of my master." Quickly, they took the bags off the donkeys and every one of them untied his bag. The steward began to search, beginning with the eldest, ending with the youngest; the cup was found in the bag of Benjamin. In despair, they began to tear their clothes, placed their bags on their donkeys, and returned into the city.

Joseph was in his house; they came to him and fell before him on the ground. "What have you done?" he asked them. "Did you not know that this land has no better diviner than I?" Judah answered, "Lord! We have nothing to answer you, nothing to say, nothing to justify ourselves! God is punishing a secret sin of your servants. We will give ourselves in slavery to my lord. May we all be your slaves, we, and the one in whose bag you found the cup." "Why should I be unfair?" asked Joseph. "Let him, in whose bags the cup was found, be my slave, but you may return to your father."

Then Judah approached him and said,

Lord! I beg you, allow me to say a few words. Do not be angry with your slave. I know that you are second only to Pharaoh. Lord! You asked your servants if we have a father or brother. And we told you that we have an elderly father and a young brother who was born when our father was already in mature years. There were two brothers from one mother. The elder . . . he died. This one remains alone, and our father has come to love him dearly. You said to your servants—bring him to me; I want to see him. We said to you that it is impossible for the young man to leave his father; if he will leave his father, he will die. And yet, you said to your slaves that if our youngest brother would not come, then we would not be allowed in your presence.

When we came to our father, we told him your words. Our father told us to go again to buy bread. And we answered that we could not go! Only if our youngest brother would come with us, then we could go, for without him we would not be allowed to stand before the face of my lord. Our father reminded us that his wife gave him two sons. One of them he sent to us, and we told him that he was eaten by animals, and from that moment, he had not seen him. If something were to happen to the second son, our father would be bowed down by his sorrow to hell itself. Thus, if I now go to your servant, our father, and the young man will not come with me—his soul is bound to the soul of this youth!—and our father will see that the young man is not with us, he will die. And we, your servants, will send our aged father with sorrow to hell. I, your servant, took the young man from my father and said to him, "If I do not bring him back to you and do not present him to you, let your anger be heavy on me for the rest of my life." Let me be a slave instead of the young man. Yes! I will be your slave . . . Let the young man go home with his brothers.

Joseph could no longer contain himself or continue to conceal himself (Gen 45). He ordered all those attending him to leave the room; even his servants and the members of his household were not allowed to stay when he revealed himself to his brothers. Everyone left; then with weeping and groaning, Joseph exclaimed to his brothers, "I am Joseph! Is my father truly still alive?" His brothers were thrown into complete confusion; they could answer him nothing. Joseph said to them, "Come closer to me." They approached.

"I am Joseph," he repeated.

I am your brother, whom you sold. Do not sorrow that you sold me . . . Let this not worry you or torture you! God, Who provides for your salvation, led me here. For two years now this land has been in the grip of a famine, and there are still five years left in which they will plough the land in vain, for there will be no harvest. God sent me before you to prepare a haven for you in this land, to feed our numerous family. It was not you who sold me here; God sent me here, making me as a father to Pharaoh, the lord over his entire house and the master of the whole land of Egypt. Hurry to return to our father and say to him that this is what his son, Joseph, says to him, "God has made me lord of Egypt; come to me, do not tarry. You will settle in the land of Goshen, you will be near me, you and your sons and the sons of your sons, and your sheep, and your cattle, and all your flocks. I will feed you, for the famine will rage over the land for five more years." Your eyes see, and the eyes of Benjamin, my brother, see that I, with my lips, say these things to you. Tell my father of all the glory and might given to me in Egypt, all that you have seen with your own eyes. Hurry and lead my father here.

He threw himself on the neck of Benjamin and embraced him, weeping, and Benjamin embraced him and wept as well.

Then, with tears, he embraced all of his brothers. Then their mouths were opened, sealed until that moment with fear and confusion. They began to speak with Joseph.

Rumor reached the house of Pharaoh that Joseph's brothers had arrived; Pharaoh rejoiced, as did his entire court. Pharaoh said to Joseph, "Tell your brothers: this is what you shall do. Fill your bags with bread and go into the land of Canaan and, having taken your father, move him and all your belongings to Egypt. The riches of Egypt are open to you."

Joseph gave gifts to each of his brothers—two changes of clothing—but to Benjamin he gave five changes of clothing and three hundred gold coins. To his father he sent many gifts on ten donkeys, and he gave his brothers ten mules laden with bread for the return journey. Having so gifted his brothers, he let them go. As he released them, he said, "Do not quarrel with each other along the way." The willful fosterlings of the wilderness needed such strict instruction; now they listened to his wise counsel, remembered it, and kept it.

The sons of Jacob returned to the land of Canaan, to their father, and said to him, "Your son Joseph is alive; it is he who rules over the entire land of Egypt." Jacob was terrified and did not believe them. They assured him and retold all the words of Joseph in detail. When the elder saw the rich gifts and the chariots sent by Joseph, then his spirit came alive and he said, "How wonderful it is for me that Joseph is yet alive! I will go and see him before the time comes for me to die."

The patriarch set out on the journey with all his household, with all his belongings; and having reached the Well of the Oath, he brought a sacrifice to God (Gen 46). In a vision at night, God said to the elder, "Jacob! Jacob! I am the God of your fathers. Do not fear to settle in Egypt; there I will make you a great nation. I will come with you to Egypt and I will lead you out of it again. With his own hands, Joseph will close your eyes."

When the family of Jacob resettled into lands belonging to Egypt, they included, in addition to Jacob and his sons, over seventy-five men. Having reached the land of Goshen, Jacob sent Judah to tell Joseph of his arrival. Joseph ordered that a chariot be prepared for him, and he rode to meet his elderly father in the land of Goshen. When he saw him, he embraced him with a cry, weeping. Jacob said to Joseph, "Now I can die, because I have seen your face. You are still alive!" When the entire family had arrived in Egypt, Joseph said to his brother, "I will go to Pharaoh and tell him of your arrival. I will say that my brothers and the household of my father that lived in the land of Canaan have come to me. They are shepherds; this is the way of our people from time immemorial. He will tell you to settle in the land of Goshen in Arabia."

This was a large area of fruitful land, very good for pasture, and it was unsettled. The reason for the settlement of the family of the patriarch in a separated and unsettled country, according to the Scriptures, was the well-known superstition of the Egyptians, who considered all those who raised sheep to be unclean.

Joseph told Pharaoh that his father and brothers with their flocks had arrived from Canaan and had settled in the land of Goshen (Gen 47). From among his brothers he chose five and presented them to Pharaoh. Pharaoh asked the brothers of Joseph, "What is your occupation?" They answered, "We, your slaves, are shepherds. This occupation was ours from childhood and the occupation of our fathers and their fathers before them. Now we have come to live in your lands; in the land of Canaan the famine rages even worse than before, and the pastures of that land are no longer capable of sustaining our flocks. Please allow your servants to settle in the land of Goshen."

Pharaoh answered, speaking to Joseph, "Your father and your brothers have come to you. Before you lies the entire land of Egypt; settle them in the most appropriate place. Let them live in the land of Goshen. If there are capable men among them, place them as chief shepherds over my own flocks." Joseph then led Jacob into Pharaoh's presence; the elder blessed the king of Egypt. Pharaoh asked Jacob how old he was. "I am one hundred thirty years old. But they are not many, and my life has been full of sorrows. I will not live as long as my forefathers lived." And, after once again blessing the king, the elder left his presence. Joseph did everything according to Pharaoh's command and settled his father in the land of Goshen. The favorite son visited his elderly father often in that place and provided him with everything necessary.

This book of the Bible has preserved some very interesting details concerning the organization of Egyptian society in the time of Joseph. In these details, we see a model of how centralized government developed, how people passed from a state of half-wildness to a state of allegiance to a particular center of government. This citizenship was at first not complete and more similar to a patriarchal system of obedience, but later, this citizenship became absolute. We also see that the man who consolidated the absolute monarchical authority in Egypt was Joseph. The court of Pharaoh of that time, though it was already majestic and luxurious, had not yet had a chance to grow out of a certain patriarchal simplicity. Joseph, who was basically Pharaoh's prime minister, sold bread by himself; another nobleman is described as carrying baskets of bread on his head; a third squeezes grapes with his own hands into the cup and hands it to Pharaoh not only during triumphant feasts, but, as is evident, every day. Egypt was at that time sparsely settled, which is why an entire fruitful region (Goshen) remained empty of people, while the inhabitants of cities did not have an opportunity to work the land or to shepherd flocks.

The book of Genesis describes a political world that is still young. The words of the God-inspired writer of this book, Moses, unpretentiously transport the attentive reader to a distant, holy antiquity; to a people who lived in wondrous simplicity; to a newly begun historical reality devoid of any sophistication. This life and this simplicity are filled with power! Whosoever immerses himself often in contemplation of the Biblical accounts will inevitably sense within his soul an extraordinary, strange impression. This impression is of a fresh and youthful fragrance, like breathing the air of a wonderful summer morning. The soul becomes younger from this distant glance at the youth of the world, from conversing with the young world. Its strength emboldens and strengthens us, just like an old man who comes alive in the company of small children. It is pleasant to bask in this freshness of the young world, to rest in it from the impression of the contemporary world, so old and corrupt as it is.

The terrible famine continued; Egypt and Palestine suffered especially badly. In these countries not a single person had his own bread, except for the bread prepared in advance by Joseph. No gold or silver remained in either land, for all the money had passed into the hands of Joseph, and he put them in Pharaoh's treasury, which, it should be noted, was in the house of the king of Egypt. The Egyptians, though they had no money, had need of bread; they first sold Pharaoh their flocks, then their lands, and then finally their own selves. This is the beginning of true Egyptian citizenship. Only the lands of the priests remained their own; they received their bread from Pharaoh for free, as an offering.

After the hungry years ended, when the Egyptians had sold their lands and even themselves to Pharaoh, Joseph gave them grain for plowing, with the condition that one-fifth of every year's harvest would be returned to the treasury of Pharaoh. All of this was enthusiastically and gratefully accepted by the people of this newly formed autocratic government. "You have saved our lives," the Egyptians said to Joseph. "You are our benefactor; we will be Pharaoh's slaves."

The writer of Genesis notes that this tribute continued to his own time, that is, nearly four hundred years later. From the much later writings of Herodotus and Diodorus of Sicily, it is evident that this same kind of tribute (one-fifth of the harvest) continued in their time. It is also evident from their writings that the land of Egypt was entirely the property of the kings of Egypt. Diodorus wrote that this tax on the land of Egypt was so profitable for the Pharaohs that no other taxes were considered necessary.[8] Joseph's profound, bright mind is obvious in his disposition, his unusual ability to rule, an ability that was revealed in him from his youth and which was so quickly noticed by Potiphar and the chief jailer. He instituted a heavy tax, but one that was effective considering the nature of the country.

What sort of tax is more appropriate for fruitful Egypt than a tax on bread? It was easy to levy such a tax in a country where a typical harvest is bountiful; it was easy to levy such a tax on fields lying next to a ship-bearing river—as are all the fruitful fields of Egypt, lying adjacent to the banks of the Nile—to be gathered in granaries in cities that lie along the same river. It was easy to overcome shortages that could happen in any given year of bad harvests, because of the tax on grain during the years of good harvest. If one can call any harvests extraordinary, in comparison with the harvests of the rest of the world, the harvests of Egypt truly were so.

It was easy for Pharaoh to gather bread in his own country. Later, when harbors were built along the Mediterranean Sea (on whose banks the entire civilized trading world lived), Egypt became the breadbasket of the civilized world, as long as the Mediterranean Sea remained its center. And it remained the center of the educated and politically active world almost until modern times, for nearly the complete lifespan of the world.

This ordinance of Joseph had unusual validity in spite of its simplicity; therefore, it remained in place for a very long time. Time itself bows before this wise civic command, preserving it through many centuries in unchanged invariability, so beneficial for governments. The power of Pharaoh was strengthened, and his autocracy founded, by the civic virtues, so obvious to all, of a former slave named Joseph. He provided a newly forming kingdom with capital and a constant stream of abundant income.

Jacob lived for seventeen years in the land of Egypt. Having reached the venerable age of 147, he felt the imminence of his death. A few days before he died, he called his beloved son Joseph to himself and said, "A great mercy I ask—do not bury me in Egypt. Let me lie with my fathers! Bear me out of Egypt and bury me in their tomb." Moved by faith—not by petty, worldly consideration—the inspired elder wished his body to be carried to Palestine and buried in the family cave in Hebron. The Apostle Paul interpreted this testament, referring to these words as inspired by God and also containing with themselves a great mystery. The holy son promised to exactly fulfill the will of his holy father (see Heb 11:21). Jacob required that this promise be sealed with an oath, and Joseph gave the oath. Then Jacob, who sat on his bed, bowed to the crossbar of Joseph's staff. The staff was proper to a magnate, either according to the custom of the time or to indicate Joseph's rank.

After a few days had passed, Joseph was informed that his father had reached the limit of his strength (Gen 48). Joseph took his two sons Manasseh and Ephraim and went to his dying father. The weak elder was lying on his deathbed, barely able to move. He was told, "Your son, Joseph, comes to you." The elder gathered his remaining strength and sat on his bed. Was it love for his son that gave him strength? Or did grace pour down on him at that moment? The dying man came back to life, renewed by divine inspiration.

Often the natural activity of the chosen ones of God is suddenly bolstered by the supernatural action of the Holy Spirit. This mighty action leads a person out of his natural state and makes him an instrument of God. Such were the last minutes of Jacob. When Joseph entered, Jacob said,

> My God appeared to me in Luz, in the land of Canaan. He blessed me and said, "I will multiply you; I will make of you a great race of people and I will give to you and to your descendants this land for their permanent holding." For this reason, your two sons, who were born to you before my coming to Egypt, will be my sons as well. Ephraim and Manasseh will be mine, just as Reuben and Simeon are mine. The sons that will be born to you after them will be yours and will be called to the inheritance under the names of these two brothers, as part of their lot. Your mother, Rachel, died in the land of Canaan, when I traveled from Mesopotamia and approached Ephratha (that is, Bethlehem). There, near the road, I buried her.

When Jacob saw the sons of Joseph, he asked, "Who are these that came with you?" Joseph answered, "These are my sons, whom God has given me here." And Jacob said, "Bring them to me; I will bless them." The eyes of the patriarch were dimmed by age; he could not see clearly. When Joseph led his sons to him, he embraced them and kissed them. Then he said to Joseph, "I never hoped to see your face, but God has shown me even your sons." Joseph led them away from the knees of the elder, and they bowed down before him to the ground. Then, taking Ephraim in his right hand, opposite Jacob's left, and taking Manasseh in his left hand, opposite Jacob's right, Joseph led them again to the elder. The inspired old man extended his hands to bless them, but then he crossed them. His right hand he placed on the head of Ephraim, and his left on the head of Manasseh. This is the first time the cross appears as part of a blessing; it will become the customary sign of blessing in the New Testament Church.

"God," said the holy patriarch: "Whom my fathers Abraham and Isaac pleased; God, Who watched over me and helped me from my childhood; Who delivered me from all my troubles—may He bless these children! They will be called by my name and the names of my fathers Abraham and Isaac; let a numerous issue come from them."

When Joseph saw that the elder placed his right hand on Ephraim, it seemed wrong to him; he took his father's hand to move it from the head of Ephraim to the head of Manasseh, the elder, and said, "My father! You have not placed your hands correctly. Here is the firstborn—place your right hand on his head." The elder did not want to do this. "I know," he said, "I know, my son; from the firstborn there will come a great number of descendants, and he will be great. But the lesser brother will be still greater; his descendants will be an entire nation." He blessed them again.

"In you," he said, "let Israel be blessed! They will say: let God accomplish that which He accomplished with Ephraim and Manasseh." To Joseph he said, "I am dying. May God be with you and may He return you from this land to the land of your fathers. In that land I give you an extra portion of land, more than your brothers. I took it with the sword and bow from the Amorites." St Isaac the Syrian, in his 1st Homily, noted that the words of inspired men are like the word of the elderly Jacob. With their words they give their listeners the spiritual strength abiding in them, acquired by them in their battle with sin, in their victories over the invisibly Amorites—sinful thoughts and feelings.

The hour of the holy patriarch's death approached. In this hour before death, the Holy Spirit poured His abundant grace on him, as though completely possessing him. In those last minutes of earthly life, in which the soul was ready to come out of the decrepit body, the Spirit of God descended, stopped the impending separation, and poured His gracious life into the remaining body and the departing soul. The dying man came to life in the life of the age to come. Quickly, the elder called all his sons to his side. Quickly they came to him and surrounded him. He still sat on his bed. When they had gathered, Jacob uttered an inspired, prophetic testament.

This testament is filled with youthful power and poetry, the eternal youthfulness of the inhabitants of heaven, their holy poetry. There is no man here! Here, the tongue of man was merely an instrument. What they heard was the voice of God. God speaks, uttering His will, with power disposing the fates of nations and their distant descendants. The testament of the patriarch is a heavenly song, sung by the Spirit for the hearing of the whole world.

This song announces the Redeemer to the world, to peoples immersed in slavery to idolatry—the illumination of the light of Christianity. "Come together," said the dying elder to his sons, speaking, as it were, from the age to come. "Come together and surround me. I will tell you the future. Come together, you sons of Jacob, hear me, hear Israel, hear your father. Reuben will lose his birthright, because he catered to his sensuality. Neither will Simeon or Levi receive it. Their tendency to spill blood is blighted with a curse, and their descendants are fated to be dispersed among the tribes of their other brothers. Over Judah has the abundance of the blessing poured forth; to him is promised political might, glory, the first place among his brothers. But above all other blessings is this predestination: he will be the forefather of the Saviour, Who is the expectation of nations."

The inspired patriarch spoke the blessing over his sons, a blessing for each, counting his sons by age. Having reached Joseph, he once again called down the blessings of heaven and earth on him and on his descendants. True and powerful was this blessing, as seen in the prosperity that the numerous descendants of Joseph later enjoyed.

With the end of the prophecy, Jacob's manner changes. He is no longer inspired by ecstasy, gravitas, heavenly majesty. He becomes like a body abandoned by the soul. God, Who spoke through the mouth of the elder, ends His mysterious declaration. The inspired prophet falls asleep; the dying elder begins to speak in his decrepitude. "I now speak," these were the last words of Jacob, "to my own people. Bury me in the cave that is on the field of Ephron the Hittite. There Abraham and Sarah are buried; there Isaac and Rebecca are buried; there I also buried Leah." Having said this, Jacob put his feet up on his bed and died. He "was added to his people" (49:33), the Scriptures say, to those holy saints whom the earth produced and raised for heaven, whom it had already given over to the province of eternity.

Seeing that Jacob had died, Joseph fell on the face of his father, kissed his face and mouth, already stamped with death, watered his face with abundant tears (Gen 50). He ordered the physicians to prepare the body for burial according to Egyptian custom. The physicians prepared his body for forty days, embalming it to prevent corruption. All of Egypt participated in Joseph's sorrow; seventy days the Egyptians wept over the death of the holy elder, the patriarch of Israel. After the days of weeping had passed, Joseph begged Pharaoh's permission to fulfill his father's testament and his last promise, bound by an oath, to bury the body of the righteous man in the land of Canaan. Pharaoh wanted the journey to Canaan to be accompanied by worthy pomp. The entire court of the king of Egypt, all of his magnates, accompanied Joseph; among them were many chariots and riders. All the sons of Jacob, all his grandsons capable of undertaking the journey took part in it. Having reached the place of burial, they honored the holy body with seven days of weeping. The Scriptures even called it "a great and very solemn lamentation" (50:10). The field in which this large assembly of people stopped and where the funeral lamentations were performed was eventually called by the locals "the Mourning of Egypt."

Having fulfilled his promise, Joseph returned to Egypt. His brothers continued to worry about the crime they committed against Joseph. They suspected that their noble brother still harbored resentment against them, but his pure, holy soul was capable only of good. Thinking that Joseph avoided seeking revenge merely not to disturb the tranquility of their elderly father, and that now he would avail himself of the quickest opportunity, they came to him and said, "Our father commanded us before his death: say to Joseph, forgive them their sin, forgive them their falsehood; they committed a crime against you, but forgive their guilt for the sake of the God of your fathers." As they were saying this, Joseph wept. Then they fell before him and said, "Look, we give ourselves up to you as your slaves."

Greathearted Joseph, Joseph who was worthy of the blessings of both earth and heaven, who was worthy of the blessings of the entire race of Christians and all who read the account of his instructive actions, answered his brothers, "Do not fear. I am God's. You conspired to do evil to me, but God transformed it into good. And His providence came to pass. And now many people are fed and their lives are preserved. Do not fear. I will be a benefactor to you and your families." A living faith in God and the pure, spiritual vision of the providence of God raise a person above all misfortunes, above the terrifying spiritual calamities of remembrance of evils and a desire for revenge.

The book of Genesis remains silent concerning the later events of Joseph's life. Likely, his life continued in peace and constant well-being. The Scriptures only say that Joseph remained for the rest of his days in Egypt, that he saw the grandchildren of Ephraim, the sons of Machir, Manasseh's eldest son, and died at the age of 110. As he departed into eternity, he uttered his testament to his family: "I am dying. God will visit you and will lead you out of this land and into the land that He promised to give to you. Then, when you resettle, take my bones from here back to the land of promise." Having made this will, he died. His body, preserved from corruption, was placed in a coffin and prepared for the promised resettlement. Joseph's body would await this resettlement, which he promised and believed in with such strong faith, for three hundred years.

May also I die and be buried in Egypt, the land of my exile. But I, a childless one, leave my children, my people, this will, and testament: they will resettle into the land of promise and take my body there with them. My children and my people are the thoughts of my mind, the emotions of my heart. O my children! O my people! Leave the land of Goshen, its fruitful pastures, useful only for raising sheep. Leave Egypt, abandon this fallen world where the flesh and sin reign, and resettle in heaven! My body will descend for a time into the dust from which it came. But when it will rise from the sleep of death, aroused by the trumpet of the resurrection, you—my thoughts and my emotions—given wings by the Spirit, will raise the resurrected body to heaven! Heaven is promised by God to the whole man; not only to his soul, but to his body as well!

So! The time will come. God will visit man; He will gather this body that has collapsed into dust and has become mixed with the earth, and He will give life to this body. And if the thoughts and emotions of a man are worthy of heaven, anointed, stamped by the Spirit, then his body will be changed, will become glorified, will be given wings, and together with the soul it will ascend to heaven.

CHAPTER 3

A Letter to the Brotherhood of the Sergiev Hermitage from the Nikolo-Babaev Monastery

My beloved fathers and brothers! I thank you for remembering me, a sinner, and for your love. May the blessing of God rest on you and on all who traverse the sea of life with the purpose of salvation, with goal of reaching the divine shore. Whoever lives exclusively for gain, advantages, and the pleasures of a transient world—to such a person I have nothing to say.

During my journey from the Sergiev Hermitage through Moscow to the Babaev Monastery, I visited many monasteries and experienced personally that which the Holy Fathers describe in their God-inspired writings. I saw in every place—both in the secluded wilderness and in the middle of the boisterous city—that those Christians who plumb the depths of the word of God and try to implement it in their life are inspired to follow the proper directions toward blessed eternity. On the other hand, those who disdain the study of God's word and who do not fulfill the holy commandments of God remain in a pitiable darkness of sin, in slavery to sin, in complete fruitlessness, even if they are ascetics living in the deep desert.

The eremitic life, when not connected with spiritual labors, only feeds, fattens, and strengthens the sinful passions.[9] This is what the Holy Fathers teach us; this is how it is in actual fact. The word of God is eternal life; he who is nourished by it "will live forever" (John 6:51). Wherever the person who is nourished by the word of God may abide—in the desert or in the midst of many people—everywhere the word of God will preserve its holy quality—the quality of eternal life. And so, no place can hinder eternal life from communicating to such a person a truly spiritual life, the only kind of true life.

When I lived with you, I always reminded you and exhorted you to study the word of God; it can give our noisy monastery the worthiness of a secluded skete. It can build a spiritual wall around our monastery, even though there is no physical wall protecting it. This spiritual wall will be stronger and higher than any wall built of bricks and stones; no sin will sneak into our monastery, and no virtue will escape it. Finding myself absent from you, I find nothing better to do than to repeat everything I have already said to you in writing. Brothers! Do not waste your life in pointless occupations; do not squander the earthly life, short as it is, given to you for the acquisition of eternal things. It will rush by, run away, and it will not come back; its loss is irreparable. Those who waste life in vain pursuits and amusements deprive themselves of eternal blessedness, prepared for us by God. Use it instead for the study of the good and perfect will of God, as it is outlined in the Holy Scriptures. "For me to write the same things to you is not tedious, but for you it is safe" (Phil 3:1).

When the merciful Lord, Who has given me a certain improvement of physical health, will return me to your blessed community and will allow me to see your faces, as the faces of the holy angels, then my word to you will be the same as it was before. Even before, I exhorted you, as you endure all things in our God-given sanctuary, only seek spiritual consolation in the word of God, not becoming distracted by vain thoughts and fantasies that give false promises of consolation, but only steal it from us. "The portion of the madman is dearth before his eyes," as the great St Isaac the Syrian said in his second homily. On the contrary, the soul that accepts with gratitude the gifts of God will reap the treasure of these gifts. This I say of our sanctuary, the Sergiev Hermitage. Gratitude to God for this sanctuary can make it a calm and pleasant refuge; but confused, embarrassed glances full of complaint pass on their darkness, their opacity even to things that, in all fairness, are worthy of our gratitude and doxology to God.

A tree that is replanted in different places loses its life force, even if it were a naturally strong tree, and eventually it stops giving fruit. Our divine Teacher has commanded us: "By your patience possess your souls" (Luke 21:19). He declared that those who bear fruit should "bear fruit with patience" (Luke 8:15). He proclaimed, "He who endures to the end shall be saved" (Matt 24:13). Finally, he said that "if anyone draws back, My soul has no pleasure in him" (Heb 10:38).

I immerse myself in the contemplation of Christ's field. How many seeds are sowed in it! How many stalks have grown! How beautifully they turn green, making a consoling and pleasing noise, excited by the wind. The time comes for these stalks to ripen, the time of harvest; they leave the field on which they were born and grew; they are gathered in the granaries, dried up, threshed, and winnowed.

Our life is exactly the same. How many different upheavals are necessary before a man sees the vanity of life, all of its uselessness! Finally, he has found the granary, the refuge of the monastery. The heavy, ripe berry, no matter how many times it is winnowed, still always falls back to the ground of the granary, while the tares and the unripe berries, those who are empty and fruitless, are easily borne away from the granary by the wind. At first they seem to be a cloud, indicating something significant; then they dissipate and eventually fade from view and completely disappear. The sorrows that we encounter in society cannot be an excuse for weak faith. A sorrow-less life and home is an unrealistic dream that only mind and hearts devoid of divine illumination seek. Such minds and hearts are deluded by the demons. To us it is commanded to seek spiritual peace in the mutual bearing of weaknesses. A change of place, which only comes from judgment of our brother, is not the fulfillment of the law of Christ. No! "Bear one another's burdens, and so fulfill the law of Christ" (Gal 6:2). Only the madman who seeks a place with no sorrow flees the fulfillment of the law of Christ. The only place and life without sorrow is in heaven; from there all sorrow and groaning flee. The earth is the place of sighs, and blessed are those who sigh on it, for they will be consoled in heaven. The place and life without sorrows is only found in a heart that acquires humility and by humility enters into patient endurance.

The word of God teaches us all this, all that is good and salvific. Therefore, the Lord Himself commands, all the prophets and apostles command, all the Holy Fathers exhort, command, beg—remain constantly in the study of the word of God, which is the source of all good things, all things that are life and light on this earth, which is the vale of tears, hunger, darkness, and death. "And the light shines in the darkness, and the darkness did not comprehend it" (John 1:5). Led by a ray of this light, the pilgrim of the earthly life wanders out to the spiritual pasture of salvation, and from here he begins his way to eternal life. Brothers, accept my words, which are nothing more than the echo of the teachings of all the saints. Thus, a deserted wild cavern—home to reptiles and all manner of other impurities—repeats in its echo the inspired sounds of divine hymnography.

I beg your holy prayers and commit myself to your holy prayers.

Archimandrite Ignatius
Nikolo-Babaev Monastery, 1847

CHAPTER 4

The Fear of God and the Love for God

Man's service to God, commanded by God, is simple and clear. But we have become so complicated and cunning, so devoid of spiritual wisdom, that we need the most exacting guidance and instruction to correctly and pleasingly serve God. Very often we approach serving God through the mediation of some method that is actually contrary to the nature of God, or is even forbidden by God, for it harms our soul. Thus some people, when they read the Holy Scriptures, learn that love is the greatest of virtues (1 Cor 13:13), that it is God Himself (1 John 4:8). So they begin to strengthen and develop in their heart the emotion of love, and their prayer, contemplation of God, all their actions become dissolved in this emotion.

But God abhors such an impure sacrifice. He requires love from a person, but only true, spiritual, holy love, not imaginative, physical love that is defiled by pride and sensuality. One cannot love God except with a heart purified and sanctified by divine grace. And love for God is a gift of God; it is poured out into the souls of true servants of God by the direct action of the Holy Spirit (Rom 5:5). Contrary to this, natural, human love is damaged by the sin that has encompassed the entire human race, the nature, and characteristics of each individual. It is futile to rush toward worship of God, union with God, through such a love! He is holy and He abides only in the saints. He is self-sufficient; futile are the efforts of man to accept God within them when God Himself does not yet wish to abide in that person, even though every person is the temple of God, created by God for the purpose of God's indwelling (1 Cor 3:16). This temple is in a pitiable state of desolation; before it can be sanctified, it needs to be renewed.

Prematurely striving to develop a sense of love for God within oneself is already self-delusion. It immediately estranges a person from right worship of God; it immediately leads to all manner of delusion; it ends with the damage and death of the soul. We will prove this with examples from the Holy Scriptures and the writings of the Holy Fathers. We will show how the way to Christ begins and is accomplished with the guidance of the fear of God. Finally, we will prove that love for God is blessed consolation in God, available only for those who have completed the invisible path to God.

The Old Testament expresses the truth by means of foreshadowing, and events that occur with the outer man become symbols of what in the New Testament is accomplished with the inner man. In it, we read of the terrible punishment of Nadab and Abihu, sons of Aaron, priests of the people of Israel. Each one of them, as we read in Leviticus, took his censer, placed incense in it, "and offered strange fire before the Lord, which He had not commanded them" (Lev 10:1). Only sanctified fire, kept in the Tabernacle of Testimony, could be used in the holy services of the Israelites. "So fire went out from the Lord and devoured them and they died before the Lord" (Lev 10:2). This "strange fire" in the censer of the priests of Israel is a symbol of the love of fallen nature that has become alienated from God in all aspects. The punishment for the bold priest is the death of the soul that dares to irrationally and criminally offer such a sacrifice of impure desires to God. Such a soul is struck down by death and perishes in its own self-delusion in the fires of its passions. On the other hand, the sanctified fire that alone can be used in worship symbolizes grace-given love. Fire for worship is taken not from fallen nature, but from the tabernacle of God.

St John of the Ladder said, "The fire that descends into the heart restores prayer. When prayer rises up again and ascends to heaven, then fire descends into the upper room of the soul."[10] "Behold! All of you [who] walk in the light of your fire and the flame" of the fallen nature that "you kindle," instead of putting it out, will perish in the fire and flames of hell. By an incorrect and criminal action in yourself, "you kindle a fire and feed" for yourselves the "flame" of Gehenna.[11]

The New Testament teaches the same thing in the parable concerning the man who entered the bridal feast not wearing a wedding garment, even though he was one of those invited. The king told his servants, pointing at the unworthy guest: "Bind him hand and foot, take him away, and cast him into outer darkness" (Matt 22:13). The action of tying the hands and feet is symbolic of the cessation of any ability to progress spiritually. This is true—the one who has taken a wrong path reaches such a state when he strives quickly toward love while still in a sinful state. However, love can only actualize the union of man with God *after* he has been cleansed by repentance. "Being cast into the outer darkness" symbolizes the fall of the mind and heart into error and self-delusion. In this state of error and self-delusion, every thought and every emotion is entirely dark, wholly opposed to God.

The servants, into whose power the unfortunate wedding guest is committed, are the demons. Even though they are infected with mad hatred toward God, they still remain His servants in the sense of His limitless omnipotence and wisdom. They take mastery only over those people who have been given over to demonic power thanks to their self-willed way of life. Only he who has embarked on a road forbidden by God is given over to demonic mastery, since he has been enticed by self-importance and has willingly rejected submission to God.

The Holy Scriptures exalt and glorify holy love. The Apostle Paul, having listed the gifts of the Holy Spirit in his first epistle to the Corinthians—including the gifts of miracle-working, prophecy, discernment of spirits, knowledge of various tongues—said, "Earnestly desire the best gifts. And yet I show you a more excellent way" (1 Cor 12:31). What can be greater than a prophet, a miracle-worker, a speaker in foreign tongues, according to the gift of the Holy Spirit (that is, not by merely human learning)?

St Paul explains,

> Though I speak with the tongues of men and of angels, but have not love, I have become sounding brass or a clanging cymbal. And though I have the gift of prophecy, and understand all mysteries and all knowledge, and though I have all faith, so that I could remove mountains, but have not love, I am nothing. And though I bestow all my goods to feed the poor, and though I give my body to be burned, but have not love, it profits me nothing. . . . Love never fails. But whether there are prophecies, they will fail; whether there are tongues, they will cease; whether there is knowledge, it will vanish away. For we know in part and we prophesy in part. But when that which is perfect has come, then that which is in part will be done away. (1 Cor 13:1–3, 8–10)

What is "that which is perfect?" Love is "the bond of perfection" (Col 3:14). One must reach perfection in all virtues before entering the perfection of perfections and their ultimate union in love. "Everyone who loves is born of God and knows God" (1 John 4:7). "God is love, and he who abides in love abides in God, and God in him" (1 John 4:16). "By this we know that we abide in Him, and He in us, because He has given us of His Spirit" (1 John 4:13). The only true sign of the acquisition of love, given to us by the very Holy Spirit, is the active presence in us of the same Holy Spirit. Whoever has not become a temple of the

Holy Spirit should not flatter himself or delude himself. He cannot be the temple of love, for he is devoid of it. Love flows into our hearts together with the Holy Spirit. It is His quality. Into whomever the Holy Spirit descends, in him also appears His quality—love (see Rom 5:5). "Whoever acquires love, together with it puts on God Himself," said St Isaac the Syrian in his 48th Homily.

Perhaps some will protest: "We are Christians! We are renewed by holy baptism, by which all the weaknesses of our fallen nature have been healed, by which the image and likeness of God are restored in their primal glory, and the Holy Spirit is implanted in us, the damage of our nature is undone, and so we are capable of love." Yes, it is so. But the grace-filled state of renewal and regeneration given by Holy Baptism needs to be upheld by a life according to the commandments of the Gospel. "If you keep My commandments, you will abide in My love. . . . Abide in Me, and I in you. As the branch cannot bear fruit of itself, unless it abides in the vine, neither can you, unless you abide in Me. . . . If anyone does not abide in Me, he is cast out as a branch and is withered; and they gather them and throw them into the fire, and they are burned" (John 15:10, 4, 6).

Whoever does not sustain the gifts of baptism, by living a life according to the commandments, loses everything he acquired. St John Chrysostom said, "An unutterable and awe-inspiring glory is given by baptism. It remains in us one or two days; then we extinguish it by directing the entire storm of life's cares against it, shutting off the rays of light with thick clouds."[12] Having come to new life in the regeneration of baptism, we once again put ourselves to death by a carnal life, by a life lived for sin, for earthly pleasures and gain. The holy Apostle Paul said, "We are debtors—not to the flesh, to live according to the flesh. Those who are in the flesh cannot please God. For to be carnally minded is death" (Rom 8:12, 8, 6).

The grace of baptism remains without effect, like a bright sun covered by clouds, like a precious treasure buried underground. Sin begins to act within us with its full power, even more strongly than before our baptism, depending on the degree to which we abandon ourselves to a sinful way of life. But the spiritual treasure given to us is not fully taken away from us before our death, and we can uncover it again in its full power and glory, but only through repentance.[13] Repentance for our sinful life, sorrow over our willing and unwilling sins, warfare against sinful habits, the struggle to defeat them and sorrow over our own defeats by them, compulsion of ourselves to fulfill all the commandments of the Gospel—this is our lot. We must beg forgiveness of God, be reconciled with Him, wipe away our unfaithfulness by our fidelity, and replace our friendship with sin by hatred of sin. To those who have been reconciled, holy love is natural. It is not so much we who seek it; rather it is God Who seeks that we become capable of accepting it.

Having accused of delusion the one who was content with himself in his conceit and blindness, the Lord called him to zealous repentance and uttered the following consolation and promise: "Behold, I stand at the door and knock. If anyone hears My voice and opens the door, I will come in to him and dine with him, and he with Me. To him who overcomes I will grant to sit with Me on My throne, as I also overcame and sat down with My Father on His throne" (Rev 3:20–21). Thus speaks all-holy Love. The feeling of love that the sinner ascribes to himself, though he has not yet stopped drowning in his sins; this feeling that he ascribes to himself so unnaturally and proudly—it is nothing other than a delusive, forced play of emotions, a nebulous creation of reverie and self-delusion. "Whoever sins has neither seen Him nor known Him" (1 John 3:6), this God Who is Love.

Let us turn to the citizens of the desert, caves, abysses of the earth, to those people of whom the world was not worthy, to the holy monastics who studied that most exalted of sciences—the science brought down from heaven by the Lord Himself. This science is the knowledge of God and—through the mediation of true, experiential knowledge of God—the knowledge of man. Vainly do the wise of this world labor to acquire such knowledge with the help of their own reason, dimmed by the Fall. Here the light of Christ is needed! Only by the light of this light can a man see God and see himself. Illumined by the light of Christ, the venerable ascetics of the desert labored over their hearts and found in them a precious jewel—love for God. In their God-inspired writing, they warn us against those calamities that usually plague the premature seeker of love. St Isaac the Syrian discusses this in an especially vivid way. From his many writings, we will offer several proofs and soul-saving instructions.

"The all-wise Lord," said the great teacher of monks, "wills for us to reap our spiritual bread in the sweat of our brow. He commanded this not out of anger, but to prevent spiritual indigestion that could lead to our death. Every virtue is the mother of the next virtue that follows it. If you leave the mother that gives birth to virtues and instead rush immediately to the acquisition of the daughters before acquiring the mother, then even these virtues will become vipers for the soul. Then, if you will not reject them from yourself, you will soon die."[14] Spiritual wisdom naturally follows the active fulfillment of the virtues. Before both must come fear and love. Again, fear must come before love. Anyone who shamelessly insists that he can acquire love "without first training himself in the former, doubtless has already laid the foundation for the death of his own soul." The Lord has mandated such a path—fear must precede love.[15]

In his 55th Homily, which is an answer to the letter of St Simeon the Miracle-Worker, St Isaac says,

> You wrote in your letter that your soul has come to love with the process of coming to love God, but that you have not yet reached the state of love, though you have a great desire to love. To this you added that you desire the eremitic life in the desert, that purity of heart is beginning to reveal itself in you and that the memory of God ignites your heart. If this is true, then it is a very great thing. But I would prefer if you did not write this to me, because there is no order in the way you describe it. If you wrote this to ask me if it is proper, then I must tell you that the proper order is different. Whoever says that his soul does not yet have boldness in prayer because it has not yet defeated the passions—how dare he also say that his soul has come to love the process of coming to love God? There is no possible way for such a soul to become aroused with the kind of divine love that urges you to go mysteriously into the desert, if the soul has not yet defeated the passions. You have said that your soul has not yet defeated the passions, but has come to love the process of loving God; there is no order in this. Whoever says that he has not defeated the passions, but also says that he loves the process of coming to love God does not know what he is saying. You may counter: I did not say love, but love the process of coming to love. This also has no place if the soul has not yet acquired purity. If you wanted to express a more typical thought, then you are not the only one who says this, for everyone says that he desires to love God. Not only Christians say this, but even those who worship God incorrectly. This word is typical for everyone. But with most people these words are just the movements of the tongue, while the soul feels nothing of what is said. Many sick do not even know that they are sick. *Hatred* is a sickness of the soul, and *delusion* is the loss of truth. Very many, infected with both of these illnesses, declare openly their health and are praised by many. If the soul is not healed of hatred and does not acquire the natural state of health in which it was created; if it will not be reborn to health by the Spirit—then the person will not be able to desire anything supernatural, inherent to the Spirit. For while the soul remains in sickness due to its passions, it remains incapable of sensing anything with its spiritual senses. It is not able to desire the spiritual naturally, but only when inspired by listening to the Scriptures or reading them.

St Isaac the Syrian writes:

The work of the cross is eminently appropriate to the two-fold makeup of human nature. The first aspect consists in the endurance of sorrows by the body, and it is accomplished together with the action of the spiritual power of zeal and is thus called properly *active doing*. The other is acquired by the subtle work of the mind, by the constant remembrance of God and constant prayer, which is accomplished by the power of the will and is called *vision*. The first, that is, *active doing*, purifies the passionate part of the soul with the power of zeal, the second purifies the intellect of the soul by the action of spiritual love or spiritual desire. Every person who passes into the second stage before becoming adept at the first stage, whoever is enticed by the sweetness of the second—let us not say that he is too lazy to complete the first—will be subject to wrath, because he has not yet put to death his "members which are on the earth" (Col 3:5). In other words, he has not yet healed the weaknesses of his thoughts by the patient persistence in the active bearing of his cross, and yet he has already dared in his mind to imagine for himself the glory of the cross. This is what is meant by what was said by the saints of old: If the mind wishes to ascend the cross before it has healed the emotions of sins, then the wrath of God will fall upon him. The ascent to the cross brings down the wrath of God when it is accomplished not by the first taste of endurance of sorrows or the crucifixion of the flesh, but by a premature striving for spiritual vision (the second stage), which only has its place after the healing of the soul. The mind of such a one is defiled by shameful passions and still rushes after fantasy and thoughts of self-conceit. To him the path is blocked by a prohibition, because he has not purified his mind by sorrows, he has not defeated carnal desires, but from the hearing and the word he rushes forward, still filled with darkness, being himself still blind. Even those who have healthy vision, who are filled with light and have found good masters filled with grace, even these are beset by calamities day and night; their eyes are filled with tears; in prayer and tears they labor day and night because of the danger of the journey, because of the dangerous rapids that await them due to the false images of truth that are still mixed up in their minds with delusive phantasms. The Fathers say that the divine comes on its own, when you least expect it. This is so! But only if the place is clean, not sullied.[16]

Whoever desires to approach God to serve Him must commit himself to the guidance of the fear of God. This sense of holy fear, which is a sense of profound reverence for God, indicates to us, on the one hand, the boundless greatness of the divine Essence and, on the other hand, our own extreme limitation, our weakness, our state of sinfulness and fallenness. This fear is prescribed for us by the Holy Scriptures, which began to replace for us the voice of the conscience and the natural law when both became darkened, when both began to give unclear, largely misleading, signs. Finally, when the Gospel appeared, it completely replaced both the conscience and the natural law. "Serve the Lord in fear, and rejoice unto Him with trembling" (Ps 2:11), the Holy Spirit teaches us. To those who submit to His command, He says, "Come, ye children, and hearken unto me; I will teach you the fear of the Lord" (Ps 33:12). He declares a promise to give the fear of God to those who truly desire to be joined to God: "I will put My fear into their hearts so they shall not depart from Me" (Jer 39:40 LXX; 32:40 NKJV).

The beginning of the great science of knowledge of God is the fear of God. The Holy Scriptures call this science "wisdom." "The fear of God is the beginning of wisdom, and there is good understanding in all who practice it . . . his praise endureth for ever and ever" (Prov 1:7 and Psalm 110:10). "The root of wisdom is to fear the Lord, and her branches are length of days. The fear of the Lord will cheer the heart and will give gladness, joy, and long life" (Sir 1:18, 10). We learn how to avoid sin by the fear of the Lord. "The command of the Lord is a fountain of life, for it causes one to turn from the snare of death. The fear of the Lord hates unrighteousness, and both rudeness and arrogance, and the ways of wicked men. Be in the fear of the Lord the whole day long" (Prov 14:28 LXX, 8:13, 23:17). By the fear of God, we are instructed in the way of God's commandments: "Blessed is the man that feareth the Lord, in His commandment shall he greatly delight. His seed shall be mighty upon earth" (Ps 111:1–2). "The angel of the Lord tarrieth round about them that fear Him, and delivereth them. . . . O fear the Lord, all ye that are His saints, for they that fear Him lack nothing" (Ps 33: 8, 10).

In vain do the dreamers who are filled with arrogance and self-delusion disdain the fear of God as something proper to despised slaves. After all, God Himself calls us to fear him, declaring that He Himself will teach us proper fear, He Himself will give us the spiritual gift of the fear of God. It is not demeaning for a person—who is a fallen, worthless, rejected, lost creature that has appropriated to himself enmity against God—to pass from a state of antagonism and perdition to a state of submission and salvation. Even such a so-called slavery is great gain! Even such slavery is great freedom! Fear is commanded for us as an essentially necessary, inevitable means for our salvation. Fear purifies a person and prepares him for love. We are slaves so that we can lawfully become children.

To the extent that we have been cleansed by repentance, we only begin to sense the presence of God. From the sense of God's presence comes the holy sense of fear of God. Experience teaches the exaltedness of this sense. Exalted and desired is this sense of the fear of God! Inspired by this sense, the mind often dulls its eyes, ceases to utter words, ceases to engender thoughts; instead, by reverent silence—so much greater than words!—it expresses its acknowledgment of its own worthlessness and utters an unutterable prayer that flows naturally from such a state.

St Isaac the Syrian describes this state superlatively:

When the humble-minded man approaches prayer or becomes worthy of it, he still does not dare to petition God or ask for anything. He does not yet know for what he should pray; all his thoughts are silent, awaiting only the mercy and the will of the God Whom he worships. His face is bowed to the earth, and the inner eye of his heart is raised to the exalted gates of the Holy of Holies. There is He Whose dominion is the darkness that dims the eyes of the Seraphim, Whose goodness inspires countless legions of angels to worship in complete silence. The boldness of this man only extends to the following words that he dares utter in prayer: "O Lord, let it be with me according to Thy will."[17]

The fear of God is a gift of God. As a gift, it is given after being asked for in prayer. The holy prophet David desired to be found worthy of such a gift, and so he begged God, "O stablish Thy word in Thy servant unto fear of Thee . . . Nail my flesh [that is, my carnal desires] to the fear of Thee" (Ps 118:38, 120). The fear of God is one of the seven gifts of the Holy Spirit that Prophet Isaiah listed so: "The Spirit of wisdom and understanding, the Spirit of counsel and might, the Spirit of knowledge and godliness. The Spirit of the fear of God shall fill Him" (Isa 11:2–3).

Our Lord Jesus Christ, Who brought peace from God and His goodwill to all men by His coming down to the earth; Who became the Father of the Age to Come and the Patriarch of the holy tribe of the saved; Who calls His children to love and union with Himself—He it is Who offers for the healing of our damaged nature, among other means, the fear of God. To the one who is subject to bursts of anger and hatred, He gives the warning of fiery Gehenna. To the one who tramples on his own conscience, He threatens imprisonment. To the one who is enticed by impure desires, He threatens eternal suffering.[18]

To the one who does not forgive his near neighbor who offends him, He declares that his own sins will not be forgiven.[19] To the lover of money and the sensualist, He gives a reminder of death that can seize them at any moment, since they do not expect it.[20]

Great is the labor of martyrdom; it is inspired and strengthened by love. But the Saviour of the world, in the instruction given to His apostles, encourages them to be sober and helps them in the terrifying trial to come. "And do not fear those who kill the body but cannot kill the soul. But rather fear Him who is able to destroy both soul and body in hell. Yes, I say to you, fear him!" (Matt 10:28, Luke 12:5). To all His followers in general, the Lord commanded the salvific fear of God, expressed in constant vigilance and watchfulness over oneself. "Let your waist be girded and your lamps burning; and you yourselves be like men who wait for their master, when he will return from the wedding, that when he comes and knocks they may open to him immediately. Blessed are those servants whom the master, when he comes, will find watching. I say to all: Watch!" (Luke 12:35–37, Mark 13:37).

The second, glorious coming of the Lord and the dread judgment over the nations is majestically described in the Gospel according to Matthew. This wondrous picture, drawn with unusual simplicity and clarity, unwillingly comes to life in the mind's eye and strikes fear in the heart. Contemplating this picture, one can describe the state into which it leads the soul with the words of Job when fear came upon him: "Shivering and trembling befell me and caused my bones to shake" (Job 4:14). With the coming of the Judgment for those cast out of heaven, the earth, the land of exile and the curse, will catch fire and the heavens will roll up like clothes being folded (see 2 Pet 3:10 and Revelation 6:14). All the dead of all times and nations, aroused by the life-giving trumpet of the word of God, will rise from their tombs and will become a boundless and countless multitude.[21] The hosts and warriors of the holy angels will come to the terrifying spectacle, to the great service. And the fallen angels will also stand before the Judge.

The Son of God will sit at the throne of glory, a glory frightening in its majesty. All rational creatures will be shaken with fear, seeing their Creator, Who called them into being from nonexistence with a single all-powerful word. They will stand before that very Word, for Whom nothing is impossible. They will stand before that Life, outside of Whom there can be no life. Truly spoke the Fathers when they said that in this terrible time all of creation, if it were not held together by the omnipotence of God and revealed thus to itself, would simply cease to exist.²² The righteous, having seen Truth face to face, will consider their own truth to have no meaning whatsoever, while the sinners will only condemn themselves if their self-justification is devoid of evangelical wisdom. Everyone's fate will be determined for eternity. Before the coming of this Judgment, the divine apostle admits that he will not be able to justify himself, even though he knows that he has not sinned, because his Judge is God.²³ All the saints, during their earthly wandering, often called to mind the dread judgment of Christ. With a timely, salvific fear, they protect themselves from the fear that will lead to despair in those who have perished. By a timely self-condemnation, they attempt to find a timely justification. With tears they ward off their future tears.

Brothers! It is necessary for us, weak and sinful ones, to frequently remember the second coming and dread judgment of Christ. Such remembrance is the most trustworthy preparation. Terrible is that judgment that awaits every person after the general resurrection; terrifying also is that judgment that awaits every person after his death. The consequences of one and the other judgment are either desired or disastrous. If earthly judges, whose occupation concerns only the perishable and passing, inspire our worry, how much more should we worry for the judgment of God? With what other purpose did the Lord give us such a clear indication of the Judgment, if not to arouse in us the kind of fear that saves the soul, that can preserve us from a sinful, negligent life that leads to our perdition? St Elijah, a monk of the Egyptian desert who led a life of silence in the Thebaid, said, "I am afraid of three times—the time of the departure of the soul from the body, the time of the court of God, and the time of the final determination of my fate by God."²⁴

Is it necessary for us to warn you that the teaching of all the Holy Fathers of the Orthodox Church concerning the fear of God agrees with the teaching of the Holy Scriptures, when the Scriptures are the source for the teaching of the fathers, and when the source of both is one—the Holy Spirit? "The fear of God is the beginning of virtue," says St Isaac the Syrian. "It is said that fear of God is also the birth of faith and only then finds root in the soul when the mind leaves the cares of this world for the sake of gathering its wandering thoughts from absentmindedness into the constant study of the age to come. . . . You would be wise to place fear of God at the very beginning of your journey, and in the matter of days you will find yourself at the gates of heaven, without the need to resort to a lengthy journey."²⁵

Among the instructions of Abba Pimen the Great, we find the following:

We need humble-mindedness and fear of God as much as we need to breathe. The three most important tasks of a monk are—to fear God, to pray to God, and to do good to his neighbor. When the bees are driven out of their hives by smoke, then the sweet fruit of their labors is taken. In the same way, carnal lust drives away the fear of God from the soul and destroys all its good fruits. The beginning and end of the spiritual way is the fear of God. The Scriptures say, "The fear of the Lord is the beginning of wisdom" (Ps 110:10). And again, when Abraham built an altar, the Lord said to him, "Now I know you fear God" (Gen 22:12).

When one of the monks responded to St Pimen by saying, "I am a part of all them that fear Thee" (Ps 118:63), the Abba answered, "The Holy Spirit said this concerning Himself." He interpreted the words of St Anthony the Great concerning St Pambo in the same way, that through the mediation of fear of God, Pambo made himself a dwelling place of the Holy Spirit.[26] St John Cassian the Roman said, "The beginning of our salvation is the fear of the Lord. By it those who are being instructed in the way of perfection are given the beginning of conversion, purification from the passions, and perseverance in the virtues. When it penetrates into the heart of man, it gives birth to disdain for all that is earthly, to forgetfulness of family, and even to hatred of the world itself."[27] In the same sermon, St John Cassian explains the words of the Lord, "And he who does not take his cross and follow after Me is not worthy of Me" (Matt 10:38), in the following manner:

Our cross is the fear of the Lord. As a crucified man can no longer turn or move his members according to the desire of his soul, so we must also direct our will and desires not according to what is pleasant or gives us joy in the present moment, but according to the law of the Lord, to do what He commanded. One nailed to the wood of the cross no longer takes pleasure in the present world or thinks of his passionate attachments. He finds no pleasure in the cares or worries of the day to come. In him is no desire for the acquisition of land. He is not aroused by any pride or any irritability. He does not sorrow for any dishonors, and he no longer even remembers the past. Though he still breathes in his body, but he already considers himself effectively dead, and he directs the eyes of his heart to that place where he has no doubt he will soon resettle. So we must also be crucified by the fear of the Lord concerning all this. That is, we must be dead not only to our carnal lusts, but even to their very inception. We must have the eyes of our soul fixed to the place where we must hope to go at any moment of the day. In such a way, we can acquire the mortification of all our desires and passionate attachments.[28]

It is easy to see that this crucifixion on the cross of the fear of God, described by St John Cassian, is the same thing that St Isaac the Syrian calls *active doing*, which consists of the crucifixion of the flesh with its passions and lusts (see Gal 5:24), the first half of the spiritual way that leads a Christian to the perfection intended for him by God.

The Holy Scriptures teach us that "the fear of the Lord is clean, enduring for ever and ever" (Ps 18:10). They also say that "there is no fear in love; but perfect love casts out fear, because fear involves torment. But he who fears has not been made perfect in love" (1 John 4:18). The Holy Fathers explain this seeming (superficial) contradiction thus:

There are two kinds of fear. One is preliminary, the other is perfect. One is proper to the beginner, that is, for the sake of their piety. The other belongs to the perfected saints who have acquired a measure of love. For example, whoever fulfills the will of God because of the fear of tortures is, as we said, still a beginner. He does not yet do good for the sake of the good, but from the fear of punishment. Another does the will of God because he loves God and loves the will of God for its own sake, and he does it in order to please God. Such a person knows what is essentially good. Such a person has come to know what it means to be with God. Such a person has the true love that the beloved apostle called perfect. This love leads him to perfect fear, because such a person fears and remains faithful to the will of God not from fear of punishments, not to avoid eternal suffering, but because, as we have said, having tasted the very sweetness of being with God, he fears falling away, fears being deprived of God's presence. This perfect fear, acting on the principle of love, casts out the preliminary fear. Therefore, it is said, "perfect love casts out fear." However, it is impossible to attain to perfect fear without first passing through preliminary fear.[29]

The majesty of God inspires holy, reverent fear in those reasoning creatures of God who, by virtue of their purity and holiness, have become worthy of the closest relationship with God. "We shall glorify God in the council of the saints; great and terrible is He over all them that are round about Him" (Ps 88:8).

But does that mean that we, because we are sinners, should not love God? No! Let us love Him, but in the way that He Himself commanded us to love Him. Let us strive with all our strength to acquire holy love, but by that path that God Himself has indicated to us. Let us not be enticed by delusive pleasures and false self-conceit! Let us not arouse in our hearts the flames of sensuality and vanity, so abhorrent before God, so pernicious for us! God commands us to love Him in the following manner: "Abide in My love. If you keep My commandments, you will abide in My love, just as I have kept My Father's commandments and abide in His love" (John 15:9–10). The Son of God Himself, having become man, revealed to us the image of this manner of life and asceticism, since "He humbled Himself and became obedient to the point of death, even the death of the cross" (Phil 2:8). Let us reject pride that ascribes any worth to ourselves. Let us venerate humility that reveals to us our own fallenness and sinfulness. Let us prove our love for Christ by our obedience to Christ, our love for God the Father by our obedience to the Son of God, Who has "not spoken on [His] own authority" to us but declared to us that the Father gave Him a "command," which is "everlasting life" (John 12:49–50). "He who has My commandments and keeps them, it is he who loves Me. . . . If anyone loves Me, he will keep My word; . . . He who does not love Me does not keep my words" (John 14:21, 23–24). The doing of the commandments of the Saviour—this is the only sign of love for God that the Saviour Himself accepts.

"For this reason, all those who pleased God did so only by leaving behind their own truth, damaged by the fall into sin, and strove to find the truth of God, written in the teachings and commands of the Gospel. In the truth of God, they found the love that is hidden from our fallen nature. And the Lord, having commanded much concerning love, commanded us first of all to seek the truth of God, knowing that it is the mother of love."[30] If we desire to acquire love for God, let us come to love the commandments of the Gospel. Let us sell our desires and passionate attachments. Let us buy a field at the cost of rejecting ourselves. This field is our heart, which without such a purchase cannot belong to us. Let us work the land of this village by the keeping of the commandments, and we will find the heavenly treasure hidden in this field—love.[31]

What awaits us on this field? Labors and sicknesses, enemies who do not easily admit defeat. The sin that lives inside us awaits us there to battle us. It lives in the mind, the heart, the body. We need an intensified struggle to bow down the proud and blind mind to the obedience of the commandments of Christ. When the mind submits to Christ, a new struggle begins—bringing the corrupted, stubborn heart into harmony with the teachings of Christ, forcing the heart to submit to the teachings of Christ, which it has so long opposed. Finally, if the mind and heart are brought to a state of obedience to Christ, the body—that clay that has been predestined for heaven—must also be brought to obedience. Every step in this unseen warfare is characterized by struggle, suffering; it is watered with the sweat of intense self-constraint. Sometimes we win, sometimes we lose; sometimes we find hope that our bondage will soon cease, sometimes we see that our chains are still whole and in no way weakened by those means that we had used to loosen them. We are defeated by natural weakness, weakness of will, a darkness of the mind that was produced by our previous sinful life, the disorder of the heart that has accumulated many sinful habits, the passions of a body that has tasted of bestial pleasures and become infected with their desire. We are attached by fallen spirits who desire to keep us in bondage.

This is that narrow and sorrowful road, paved by endurance, along which the sinner's tears of repentance lead to reconciliation with God. Along the way, the sinner is aided by works of repentance, labors of humility, and the doing of the commandments of the Gospel, inspired by the fear of God.

This union of fear of God with divine love is superlatively described by the Spirit-bearing fathers Isaac the Syrian and Symeon the New Theologian. We will embellish our own poor words with their magnificent writings.

Repentance is given to people by grace for the increase of grace. Repentance is our second birth from God. We expect that thanks to repentance we will be given that which we accepted as a pledge by faith. Repentance is the door of mercy that opens to those who seek it fervently. Through this door, we enter God's mercy. Other than this entrance, there is no way to His mercy; as the divine Scriptures say, those who have sinned will be "justified freely by His grace" (Rom 3:23–24). Repentance is the second grace and is born in the heart of fear and faith. Fear is the fatherly staff that rules over us until we become worthy of the spiritual goods of heaven; when we reach them, fear leaves us and goes back. Heaven is the love of God, in which is the enjoyment of all blessedness, where the blessed Paul was nourished by supernatural food. Having tasted of the Tree of Life, he declared, "Eye has not seen, nor ear heard, nor have entered into the heart of man the things which God has prepared for those who love Him." (1 Cor 2:9)

To eat of this tree was forbidden to Adam because of the snare prepared by the devil. The Tree of Life is love for God, from which Adam fell, and so joy did not meet him afterward, but he worked and labored over the land of thorns. Those who have lost the love of God, even if they walk the right way, they still must eat their bread in the sweat of their labors in the same ways as was commanded to the first man after his fall. As long as we still strive for love, so long do we have to work the land of thorns. We sow and we reap among thorns. Even if our harvest is the harvest of truth, we are hourly wounded by thorns, and, no matter how much we labor for truth, we still labor in the sweat of our brow. When we do acquire love, then we will be nourished with the bread of heaven, then we will be strengthened without labor or without works. Christ is the living bread "which comes down from heaven and gives life to the world" (John 6:33). This is the food of angels. Having found love, he eats Christ every day and hour. "If anyone eats of this bread, he will live forever" (John 6:51). Blessed is he who eats the bread of love, which is Jesus. And whoever has love for his food has Christ, Who is God over all, as his food as well, as John witnesses, saying, "God is love." (1 John 4:8)

Then, he who lives in love finds enjoyment in his life that streams from God and, being in this world, already breathes the air of the resurrection. The righteous will enjoy this air after the resurrection. Love is that mystical kingdom that the Lord promised his apostles. He said, "that you may eat and drink at My table in My kingdom" (Luke 22:30), which means what, if not Love? This love is enough to feed a person instead of food and drink. It is the wine that gladdens the heart of man (Ps 103:15). Blessed is he who drinks this wine. Those with no self-control drank it, and they became reverent. The sinners drank it and forgot the path along which they stumbled. The drunkards drank it and became ascetics. The rich drank it and desired poverty. The poor drank it and were enriched with hope. The weak drank it and became strong. The ignorant drank it and became wise. Just as it is impossible to cross the great sea without a ship, so no one can reach love without fear. The foul-smelling sea that lies between us and the noetic heaven can be sailed over in the ship of repentance, whose oars are manned by fear. If these oarsmen—that is, holy fear—do not direct the ship of repentance on which we sail over the sea of the world toward God, then we will sink in the foul-smelling sea. Repentance is the ship. Fear is the helmsman. Love is the divine shore. Fear leads us into the ship of repentance and carries us over the foul-smelling sea of life, directing us toward the divine shore, toward love, to which those who "labor and heavy laden" (Matt 11:28) with repentance strive. If we reach love, then we have reached God. Our journey has ended. We have landed on the island of the world where the Father and the Son and the Holy Spirit are.[32]

The heading of the 2nd Homily of St Symeon, written in verse, contains a summary of our entire subject, and so we offer it here in full: "From fear is born love; by love is fear banished from the soul, and then love alone abides in the soul, being the divine and Holy Spirit." The actual homily begins thus: "How can I hymn, how can I glorify, how can I worthily praise my God Who has despised my many sins? How will I gaze at heaven? How will I open my eyes? How will my lips open, O Father? How will I move my lips? How will I raise my hands to the height of heaven? How will I come up with the words? What utterances will I offer? How will I dare begin the conversation? How can I ask forgiveness of my limitless sins? Truly I have done things that do not deserve forgiveness. You know, Saviour, what I say! I have fallen lower than any nature; I have done acts that contradict my humanity. I have been found worse than the irrational beasts, worse than all the creatures of the sea, all the beasts of the earth, truly worse even than the reptiles and snakes, for I have broken your commandments more than is possible for the nature of the irrational beasts. I have defiled my body and I have dishonored my soul. How will I reveal myself to You? How will I see You? How will I dare stand before Your face? How can I not flee from Your glory, from the light with which Your Holy Spirit glistens? How will I avoid falling into darkness alone, having done all the works of darkness? I will be banished from the multitude of saints!"

How will I endure Your voice that sends me into the darkness? I already bear the condemnation of my deeds, and I fear and tremble. Possessed by fear and horror, I cry to You: my Saviour! "I know, O Saviour, that none other hath sinned against Thee as have I, nor hath wrought the deeds that I have done. But this again I know, that neither the magnitude of mine offences nor the multitude of my sins surpasseth the abundant long-suffering of my God and His exceeding love for mankind; but with sympathetic mercy Thou dost purify and illumine those who fervently repent and makest them partakers of the light, sharers of Thy divinity without stint. And, strange to angels and to the minds of men, Thou conversest with them oftimes, as with Thy true friends. These things make me bold, these things give me wings, O Christ."[33] This is why I fall before You and cry to You! As You accepted the prodigal and the harlot who came to you, so also accept me, O merciful One, for I repent with my whole soul. Impute my tears, O my Christ, as drops of water pouring from a never-ceasing fountainhead, and with them wash my soul. With them purify also the defilement of my body, produced by passions; wash also my heart from any evil, for it is the root and source of all sin. Evil is the seed of the evil sower. Wherever it is found, there it takes root and rises toward the heights and gives rise to many branches of evil and danger. Its roots are from the depths of history, O my Christ, and so purify the fields of my soul and heart. O merciful One! Plant in them Your fear. Let it take root and bud and grow tall, increasing by the keeping of Your commandments and by the constantly increasing river of my tears. Let this fear, nourished by them more and more, grow taller and more strong.

Together with fear, in equal measure, let humility grow as well. All the passions make way before humility, and with them all the hosts of the demons flee. All the virtues come after these two, and surround them like ladies in waiting surrounding a queen. When the virtues gather and unite with each other, then among them will flower, like a tree at the source of a river, the fear that You have planted, and little by little it will give rise to a strange flower. I say 'strange' because every natural thing gives its proper fruit, and every tree is found in its own seed, but Your fear produces a flower foreign to nature, and a fruit equally strange and foreign to its nature. This fear is naturally filled with lamentation, and the one who acquires it must constantly sorrow as a slave worthy of much punishment, as one expecting every hour to be executed, as one who sees the sickle of death, but does not know the hour of death, having no hope or news of his complete pardon, but fearing the end, not knowing the ruling of the Just Judge, O my God.

The flower produced by fear is indescribable in its form, and even more indescribable in its image. It seems to be flowering, but immediately hides itself, which is unnatural and not usual, which is greater than nature, superseding any nature. However, the flower appears beautiful as well, beyond any description, and it ravishes my entire mind, not allowing me to remember any of that knowledge given by fear, producing in me forgetfulness of all this, and then it flies away quickly. And the tree of fear again remains without a flower. I sorrow, I sigh, and I cry to You fervently! And again, I see the flower on the tree! O my Christ! Keeping my eyes fixed on the flower alone, I then do not see the tree of fear. But the flower appears more and more often, and, drawing me to itself with a strong desire, ends in the fruit of love. Again this fruit does not endure to remain long on the tree of fear. On the contrary, when it flowers, it alone is visible, and the tree is not. For fear is not found in love, just as, in opposition to this, the soul does not flower without fear.

Truly this is a miracle beyond all words, greater than any thought! The tree flowers with difficulty and brings a fruit, but the fruit then uproots the whole tree, and remains a fruit alone. How can a fruit be without its tree? I cannot explain it! However, it does exist, this love without the fear that gave birth to it. This love is truly the greatest joy that fills the one that acquires it with joy and spiritual sweetness, and it even casts one out of this world by the senses, something that fear can never do. Fear, being of the visible and of the physical, how can it place its acquirer far from everything and completely unite him with the invisible means of (spiritual) purification? Truly, it cannot. The flower and the fruit produced by fear are found outside this world. Do they ravish the soul even here, and raise it up, and place it beyond this world? How, tell me, can this love transport someone beyond the world? I wanted to know this quantifiably. But it is indescribable. Love is the divine Spirit.[34]

In what manner does this transformation occur within the heart? In what manner does it accomplish the inconceivable transformation from fear to love? We offer an answer from the experience of the holy saints of God. Our contemporary and fellow Russian, the adornment and glory of contemporary monasticism, St George the recluse of the Zadonsk monastery, a man who achieved Christian perfection, says the following in a discussion concerning trust of one's neighbor.

I want to say a few words concerning the essence of love. It is the subtlest fire, surpassing any mind and lighter than any mind. The actions of this fire are quick and wondrous; they are holy and poured out on the soul from the holy, omnipresent Spirit. No sooner does this fire only touch the heart than every restless thought and feeling immediately transform into silence, humility, joy, and sweetness that overcomes everything. I have been open with you about many things concerning myself, and I intend to be even more open. I had spent, I think, six years in reclusion when it pleased the Lord to completely break my heart. Then I thought that I had already perished and that the wrath of God would consume my iniquitous, despairing, and slothful soul. . . . I fell into a great exhaustion and was barely breathing, but constantly repeated in my heart the words: Lord Jesus Christ, Son of God, have mercy on me, a sinner. Suddenly, in a single moment, all the weakness fell away, and the fire of pure love touched my heart. I was filled with strength, emotion, sweetness, and unutterable joy. I was so ecstatic that I even desired that I would be tortured, torn apart, mocked; I desired it only to preserve within myself the sweet fire of love for all. It is so strong and so sweet that there is no bitterness, no insult that it would not immediately transform into sweetness. The more logs I place on a fire, the stronger the flame; this is how sorrows and troubles from others act on us. The more we are attacked, the more the heart burns with holy love. And what freedom, what light! There are no words to describe it. I would have been happy if someone had deprived me of my eyes, so that I would no longer look at the vain light. I would have been happy if someone had taken me like a prisoner and walled me in, so that I would no longer have to listen to a human voice, or even see a human shadow.[35]

That which is God's comes of itself and in a time when we least expect it or hope to receive it. But if God's goodwill is to come to us, we must first purify ourselves with repentance. All the commandments of God are contained in repentance. Through repentance, a Christian is led first to fear of God and then to divine love.

Let John, the virgin and theologian, the disciple whom Jesus loved, recline on the breast of Jesus! Let all the other saints of God, the initiates of holy love, join him there! But that is not our place. Our place is in the assembly of the lepers, the paralytics, the blind, the deaf, the dumb, the possessed. We belong to those because of the state of our souls. Let us approach our Saviour as members of that assembly. Our Mother, the Holy Church, places us in that group, as she places the prayers of the Akathist to the Sweetest Jesus—so full of the heart-wounding feeling of the acknowledgment of sinfulness—into the mouths of her children. Our spiritual Mother gives us a trustworthy instruction on how to receive God's mercy. The Lord adopted us by Holy Baptism, but we have broken the holy union with Him by disregarding His holy commandments through our adulterous union with vile sin. "You rulers of Sodom . . . Give ear to the law of our God, you people of Gomorrah" (Isa 1:10), as the Lord calls the people after they fell into iniquity, that same people about whom God said before, "For the Lord's portion became the people of Jacob; the allotment of His inheritance is Israel" (Deut 32:9).

The prodigal son, having wasted his inheritance in a foreign land and having been subjected to all manner of disasters, began to think of returning to his father. As he thought this, instructed by his own troubles and the great riches of his father, he determined for himself the wisest course of action. "I will arise and go to my father, and will say to him, 'Father, I have sinned against heaven and before you, and I am no longer worthy to be called your son. Make me like one of your hired servants'" (Luke 15:18–19). This humility that arose in the thoughts was accomplished in deed, and "he arose and came to his father. But when he was still a great way off, his father saw him and had compassion, and ran and fell on his neck and kissed him" (Luke 15:20). So also we—having lost the beauty of sonship, gifted us by the Heavenly Father, in our vain and sinful occupations—must approach (when we have decided to turn to Him) the throne of glory and majesty with profound humility and reverent fear. Our first action should be the acknowledgment and confession of our sins, the abandonment of our sinful life, and the beginning of a life lived by the commandments of the Gospel. The sensation of repentance should be imbued with heartfelt prayer and pious labors. With complete conviction, we should consider ourselves to be unworthy of love, unworthy of being called sons and daughters of God. "Make me," says the repentant prodigal son, "like one of your hired servants," who work the fields of repentance under the severe watchful eye of the overseer—fear. Let us not seek that which we cannot acquire on our own, for which we have not yet matured.

Like the centurion mentioned in the Gospel, while we remain "under authority," while our sins rule over us along with the fallen spirits, let us witness and confess together with the wise centurion, "Lord, I am not worthy that You should come under my roof. But only speak a word, and my servant will be healed" (Matt 8:8). You are all-holy and all-pure, and you abide only in the pure and the holy, but I, a defiled one, "am not worthy that You should come under my roof."

"I think," says St Isaac,

> that just as a son does not doubt his father and does not ask him the following—teach me a trade, or give me this or that—so also a monk should not think of asking God to give him this or that. He should know that God provides for us more than a father cares for his son. Consequently, we must lead ourselves to humility, weep over the reasons for our unwilling sins, committed by us either in thought or deed, and from a broken heart say the words of the publican, "God, be merciful to me, a sinner!" (Luke 18:13). As the ailing son of a king does not say to his father, "Make me king!" but instead does everything possible to heal himself (for after his improvement the kingdom of his father will automatically fall to him), so also a repentant sinner, having worked for the health of his soul, enters together with the Father into the land of virtuous, untainted nature and reigns in the glory of his Father.[36] Amen.

Sergiev Hermitage,
1884

CHAPTER 5

The Judgments of God

There is no such thing as blind chance. God directs the world and everything occurs in heaven and under the heavens according to the judgments of the all-wise and omnipotent God, Who is unfathomable in His wisdom and omnipotence, incomprehensible in His mastery of the world.

God directs the world. Let His reasoning creatures submit to Him, and let His servants reverently contemplate His majestic mastery of the world, praising it in wonder and in bewilderment, for it surpasses their knowledge.

God directs the world. Only blind sinners do not see His direction. They invented blind chance, so devoid of any reasoning. The incorrectness of their views, the stupidity of their point of view, their darkened and perverted judgments—these they do not acknowledge. They claim that the direction of God has no righteousness or meaning. They blaspheme God's direction and activity in the world, so full of wisdom, calling it irrational.

"He is the Lord our God; His judgments are in all the world" (Ps 104:7). "The judgments of the Lord are true, and righteous altogether" (Ps 18:10). There is nothing unjust in them! There is nothing unwise about them! They are justified by their consequences, their spiritual fruits; they are justified by the perfection of their all-perfect Source.

"Praise the Lord, O Jerusalem! Praise thy God, O Zion! For He hath strengthened the bars of thy gates; He hath blessed thy children within thee" (Ps 147:1–2). Only the Orthodox Church is capable of praising God in a manner pleasing to God; only her true sons, faithful to her dogmatic and moral tradition, are capable of inheriting His blessing. God, "Who declareth His word unto Jacob, His statues and ordinances unto Israel"[37] (Ps 147:8), reveals His salvific teaching to all the members of the Orthodox Church; but the mystery of evangelical truth and His judgments He only reveals, as much as this is possible, to His chosen ones who are capable of seeing God in His providence and in His direction of the world with a purified mind. God "hath not dealt so with every nation, neither hath He revealed His judgments unto them" (Ps 147:9).

The vision of God's judgments is a spiritual vision. The mind of a Christian who labors properly in asceticism is raised by God's grace, in His own time, to this vision. The spiritual vision of the mind harmonizes with the heart in a spiritual, holy sensation, which it imbibes as though it were a sweet and fragrant drink that fills with nourishment, courage, and joy. I gaze into your judgments, O my Lord. "Thy judgments are as the bottomless deep" (Ps 35:7). Neither the mind of man nor the mind of angels can examine this depth, just as our physical eye cannot see the vaults of the heavens that hide beyond the azure of the sky.

It is impossible to correctly and exactly fulfill God's will without first coming to know the judgments of God. What are the commandments of God? They are God's will, declared by God to mankind to guide all the actions that depend on their free will. What are the judgments of God? They are those things that God either allows or accomplishes directly, according to His will, over which the free will of man has no influence whatsoever. It is evident that for the complete fulfillment of God's will by man, it is necessary for man to orient himself properly both with respect to the commandments of God and the judgments of God. The true servant of God said, "I have kept the ways of the Lord, and have not forsaken my God. For all His judgments are before me, and His statutes have not departed from me" (Ps 17:22–23). O my Lord, "teach me Thy judgments" (Ps 118:108). "I will thank Thee with an unfeigned heart, when I shall have learned the judgments of Thy righteousness" (Ps 118:7).

"The sinner," that is, the willful servant of the demons, "hath provoked the Lord; he is so wrathful, that he careth not; God is not before him. His ways are always defiled; Thy judgments are far above out of his sight" (Ps 9:25–26). Disdain of the commandments of God of necessity unites itself with the rejection of God's direction of the world and God's providence for the world. Disdain of the commandments of God is a natural consequence of such rejection. The willful sinner equates the actions of the ruler of the cosmos, the first principle of everything that occurs in human society in general, and with every person in particular, with human reason or blind, pointless chance. This sinner places himself, in his way of thinking and in the disposition of his soul, in direct opposition to the Lord and to His holy Gospel. Such a sinner fearlessly tramples all the commandments of God and fearlessly satisfies all his passionate, sinful desires.

Whoever takes God out of the providence for the world sees no divine dispensation in the commandments of God. However, he who acknowledges God's mastery over the universe reveres this providence and the judgments of God so much that he has nailed his flesh to the fear of God (Ps 118:120). He has crucified his own will and his carnal and sinful mindset on the cross of the commandments of the Gospel. To see God in His providence, it is necessary to have a pure mind, heart, and body. To acquire this purity, it is necessary to live according to the commandments of the Gospel. From the vision of the judgments of God comes, in great abundance, the mother of this vision—the life of piety.

God directs the universe; He also directs the life of every person down to the smallest detail. This providence, concerning even the tritest, apparently most worthless conditions of the life of mere creatures, corresponds to the endless perfection of God's qualities. The law of this direction is revealed in nature; it is also revealed in the social and private life of men; it is revealed in the Scriptures. The Saviour said, "Are not two sparrows sold for a copper coin? And not one of them falls to the ground apart from your Father's will. But the very hairs of your head," you constant and faithful servants of God, "are all numbered" (Matt 10:29–30). I believe these all-holy words! I cannot fail to believe them, for they describe the perfections of my God exactly.

O my Lord, "from Thy presence shall my judgment come forth" (Ps 16:2). I belong to You completely! My life and my death are hourly in Your hands! In all my deeds, in all the circumstances of my life, You are present. You help me to please You; You are long-suffering to my self-willed, sinful, mad deeds. Constantly You guide me to the right path by Your right hand! Without Your right hand, I would have become hopelessly lost a long time ago; I would have perished irrevocably. You, the only One capable of judging man, judge me and decide my fate forever according to Your righteous judgment, according to Your unutterable mercy. I am Yours, both before I was, now as I am, and even beyond the limits of earthly life, of my earthly wandering!

The judgments of God govern all that occurs in the entire cosmos. Everything occurs as a consequence of the judgments and dispensation of God. Nothing can, nothing does occur apart from God or independent of His will. Some events occur by God's direct will, others by His permission; however, everything occurs by the judgment and dispensation of God. For this reason, the judgments of God are often called the judgment seat of God. The judgment seat of God is always righteous; as the prophet said, "Righteous art Thou, O Lord, and true are Thy judgments" (Ps 118:137).

By the actions of God's will were the visible and invisible worlds created. Man was created and redeemed, and all events—social or private—were accomplished and are accomplished in light of God's goodness, God's omnipotence, God's wisdom, shining like the sun in the sky to illumine all the earth. By God's permission, and by the free will of created beings, evil appeared, with all its attendant consequences. By God's permission, and by their own free will, the angels fell; man fell, and mankind did not accept God and abandoned Him, though they were redeemed by God Who became man. By God's permission, and by the evil will of the rejected angels and the fallen men, the earth was corrupted by the crimes and iniquities of fallen angels and men. By God's permission and judgments, the universe was, and will continue to be, smitten by various sorrows and disasters, both general and particular. By God's permission and according to His judgments, eternal suffering in the fiery, dark abyss of hell awaits the enemies of God and those who have abandoned Him, for they have prepared it for themselves willingly.

The Apostle Paul saw with a mind purified, a mind illumined by the rays of holy truth; he saw the unreachable height of the judgments of God and, in sacred terror from the vision of these judgments, exclaimed, "Oh, the depth of the riches both of the wisdom and knowledge of God! How unsearchable are His judgments and His ways past finding out! For who has known the mind of the Lord? Or who has become His counselor?" (Rom 11:33–34).

The apostle exclaimed these words when he spoke of the horrible crime, the willing rejection of the Redeemer by the Jews, a maddened rejection that was crowned with a horrifying evil—the murder of the Redeemer. Speaking of this crime, which completely depended on the free will of the perpetrators, the apostle still expresses himself as though the crime were accomplished by God: "For God has committed them all [the Jews] to disobedience" (Rom 11:32). "God has given them a spirit of stupor, eyes that they should not see and ears that they should not hear" (Rom 11:8).

In Scripture, what God allows is equated with what God does. It is as if the One Who is limitless in power and might, as it were, limited Himself by not infringing on human free will, by not stopping human actions that are done in stubborn opposition and hardened antagonism to the will and actions of God. The free will of creatures could not possibly oppose the almighty right hand of the Creator. And that is not what happens, for all occurs according to the judgments of God. To comprehend them fully is impossible, since they transcend the reasoning capacity of thinking creatures.

Examination of that which cannot be comprehended is a useless labor, devoid of reason. Any examination of the judgments of God is forbidden by God. It is an endeavor inspired by blind arrogance, an endeavor inspired by a false seeing of an object, an endeavor leading to inevitable delusion, blasphemy, and the loss of one's soul. Following the example of the apostle, one must see and contemplate the judgments of God with the eye of faith, the eye of spiritual wisdom. Not allowing ourselves any pointless conclusions of human reason, we must immerse ourselves reverently into holy ignorance, into a holy, spiritual darkness that is also a miraculous light that hides God from the mental gaze both of angels and men.[38]

"Evil has no substance," the Fathers say, "it appears as a result of our laziness to do good and it disappears as soon as we fervently live for virtue."[39] Evil, being nothing other than the absence of good, can refer only to reasoning creatures in whom good is limited. This limitation has no place in eternity and is inaccessible to it. God is eternal, and His good is limitless. That which is limitless in its nature does not lessen, no matter how much or how little we try to count it. Neither evil nor the good of creatures has any influence on God (nor can it), nor can it influence His actions. The judgments of God stand on an unassailable and untouchable height. They stand on a height that does not depend on the actions either of demons or of men. The actions of God abide in their own proper nature and significance, no matter what sort of demonic or human activity may appear to be united with an action of God.

A striking example of such a situation is this great event—the suffering and death of the God-Man. On the one hand, the incarnate God, according to His own holy will, subjected Himself to this suffering and death. On the other, the high priests of the Jews, led also by their own free will, subjected the incarnate God to humiliating dishonor, cruel tortures, and a shameful death. In the evil actions of these men demons also cooperated, as the masters of all evil.[40] Here the actions of God were united, according to a superficial perspective, to the actions of men and demons.

However, in essence these two actions—God's and man's—were completely distinct. The Apostle Peter said to the Jews: "You denied the Holy One and the Just, . . . and killed the Prince of life . . . But those things which God foretold by the mouth of all His prophets, that the Christ would suffer, He has thus fulfilled" (Acts 3:14–15, 18). All the apostles expressed the same thought in the prayer that they uttered when they heard of the beginning of persecutions against the Church in Jerusalem. They said, "Lord, you are God, who made heaven and earth and the sea, and all that is in them, who by the mouth of Your servant David have said: 'Why did the nations rage, and the people plot vain things? The kings of the earth took their stand, and the rulers were gathered together against the Lord and against His Christ.' For truly against Your holy Servant Jesus, whom You anointed, both Herod and Pontius Pilate, with the Gentiles and the people of Israel, were gathered together to do whatever Your hand and Your purpose determined before to be done" (Acts 4:24–28).

The judgments and actions of God go their own way; the actions of men and demons also go their own way. Crimes and iniquities do not cease to be crimes and iniquities with respect to the perpetrators, even if the evil committed, with evil intention, was also an instrument in the hand of God. The latter is a consequence of the limitless wisdom of God, the unlimited might of God, which makes it possible for created beings, acting according to their own free will, to remain at the same time inevitably within the authority of the Creator. In such cases, they do the will of the Creator, though they do not know that they do it.

The judgments of God are present and act within the sphere of events accomplished by people and demons, like a subtle wind in the midst of dense matter, which does not depend on the matter, is not inconvenienced by the matter, and does not react to the force of the matter. The judgments of God are the almighty actions of the all-perfect God in the cosmos, the One Spirit[41], in the proper sense, Who fills the cosmos and everything that is beyond the cosmos with His presence. The physical world, subject to our senses, cannot encompass God. Neither can the world of the spirits, which is not subject to our senses. The actions and judgments of God correspond to God; they are boundless. Let both men and angels remain in reverent silence before them!

Compared to God, the immaterial spirits are material; they differ from God both in their essence and in their qualities. They differ from God with a difference that is beyond measurement. They differ from God as much as they differ from the material world.[42] This is the law for the relation of the eternal to the limited and finite. No matter how much difference there is among different limited objects, no matter how great or small they can become, their difference from the eternal never changes and can never change. It is always the same, for it is infinite.

"Woe to the world because of offenses! For offenses must come, but woe to that man by whom the offense comes" (Matt 18:7). This was said by the Saviour of the world, our Lord Jesus Christ. This was said about the events that occur before our very eyes and must still occur, in which the all-holy judgments of God come together to mingle with the criminal and pernicious consequences of the sinful, passion-loving free will of man that is at enmity with God.

"Offenses must come"—these words announce God's predetermination and His judgments, unattainable for man and inconceivable to human reason. "Woe to that man by whom the offense comes"—these words declare God's wrath against the servants, preachers, benefactors of evil, the sowers and spreaders of sin in human society, the enemies and persecutors of true knowledge of God and service of God. Their frame of mind and their activity have already been condemned by God; already God's threats against this frame of mind and this activity have thundered. For their retribution the eternal hell with its prisons is prepared, with its horrifying tortures and punishments. But the activity and frame of mind of people who are antagonistic to God and who oppose God are still permitted by God. These are the judgments of God.

No evil of created beings can destroy God's immutability in goodness. No evil can prevent the limitless Wisdom of God from accomplishing His all-holy, almighty will.

What is the "predestination of God"? This is an expression that is used by Scripture to express the majesty of God, greater than any description. The idea of "predestination" is in many ways similar to the idea of "judgments"— they are often used interchangeably. We will try to explain, as much as we are able, this predestination of God, concerning which the Scriptures speak,[43] but which has been interpreted incorrectly by many, leading them into a disastrous abyss of delusion.

God is not subject to time.[44] Time simply does not exist for God. The word "time" expresses an idea created in reasoning creatures from the impression of changes of phenomena in nature. This is also how science views time. "And there was evening and morning, one day" (Gen 1:5). This is how Scriptures understand the idea of time, which is completely consonant with the latest findings in physics. It is obvious that external stimuli can have no effect on God; otherwise, He would not be perfect and would be subject to addition or subtraction, which is not inherent to the Limitless. There is no time for God. There is no future tense for Him. That which will happen has already occurred before the face of God, and the eternal fate of every person, which naturally must flow from his willed activity on earth, is already known to God (and therefore already determined by God). "Thine eyes did see my unformed being," O all-perfect God! (Ps 138:16). The inspired prophet confessed this; and every person, by logical necessity, must confess the same thing.

I am predestined! I have no ability to resist this predestination, to change or destroy the predestination of God. Why, then, should I force myself to the inexorably strict life of Christian virtue? Why should I subject myself to countless deprivations and live by constantly rejecting my life? I will live as I wish and as it pleases me! I will rush to whatever pleasures my imagination can conjure in enticing visions before my mental eyes. I will satisfy myself to the full with all pleasures, even if they be sinful! In abundance are they scattered about in the world, and my insatiable curiosity pushes me to taste and to know them all by experience! If it is predestined for me to be saved, then, in spite of all my sinfulness, God will save me. If it is fated for me to perish, then I will perish, in spite of all my efforts to acquire salvation.

Such nonsense is declared by one ignorant of the mysteries of Christianity! It is uttered as so-called wisdom and reveals a carnal mindset. These words contain a terrible blasphemy that people do not fully comprehend. Many accept this pitiful, incorrect mindset as incontrovertible truth. It is the foundation of the self-willed, iniquitous, and debauched lifestyle of many. A life founded on sin is an endlessly bitter life now and a life of constant calamities in the age to come.

This false, soul-destroying mindset concerning predestination and God's judgments arose from confusing the actions proper to God with the actions that depend exclusively on human will. One error leads to another; in summary, many errors are made if the first premise is false. A person who has confused his own actions with the actions of God has already, as it were, subjected both to a single law, a single judgment—the judgment of his own reason. This opens up an entire arena of errors. Having placed himself as a judge of God's action, he, by necessity, has ascribed to God the same reference to good and evil as man has. He has equated the qualities of God with human qualities. He has subjected God's mindset to the laws of human reason. He may have mentally distinguished them, but this distinction is amorphous, devoid of any correctness or meaning.

From His beginningless beginning, God has been and is content with His Word alone. His Word is also His thought: "The Word was God. He was in the beginning with God" (John 1:1–2). This is the quality of a limitless mind. According to His limitless perfection, God has only one thought, even if that single thought is expressed in the sphere of the reasoning creatures as a countless multitude of thoughts. We must separate God's essence, God's qualities, and God's actions from ourselves to an eternal distance, and only then can our assertions concerning God's judgments or predestination be considered valid. The predestination of a person's fate is completely proper to God according to the unlimited perfection of the mind of God, according to God's total independence from time. This predestination—which reveals God's might and remains mysterious to human minds, known only to God—in no way limits the free will and activity of man in life. It has no influence on man's actions. In fact, it has no reference to man's actions at all. Since it has no influence on man's actions, the predestination of God does not have, and cannot have, any influence on the consequences of these actions, on the salvation or the perdition of a person.

The things that do guide our behavior are, on the one hand, reason and free will, and on the other, the revealed teaching of God. The revealed teaching of God declares the will of God for salvation with satisfactory exactness. It declares God's good desire for all people to be saved, but it also declares eternal suffering for those who trample the will of God. Thus, the logical consequence is clear—the salvation or perdition of man depends entirely on his own will, not on the judgments of God, which man cannot know.

Why is one person born in riches and with distinction, while another is born in poverty among people who are despised and oppressed, cursed for a lifetime of physical work in the sweat of the brow, deprived of all means to develop the mind? Why does one person die a decrepit old man, while another in the flower of youth or in the prime of life, while still others in childhood or even in infancy? Why does one person enjoy constant health and prosperity, while another suffers through constant diseases, passing from sorrow to sorrow, from disaster to disaster? These and other similar questions were asked once by the great ascetic of the desert, St Anthony. Futile was his desire to find the answer using his own intellect, even though it was illumined by God's grace and capable of immersing itself into, and investigating, the mysteries of God. When the holy elder became exhausted with these fruitless thoughts, a voice from heaven came down to him: "Anthony! These are the judgments of God. Examination of them is harmful for your soul. Be attentive to yourself."[45]

"Be attentive to yourself," O man! Limit your mental exertions to things that are essentially necessary for you. Determine in detail your own relationship to God and to all of the immense creation that is known to you. Determine what is possible for you to understand, what is given to you solely for contemplation, and what is hidden from you. Determine the degree and limits of your own ability to think and understand. This ability, proper to a limited creature, has its natural degree and its natural limitation. Science sometimes declares that some human concepts are completely understood, but they still remain so only with reference to the human ability to think and understand. They are complete only as much as a human being is complete. You must come to the important conclusion that completely understanding something is unnatural and impossible for a limited mind. A complete understanding of anything is proper only to a perfect mind.

Without acknowledging this as fact, even a genius will always be unable to acquire a correct attitude or way of life. Here we mean a spiritual attitude and way of life, that is, every person's duty to develop himself as much as possible in virtue, as the Creator has determined and predestined for every reasoning creature. We are not speaking here of those temporary attitudes or actions that refer only to our short wandering on this earth as members of a specific human society.

It would seem that nothing is more intimate to me than my own self. Whom do I know so well as my own self? I am constantly with myself. By necessity, I must constantly pay attention to myself, and I only pay attention to other objects as much as it is necessary for me. God Himself has commanded that I love myself as much as I love my neighbor. And yet I, who endeavor to plumb the mysteries of the depths of earth and sea and sky, am perplexed, completely confused, and I do not know what to answer myself when I ask, "Who am I? What am I?" Am I a living being? But I am subjected to extraordinary upheavals from the day of my conception to the day of my death. A being, in the full sense of the word, should not be subject to any changes; the life force should be constant and immutable. There is no proof of life within me, nothing that is completely self-sufficient. I am subject to a complete exhaustion of my life force; I am dying. Not only my perishable body is subject to death, but even my soul does not have within itself the conditions for eternal life—this I am taught by the Holy Tradition of the Orthodox Church. The soul, just like the angels, is given immortality by God; immortality is not inherent or natural either to my soul or to the angels.[46]

The body, to continue living, needs to breathe air and eat the fruits of the earth. The soul, to preserve and uphold its immortality, needs nourishment through the mysterious sustenance of God's right hand. Who am I? Am I a phantom? But I sense my own existence.

For many years, a certain person contemplated a suitable answer to this question. He thought; he descended to the depths of self-investigation in the light of the Spirit of God. He summarized his contemplation of many years in the following way: "Man is a spark of Being and takes from this Being his manner of existence."[47] God, the Only One Who Is (see Exod 3:1) is reflected in the life of a person in the same way that the sun depicts itself in a pure drop of rain. In this drop of water, we see the sun; at the same time, what we see is *not* the sun. The sun is there, in the unattainable high places.

What is my soul? What is my body? What is my mind? What are my heart's emotions? What are my body's senses? What are the powers of my soul and body? What is life? These questions have not been answered and cannot be answered! Over the millennia, the human race has approached these questions for discussion and has tried to resolve them, only to step away from them, having become assured that answering them is impossible. What can be more familiar to us than our own body? Having senses, it is subject to their influence. Knowing of the body should be the most satisfying endeavor, since it is conceivable both by the reason and the senses. And yet the opposite is true!

It is exactly the same with knowledge of the soul, its qualities and powers, as well as knowledge of objects that are not subject to the body's senses. Ultimately, human knowledge is completely unsatisfactory.[48]

In order to know the significance of any element, science is required to deconstruct it to its constituent parts and from them to rebuild the element back to its original form. Whatever knowledge is gleaned about the element is then considered as authoritative by science. Hypotheses, until they are not proven positively, are not accepted into the body of knowledge, into the treasure house of science, even though it is human arbitrariness that declares them—orally and in writing—to be absolute truth, mocking the ignorance and gullibility of the mass of mar   nd. But here is a problem. To fully and satisfactorily deconstruct a human be   it must still be alive. There is no possibility of determining the meaning of .   except by catching it and examining it on its own. The truth of this decons   ction must be proven by the subsequent reorganization of the living parts c   human body back to a living human being. This is, of course, impossible.   'e dissect only corpses, not knowing what life is left in the decomposing bo .y, bereft of its soul, and what life has fled with the soul. By dissecting bodies, we come to understand the makeup of the machine that is hidden inside the body, but a machine that is no longer capable of movement is a machine that is deprived of its essential purpose. So what do we actually know about our own bodies? Something. But it is far from a complete and satisfactory knowledge.

Let us make a request of our mind, that most important instrument for the acquisition of knowledge, to give us an essential definition of itself. What is it? Is it a power of the soul? But this phrase merely expresses concepts revealed by impressions produced by the action of the mind, but it does not define the essence of "mind." We are forced to say exactly the same about the spirit of man, that is, of those exalted emotions of the heart that animals are deprived of—those emotions by which the heart of man differs from the hearts of beasts.

The spirit is a power of the soul. But in what manner are the powers of the soul united with the soul itself? The manner of union is unfathomable, just as the manner of the body's union with its senses—sight, hearing, and the others—is also unknown. The senses of the body leave the body at the same time as life leaves the body. They are carried away from it by the departing soul. That means that the body's senses do not belong to the body at all, but to the soul, and when it abides in the body, then they are borrowed by the body. Thus, the logical conclusion: the soul is able to feel everything that the body feels. There is affinity between the body and soul, not the complete opposition that recklessly is ascribed by some to the soul and the created spirits, which is an ignorant proposition.[49]

There is a gradation among creatures, and from this gradation comes difference, similar to the difference between numbers. This difference can be very great, but it does not automatically destroy any similarity that may exist between them, nor the gradation itself. In this gradation, some creatures are crude in comparison with us, while with others, the differences are subtler. However, everything created, limited, existing within space and time cannot be devoid of materiality, that integral appurtenance of all that is limited. The only One Who is immaterial (in the sense of having no matter) is God. He differs absolutely from all creatures. He is opposite to them by His being and qualities just as infinity is opposite to numbers, to all without exception, even the largest. This is all we know of our soul, our mind, our heart! What do we know? Something! The most limited *something*.

Who has sufficient knowledge of these things? Only God. He, by His nature eternal, has complete understanding of all things. He is devoid of any limitation, and He proved this completeness of knowledge with a total proof: He created countless worlds, both visible and invisible, known and unknown, from absolutely nothing. It is proper for the Eternal to give life to the nonexistent, to give being to that which is not. No quantity (i.e., nothing created) is capable of doing this, no matter how great. The proof of the limitlessness of the Mind that directs the cosmos continues to be expressed by the continuation of the existence of all that exists.[50] Only the smallest number of the laws of nature have been understood by man (and these only to a certain degree). We have come to know that there are natural laws that encompass nature completely and that they are beyond man's full comprehension. If a mind is needed to understand this small part of the laws, then naturally a Mind is necessary to construct them.

Man! "Pay attention to yourself!" Watch yourself. From a clear understanding of yourself (as much as this is possible) you will more clearly and properly examine everything that is outside yourself. In what manner, for what reason did I enter existence and appear on the stage of earthly life? I have appeared on this stage unwillingly and without consciousness. The reasons why I entered existence from nonexistence are unknown to me. I contemplate, I search for the reason, but I cannot fail to admit, by necessity, that I am subject to an unlimited, unknown, unfathomable Will. I am subject to Him absolutely.

I came to exist, with abilities of soul and body that are like temporary belongings (that is, they are given to me, and not chosen by me). I have appeared with various weaknesses, as though I were already stamped with a punishment in advance. I have appeared, and already I suffer, as one who cursed to suffer. I entered the circumstances and situation of my life—did I find them or were they prepared for me? I do not know! On the path of this earthly wandering only rarely can I act according to my own desires or fulfill a wish completely. Almost always I am led forcefully by some invisible, all-powerful Hand, by some inexorable current against which I cannot swim. Almost constantly, I encounter only the unexpected and unforeseen.

I am taken from this earthly life, more often than not, suddenly, without my own consent, without any attention to my earthly needs, to the needs of those surrounding me, for whom I am necessary, according to my self-opinion. I am taken from the earth forever, and I do not know where I will go! I am taken away in terrifying solitude! Only the new and previously unseen will greet me in the unknown land into which I journey after death. To enter this unknown land, I must leave everything earthly behind on this earth. I must even cast off my own body. From there, from that undiscovered country, I cannot give anyone on earth any news concerning myself, because there is no possibility for anyone enclosed in an earthly, crude shell to hear anything from there.

My life in this visible word is constant warfare with death; it is so from my cradle to my grave. I can die any day and any hour, but I still do not know the day or hour of my death. It is clear to me that I will die; there is not the slightest doubt of this, but I live as though immortal, feeling myself to be so. The sense of coming death is taken from me, and I would never have believed that man can die, until I saw with my own eyes that death is the inevitable fate of every person. The Gospel beautifully expresses the weakness of our authority over our own selves. No matter how much you try, says the Gospel to man, you cannot add to your height even "a cubit" (Matt 6:27), nor can you transform a single white hair into black (Matt 5:36).

> Why is this so? I cannot help but admit that much of what is written here is obviously true . . . The suffering state of mankind on earth, the state that lies before the gaze of everyone, must have its proper reason. But how can we, the descendants, be guilty of the sin of our ancestor who is so distant

from his descendants? The descendants are punished—this is obvious. Why are we, the innocent ones, punished? Why do we bear this horrible, eternal punishment? The curse passes from one generation to the next and so on, weighs heavily on them all, wipes every generation from the face of the earth, having first subjected each to countless torments. Every generation appears on the face of the earth without consciousness, unwillingly, by force. Every person enters the earthly life without the chance to willingly act on his abilities (which in childhood are more properly likened to seeds than shoots). Why do the descendants participate in the sin of the forefather—this participation that leads to such horrible punishments—when there was not, and cannot be, any possibility for the descendants to directly participate in Adam's sin either by the subtle agreement of the heart, or by the slightest transgression of the mind? Where is God's justice? Where is His goodness? What I see only proves the opposite!

Thus groans the weak man, blinded by his sinful, earthly life. Thus he groans and calls the judgments of God to account.

This is the groaning of ignorance of God! This is the groaning of human pride! This is the groaning of man's ignorance of his very self! This is the groaning of a false understanding of the self and the human condition! Thus do they cry out, and no one listens to their wails. By means of these groans, man (though he does not understand this) discovers only the sickness of self-conceit and self-delusion that has enveloped him. Through these groans, man unwillingly reveals the hidden desire to be the ruler of the cosmos, to be the judge and instructor of God in His governing of the world. But no one gives him any exalted throne above the clouds, on which the rebellious angels tried to sit long before rebellious man. Irrationally, man wallows in his irrationality, as though in a dark prison, tearing apart the sacrifices to which he has given himself, heedless of his life, tearing them apart in pointless suffering, bound by unbreakable chains. But events continue to go their own way, and in the divine economy that governs the world, nothing changes. The judgments of God remain immutable. The worthlessness and self-delusion of man are thus proved positively and irrevocably by bitter experience.

The most exacting mathematical arguments can explain the infinite difference between a person and God with complete certainty, both in being and in characteristics, though we use the same words to express both human and divine realities because of the poverty of human language. The limitless has completely different laws than everything that can be defined qualitatively by positive science, upon which all other sciences are built as the whole man is built on top of the skeleton. From this axiom naturally flows another axiom: the actions of the infinite are naturally unfathomable for any reasonable creatures who are subject to qualitative description.

No matter how large a number is, it still remains a number, and it is set apart from infinity by an infinite distinction, the same distinction that differentiates *all* numbers from infinity. The striving to understand the unfathomable is nothing other than the consequence of false knowledge, built on false hypotheses. Therefore, such striving can only end with false results. In fact, it must lead to the most pernicious consequences, as is proper for all actions that proceed from falsehood. From where does such false striving come? This is obvious: from a prideful, delusional arrogance that entices a person to give himself far more significance than he actually has in the boundless cosmos.

I examine myself! And this is the spectacle that manifests itself before my eyes when I examine myself. This is how I am, indisputably, drawn with clear lines, vivid colors, drawn by the very experiences and events of my own life. What sort of conclusion must I make from such a spectacle? The conclusion that I am not self-existent. I am not an independent creature. I am deprived of the most essential, most vital knowledge concerning my own self. And so I find it necessary that another explains myself to me more satisfactorily than I can myself. Let someone else declare my calling; let someone else indicate the right course of action for me, thereby preventing me from living without purpose or without a goal.

God Himself admitted that this is an imperative need, a necessity for man. He admitted it and gave man the revealed teaching that would lead us to the knowledge that is not attainable by man himself. In the divinely inspired teaching of God, He revealed Himself to man as much as the infinite and indescribable God can be explained and revealed to limited man. In this divinely inspired teaching, God revealed the meaning and calling of man to man, his relationship to God and to all the worlds, both visible and invisible. God also gave man self-knowledge, as much as such knowledge is possible for the mind of man. A complete and total knowledge of man, as of any other creature, is only possible for One Who is in Himself complete and capable of total knowledge of everything—the all-perfect God.

The divinely inspired teaching, together with the knowledge gained by man after a detailed examination of himself, is confirmed by this self-examination. Thus this knowledge so acquired stands before man in the bright light of incontrovertible truth.

The divinely inspired teaching tells me, and my own life experience proves to me, that I am a creation of God. I am a creation of my God! I am a slave of my God, a slave, because I am completely subject to the authority of God. I am encompassed and contained by His might, a might that is limitless and autocratic (in the proper meaning of the word, that is, "self-governing," not "authoritarian"). Autocratic power does not hold consultation with anyone; it does not give account of its dispensations or actions to anyone. No one—not any man or any angel—is capable of giving God counsel, nor of hearing or even understanding God's account of His own actions. "[The Word] was in the beginning with God" (John 1:2).

I am a slave of my God, even though I have been given a free will and a reasoning mind to direct that will. My will is free almost exclusively in one aspect—the choosing of good or evil. In all other respects, my will is fenced about on all sides. I can desire all I want, but when my desires encounter a contrary will of another person or the opposition of insurmountable circumstances, they remain more often than not unfulfilled. I can desire much, but my own weakness makes a most of my desires fruitless.

When my desire remains unfulfilled, especially when this desire appears wise, beneficial, and necessary to me, then my heart is struck with sorrow. The more important the desire, the greater the sorrow. Often it becomes depression or even despair. What can console a man in the dark times of spiritual calamity when all human help is either powerless or impossible? Only this— the acknowledgment that I am a slave and a creation of God. This consciousness alone has the power to console. No sooner does a person prayerfully turn to God with his whole heart—"Let Your will, my Lord, be done in me"—than the storm of the heart subsides. From these words, if uttered sincerely, the heaviest of sorrows lose their power over man.

What does this mean? This means that man, having confessed himself a slave and a creation of God, having committed himself completely to the will of God, immediately enters with his entire being into the realm of holy truth. Truth gives the correct disposition to the spirit and to life. He who has entered the realm of truth and has submitted to truth receives moral and spiritual freedom, moral and spiritual joy. This freedom and this joy do not depend on any other people or any of life's circumstances.

"If you abide in My word," said the Saviour to the Jews, "you are My disciples indeed. And you shall know the truth, and the truth shall make you free . . . Whoever commits sin is a slave of sin . . . . Therefore, if the Son [Who is Truth Himself] makes you free, you shall be free indeed" (John 8:31-36). Service to sin, lies, vanity is slavery in the truest sense, even if it superficially seems to be the most brilliant freedom. This slavery is eternal slavery. Only the true slave of God is completely and truly free.

I descend even deeper into self-examination, and a new spectacle reveals itself before my eyes. I see the complete disorder of my own will, its insubordination to the reasoning mind. In my mind, I see the loss of the ability to direct the will properly. I see that I have lost the ability to act correctly. In my distracted life, I rarely notice this state, but in solitude, when I am illumined by the light of the Gospel, this disorderly state of my spiritual powers is illustrated in a huge, dark, terrifying picture. The Gospel is an unbiased witness that I am a fallen creature. I am a slave of my God, but a slave who has enraged my God. I am a rejected slave, a slave punished by the hand of God. Divine Revelation declares this truth about myself to me.

My state is one that is common to all mankind. Mankind is a group of creatures that all suffer in various troubles. All men are condemned to suffer. It cannot be otherwise! I am surrounded, both outside myself and within myself, with proofs of this. If I were not an exile on the earth, like all my brother-men, if my earthly life were not a punishment, then why must this entire life be an arena of constant labor, constant conflict, and insatiable strivings? Why must the earthly life be a path only of sufferings, sometimes stronger, sometimes weaker, sometimes felt, sometimes drowned out by the pleasures of earthly cares and amusements? Why must there be sickness and so many other misfortunes, both individual and societal? Why must there be quarrels, insults, murders in the society of men? Why must there be all manner of evil, indefatigably battling against good, oppressing and persecuting good, nearly always triumphing over good? Why is every person infected with passions, suffering from them incomparably more than from external sorrows? Why must death be, death that mercilessly consumes all? What is this phenomenon—the generations replace each other, each coming from nonexistence, entering life for a short span, and again plunging forever into obscurity?

What sort of a phenomenon is the activity of every generation on this earth, which while it lasts seems so eternal, until it fades forever? What is this phenomenon, this human activity that constantly contradicts itself, constantly builds with great labor, even on streams of human blood, like cement, and yet constantly destroys its own work with the same enthusiasm and the same shedding of blood? The earth is a vale of exile, a vale of constant disorder and confusion, of unbroken suffering of creatures who have lost their primordial dignity and home, bereft of their good sense. People suffer in countless ways in this dark and deep vale! They suffer under the yoke of poverty and in the excess of riches. They suffer in miserable hovels and in glorious, kingly palaces. They suffer from external misfortunes and from that horrible disorder that has corrupted the nature of every person, that has stricken both his soul and his body, that has perverted him and blinded his mind.

This is how you should see yourself! My own experience, as well as everything that has taken place and is occurring with all mankind, leads me to this incontrovertible, palpable conclusion. This is how Divine Revelation describes me, revealing gates to the region of knowledge that is a gift of my God, gates that are shut, gates that I can only approach if I rely on my mind alone. It becomes clear by Divine Revelation that the first man was created by God from nothing. He was created in the beauty of spiritual refinement; he was created immortal, devoid of evil. This account cannot but be truth, for I feel myself to be immortal, and evil is repulsive to me. I hate it; I suffer from it, and even if I am enticed by it, it is still a flatterer and a tyrant. Man, created on earth, was taken into the part of heaven called Paradise. Here, in blessedness that was not disturbed by anything, he poisoned himself with a self-willed taste of evil. In himself and with himself he poisoned and destroyed all of his descendants. Adam—so was the first man called—was struck down by death, that is, by sin, irreparably disordering the nature of man, making him incapable of blessedness.

Killed by this death, though still not denied life, making death even more horrible, since it was evident to his senses, Adam was cast down to earth in chains—transformed from a dispassionate, holy, spiritual body into crude, much-suffering flesh. The entire earth was cursed for the crime of man. Having lost its primordial state,[51] it was transformed into a home worthy only of an exile from heaven, all because Adam trampled the commandment of God in heaven. And now, Adam encounters enmity from visible nature at every step! At every step, we humans encounter nature's reproach, its censure, its disagreement with our behavior! All of creation—animate and inanimate—refused to submit to man, who had rejected submission to God. Creation was submissive to man while he remained submissive to God. Now it only forcibly submits to man; it pushes back and often breaks its bonds, often strikes back at its master, cruelly and unexpectedly rising up against him.

The law of the propagation of the human race, established by the Creator immediately after creation, was not canceled; however, it was now subject to the new reality of the Fall. It changed and became perverted. Parents began to quarrel in spite of their physical union.[52] They were subjected to birth pangs and the difficulties of child-rearing.[53] Their children, conceived in a perishable womb and in sin (Ps 50:7 LXX), entered the realm of life as victims of death. Every person was given only a short time on the earth, and only among much varied anguish. After the passage of the time allotted by the inscrutable God, every person had to descend into the eternal prison, into hell, symbolized by the immense interiors of planet earth. What is mankind, so filled with prideful fantasy, so maddened by vain and false imagination? Man is refuse, useless for heaven, thrown out of it, cast first to the mouth of the pit, then gradually falling into the pit itself. The pit is called an abyss, and so it is for mankind. There is no release from it. Its "bars of which are everlasting barriers," the Scriptures say (Jonah 2:7).

Listen to the account of Divine Revelation and admit it to be true. It is impossible to admit otherwise! The limitless God is the perfect good; man's nature differs from God's nature with an infinite difference. As for his characteristics, he uses them intentionally to take an opposing position of hostility to God. If man, such a nothingness before God, is at the same time an enemy of God, then what sort of significance can he have before the holiness and majesty of the Divinity? He is merely a despised impurity and a stain, according to the Scriptures.[54] He must be exiled from the face of God, hidden, as it were, from the gaze of God.

Divine Revelation teaches man that he is the creation and slave of God, a guilty slave, a rejected creature, wallowing and perishing in his own fallenness.[55] Poisoned by his intercourse with the source and father of evil, with the insane and stubborn enemy of God, with the fallen angel, and deprived of natural freedom by this submission to the all-hateful spirit, man has perverted his natural relationship with God. He became, like the fallen angel, the enemy of God.[56] Some people were content with this state, not understanding or not imagining any other possible state, finding pleasure in service to sin. Others, instructed by God and the remnant of His good will, began an exhausting war against sin, but they could not purify their nature of the unnatural adulteration of evil. They could not tear apart their bonds of slavery, nor could they cast off the yoke of sin and death. Only the Creator of human nature could restore it again.

Mankind suffered in this horrifying slavery for more than five thousand years, according to the unfathomable judgments of God. Mankind suffered in slavery, and the prisons of hell were filled to the brim, but mankind received the promise of deliverance from God in the very hour of their fall into slavery. "With the Lord one day is as a thousand years, and a thousand years as one day" (2 Pet 3:8). The promise was uttered in the same breath as the declaration of the punishment for the transgression. Humanity was favored with this promise because the reason for their fall was delusion and enticement, not an intentionally premeditated plan. After five thousand years had passed, the Redeemer—the incarnate God Himself—came down to earth, to the exiles, into the country of their exile. He visited the doorway of our prison—the surface of the earth—and the prison itself—hell. He gave salvation to all mankind, offering to their free will the choice either to accept His salvation or to reject it.

He freed all who came to believe in Him; those imprisoned in the bowels of the earth He raised to heaven, while those who wandered the surface of the earth He led to communion with God, having torn apart their communion with Satan. The God-Man, taking on Himself all the consequences of man's fall (except for sin), accepted the form of an earthly life, inherent to those who have fallen and been rejected and punished by the justice of God. He acknowledged the Fall, confessed the justice of God by the patient endurance of all troubles. Through His actions, He revealed a model for every man to emulate in the arena of earthly life.

The Gospel stresses two distinct qualities in the Saviour's earthly activity:

1. His exact fulfillment of the will of God in all actions that depend on human will, and
2. His complete submission to the will of God in the judgments of God, which do not depend on human will.

The Lord said, "For I have come down from heaven, not to do My own will, but the will of Him who sent Me" (John 6:38). "Shall I not drink the cup which my Father has given me?" (John 18:11). The God-Man expressed this exact fulfillment of the will of God and submission to the judgments of God throughout His entire life. The God-Man brought the great virtue of obedience—the foundation for all the virtues that Adam had lost in Heaven—from heaven to mankind, who were languishing in the perdition that they had caused for themselves by transgressing God's command.

This virtue was especially evident in all its glory when the Lord accepted horrible tortures. He, "being in the form of God," not ceasing to be God, "made Himself of no reputation, taking the form of a bondservant, and coming in the likeness of men. And being found in appearance as a man, He humbled

Himself and became obedient to the point of death, even the death of the cross" (Phil 2:6–8). Because of such complete submission to God, the Lord was the only true Slave of God in His human nature.[57] He was the complete Slave of God, never turning away from the fulfillment of the will of God and from submission to His will. Not one of the righteous men in history had satisfactorily fulfilled this holy duty of mankind before God.

The Lord declared to the congregation of the Jews, "I do not seek my own will but the will of the Father who sent me" (John 5:30). Before He began His sufferings and death, which gave life to the human race, the Lord revealed within Himself the weakness of fallen man before the chastising judgments of God. He began to sorrow and was deeply distressed. He even told His chosen disciples about the pain in His soul: "My soul is exceedingly sorrowful, even to death" (Matt 26:38). Then He prayerfully turned to the only trustworthy refuge in misfortunes and temptations. He "fell on His face" (Matt 26:39) and was (in His humanity) so belabored that "His sweat became like great drops of blood falling down to the ground" (Luke 22:44). Despite this strenuous state of His human nature, His prayer expressed the presence of a human will within Him and a full submission of His human will to the will of God. The prayer of the God-Man in Gethsemane, offered before His passion, is a precious spiritual inheritance for the entire race of Christians. It is capable of pouring consolation into a soul that is laboring under the yoke of the heaviest sorrows. The Lord said in this prayer, "Father, if it is Your will, take this cup away from Me; nevertheless not My will, but Yours, be done" (Luke 22:42). The Lord calls the judgments of God a cup. This cup was given to man by God for his salvation.

The God-Man willingly accepted death on the cross and all the preceding mockery, beatings, and tortures. As the Son of God and God, having a single will with His Father and the Spirit, He laid the punishment on Himself, on the only One Who was not guilty of sin, on the Son of man and the Son of God equally, for the redemption of mankind, who were guilty of sin. Daring to use human means to protect mankind, in a kind of opposition to the judgments of God, the Lord said, "Put your sword in its place, for all who take the sword will perish by the sword. Or do you think that I cannot now pray to My Father, and He will provide Me with more than twelve legions of angels? How then could the Scriptures be fulfilled, that it must happen thus?" (Matt 26:52–54).[58]

Christ expressed the same understanding of the inexorable judgments of God before Pilate. The proud Roman, offended by the silence of the Lord, said, "Are You not speaking to me? Do You not know that I have power to crucify You, and power to release You?" The Lord answered him, "You could have no power at all against Me unless it had been given you from above" (John 19:10–11). The judgments of God act; the power of God acts; and you, Pilate, are an instrument, though you do not realize it. But even such an instrument is gifted with reason and a free will, of which he is convinced, and expresses it with brazenness and vanity. He acted without any understanding of the judgments of God; he acted freely and willfully. His activity was declared a sin, which has its weight and measure before the judgment seat of God.

Opposition to the judgments of God can also be considered a demonic endeavor. When the Lord announced to His disciples that He would soon suffer and die violently, "Peter took Him aside and began to rebuke Him, saying, 'Far be it from You, Lord; this shall not happen to You!' But He turned and said to Peter, 'Get behind Me, Satan! You are an offense to Me, for you are not mindful of the things of God, but the things of men.'" (Matt 16:22–23). Peter was, by all appearances, inspired by a kind emotion, but he acted out of a frame of mind and desire for good that belongs only to fallen human nature. The reasoning and "virtue" of fallen human nature are at war with the will of God and His all-holy goodness. They vilify and condemn the judgments of God. Human reason and will, in their blindness, are ready to oppose and act against the judgments and dispensations of God, not understanding that such an endeavor is ludicrous, for it is the war of a limited, worthless creation against the almighty and all-perfect God.

"It is not for you to know times or seasons which the Father has put in His own authority" (Acts 1:7), said the Lord to the apostles when they asked Him about the coming of the earthly kingdom of Israel. This answer of the Lord is an answer to all curiosity and pride concerning the judgments of God. It is not for you, O man, to know that which God has placed under His own authority! Your understanding is limited by your mind; you are not capable of understanding the thoughts of a limitless Mind.

Your way of life, O man, must completely be confined within the fulfillment of the law of God. The perfect Man, God Who took humanity on Himself, gave us a model of this way of life, the rules that govern this way of life. Moved by the power of proper faith in God, you must follow the commandments of the Gospel diligently and submit reverently to the judgments of God.

What leads to such violation, such trampling upon the commandments of Christ, such opposition to the judgments of God, useless striving, complaints, blasphemy, despair? This—forgetfulness of eternity, forgetfulness of death, forgetfulness that we are short-lived pilgrims on this earth, rejection of the thought that we are exiles in search of our true homeland, a striving to please the passions and lusts, a desire for satiation with sinful and carnal pleasures, a pernicious lie and self-delusion, under whose influence man madly misuses his power over himself and his free will, bringing himself as a sacrifice to earthly vanity, destroying for himself the eternal blessedness that was returned to him by the suffering labors of the Redeemer, preparing for himself an eternal tomb in hell, a tomb for the body and the soul.

"Let this mind be in you which was also in Christ Jesus" (Phil 2:5). The Apostle Paul exhorts the Christians, pointing at the obedience of the God-Man to the judgments of God, to His uncomplaining submission that extended even to accepting the kind of execution that was reserved for capital criminals from the barbarian nations. No Roman citizen could ever be crucified. "Let us lay aside every weight, and the sin which so easily ensnares us, and let us run with endurance the race that is set before us, looking unto Jesus, the author and finisher of our faith, who for the joy that was set before Him endured the cross, despising the shame, and has sat down at the right hand of the throne of God. For consider Him who endured such hostility from sinners against Himself, lest you become weary and discouraged in your souls" (Heb 12:1–3).

"Therefore Jesus also, that He might sanctify the people with His own blood, suffered outside the gate. Therefore let us go forth to Him, outside the camp, bearing His reproach" (Heb 13:12–13). Going outside the camp and setting aside all pride is what we call rejecting the love of the world. The apostle reminds us of divine consolation, given by God to those of His chosen whom He adopted to Himself and whom, as proof of their sonship, He visits with sorrows: "My son, do not despise the chastening of the Lord, nor be discouraged when you are rebuked by Him; for whom the Lord loves He chastens, and scourges every son whom He receives" (Heb 12:5–6).

The holy Apostle Peter said, "Christ also suffered for us, leaving us an example, that you should follow His steps. . . . But when you do good and suffer, if you take it patiently, this is commendable before God. For to this you were called" (1 Pet 2:21, 20–21). These are the judgments of God! These are the dispensations of God! This is the calling of true Christians for the entire time of their earthly wandering! O Christians, beloved of God and heaven, do not be surprised, as though it were a strange, unnatural, disorderly catastrophe, when you are sent a "fiery trial" for your testing (1 Pet 4:12). Instead, rejoice when the temptations come!

Just as here, on earth, you become communicants of Christ's sufferings, so in the future life you will become communicants of His glory and triumph. The house of God is subject to God's judgment; it requires such a judgment (1 Pet 4:17). The house of God is the entire Church of Christ, as well as every Christian individually. This house requires God's visit and purification, as one who is constantly subject to defilement and damage. Even with the great aid of sorrows, which humble the spirit of man that so easily inclines to self-aggrandizement, it is still very difficult to be saved. "If the righteous one is scarcely saved, where will the ungodly and the sinner appear?" (1 Pet 4:18). What will happen to "those who do not obey the gospel of God?" (1 Pet 4:17). Thus, "be clothed with humility, for God resists the proud, but gives grace to the humble" (1 Pet 5:5).

You will feel the coming of grace in the wondrous calm and consolation that will be poured into your hearts when you confess that God's judgment over you is righteous, and you yourselves are worthy of punishments, in desperate need of them. When temptations do come, do not surrender to sorrow, hopelessness, despair, complaints, or any other manifestations of pride and faithlessness. On the contrary, enlivened and strengthened by faith, "humble yourselves under the mighty hand of God, that He may exalt you in due time, casting all your care upon Him, for He cares for you" (1 Pet 5:6–7).

O, you who suffer! Know that you suffer by God's will; be convinced that without the will of God, without God's permission, no sorrow would so much as touch you. The Lord has looked upon you with mercy; He has blessed you; He has admitted your heart and life to be pleasing to Him and therefore He has extended His right hand to help you through His judgments. He sent or allowed the suffering to come to you to purify you, to protect you, as a means to acquire perfection.

O, you who suffer according to God's will! When the sorrows come, surrender yourself completely to the will and mercy of God and with particular diligence apply yourselves to the fulfillment of the commandments of God. The time of suffering is a blessed time, in which God builds the soul of His beloved one, chosen from among the people.

The narrow and sorrowful path was established by God to lead from the earthly life to heaven. We are commanded to walk this way, weighed down by our cross, for this was the way that the Commander of the Christian nation, the incarnate God, walked, weighed down by His cross. The cross is endurance in the Lord of all offenses and assaults that are allowed by the providence of God. This is the judgment of God. On what is it founded? On the fact that man on earth is a criminal in a land of exile. This criminal is given a term, lasting the entirety of his earthly life, only so that he can realize his fallen state, his rejection, and the necessity for him to be saved, so that he will acquire salvation through the mediation of the Redeemer of mankind, our Lord Jesus Christ. The criminal who confesses himself to be a criminal, who seeks mercy, must by his very life express this confession of sinfulness. This confession cannot be admitted to be sincere when it is not proven by corresponding behavior. The criminal is required to prove the truth of his conversion toward God by the fulfillment of the will of God and by obedience to this will. He is required to offer the just and merciful God his patient endurance of God's chastisement, to bring his humble endurance as a sweet-smelling incense, as an acceptable sacrifice, as a convincing witness to faith.

All the saints, without exception, walked the dolorous path.[59] They all walked the earthly life through thorns, nourishing themselves with the unleavened bread of deprivations, sprinkled over with bitter hyssop. They constantly drank the cup of trials. This was necessary for their salvation and their perfection. Their sorrows were their spiritual education, medicine, and punishment. No human being has ever managed to avoid bearing the fruits of sin, inherent to a damaged and perverted nature. Our damaged nature constantly requires both an antidote for the poison of sin and sorrows for sin's correction. Together, they extinguish our sympathy for the sinful poison of passions, especially pride, the passion that is most poisonous and pernicious among all the passions. Sorrows lead the servant of God from a pompous, incorrect vision of himself to humble-mindedness and spiritual wisdom. A pompous self-opinion always proves that a superficially virtuous life actually lacks all correctness and dignity.[60]

"I have understood, O Lord, that Thy judgments are righteousness, and justly didst Thou humble me" (Ps 118:75). Your judgments are good, in spite of their severe aspect. Their consequences are beneficial; life-giving and sweet is their fruit. "It is good for me that Thou didst humble me, that I may learn Thy statutes" (Ps 118:71). "I have chosen the way of truth, and Thy judgments have I not forgotten" (Ps 118:30). "I have not turned aside from Thy judgments" (Ps 118:102), for without obedience, I am unable to please You by their fulfillment. In the midst of heavy temptations and trials, I find help nowhere, "I remembered Thine everlasting judgments, O Lord, and was comforted" (Ps 118:52). "In Thy judgments have I hoped!" (Ps 118:43). "Thy judgments shall help me" (Ps 118:175). "Seven times a day," that is, constantly, "have I praised Thee, because of Thy righteous judgments" (Ps 118:164). A way of life that corresponds to the actions of God in His unfathomable judgments is a constant glorification of God. Through the glorification of God, thoughts of unbelief, weak faith, complaining, blasphemy, despair are all cast out. Instead, holy and divine thoughts are led into the mind. The apostle said, "But when we are judged, we are chastened by the Lord, that we may not be condemned with the world" (1 Cor 11:32). Amen.

CHAPTER 6

A Meeting of the Soul and the Mind

Soul:

I sorrow unbearably. Nowhere can I find joy. I find no joy or consolation, either within myself or outside myself. I cannot look at the world, so filled as it is with constant delusion, lies, and murders. My frivolous contemplation of the world, my several unguarded glimpses of its temptations, my lack of knowledge concerning the poison of its impressions, my childish, inexperienced credulity toward the world have caused its arrows to strike me and fill me with fatal wounds. Why do I look at the world? Why am I curious about it; why do I examine it or grow attached to it when I am a mere short-lived wanderer in a world I will doubtless leave, and I do not know when I will leave it. Every day, every hour I must be ready for the call to go into eternity. No matter how long my wandering in the desert of the world, it is still an insignificant time compared with immeasurable eternity, before which hours, days, years, centuries are all equally insignificant. The very world, with all its massive pandemonium, is already passing: "both the earth and the works that are in it will be burned up" (2 Pet 3:10).

These works will all be consumed—the fruits of the Fall and the rejection of man. The wounds I received from the world have made it abhorrent to me, but they do not protect me from new wounds. I do not wish to remain in the world! I do not want to submit to it! I do not want to take any part in serving it! I do not even want to see it. But it persecutes me at every turn. It violently encroaches and appears in enchanting beauty to my gaze, weakening and wounding me, striking me down, destroying me. I myself, constantly bearing and containing within myself the principle of self-delusion and falsehood, into which I have been cast by sin, continue to be deluded by the world. Though I hate it, I unwillingly am attracted to it and greedily drink its poison. I deeply pierce myself with the arrows that it casts at me. I turn my sorrowing and inquisitive gaze from the world to my own self. But here I find nothing consoling. Inside me, sinful passions roil! I constantly defile myself with various sins. Either anger or remembrance of evils tortures me, or I feel like I am on fire with carnal lust. My blood boils; my imagination catches fire, incited by some other action, foreign to my self, at enmity with me, and I see before myself tempting images that entice me to sins of thought, to accepting the pleasures of pernicious temptation. I have no strength to run away from these enticing images. Unwillingly, by force, my sickened eyes become bound to them. And I have nowhere to run.

I ran into the desert, but the sinful visions came into the desert with me. Or perhaps they came to the desert before me—I do not know! In the desert they appeared before my eyes with even greater, more fatal vividness. These images are not real—both the images and their existence and the beauty they put on are lies and delusions. But still, they are so alive! And nothing, not time, not old age, can kill them completely. A tear of repentance would wash them out of my imagination, but I have no tears of repentance. Humble prayer, accompanied by the weeping of the heart, would wipe them out of my imagination. But I have no such prayer. My heart is devoid of compunction, deprived of soul-saving tears. My heart is unmoved, like a shard of a senseless stone. Despite my terrible sinfulness, I rarely see my sinfulness. Despite the fact that good is mixed with evil in me and has itself become evil, as delicious food becomes completely noxious with the addition of a little poison, I forget the calamitous state of the good that I was given at my creation, which was then damaged and twisted by the Fall.

No sooner do I begin to see the good inside me whole and free from poison than I begin to grow proud of it! My vanity bears me away from the fruitful and rich soil of repentance into a far country—a country whose soil is rocky and unable to give fruit, a country of thorns and tares, a country of lies, self-delusion, and perdition. I leave behind the doing of Christ's commandments and begin to cater to the desires of my heart, to follow its emotions and its will. I brazenly pretend that the senses of a fallen nature are good, and its actions I declare to be beneficial. This good and this virtue I declare to be worthy of earthly and heavenly rewards, the accolades of man and God.

When I tried to keep the commandments of Christ, not listening to the will of my heart and forcing it to follow, I admitted myself to be a debtor before God and man, an unworthy and unfaithful slave. Following self-delusion, sorrow, despair, and a kind of terrible darkness appear inside me. Sorrow deprives me of moral action; despair removes the strength to battle with sin, while the darkness—the consequence of sorrow and despair—a thick darkness hides God and His impartial and terrible Judgment Seat, as well as the promised rewards for Christian virtue, as well as the promised punishments for the rejection of Christianity and its all-holy tenets. I begin to sin without fear, while my conscience remains silent, as though killed or in a deep sleep. Rarely, very rarely a moment of compunction, a moment of hope and light gleams through. Then I feel myself to be different. But this light-filled moment is short. Rarely do my skies remain unclouded. Like dark clouds, once again my passions attack me, and once again they plunge me into darkness, confusion, disturbance, and perdition. Oh my mind! You are the director of the soul. Guide me! Lead me into blessed consolation! Teach me how I must shut out the impressions of the world. Teach me how to rein in and defeat the passion arising inside me. The world and the passions have exhausted me with their tortures.

Mind:

My answer will not be consoling. I am also sickened with sin, O my soul! Everything you have said is completely familiar to me. How can I help you when I myself have been fatally wounded, when I am deprived of the strength to act according to my own will? In my constant activity, given me by the Creator and characterizing my nature, I am ceaselessly subject to external influence. This influence is the influence of sin by which I am damaged and disordered. This influence constantly distracts me from God, from eternity. The vain and moribund world seduces me, sin seduces me, pride seduces me, the fallen angels seduce me. My essential limitation is my constant distraction. Struck by diversion, I soar, I rush about the entire cosmos without any need or without any benefit (like other rejected spirits). I would like to stop, but I cannot. Diversion once again snatches me and carries me away. Seized by diversions, I cannot stop long enough to see properly—not myself, not you, O my soul. I cannot properly attend to the word of God because of my distractions. On the surface, I appear to be attentive, but while I try to listen, I unwillingly turn aside to every direction. I am borne very far away to completely unrelated subjects, which is not only unnecessary for me but is extremely harmful.

Because of this fatal distraction, I cannot offer God any strong, active prayer, nor can I be stamped with the fear of God, which would easily destroy my distraction and would make my thoughts obedient to me; and then you, O my soul, would receive your desired repentance and compunction. Because of my distraction, you remain cold and stony, and while you are hardened and unfeeling, I divert myself even more. These diversions are the reasons for my weakness in battling sinful thoughts. Because of these diversions, I feel darkness and heaviness, and when a sinful thought comes to me, I do not immediately see or recognize it, especially if it hides itself with a good justification. Even if it is obvious, then I, arming myself against it, still do not find any definitive and complete hatred for it, and I begin to converse with my own murderer. I find pleasure in his fatal poison as he pours it into me. Rarely am I a victor, and often I am defeated. Because of my distraction, forgetfulness has enveloped me. I forget God; I forget eternity; I forget the vicissitude and falseness of the world; I am attracted by it, and I take you, O my soul, along with me. I forget my own sins. I forget my fall; I forget my calamitous condition. In the darkness of self-delusion, I begin to find merits both in you and myself. I begin to seek and require that the world admit these merits, and the world is instantaneously ready to accede to my request, the more to mock it afterward.

You and I have no merits; the dignity of a human being has been completely defiled by the Fall, and man only then correctly thinks of himself when he, as a certain great ascetic said, considers himself to be filth.[61] What else but filth is such a weak, pitiful being, who was called by the all-powerful Creator of all that is visible and invisible into being from nonexistence and who answered by arming himself against his Creator? What else but filth is a being that has nothing properly belonging to himself, for he has received everything from God, and still he has risen up against God? What else but filth is a being who was not ashamed of Eden and allowed himself, amid the blessedness of heaven, to eagerly listen to horrible slander and blasphemy against God, and even showed sympathy with the slander and blasphemy by actively trampling upon the commandment of God? What else but filth is a mind when it is the treasure trove, a constant producer, of filthy and angry thoughts, in all ways hostile to God? What else but filth is a soul in which fierce and bestial passions constantly roil, like poisonous snakes, basilisks, and scorpions in a deep pit? What else but filth is a body that was conceived in sin, birthed in sin, that became an instrument of sin in its entire short life, a source of death-bearing stench after the end of its earthly life? We, O my soul, are one single spiritual being: I think, and you feel. But we are not merely damaged by sin; we are cloven by it as though we were two separate beings, acting nearly always in opposition to each other. We are disunited; we are placed at odds against each other; we are separated from God! The sin that lives in us forces us to oppose even the all-holy and all-perfect One!

Soul:

Your answer is grievous, but true. There is but small consolation in our calamity being mutual, and we can share our sorrow and help each other. Give me advice. How shall we leave this disorderly state? I have noticed that my emotions always correspond with your thoughts. The heart cannot battle for long with the mind—it always submits, and even when it fights, it does so only for a short time. O my mind! Be a guide to our mutual salvation!

Mind:

I agree that the heart does not oppose the mind for long. But after being submissive for a moment, the heart rebels anew against every perfect and God-pleasing thought, rebels with such force and bitterness that it almost always deposes me and entices me. Having dethroned me, it begins to engender in me the most absurd thoughts, the expressions and revelations of hidden passions. What can I say about my own thoughts? Because of my disorderliness and my damage from sin, my thoughts are incredibly inconstant. In the morning, for example, I think about our spiritual life, of our invisible, much-laboring toil, of our earthly state, relationships, circumstances, and our eternal fate, and these thoughts seem to me to be profound. Suddenly, by noon, or even earlier, these thoughts disappear of their own accord or because of some unexpected encounter, and they are replaced by others that, in their own turn, demand attention. By the evening, still new thoughts with new justifications arise. At night, I am swept away by still other thoughts that were hiding somewhere during the day, as though waiting in ambush, to unexpectedly appear before me in the time of night's silence and to disturb me with the enchanting and fatal vividness of sin. In vain do I admit (instructed by the word of God) as correct only those thoughts that inspire in you, O my soul, a state of profound calm, humility, love for others. In vain am I convinced that all such thoughts—not only those that provoke suffering and disorder in you, but those that are joined with the least bit of confusion or lack of feeling—are lacking in truth, are completely false, delusive, pernicious, no matter how convincing their mask of righteousness. Futile is this knowledge! Futile is that trustworthy sign that so definitively divides good from evil in the spiritual world! Because of the unfathomable sickness that lives in me, which I come to know only by experience, I cannot tear myself from death-dealing thoughts, thoughts that are produced by the sin in me. I cannot subdue them, nor can I uproot them when they begin to roil inside me like worms. I cannot fight them off; I cannot push them away when they attack me from without like brigands, like fierce, bloodthirsty predators. They hold me in thrall; they force me to labor heavily. They torture, oppress me and every hour are ready to tear me apart, to defeat me with eternal death. I unwillingly tell you of these tortures, O my soul, and I also tell our body about them, for it is sick and weak because it is stricken by countless wounds; it is pierced with both the arrows and the swords of sin. O my soul, poisoned as you are by the venom of eternal death, you sorrow unbearably and seek joy, but you find it nowhere. In vain do you think to find this joy in me. I am killed together with you; together with you I am buried in the dark and constrained tomb in which we can neither see nor know God. Our relationship with the living God is as to an nonexistent or dead creature. This is the surest proof our own destruction.

Soul:

O my guide! O my eye! My highest spiritual power! My mind! You are leading me into hopelessness. If you, the light of my eyes, admit yourself to be darkness, then what should I expect of my other powers, which are the same as in any irrational beast? What should I expect of my will or desire, from my zeal or my natural anger? They can only be different from the desire or the anger of cattle, beasts, or demons when they are guided by you. You told me that, despite all your weakness, despite all your darkness, despite all your lifelessness, the word of God still acts within you and gives you at least an echo of an ability to distinguish good from evil—an extremely difficult thing to do! And now, I have become a participant in this saving knowledge. Already now, when I begin to sense confusion and disorder, I begin to acknowledge the incorrectness of this state. I begin to distrust and hate this state and try to throw it off me, for it is unnatural and hateful to me.

Not only that, but if you remain, even for a moment, in the familiar embrace of thoughts gleaned from the word of God, I feel such consolation! Such glorification of God begins to rise up from my depths, from the very treasure stores of my heart! What reverence for the greatness of God encompasses me then! What a worthless mote of dust do I seem to myself then, before the great and various beauties of creation! What grace-filled silence, as though brought down by a breeze from heaven, begins to blow within me and to cool me, who am so overwhelmed by heat and drought. What a sweet and healing tear has arisen in the heart and poured out on my scorched cheek from a humble and meek eye that now looks on everything and everyone so peacefully, with such love! Then I feel the healing of my nature! Then the inner warfare stills! Then my powers, so fragmented and cloven by sin, come together and unite. Having become one with you and with my other powers, and having attracted to this unity even the body, I feel the mercy of the Creator to His fallen creation. I come to know by experience the meaning and power of the Redeemer Who heals me by His all-powerful and life-giving commandment. I confess Him! I see the action of the all-holy Spirit, worthy of worship, Who proceeds from the Father and is sent by the Son! I see the action of God the Spirit, presented by God the Word, revealing His divinity by His creative power, through Whose mediation this broken vessel appears as though it were never broken, appearing in its primordial wholeness and beauty. O my mind! Turn to the word of God from which we have already taken so many countless benefits, which we have lost by our sloth, our apathy to the gifts of God. We have bartered these priceless spiritual gifts for delusive phantasms, the poison of sin and the world presented in the form of a gift. O my mind! Turn to the word of God! Seek my joy there, for in this moment my sorrow is unbearable, and I fear that I will fall to ultimate perdition—into despair.

Mind:

O my soul, the word of God resolves our disturbance with the most satisfactory articulations. But many people, having heard the word of the Spirit and having interpreted it with their own carnal mindset, have said about the life-giving word of God: "This is a hard saying; who can understand it?" (John 6:60). Listen, O my soul, to what the Lord said, "He who finds his life will lose it, and he who loses his life for My sake will find it" (Matt 10:39). "He who loves his life will lose it, and he who hates his life in this world will keep it for eternal life" (John 12:25).

Soul:

I am ready to die, if God commands it. But how can I, an immortal soul, die? I do not know the instrument that would be capable of depriving me of life.

Mind:

Do not think, O my soul, that the command of Christ intends for you to die alone, and that I am not condemned as well. No! I must share the cup of death with you, and I must drink it first, since I am the main culprit in our mutual fall, rejection, calamity, and our mutual temporary and eternal death. The death and loss required of us by God do not consist in the ceasing of our existence. They are the death of self-love, which has become for us a second life. Self-love is the perverted love of fallen man for himself. Self-love deifies fallen, so-called reason and tries in all things and constantly to satisfy its fallen, incorrectly oriented will. Self-love is expressed toward others either as hatred or base flattery, that is, satisfaction of human passions with respect to the objects of the world (which it always misuses) in the form of passionate attachment. Just as holy love is "the bond of perfection" (Col 3:14) and is made up of the fullness of all other virtues, so self-love is that sinful passion that is created from the fullness of all other various sinful passions. In order to destroy self-love in ourselves, I must reject all my own reasoning, even if I am very rich with the understanding transmitted by the study of the world and its natural processes.[62] I must submerge myself into poverty of spirit and, uncovered by this poverty, be washed away by tears, smoothed over and softened by meekness, purity, and mercy. I must accept the reasoning that the right hand of my Redeemer will so kindly inscribe on me. This right hand is the Gospel. And you, O my soul, must reject your own will, no matter how difficult this is for the heart, even if the feelings and inclinations of the heart seem to you to be very righteous and noble. Instead of your own will, you must fulfill the will of Christ, our God and Saviour, no matter how abhorrent or cruel this seems to the self-loving heart. This is the death that God requires of us, so that we, by this willing death, would destroy the death that lives in us forcibly and receive as a gift resurrection and life, flowing from the Lord Jesus.

Soul:

I have decided on self-rejection. Even from uttering words about self-rejection, I already began to feel joy and hope. Let us leave the life that gives rise to hopelessness and let us accept death—the pledge of salvation. Lead me, O my mind, in the footsteps of God's commands, and I will unswervingly remain in that Word, Who spoke concerning Himself: "He who abides in Me, and I in him, bears much fruit; for without Me you can do nothing" (John 15:5). Amen.

CHAPTER 7

Seeing One's Sins

That frightening time will come, that frightening hour will approach when all my sins will appear uncovered before God the Judge, before His angels, before all mankind. I foretaste the state of my soul in this terrible hour, and I am filled with horror. Under the influence of this vivid and strong foretaste, I hurry with trepidation to plunge deeply into myself, to examine myself, to inspect the book of my conscience for the sins of deed, word, and thought that are written within.

Books that have been left a long time unread in cabinets become filled with dust and can be eaten away by moths. If someone tries to read such a book, he finds it quite difficult to make out the words. This is my conscience. It has long remained uninspected; it can hardly even be opened. Having opened and read it, I do not find the contentment I expected. Only my grievous sins are clearly written. The smaller sins, which are very many, have been almost completely effaced. And now, I can hardly make out what was written.

God, God alone can return clarity to the faded words and deliver man from an evil soul.[63] God alone can give a man the vision of his own sins. Only through God, can man see his sin and the fall that is the germ, the seed, the summation of all human transgressions.

Having called on God's mercy and power with ardent prayer, wise fasting, and the sorrow and groaning of the heart, once again I open the book of my conscience. Once again I look at the number and quality of my sins. Once again I examine the consequences of the sins I have committed.

I see: "For my wickednesses are gone over my head; like a sore burden have they become too heavy for me . . . yeah, they are more in number than the hairs of my head" (Ps 37:5, 39:13). What is the consequence of my sinfulness? "Innumerable troubles are come about me; my sins have taken such hold upon me, that I am not able to look up . . . and my heart hath failed me" (Ps 39:13). The consequences of a sinful life are the blindness of the mind and the hardening and insensibility of the heart. The mind of a confirmed sinner sees neither good nor evil. His heart loses its spiritual senses. If, after having left his sinful life, this person turns to pious labors, his heart, as though foreign to him, does not sympathize with his striving toward God.

When the action of divine grace reveals to the ascetic the multitude of his sins, then it is impossible for him not to become extremely perplexed and be plunged into deep sorrow. "My heart is troubled" at this vision of my sins, "my strength hath failed me, and the light of mine eyes, even that is gone from me. For my loins are filled with sores"; that is, my life is full of troubles from habitual sin that forces me to sin anew. "My wounds stink, and are corrupt, because of my foolishness"; that is, the sinful passions have become habits and have terribly harmed me because of my inattentive life. "There is no healing in my flesh," no healing possible from my personal exertions, for my entire nature is stricken and infected with sin (Ps 37:11, 6, 8).

By admitting my sins, by repenting of them, by confessing them, by regretting them, I cast their multitude into the abyss of God's mercy. To avoid sin in the future, watch closely, having descended deep into yourself, how sin acts against me, how it approaches me, and what it says to me. It approaches me like a thief. Its face is hidden; its words drip with oil (see Ps 54:22 LXX); it speaks lies to me when it offers me iniquity. Its mouth is filled with poison. Its tongue is a death-dealing stinger.

"Take pleasure in it!" quietly and cajolingly whispers sin. "Why should pleasure be forbidden you? Enjoy! What sin is there in that?" And it offers you—the villain!—transgression of the commandments of the all-holy Lord.

I should pay no attention to sin's words. I know that sin is a thief and a murderer. But some kind of inexplicable weakness of will defeats me! I listen to the words of sin and I gaze at the forbidden fruit. In vain does my conscience remind me that to eat of this fruit is to taste of death.

If there is no forbidden fruit before my eye, then immediately it draws itself in my imagination vividly as though with the hand of enchantment.

The emotions of my heart incline toward this seductive painting, as to a harlot. Her external beauty is captivating, and she radiates temptation. She looks expensive and rich, but it is all plating, for her lethal infection is carefully hidden. Sin seeks a sacrifice of the heart when the body cannot bring itself, in lieu of the actual object.

Sin acts in me through sinful thoughts, through sinful emotions of the heart and body—through the body's senses and through the imagination.

What conclusions can I make after seeing myself thus? Only one—in me, in my entire being, sinful damage abides, which sympathizes and aids the sin that attacks me from without. I am like a prisoner chained with heavy chains, and everyone who wishes can grab the prisoner and lead him wherever he wants, because the prisoner, being bound in chains, has no ability to resist.

Once, sin even infiltrated sublime Eden. There it offered my ancestors to eat of the forbidden fruit. There it seduced them, and the seduced were struck down with eternal death. And I, their descendant, contently hear the same proposition from sin, and I, their descendant, am constantly seduced and destroyed by sin.

Adam and Eve were immediately cast out of Eden after sinning, from the garden into the country of woe (Gen 3:23–24). I was born in this country of sorrow and calamity. But this does not justify me; the Redeemer has brought down Eden to me and planted it in my heart. And yet I banished Eden from my heart, because I sinned. Now my heart is a confusion of good and evil; now it is a battlefield of good against evil. Now my heart is filled with the clash of countless passions. Now it is filled with tortures, the foretaste of hell's eternal pain.

In myself I see the proof that I am the son of Adam. I keep his inclination to sin; I agree with the propositions of the enticer, though I know with conviction that he offers me a lie and that he prepares to murder me.

In vain do I begin to blame my forefathers for the sin I inherited from them, for I have been freed from sinful bondage by the Redeemer, and now I fall into sin not from constraint, but willingly.

My forefathers once transgressed a single command of God, but I, though I am in the bosom of the Church of Christ, constantly violate all the divine commandments of Christ, my God and my Saviour.

How my soul is disturbed by anger and remembrance of evils! In my imagination, a knife glints over the head of my enemy and my heart revels in the satisfaction of revenge, even committed by the imagination. Or I imagine piles of cold coins at my feet! Immediately majestic palaces, gardens draw themselves in my imagination, all sorts of objects of luxury, sensuality, pride that can be bought with gold and for which reason sin-loving man so readily worships this idol, for it is a means to the satisfaction of all earthly desires. Or I am enticed by honors and power! I am drawn and absorbed by reveries of ruling people and nations, of earthly profits gained from it, and perishable glory for myself. Or my imagination conjures up realistic visions of tables with steaming and pleasant-smelling food. How pitifully and comically I find pleasure in these enticements that present themselves to my imagination! Or I suddenly imagine myself to be righteous or, more specifically, my heart flatters itself by forcibly trying to assimilate righteousness to itself. My heart flatters itself and worries about human praise and how to attract more of it!

The passions quarrel over me, and I am constantly passed along from one to another. They confuse me and harass me. And I do not see my own pitiable condition. My mind is shrouded by an impenetrable curtain of darkness; my heart is crushed by a heavy stone of unfeeling.

Will my mind awaken and will it desire to turn to the good? My heart resists it, having grown used to sinful pleasures. My body resists it, having hoarded bestial desires. I have even lost the understanding that my body, created for eternity, is capable of divine desires and movements and that bestial striving is a sickness that infected it after the Fall.

The heterogeneous parts that make up my being—my mind, heart, and body—are fragmented, separated. They are in discord and oppose one another. They only act in a fleeting harmony (abhorrent to God) when they work together for sin.

This is my state! It is the death of the soul while the body still lives. But I am content with my state! I am content not because of humility, but because of my blindness, because of the hardness of my heart. My soul does not even know it is dead, and neither does the body, though it is parted from the soul by death.

If only I would feel my death, then I would remain in constant repentance! If only I would feel my death, then I would work toward my resurrection!

But I am busy entirely with the cares of the world, and little do I care for my spiritual calamity! I cruelly judge the slightest sins of my neighbors; yet I am filled with sin, blinded by it, transformed into a pillar of salt like Lot's wife, incapable of any spiritual movement.

I have not inherited repentance, for as yet I do not see my own sin. I do not see my sin because I am still enthralled to sin. He who takes pleasure in sin and allows himself to taste of sin—even in thought or with a mere sympathetic inclination toward sin in the heart—cannot see his own sin. Only he who has definitely decided to cut off any friendship with sin can see his own sin. Only he who has stood watch all night at the gates of his house with a naked sword in hand—the word of God—and who repels and cuts sin down with this sword, in whatever form it approaches him—can know his own sin.

Whoever will do this great deed—to begin war against sin, forcefully repelling his mind, heart, and body from it—to him will God give a great gift—to see his own sin.

Blessed is the soul that has seen sin nesting inside itself! Blessed is the soul that has seen within itself the fall of the forefathers, the decrepitude of the old Adam. Such seeing of one's own sins is spiritual sight, the sight of a mind healed of blindness by God's grace.

The Holy Eastern Church teaches us to ask for this seeing of our own sins with fasting and with prayer on bended knees.

Blessed is the soul that constantly learns the law of God! In it, the soul can see the image and the beauty of the New Man and can use Him as a ruler by which to see and measure its own shortcomings.

Blessed is the soul that has bought the field of repentance with the mortification of the self to all sinful inclination! In this field, it will find the priceless pearl of salvation.

If you have acquired the field of repentance, cry like a child before God. Do not ask anything of God if you can help it; instead, commit yourself with self-rejection to His will.

Understand palpably that you are a creature, and God is the Creator. Give yourself completely into the will of the Creator and bring to Him only your tears, as a child. Bring Him a silent heart that is ready to follow His will and be impressed with the stamp of His will.

If, in your spiritual infancy, you cannot plunge into prayerful silence and weeping before God, then utter before Him a humble prayer for the forgiveness of sin and the healing from sinful passions, these terrifying moral illnesses that are formed from the willful repetition of sins over the course of a very long time.

Blessed is the soul that has acknowledged itself completely unworthy of God, that has condemned itself as accursed and sinful! It is on the path to salvation; there is no self-delusion in such a soul.

On the contrary, whoever considers himself ready to accept grace, whoever considers himself worthy of God, who expects and asks for His mystical visitation, whoever says that he is ready to accept, hear, and even see the Lord—that person lies to himself and flatters himself. He has only reached the heights of pride, from which he will fall into the dark abyss of destruction.[64] All those who have prized themselves higher than God fall into that pit, all those who have shamefully dared to consider themselves worthy of God. Such men have in their delusion and arrogance said to God, "O Lord, speak, for Your servant hears" (1 Kgdms 3:9).

The young prophet Samuel heard the voice of the Lord calling to him and, not acknowledging himself worthy of conversation with the Lord, came before his elderly mentor and asked him for instructions concerning his behavior. Samuel heard the same voice calling a second time and again assumed it was his teacher. Then the elderly teacher understood that the voice calling Samuel was the voice of God. He commanded the youth to answer the voice that calls him thus: "O Lord, speak, for Your servant hears."

The sensual and arrogant dreamer dares to say the same as Samuel, though no one has called him! Drunk on his own vain self-opinion, he invents voices and consolations for himself that only flatter his own arrogant-up heart. He only lies to himself and his gullible followers.[65]

O child of the Eastern Church, the Only Holy and True Church! In your unseen labors, be guided by the instructions of the Holy Fathers of your Church. They all, in one voice, tell you to turn away from any vision, any voices within or without, until you are renewed by the palpable action of the Holy Spirit, for otherwise you will fall to self-delusion.[66]

Let us preserve our minds free of visions; let us reject all images and fantasies that approach, because through them truth will be replaced by a fall. Clothed with repentance, stand with fear and reverence before the great God Who has the power to purify you of your sins and to renew you by His all-holy Spirit. The Spirit Who will come "will guide you into all truth" (John 16:13).

The only emotion required by the soul that approaches the Lord with the intention of receiving forgiveness of sins is sorrow and repentance. This is "that good part" (Luke 10:42)! If you have chosen it, it "will not be taken away" from you! Do not exchange this treasure for empty, delusional, forced, falsely gracious emotions. Do not destroy yourself by flattering yourself.

"If some fathers," said St Isaac the Syrian in his 55th Homily, "wrote to explain what is purity of the soul, what is health for the soul, what is dispassion, what is *theoria* (that is, spiritual vision), then they wrote it not so that we would seek these too early or with expectation. For the Scriptures say, 'The kingdom of God does not come with observation' (Luke 17:20). Those who have such expectation have only acquired pride and the fall. . . . Seeking the exalted gifts of God with expectation is rejected by the Church of God. This is not a sign of love for God; this is a spiritual sickness."

All the saints have admitted that they were unworthy of God. By this have they shown their worthiness, which can only be found in humility.[67]

All those who are self-deluded consider themselves to be worthy of God. By this have they revealed the pride and demonic delusion that have enveloped their souls. Some of them accepted the demons who appeared before them in the form of angels and followed them. To others the demons appeared in their proper form and pretended to be defeated by their prayer, leading the false ascetics to an exalted self-opinion. Others incited their imagination, warmed their blood, forcibly produced within themselves certain movements of the nerves, and considered this to be the pleasures of God's grace. By this, they fell into self-delusion, into complete darkness, and have been ranked, according to their spirit, among the rejected spirits of darkness.

If you have the need to speak with yourself, then offer self-condemnation, not flattery, to yourself.

Bitter medicine is helpful to us in our fallen state. Those who flatter themselves have already received their reward on this earth—their self-delusion, as well as the praise and love of the world that hates God. Those who flatter themselves should expect nothing in eternity except condemnation.

"My sin is ever before me," said St David (Ps 50:5 LXX). His sin was an object of constant scrutiny. "For I will confess my wickedness, and be sorry for my sin" (Ps 37:19).

The holy David condemned himself and denounced his own sin, even after the sin was forgiven and the gifts of the Holy Spirit were returned to him. This was not enough. He condemned his own sin and confessed it for the entire cosmos to hear (see Ps 50).

When the Holy Fathers of the Eastern Church, especially the desert ascetics, achieved the heights of spiritual ascesis, all their labors flowed together into a single stream of repentance. Repentance embraced their entire life, their entire activity. This was the consequence of their seeing their own sins.

A certain great father was asked what is the essence of the work of a solitary monk. He answered, "Your mortified soul is laid bare before your gaze, and you are asking me what your work should be?"[68] Tears are the essential task of a true ascetic of Christ; tears, from the moment he begins his labors to the time of the completion of his labors.

Seeing one's own sins and the repentance that comes of such vision—this is a labor that has no end on this earth. The vision of sin inspires repentance. Repentance gives purification. The gradually purified eye of the mind begins to see ever more shortcomings and scars in man's entire being, which he previously, in his darkness, did not even notice.

Lord! Give us the gift of seeing our own sins, so that our mind, drawn completely toward attentiveness to our own sins, ceases to see the sins of others. Thereby, we will see all our neighbors as good. Help our hearts abandon the pernicious attention given to the sins of our neighbor, and let all our cares be united in a single desire to acquire the purity and sanctity that You have commanded and prepared for us. Help us, who have defiled our spiritual clothing, to whiten them once again. They have already been washed clean once by the waters of baptism, but they now require, after defilement, to be washed clean by the streams of repentant tears. Grant us to see, in the light of Your grace, the many sicknesses that live within us and destroy all spiritual movements in the heart, instead inspiring in it sinful movements of the flesh, so hostile to the Kingdom of God. Give us the great gift of repentance, preceded and birthed by that greater gift—the vision of our own sins. Protect us by these great gifts from the abyss of self-delusion that opens up in the soul from its unnoticed and unacknowledged sinfulness, from the actions of unnoticed and unacknowledged sensuality and vanity. Preserve us by these great gifts on our path to You, and let us reach You, Who calls repentant sinners and rejects self-admitted righteous ones. And we will eternally praise You in eternal blessedness, the Only true God, the Redeemer of the imprisoned, the Saviour of the lost. Amen.

CHAPTER 8

The Image and Likeness of God in Man

"Let us make man in Our image, according to Our likeness" (Gen 1:26). This was the mystical counsel of God the Trinity within Himself and with Himself before the creation of man.

Man is the image and likeness of God. God, unapproachable in His greatness, God, surpassing any image, vividly invested man with His image in glory. Just so is the sun depicted in a humble drop of water. The being of man, his sovereign power, that which differentiated him from all the beasts of the earth, by which he is equal to angels—his spirit—is the image of the being of God. The characteristics of the human spirit, in their pure state, are the likeness of the characteristics of God, Who, having drawn with His almighty right hand His own likeness on man, still remains beyond all likeness and comparison.

What a superlative creature is man, so filled with various advantages, such multifaceted beauty!

For him the Creator created all visible nature, and all nature was intended to serve him. All of nature was his miraculous setting.

When the Creator created all the other creatures out of nothing, He was content to merely utter His almighty command. However, when He wanted to complete the work of creation by making a refined, perfect creation, He preceded it with a council.

All the vastness of matter, in all its boundless and countless variations, created before man, was—we will say this definitively, for we speak the truth—a premeditated creation.

Thus, an earthly king prepares and decorates a majestic frame in which to set his portrait.

The King of kings and God of gods prepares all of visible creation, in all its harmony, in all its visible and wondrous grandeur. But this is all but a frame, into which He places His image, the final purpose of all that He created.

After He finished the creation of the world, before He created man, God looked over His creation and found it satisfactory: "God saw that it was good" (Gen 1:25).

After the creation of man, once again God looked over all that He had done, and now he found it refined, full, perfect: "Then God saw everything He had made, and indeed, it was very good" (Gen 1:31).

O man! Understand your worth!

Look at the meadows and fields, the wide rivers, the endless seas, the high mountains, the luxurious trees, all the animals and beasts of the earth, all fish and creatures that travel the expanse of the waters; look at the stars, the moon, the sun, the sky. All this is for you! All this was intended to serve you.

Other than the world that we see, there is yet another world, invisible to the physical eyes, and it is incomparably greater than the visible world. Even this invisible world is for man!

How greatly has the Lord honored His image! What a great calling He intended for him! The visible world is only the preparatory threshold of a domain that is incomparably more glorious and expansive. Here, as in a threshold, the image of God gradually receives complete likeness with its all-holy, all-perfect Archetype, so that it can enter bridal chamber in the beauty and refinement of this likeness, in which the Archetype inconceivably presides, as though limiting his limitlessness to reveal Himself to His beloved, reasoning creatures.

The image of God the Trinity is man the trinity.

The three persons of man the trinity are the three powers of his soul, by which the existence of the spirit is manifested. Our thoughts and spiritual senses manifest the existence of the mind, which, while expressing itself in complete obviousness, is at the same time totally completely invisible and unattainable.

In the Holy Scriptures and the writings of the Holy Fathers, the soul is sometimes called "the spirit" outright, and sometimes the "spirit" is one of the three powers of the soul. The Fathers also call this power of the soul the "ability to form speech." The Fathers generally divide the soul into three powers—the mind, the thought (or the word), and the spirit. The mind they call the source, the principle, both of thoughts and spiritual sensations. The spirit, in this specific meaning, they call the ability to sense spiritual realities. Often in the writings of the Fathers, the reasoning power (that is, the spirit) is also called the mind (or "intellect," *nous* in Greek). This is why the created spirits are called "minds." The whole receives its name from its most important constituent part.

The very essence of our soul is the image of God. Even after the fall into sin, the soul remains the image of God! Even cast into the flames of hell, the sinful soul, within the flames themselves, remains the image of God! This is the teaching of the Holy Fathers.[69]

The Holy Church cries aloud in its hymnography: "I am the image of Thine unutterable glory, though I bear the wounds of sin" (see the Troparia in the Funeral Service of the Orthodox Church [Or in Memorial Saturdays / Soul Saturdays]).

Our mind is the image of the Father; our word (the unuttered word is usually called the thought) is the image of the Son; our spirit is the image of the Holy Spirit.

As in God the Trinity the three Persons comprise a single divine Essence without confusion or division, so also in man the trinity three "persons" comprise a single human essence, without confusion into a single "person" or without fully dividing into three distinct entities.

Our mind gave birth to, and never ceases to give birth to, thought. The thought, being born, does not cease being begotten again, though at the same time it remains begotten, hidden in the mind.

The mind could not exist without thought; neither can thought exist without the mind. The beginning of the first is always the beginning of the second as well. The existence of the mind is the existence of the thought.

In the same way, our spirit proceeds from our mind and acts together with thought. Therefore, every thought has its spirit. Every way of thinking has its distinct spirit. Every book has its unique spirit.

Thought cannot be without spirit; the existence of one must accompany the existence of the other. In the existence of both one and the other, the existence of the mind is revealed.

What is the spirit of man? It is the fullness of the heart's emotions that belong only to a soul that is reasoning and immortal, absent in the souls of beasts and animals.

The heart of man differs from the hearts of beasts by its spirit. The hearts of animals have emotions that depend on blood and nerves, but they have no spiritual sensations. This characteristic of the divine image is the exclusive inheritance of man.

The moral authority of man is his spirit.

Our mind, word, and spirit, whose beginning and mutual relation is simultaneous, are images of the Father, Son, and Holy Spirit, Who are co-eternal, equally without beginning, equally worthy of praise, consubstantial.

"He who has seen Me has seen the Father," said the Son, "I am in the Father, and the Father in Me" (John 14:9–10). The same can be said of the mind of man and his thought—the mind, invisible on its own, is revealed in the thoughts. Whoever comes to know the thought also comes to know the mind that produced this thought.

The Lord declared the Holy Spirit to be "Power from on high" (Luke 24:49), and "the Spirit of truth" (John 14:17), the Truth being the Son. Human spirit also has as its characteristic "power," being also the spirit of a man's thoughts, whether they be true or false. It is expressed in the hidden movements of the heart, in the manner of thinking, in all the actions of a person. By the spirit of man, man's mind and manner of thought are also revealed. The spirit of every action reveals the thought that directs the man toward that action.

The merciful Lord decorated His image with His likeness. The image of God is the very essence of the soul, but the likeness is the soul's attributes.

The newly created image of God—man—was like God immortal, wise, good, pure, incorruptible, holy, devoid of any sinful passion, any sinful thought, any sinful emotion.

The trained artist first draws the outline and the general features of the face that he will later paint as a portrait. Having carefully drawn these outlines, he gives the face and clothing the light and colors of the original, and by doing this, he completes the likeness. God, having created His image, decorated him with His likeness. It is proper to the image of God to have similarity with God in all things. Otherwise, the image would be incomplete and unworthy of God, for it will neither have fulfilled its original purpose nor conformed to it.

Alas! Alas! Weep, O heavens! Cry out, O sun and all luminaries. Weep, earth! Weep, all the creatures of the heavens and the earth! Weep, O Nature! Weep, you holy angels! Weep bitterly, inconsolably! Put on your profound sorrow like a cloak, for a calamity has occurred, for a calamity it can truly be called without exaggeration—the image of God fell!

Honored by God with free will—one of the bright, living flowers of the likeness of God—yet seduced by the angel who had fallen before him, man communed with the thoughts and spirit of the dark father of lies and all evil. This communion was actualized by action—division from the will of God. By this, man banished the Spirit of God from his side and perverted the divine likeness. Man befouled the very image of God.

Vividly and exactly did the Teacher describe the calamity of the Fall: "That which has become crooked cannot be made straight, and what is lacking cannot be counted" (Eccl 1:15).

The disorder of the image and the likeness is easily glimpsed within. The beauty of the likeness, consisting of the fullness of all virtues, is defiled by dark and foul-smelling passion. The outlines of the image have lost their precision, and they no longer look harmonious. The thoughts and the spirit battle each other, rebel against the mastery of the mind and rise up against it. The mind itself is in constant confusion, in terrible darkness that closes it off from God and the holy and sinless way toward God.

The disorder of the image and likeness of God is accompanied by torturous pain. If a person examines himself carefully in solitude for a long time, constantly, he will be assured that this pain acts without ceasing. The pain rises or falls only depending on how much it is muted by distraction.

O man! Your distractions and pleasure are the exposers of the pain that is inside you! You seek to mute it with the cup of boisterous amusements. O miserable one! No sooner does a moment of sobriety come for you than you once again are convinced that the suffering that you tried to destroy with amusements still resides in you. Amusements are only food for the pain, a means for its strengthening. Having rested under the cover of distraction, the pain reawakens with renewed power. It is the witness, living within man himself, of the fall of man.

The very body of man is stamped with the proof of the Fall. From the moment of his birth, the body is at war with everything that surrounds it and with the soul within it. All elements attack it; finally, exhausted by inner and outer warfare, stricken with sickness, brought low by old age, the body falls prey to death's sickle, and even though it was created to be immortal, it falls apart into dust.

And once again the greatness of God's image appears! It is revealed even in the very Fall, in the way that man was rescued from this fall.

God, by One of His Persons, took His image upon Himself. He became man. By His own Self he rescued him from the Fall and restored him to his former glory, raising him up to an even greater height that was given to him at the creation.

The Lord is just in His mercy. By His redemption, He magnified His image even more than at the first creation. Man himself did not invent the Fall, as did the fallen angel. Man was enticed to the Fall by envy; he was deluded by evil that hid behind a mask of goodness.

All the Persons of God the Trinity took part in the work of Incarnation, even hypostatically. The Father abides as the begetter; the Son is begotten, and the Holy Spirit acts.

Here also we see how man is exactly God's image. The Son takes humanity on Himself; through Him God the Trinity enters into communion with mankind. Our own thought, in order to communicate with other people, is incarnated into sounds. The immaterial is joined with matter; through it, the spirit and the mind enter this communication as well.

The Son, God the Word, the Divine Truth—He was incarnate. Our own thought was corrected and purified by Truth, and our own spirit became capable of communion with the Holy Spirit. The Holy Spirit then revivified our spirit, which was mortified by eternal death. Then our mind could enter into the knowledge and vision of the Father.

Man the trinity is healed by God the Trinity. The Word heals the thought and leads it from the dominion of falsehood, from the dominion of self-delusion, into the dominion of truth. The Holy Spirit vivifies the spirit and leads it from carnal and sensual emotions to spiritual ones. The Father appears to the mind, and the mind becomes the mind of God. "We have the mind of Christ," said St Paul (1 Cor 2:16).

Before the coming of the Holy Spirit, man, as one with a dead spirit, begged, "Lord, show us the Father" (John 14:8). After accepting the Spirit of adoption, having sensed his sonship to God, reviving in spirit for God and salvation by the action of the Holy Spirit, man now refers to the Father as an intimate, as to a Father, crying "Abba, Father!" (Rom 8:15).

In the font of baptism, our fallen image is restored, and man is born into eternal life by water and the Spirit. From this moment, the Spirit, who had come away from man at his fall, begins to accompany him during his earthly life, healing the damage inflicted by sin after baptism through repentance. Thus, He makes it possible for him to be saved through repentance, even to the last breath.

The beauty of the likeness was restored by the Spirit, just as the image was in baptism. It develops and perfects itself by the keeping of the commandments of the Gospel.

The model for this beauty, the fullness of this beauty is the God-Man, our Lord Jesus Christ.

"Imitate me, just as I also imitate Christ" (1 Cor 11:1), exhorts the apostle, calling the faithful to restore and perfect the divine likeness in themselves, indicating to them the Holy Archetype of perfection for the new man who was recreated and renewed by the Redemption. "Put on the Lord Jesus Christ" (Rom 13:14).

God the Trinity, when He redeemed His image (man), gave him such an opportunity to succeed in the perfection of the likeness, that the true likeness becomes a union of the image with the Archetype, the union of impoverished creation with its all-perfect Creator.

Wondrous, miraculous is the image of God, that image through which God Himself shines and acts. Peter's very shadow could heal the sick! The man who lied to his face immediately fell down dead, as though he had lied directly to God. Paul's kerchiefs and head-coverings performed miracles. Elisha's bones raised a dead man, when the careless undertakers accidentally touched his body to the bones of the long-dead spirit-bearer.

The closest likeness and union is effected and preserved by the constant abiding in the commandments of the Gospel. The Saviour commanded His disciples, "Abide in Me, and I in you. . . . I am the vine, you are the branches. He who abides in Me, and I in him, bears much fruit" (John 15:4–5).

The most blessed of states is when the Christian, with a conscience purified by the abandonment of all sin and the exact fulfillment of the commandments of the Gospel, communicates of the all-holy Body and Blood of Christ, and together with them he unites with God. "He who eats My flesh and drinks My blood abides in Me, and I in him" (John 6:56).

O reasoning image of God! Look carefully at the glory, the perfection, the majesty that you are called to, that you are predestined for by God!

The unattainable wisdom of the Creator has provided for you to make of yourself what you will.

O reasoning image of God! Is it possible that you do not want to remain a worthy image of God? Is it possible that you want to pervert yourself, to destroy the likeness, to assume the image of the devil and to descend to the level of the dumb beasts?

Has God poured forth His benefits in vain? Has His wondrous creation been for naught? Has He considered His counsel before the creation of His own image to be pointless? Did He redeem man from the Fall without expecting recompense? No, He will expect an account from all who received gifts from Him. He will judge how His generosity was used, how His incarnation was appreciated, how His blood was valued, the blood that was poured to redeem us from the Fall.

Woe, woe to any creatures who disdain the benefits of God, the Creator and Redeemer!

Eternal fire, the pit of inextinguishable fire, lit a long time ago, prepared for the devil and his angels—this is what awaits the perverted images of God who have become worthless. They will burn eternally but will not be consumed for eternity!

Brothers! While we wander this earth, while we are on the threshold of eternity (this visible life) let us try to correct the outlines of the image of God within ourselves, as God has drawn on our souls. Let us add shading and color to fill out the beauty, vividness, and freshness of the likeness; and God, at the terrible judgment, will judge us worthy of entering His eternal, blessed bridal chamber on His eternal day, His eternal feast and triumph.

Let us take heart, we who are weak in faith! Let us rise up, slothful ones! Remember Saul of Tarsus who like us was filled passions—he who first persecuted the Church of God in his darkness, who was an enemy and adversary of God—so completely corrected the God-given image within himself after his conversion, so perfected the divine likeness, that [St Paul] boldly said concerning himself, "It is no longer I who live, but Christ lives in me"; [Saul was renamed Paul after he became a Christian] (Gal 2:20).

Never doubt the truth of this voice! This voice was so filled with all-holy Truth, the Holy Spirit so cooperated with him, that the voice of Paul raised the dead. At the voice of Paul, demons were cast out of the people they tortured; demonic oracles fell silent; the enemies of the Light of God were deprived of the light of their eyes; pagans rejected their own idols and came to know Christ, the true God, and worshipped him. Amen.

CHAPTER 9

A Reflection on the First Epistle of the Holy Apostle Paul to Timothy, Referring Primarily to the Monastic Life

The word of God is a testament. To those who have received the word of God, it delivers salvation and blessedness (see 1 Tim 1:15).

Love is born of purity of heart, blamelessness of soul, and un-hypocritical faith.

Cultivate these virtues, preserving attentiveness to yourself and silence, so that you may acquire love, which is the height and fullness of Christian perfection.

Purity of heart is destroyed by the acceptance of sinful thoughts, especially lustful thoughts. The blamelessness of the conscience is destroyed by willful sin. Faith weakens when one puts all one's trust on one's own reason. Faith is weakened by insincerity and self-love.

Whoever wants to speak about truth without illumination from on high will only engage in empty babble and contentions, and he will have left the path that leads to love (see 1 Tim 1:6–7).

Untimely, vain discussions about the truth (which surpasses knowledge) gave birth to heresy, delusions, and blasphemy against God.

Constancy in the Orthodox confession of the dogmas of faith is maintained and preserved by the works of faith and the blamelessness of the conscience.

Those who are not guided by faith in their actions and who destroy the blamelessness of their conscience by willful sin will not be able to preserve their knowledge of the dogmas in the necessary purity and correctness. This knowledge, like knowledge about God, requires an essential purity of mind that is only characteristic of the virtuous and the chaste (see 1 Tim 1:18–19).

"There is one God and one Mediator between God and men"—the God-Man, Jesus Christ (1 Tim 2:5). No one can approach or come near to God without this Mediator. Whoever rejects this Mediator rejects God also. "Whoever denies the Son does not have the Father either" (1 John 2:23). "He who believes in the Son has everlasting life; and he who does not believe the Son shall not see life, but the wrath of God abides on him" (John 3:36).

Spiritual wisdom consists in knowledge of the truth by faith. At first, one acquires the knowledge of faith; then faith, having become assimilated by the Christian, changes his reasoning mind by the revelation of the Truth—that is, Christ Himself.

Those who have reached a mature age in Christ receive the gift of constant prayer, which they utter in the secret cell of the spirit, in any place or time. The Christian only receives ceaseless prayer when his will and his activity (which depends on the will) are overwhelmed by the knowledge, desire, and fulfillment of the will of God. Through this, true faith enters into the heart, along with evangelical simplicity and the peace of God, devoid of any confusion.

Such a wise child ceaselessly sees his own weakness, ceaselessly believes, ceaselessly hungers and thirsts for divine righteousness, and thus ceaselessly prays (see 1 Tim 2:8).

The virtues most necessary for a hesychast are the following: meek submission to God, a disposition tending to silence, distancing oneself from conversations, even beneficial ones that nonetheless distance one from God and disturb the silence of the heart. Especially in the beginning of his labor, the hesychast is capable of being distracted by external impressions. Careful attention to remaining inside one's cell, avoiding meeting one's acquaintances and all manner of other amusements—these counteract the distraction of the novice hesychast.

A newly tonsured monk should not be given important responsibilities in the monastery, because he is likely to grow proud and be subject thereby to other snares of the devil (1 Tim 3:6–7).

The mystical knowledge and sense of faith is preserved by a pure conscience.

The Church of the living God is the pillar and foundation of truth. Therefore, God is called "living," because He acts. He acts in all the faithful through the sacraments, while in the chosen few, He acts through various obvious gifts of the Spirit, in addition to the sacraments. This proves that the Eastern Church is firm and unconquerable in the truth. On the contrary, heterodox churches, though they adorn themselves with the name "Churches of Christ," though they acknowledge God, they acknowledge an inactive God, as though

He were dead (for the dead, even a living man is also dead). This reveals that they waivered and did not stand firm in the truth.

"Great is the mystery of godliness!" (1 Tim 3:16). God appeared in the flesh; He proved that He is God by His Spirit, that is, His teaching, which is Spirit and life. He proved it by His actions, which were accomplished by the finger of God. He proved it by the giving of the Holy Spirit to mankind. Having been clothed in flesh, He became visible not only for men but for angels as well, for whom by His divinity He is invisible.[70] The pagans, perishing from ignorance of God, heard the preaching unto salvation. It is not earthly wisdom, not exalted reasoning, not expansive erudition, not the rich, exalted, and glorious of the world that accept the teaching of God. Rather, one accepts God's teaching by the humble pledge of the heart by faith. Those who have believed in God are adopted by Him and, being raised by grace higher than all that is temporal, they receive mystical, experiential knowledge that He ascended into heaven and lifts up all who believe in Him.

Those who have not believed and who have not cultivated their faith by the works of faith are easily seduced by false teaching that hypocritically puts on the mask of truth (1 Tim 4:1).

"For bodily exercise profits a little" (1 Tim 4:8), that is, its effectiveness is limited to the taming of the passions, but it is not able to uproot them. Godliness, on the other hand, which is the invisible training of the mind and heart within the Orthodox faith, "is profitable for all things," and only through godliness can a person palpably sense the eternal life that is tasted by the saints partially while still on this earth, as though they were the betrothed of God who would only be fully married to Him after the departure of the soul from the body. Eternal life is found in the diverse actions of grace in the soul, which is sensed in proportion to how much the passions have been purified. This saying, coming from spiritual experience, is true. It is worthy of being accepted as a principle by which a Christian can rise up to unutterable good things, proposing ascents in his heart (see Ps 83:6).

Faith and attentiveness lead to the knowledge of the Cross of Christ, which itself leads to patient endurance of sorrows, a virtue that arises and is strengthened by trust in the living God. Such a sufferer in Christ is moved by the consolation of grace acting in the heart (1 Tim 4:10).

When the consolation of grace acts together with the mystical knowledge of Christ and His providence, then a Christian never judges anyone, whether he be a Jew, a pagan, or an openly lawless man.[71] Instead, his heart is afire toward all with a quiet, blameless love. With the purity of his mind, he contemplates how from the time of the coming of Christ the only dignity, value, praise, and salvation for man is found in Christ, not in the natural virtues of humanity. He constantly desires to be crucified because his hearing has been opened, and he hears the voice of Christ his God, saying to him: "He who does not take his cross and follow after Me is not worthy of Me. He who finds his life will lose it, and he who loses his life for My sake will find it" (Matt 10:38–39). He considers the cup of sufferings to be the cup of salvation, the proof of his election, the gift of God. He cannot have any enmity or enemies, for those who subject him to sorrows are, in his eyes, nothing more than the instruments of divine providence.[72] He excuses them, justifying them by their ignorance. He blesses them as instruments of the God who provides for him. He says to himself, "Can I condemn those who now, before me, fall into obvious sins when Christ has already redeemed all their sins—past, present, and future—when in Christ they already have justification and salvation that they cannot fail to attain unless they continually reject Christ, until the last possible moment?"[73]

We must not lead our neighbors into temptation by our behavior (1 Tim 4:12). Therefore, preserve godliness both in soul and in body. Be modest and simple in words and in the movements of your body. In your home life, be restrained, chaste, not brazen. In your soul, be meek, gentle toward all, truthful, wise. Never permit any duplicity or hypocrisy in yourself. Instead of them, have faith that will teach you that the world and the fates of every individual person are directed by God's providence, not the contrivances of human reason. Therefore, one must always observe meek Christian correctness in one's acts, words, and thoughts.

"Until I come to you," says the grace of God to the righteous man of God, "and replace the need for external instruction by abiding within you, you must read spiritual books diligently, train yourself in prayer, and listen to the instructions of the spiritually mature. Do not allow yourself to grow slothful, and constantly remain vigilant over yourself. Then, your gradual spiritual growth will be evident. You will acquire salvation and with your instructive and salvific word become profitable to all who hear you." Read 1 Timothy 4:14–16.

Whoever truly senses the poverty of Adam's nature, whoever has come to know that his nature is bitterly fallen and lost—he will of course also come to know with conviction that for man's salvation, he must become united with Christ. Such knowledge is the sign of a true widow. She is permitted to enter in silence, to remain in prayer and petitions night and day, so that the image of Christ can palpably draw itself inside her (see 1 Tim 5:5).

As the helmsman looks at the stars and directs the ship by their position in the sky, so the hesychast must constantly look to God, see Him with the eyes of faith, and hope to preserve himself in constancy and endurance. On the sea of hesychasm, unutterable calm is always preceded by extraordinary storms.

The hesychast who is enticed by gluttony, excessive sleep, self-pampering, or even sensuality and self-love only proves that he is spiritually dead, though his body is alive (see 1 Tim 4:6). Christ, the true Life, only abides in the crucified ones.

The age of the widow who is capable of hesychasm is determined to be sixty years (see 1 Tim 5:9), which in a spiritual sense means the half-way point in one's spiritual ascent, expressed in the Gospels by the numbers 30 (spiritual infancy), 60, and 100 (spiritual perfection). In this half-way point are found those who, though they are still mastered by the realm of the senses, have acquired some power from prayer to defeat enemies in the invisible warfare. To these, the mystery of the Cross has been revealed, and they palpably sense the action of grace within their souls during sorrows that attack them from without. This action of grace serves both as light and consolation for their hearts.

Before the hesychast can take on the life of silence, he must prove himself by his virtuous deeds. Examine yourself, you who desire to reach the refuge, or rather, the sea, of silence! Have you done every good deed, not by the nature of the old Adam, but according to the qualities of the New? (see 1 Tim 5:10). In other words, have you accepted the yoke of humility and meekness? Have you tasted that this yoke is easy and this burden is light? In other words, have you studied the commandments of the Gospel? Have your mind and your heart been inscribed with them like stone tablets? Do you not still seek truth outside the Cross? If you do, then you are not capable, not ready for silence, for it is calamitous to enter the hesychastic life without first having condemned yourself, while still condemning others.

Those ascetics who are young in spiritual age, though they be old in body, though they have rejected the world and have been found worthy of the name "widow," should still not be allowed to attempt the hesychastic life (see 1 Tim 5:11). Because of the deficiency of their spiritual wisdom, they cannot remain constantly in the thought that only Christ is essential for salvation. They will not endure their own deadness, and they will want to revivify their ego in good deeds that belong to the sensual man. By doing this, they will cast the yoke of Christ from their shoulders and will live again by the nature of the old Adam. It is better for such to train in active virtues; it is better for them, rejecting all that is beneath their nature, to remain *in* their nature, rather than to strive prematurely and incorrectly toward what is above their nature.

They are also not forbidden to strive to renew themselves in the Lord, but they must strive properly—let them try to correct their temperament by the example of Christ as described in the Gospels. With the gradual correction of the temperament comes the healing of the mind. The mind, having received healing, that is, having become pure, clearly sees the truth, acknowledges it, and confesses it. After this, if it is pleasing to the Truth, and only by His blessing and choosing, can the disciple ascend the mountain and become a contemplator of the Transfiguration. If not, then remain under the mountain and work on casting the demon from the youth. That demon is cast out by faith, prayer, and fasting. By "fasting," we understand not only abstinence from overeating but also abstinence from all sinful endeavors. Only the one who thoroughly scrutinizes his own state and the state of all mankind—infected with sin, enslaved to the spirits of darkness—can understand the mystical answer given to the Saviour by the father of the possessed youth, after Christ asked when the possession had begun: "from childhood" (Mark 9:21).

An attempt to master hesychasm prematurely will lead to inevitable calamitous consequences. The brazen, self-reliant, dark, ignorant ascetic will not find food for his soul in hesychasm, and because of this he will inevitably fall to despair, which in hesychasts acts with especial power and harm, abandoning them to various evil thoughts and fantasies. The hesychast's nourishment is the illumining consolation of grace revealed by the mystery of the Cross of Christ. It is a gift from above, not knowledge that is natural to humanity. It is impossible to replace the spiritual with the emotional. If anyone tries to forcibly replace one with the other, then he will only assimilate lies instead of truth, falsehood masquerading as truth. The fruit of falsehood is disorder, and the same is true of the fruit of despair. However, the disorder that comes of falsehood is different from the disorder given birth by despair. The first is revealed as self-delusion, exalted self-opinion, boasting in one's apparent virtues and gifts accompanied by disdain and condemnation of others. It ends with pride, *prelest* (spiritual delusion), madness. Sometimes it leads to carnal sins, sometimes to suicide, most often to possession and mental damage that is usually labeled as insanity.

The second is revealed in sloth, laziness, leaving one's cell, attraction toward the pleasure of conversations, frequent abandonment of one's monastery, wandering about in search of one's place, and turning to earthly wisdom and knowledge. With the awakening of this "emotional reasoning," characteristic of the old Adam, faith is rejected and the providence of God is hidden from the eyes of the mind. Man, as though he were eternal on this earth, strives completely toward the earthly and gradually falls to a sub-natural state—a carnal, passionate state that is, with reference to the true life in Christ, the death of the soul (see 1 Tim 5:12–13).

Whoever has fallen to both these kinds of disorder, especially the first, becomes most often incapable of living the ascetic life. However, humility is capable of healing even such diseases that are incurable.[74]

Whoever desires to be a pure fulfiller of the commandments of Christ must be extremely careful to avoid passionate attachments. When the heart is infected with passionate attachment, it cannot fulfill the pure and holy will of Christ with proper holiness and purity. Fulfilling our own will instead of the will of Christ and still insisting that we do fulfill the will of Christ, we become hypocrites. We often say, and even perhaps think, that we do the will of Christ, but in actual fact we do the will of the devil.

Those who try to come to know Christ's teaching not for His sake but for tangential, earthly purposes, for the purpose of acquiring gain or honor, can never receive true spiritual wisdom, for it is a gift of God, given to the humble according to the measure of their faith, their purification from the passions, and their self-denial.

If you see that those who call themselves teachers, who claim to know Christ, are in actual fact argumentative, envious, slanderous, suspicious, hateful, filled with passions, then know that they only have the dead knowledge that comes of hearing. Their minds and hearts are in darkness and sickness, as those who are not healed and not purified by the doing of the commandments of the Gospel (1 Tim 6:4). The words of the Lord Himself clamor against them: "I do not know you!" Thus speaks Truth Himself, Christ, to those who think that they know Him not by the works of faith, but only by hearing. Whoever has come to know that the race of man is fallen, that the earth is the land of our exile and a prison where we spend but a short time before we leave it to receive either eternal blessedness or eternal punishment—such a person has come to know that the only treasure for man on earth is Christ, the Saviour of the lost. Consequently, the only (sadly underappreciated) acquisition for man on earth is the knowledge of Christ and union with Christ. Will he who desires to acquire this treasure desire merely temporary gain and pleasures? On the contrary! He will avoid them, fearing that they will distract him. He will be content not only with necessities, but even with dearth. And the content is far richer than the rich! (1 Tim 6:6).

Brothers! We have entered naked into this world. When we leave it behind, we will even abandon our bodies. Why do we seek perishable acquisitions? Why do we search for that which we will imminently leave behind? Let us not lose precious time for perishable things, lest we lose our only treasure—Christ. To Him we must rush with our mind and heart. Having food and clothing, let us be content. Let us not allow ourselves any excesses or caprices, lest they gradually attract our love toward them and deprive us of Christ (1 Tim 6:7–8).

Those who desire to get rich fall into many traps and snares that their own striving toward wealth prepares for them. The first fruit of this striving is the increase of cares and worries that distract the mind and heart from God. The soul pursues God faintly, coldly, carelessly. It acquires crudeness and becomes insensible. The fear of God fades from it. Remembrance of death abandons it, and the mind becomes dark and ceases to see the providence of God, which leads to loss of faith. Hope, instead of being founded on God, turns to the idol of wealth, and eventually love is also brought to its pedestal. Then the person dies to virtue, abandons himself to lies, cunning, cruelty, in short, to all passions, and falls to complete perdition, having become the vessel of the devil. "For the love of money is a root of all kinds of evil," since it contains in itself the reason and cause of all sins (1 Tim 6:10).

Even those who had not been completely destroyed by love of money (because they did not fully abandon themselves to it, seeking only moderate enrichment) still suffered many troubles. They entwined themselves in many heavy cares, they fell to various sorrows, they were forced often to compromise their conscience, and they suffered a great wound in their spiritual warfare and saw in themselves a significant deviation from faith and spiritual wisdom.

For a Christian, evangelical poverty is more desirable than all the treasures of the world, for it guides to faith and the fruits of faith. The more the ascetic of Christ remains free of the world, the safer he is; no sooner has he reached out to the world than he has already been defeated.

Babblings "falsely called knowledge" (1 Tim 6:20) is a manner of thinking and reasoning that becomes natural to the mind after the fall of man. As a consequence of the Fall, it is prone to self-delusion. As a consequence of its falsehood and deception, it does not accept the Truth, Christ. Since it highly values everything earthly (despite the earth being the place of exile for the fallen), it is at odds with faith and the spiritual wisdom that comes of faith, which looks at everything on earth through the eyes of a sojourner. The subject of this false knowledge is temporary and perishable. When the subject of its contemplation becomes the eternal and the spiritual, then it makes completely unfounded and erroneous conclusions. It lacks the illumination from on high that explains spiritual subjects. Left to its own devices, without Revelation, these subjects remain unattainable to false knowledge. The light surrounding false knowledge is the glow of the dark spirits of falsehood. All its conclusions are made by physical senses, but they are damaged by the Fall. When the invisible becomes attainable to its physical eyes by some means (such as by forces of magnetism, for example), this only magnifies its tendency toward errors, strengthening its darkness and self-delusion, since it remains in the domain of falsehood, which acquires only perverted knowledge.

Those who follow such false knowledge constantly disagree with one another, contradict each other, and even themselves. It does not require good behavior of its followers; on the contrary, it gives them the freedom to sin. It considers itself the ruler of the world, which is why it rejects the providence of God (if not only in words, then always in action). It contains in itself the kernel of godlessness, which is the main aspect of the essence of every error, whether to greater or lesser degree. Finally, it is the unfavorable portion of the fallen spirits and those people who are in communion with the fallen angels.

Let us abandon the wisdom of this world, let us stop trusting it, and let us approach God's wisdom and power with faith and humility, to the holy Truth, Christ, Who came into the world "that the world through Him might be saved" (John 3:17). He is the Light that the darkness did not understand or accept (John 1:5). Only he who has come to love righteousness is capable of accepting Him. "For everyone practicing evil hates the light" (John 3:20). "He who does not believe is condemned already" (John 3:18). "And this is the condemnation, that the light has come into the world, and men loved darkness rather than light, because their deeds were evil" (John 3:19) (see also 1 Tim 6: 11 and 16). Amen.

CHAPTER 10

The Essential Work of a Monk

The essential work of a monk is prayer, since it is that which unites man with God. All other tasks serve either as preparation or aids to prayer or are given to those who by their moral weakness or mental insufficiency cannot devote themselves completely to prayer. St Mark the Ascetic said, "For those who cannot endure in prayer, it would be well to find some service (to work physically or with the hands in obedience), lest they lose one and the other. However, those who can, should not be slothful concerning the best."[75]

St Mark, in his explanation of these words of the Lord: "Do not labor for the food which perishes, but for the food which endures to everlasting life" (John 6:27), says that we must seek the kingdom of heaven that is within us, as the Lord said (Luke 17:21), Who promised to give all earthly necessities by His divine providence to those who seek the kingdom of heaven.

St Paul said, "And do not be conformed to this world, but be transformed by the renewing of your mind, that you may prove what is that good and acceptable and perfect will of God" (Rom 12:2). St Mark explains that the apostle teaches us to fulfill the complete will of God, since he desires that we not be culpable in anything. Knowing that prayer helps the accomplishment of all commandments, he does not cease to command this repeatedly and in various ways: "praying always with all prayer and supplication in the Spirit, being watchful to this end with all perseverance and supplication for all the saints" (Eph 6:18). From this, we know that one kind of prayer differs from another; it is one thing to contemplate God with a focused mind; it is a different thing to stand in prayer with the body alone, with the mind wandering about in the clouds. It is one thing to pray at the appropriate times and begin and end every earthly conversation and endeavor with prayer, but it is another thing to prefer prayer as much as possible to all earthly cares, according to the instructions of the apostle who said that the Lord is at hand. "Be anxious for nothing, but in everything by prayer and supplication, with thanksgiving, let your requests be made known to God" (Phil 4:6). The blessed Apostle Peter said something similar: "Therefore be serious and watchful in your prayers . . . casting all your care upon Him, for He cares for you" (1 Pet 4:7, 5:7).

First and foremost, the Lord Himself, knowing that everything is confirmed by prayer, said, "Therefore do not worry, saying, 'What shall we eat?' or 'What shall we drink?' or 'What shall we wear?' . . . But seek first the kingdom of God and His righteousness, and all these things shall be added to you" (Matt 6:31, 33). Perhaps by these words the Lord is calling us to greater faith, for who, having rejected all cares for the temporary and not been subjected to dearth, will not believe God concerning the eternal good things. Explaining this, the Lord said, "He who is faithful in what is least is faithful also in much" (Luke 16:10).

However, even in this case He has condescended to our level as the Lover of mankind. Knowing that daily worries about the body are inevitable, he did not reject one's daily cares. Instead, allowing the cares for this current day, He commanded us not to worry about tomorrow. He commanded this very properly, reverently, and lovingly, because it is impossible for enfleshed people to not care at all about what happens to the life of the body.

What is possible is to reduce the cares to a minimum with the help of prayer and moderation, but to completely despise everything referring to the body is impossible. Therefore, whoever desires, according to the Scriptures, to "come to the unity of the faith and of the knowledge of the Son of God, to a perfect man, to the measure of the stature of the fullness of Christ" (Eph 4:13), should not prefer various bodily labors to prayer without need. He should not assume them as a pretext to avoiding prayer, but neither should he reject them outright when he encounters them by need or by the providence of God. Otherwise, one runs the risk of not admitting that one commandment can be higher than another, as we see in the Scriptures, and not wanting to direct oneself toward all the commandments (see Ps 118:128) as one encounters them, as the prophet recommends. Everything that we encounter that is necessary or providential is also inevitable, and we must always reject untimely activities, preferring prayer to them, especially those tasks that lead us either to the gathering or the spending of money in excess.

As much as a monk limits extraneous tasks and their objects, the more he will keep his mind from wandering during prayer, the more he will rein in his thoughts, the more he will give place to pure prayer and will prove his faith in Christ. If anyone cannot act thus because of weak faith or some other weakness, then at the very least let him accept the truth about himself and labor forcefully as much as he is able, accusing his own spiritual infancy. It is better to take responsibility for weakness than to fall prey to self-delusion and false exaltation. Remember the example of the Lord's parable, which vividly expressed the former state through the publican, the latter through the Pharisee (see Luke 18:9–14).

Let us try to lay aside all earthly cares through hope and prayer. If we are not able to do this as we must, then let us bring our confession to God in our insufficiency. However, in no way must we cease training ourselves in prayer. It is better to be subjected to rebukes for our frequent lapses than for complete abandonment. In all that we here say concerning prayer and our inevitable service, much discernment is needed from God to understand which tasks we should allow to interfere with prayer, because every person who labors at a work that pleases him thinks that he is doing his duty, not knowing that he must examine his service with respect to pleasing God, not pleasing himself. What makes discernment so difficult in this situation is that there are many commandments of different orders of importance, and sometimes one must follow some commandments, at other times—others. Not every kind of service should be accomplished at any time, but only in its appointed time, while the service of prayer is commanded to be constant, which is why we must prefer it to all tasks that are not absolutely necessary at the given moment. All the apostles, teaching this distinction to the people, wanted to attract them to the service of unceasing prayer, saying, "It is not desirable that we should leave the word of God and serve tables. Therefore, brethren, seek out from among you seven men of good reputation, full of the Holy Spirit and wisdom, whom we may appoint over this business; but we will give ourselves continually to prayer and to the ministry of the word. And the saying pleased the whole multitude" (Acts 6:2–5).

> Let us begin our work. Advancing gradually, we will find that not only hope in God, but revealed faith, un-hypocritical love, lack of remembrance of evil, love for our fellows, moderation, endurance, depth of wisdom, deliverance from temptations, the giving of gifts, the confession from the heart, abundant tears—all these are given to the believer by prayer. Not only this, but also endurance in sorrow, pure love for others, knowledge of spiritual laws, acquisition of the righteousness of God, the inspiration of the Holy Spirit, the reception of spiritual treasures—in a word, everything that God promised to give the believer in this age and in the age to come. It is impossible for the soul to restore in itself the image of God without God's grace and his own faith, when he abides mentally in undistracted prayer and great humble-mindedness.[76]

Like St Mark, St Macarius says, "The crown of any good desire and the summit of all virtues is constantly abiding in prayer, through which we acquire all other virtues cooperating with the Giving Hand of the One Who called us to this service. For the giving of mystical strength to those who seek holiness, and the control over their thoughts, and the union with God of the very soul that ardently loves the Lord—all this is unutterably given to the worthy in prayer. For it was said, 'Thou hast put gladness in my heart' (Ps 4:8). And the Lord Himself says, 'the kingdom of God is within you' (Luke 17:21)."[77]

St John of the Ladder calls prayer the mother of all virtue.[78]

St Symeon the New Theologian says this about attentive prayer:

> Our holy father, hearing the words of the Lord in the Holy Gospel, that "For out of the heart proceed evil thoughts, murders, adulteries, fornications, thefts, false witness, blasphemies. These are the things which defile a man" (Matt 15:19–20), also heard in another place of the Gospel that the Lord commands us to "cleanse the inside of the cup and dish, that the outside of them may be clean also" (Matt 23:26). And so they abandoned all other tasks and labored with all strength in that work that is in the deep places of the heart, knowing assuredly that with this work they will easily acquire all other virtues, and that without this work they can neither acquire nor receive a single other virtue. Some of the fathers called this work "the silence of the heart," other called it "attention," others—"vigilance" and contra-diction (that is, the opposite of speech). Others called it the testing of the thoughts and the "preservation of the mind," because all of them labored in this work and through it were found worthy of divine gifts. Concerning this, the Preacher says, "Rejoice, O young man, in your youth, and let your heart cheer you in the days of your youth, walk in the ways of your heart blameless and pure, and keep your heart away from thoughts."[79] The Preacher continues: "If the spirit of the ruler (i.e. the devil) rises against you, do not leave your post," (Eccl 10:4) that is, do not let him enter your place, which here means the heart. The Lord Himself speaks of it in the Holy Gospels: "Do not have an anxious mind," that is, do not let your mind be scattered here and there. In another place He said, "Blessed are the poor in spirit" (Matt 5:3), that is, blessed are those who have not acquired in their hearts a single thought of this world, but are poor, not having a single earthly thought to call their own. And all our divine Fathers wrote much concerning this. Whoever wants to read their writing will see what the ascetic Mark has written, or the holy John of the Ladder, or St. Hesychius, or Philotheos of Sinai, or Abba Isaiah, or the great Barsonuphius, and many others. In short: whoever does not

pay attention to the preservation of his mind cannot be pure in heart and will not be worthy of seeing God. Whoever does not practice attentiveness, that one cannot be poor in spirit, he cannot weep and lament, he cannot be meek and humble, he cannot hunger and thirst after righteousness, he cannot be merciful or a peacemaker, nor can he be persecuted for the sake of righteousness. In general, I will say this: it is impossible to acquire any other virtue in any other way, save through attentiveness. Therefore, you must work on this much more than you do on any other task, so that in actual fact you can acquire that of which I speak.[80]

Then St Symeon suggests that his listeners constantly pray the Jesus Prayer by uniting the mind with the heart. Moreover, the ascetic can constantly remain in vigilance and turn aside every sinful thought by the name of Jesus, no matter what direction the thought comes from, to cut it off before it could enter and become an image. Through such work, experiential and actual knowledge of the fallen spirit is gained; having come to know them, we then begin to hate them, we enter the fray in the constant warfare, we raise up our natural zeal against them. We persecute them, defeat them, destroy them.[81]

The Blessed Nicephorus defines attentiveness thus:

One of the saints called attentiveness the *vigilance of the mind*. Others have called it *the preservation of the heart,* others *moderation*, others *silence of the thoughts*, and so on. All these terms describe the same reality, as though one person were saying "bread," and other "hunk," and another "slice"—this is how you should understand this. What is attention and what are its qualities—this you must diligently study. Attention is knowledge given by pure repentance; attention is the cry of the soul, the hatred of the world, the ascent to God. Attention is rejection of sin and acceptance of virtue. Attention is the undoubted conviction of the forgiveness of sins. Attention is the beginning of the vision of the mind, or rather, the cause of the vision of the mind, for God, through it, comes down and appears to the mind. Attention is the lack of confusion of the mind or, more properly, its firmness, given to the soul by God's mercy. Attention is the defeat of thoughts, the temple of the remembrance of God, the treasure-store of endurance when encountering dangers. Attention is the cause of faith, hope, and love.[82]

St Nicephorus, like St Symeon the New Theologian, offers the constant practice of the Jesus Prayer as the best means for attention, accomplished by the union of the mind in the heart. Inviting all monks who desire to acquire true spiritual advancement to this labor of attention and constant prayer, Nicephorus says,

> You, who desire to be given the majestic, divine light of our Saviour Jesus Christ; you, who desire to palpably sense the fire of heaven in the heart; you, who endeavor to receive essential reconciliation with God; you who have left all that is earthly for the acquisition of the treasure hidden in the field of your heart; you, who desire that your spiritual candles would be lit brightly and therefore rejected all that is temporary; you, who want to wisely and experientially understand and accept the kingdom of heaven that is found within you! Come. I will teach you the science and art of the eternal, heavenly life, leading the doer with no labor or sweat to the harbor of dispassion, where you will fear no fall, no delusion of the demons. We only fall when we, by reason of our sin, remain outside this land, in some faraway country like the old Adam. He, having disobeyed the command of God, having befriended the serpent and admitted him as truthful, ate his fill of the fruit of delusion and was cast out miserably into the pit of death, darkness, and corruption—he and all his descendants. It is impossible for us to receive reconciliation and union with God if we, first of all, do not return to ourselves, if we do not enter into ourselves. It is wondrous to reject from ourselves all communication with the world and to reject all vain worries, instead untiringly observing the kingdom of heaven that is found within us. For this reason, the monastic life is called the science of sciences and the art of arts This venerable lifestyle supplies not some kind of perishable object in which we can bury our minds, being distracted from the better; instead, it promises the frightening and unutterable benefits that eye has not seen, that ear has not heard, that is entirely unknown for the heart (see 1 Cor 2:9). Therefore, "we do not wrestle against flesh and blood, but against principalities, against powers, against the rulers of the darkness of this age" (Eph 6:12). If this age is darkness, then let us flee from it, let us run, thinking that we have nothing in common with the enemy of God. Whoever desires friendship with that enemy becomes the enemy of God (see Jas 4:4), and who can aid the one who has become the enemy of God? Therefore, let us emulate our fathers and, like them, let us work on finding the treasure that is hidden in our hearts. When he have found it, let us hold it firmly, cultivating it and keeping it. This is our calling from the very beginning.[83]

St Nilus of Sora advises those who desire to practice the silence of the heart to reject all thoughts outright and to replace them with the name of the Lord Jesus, that is, to pray the Jesus Prayer: "It is necessary to enforce the silence of the thoughts and to cut off even thoughts that pretend to be beneficial, instead looking constantly into the depths of the heart and saying: Lord Jesus Christ, Son of God, have mercy on me."[84] So desirable is this practice, so expansive, so filled with spiritual abundance, that the holy Apostle Paul preferred it to all other thoughts and reflections: "For I determined not to know anything among you except Jesus Christ and Him crucified" (1 Cor 2:2).

The blessed elder St Seraphim of Sarov said, "Whoever has truly determined to serve the Lord God must exercise himself in the remembrance of God and constantly pray to Jesus Christ, saying with the mind: Lord Jesus Christ, son of God, have mercy on me, a sinner."[85] "The gifts of grace are received only by those who have the inner practice of the mind and who are vigilant over their souls."[86]

In his 4th homily, St Mark the Ascetic calls prayer the most important work of a monk. This work must envelop all his other tasks, his entire life. In his 1st Homily he calls the most important and only work of a monk "repentance," and the command to repent the most important commandment that encompasses all other commandments. This contradiction is only apparent at a cursory glance. It means that the work of repentance must be combined with the work of prayer, into a single labor. The Lord united them: let no man put them asunder. The Son of God said, "And shall God not avenge His own elect who cry out day and night to Him, though He bears long with them?" (Luke 18:7). Here the Lord speaks of the work of His elect, their constant prayer. He calls it a "cry" that is, an expression of weeping and repentance.

"Repentance," said St Mark,

as I see it, is not limited by time or any action. It is accomplished by fulfilling the commandments of Christ, proportionate to their fulfillment. Certain commandments, of a more general nature, contain in themselves many of the other more specific ones, and their fulfillment can cut off many different sins at once. For example, the Scriptures say, "Give to everyone who asks of you. And from him who takes away your goods do not ask *them* back," (Luke 6:30) and "Give to him who asks you, and from him who wants to borrow from you do not turn away" (Matt 5:42). These are partial commandments. The general one that contains them within itself is the following: "Go, sell what you have and give to the poor" (Matt 19:21), "come, take up the cross, and follow Me" (Mark 10:21). By the cross, He means endurance of all sorrows that may come. Whoever gives everything to the poor and takes up his cross has fulfilled all the aforementioned commandments at once. Again, the Scriptures say, "I desire therefore that men pray everywhere, lifting up holy hands" (1 Tim 2:8), but the general command is "You, when you pray, go into your room, and when you have shut your door, pray to your Father who is in the secret place" (Matt 6:6) and "pray without ceasing" (1 Thess 5:17). Whoever has entered his cell and constantly prays has fulfilled the command about men "praying everywhere." Again, it is said, "Do not fornicate, do not commit adultery, do not murder," and so on, but the general command is this: "casting down arguments and every high thing that exalts itself against the knowledge of God, bringing every thought into captivity to the obedience of Christ" (2 Cor 10:5). Whoever casts down his thoughts has put up barriers against all forms of sin. For this reason, the lovers of God and the faithful force themselves to keep the general commandments and so do not fail to keep the partial ones as well, when circumstances require it. From all this, I conclude that the work of repentance is accomplished through the mediation of the following three virtues: purification of thoughts, constant prayer, and endurance of sorrows. These three virtues must be fulfilled not only externally, but by the work of the mind, so that anyone who has become mired in the passions may become dispassionate. And since the work of repentance cannot be accomplished without these three virtues, I believe that repentance is appropriate at all times for all people who wish to receive salvation, both the sinners and the righteous, for there is no level of perfection where one would not need to exercise the aforementioned three virtues. Through them, the beginner finds his entrance into godliness, the intermediate finds spiritual advancement, and the advanced finds confirmation and habitation in perfection.

Like St Mark in his 4th homily, so all the other aforementioned Fathers witness that endurance of all sorrows and successful cutting off of thoughts is given only by prayer; they call prayer the source of repentance. It is both the mother of repentance and her daughter. This quote of St John of the Ladder concerning prayer and remembrance of death can also fairly be applied to prayer and repentance: "I praise the two natures in a single hypostasis."[87] The work of repentance and prayer are one, but this single work contains in itself two different kinds of virtue.

The cutting off of sinful thoughts and emotions is accomplished with the help of prayer. It is a labor united with prayer, inextricable from prayer, constantly in need of the cooperation and action of prayer. St Nilus of Sora, citing St Gregory of Sinai, says,

> The Blessed Gregory of Sinai knew with conviction that we, passionate ones, cannot defeat evil thoughts. He said the following: no beginner can rein in his mind and banish thoughts if God will not restrain the mind and not send away the thoughts Himself. To restrain the mind and cut off thoughts is proper to the strong, but even they do not do this on their own. They labor in preparation for the fray, having God at their side, being clothed in His grace and His armor. If you see the impurity of the evil spirits, that is, the murky thoughts in your mind, do not fear or be amazed. If good thoughts concerning various things appear, do not pay attention to them but, restraining your breath as much as possible and keeping the mind in the heart, instead of rising to battle, call to the Lord Jesus often and diligently. They will flee, being invisibly burned by the divine name. When the thoughts begin to wear you down, stand up, pray at them, and again begin your previous work [the invocation of the name of Jesus Christ].[88]

St John of the Ladder in his "Homily on Prayer" says, "Repel the coming dog—sinful thoughts—with this weapon, the weapon of prayer, and no matter how many times he tries to attack, do not weaken in your defense." St Nicephorus says,

> Satan and his enthralled spirits gained the right to attack us from that moment when, with the aid of human sin, he subjected man to exile from Paradise and separation from God. Now, they invisibly agitate the reasoning mind of mankind—some more, some less—and the mind has no way of protecting itself other than by the constant remembrance of God. When, by the power of the Cross, the remembrance of God becomes impressed in the heart, then the intellect will be unshakeable. The work of the mind leads to this (that is, constant prayer), and every Christian working the field of Christ must labor in this. If man does not attain constant prayer, then all his labors are in vain. All labors of anyone who suffers for the sake of God with the purpose of calling down God's mercy to himself (that is, anyone who asks help to return to man's original dignity, so that Christ will become impressed on the mind) eventually lead to success in the work of the mind.[89]

Constant prayer, though it is the essential work of a monk, requires preliminary instruction, as we see from the quote of St Nicephorus, who, remembering St Sabbas, says that when this leader of a great community of monks saw that a monk had completely learned the rules of monastic life, only then would he consider him capable of battling contrary thoughts and holding vigil over his mind. Only then would he allow this monk to exercise silence in his cell. The preparatory training for constant prayer was accomplished with the help of obedience and physical labors in the monastery.

St Philemon says, "God wishes us to show our striving toward Him first in labor, and only then in love and constant prayer."[90] Nothing so prepares one for prayer as the obedience that mortifies us for the world and for our very selves. The great benefit of prayer flows from obedience, said St Symeon the New Theologian.[91] Those who are under obedience and do physical monastic work should in no wise consider themselves free of the necessity of exercising in prayer. Without this, their very labors, and even their obedience, will be fruitless. What is more, they may bring the harmful fruit of vanity and other sins that always appear in the disastrously empty soul, in which there is no power or sweet fragrance of prayer. Those who do physical work in the monastery or work with their hands should pray often if they cannot yet pray constantly. They should return to prayer as soon as they call it to mind. Eventually, the prayer will become habitual, and frequent prayer will unnoticeably become constant.

"The ascetics under obedience use their feet in various ways. Some of them move in service, others are immovable in prayer."[92] By "feet," St John means the entire activity of a monk. "I have seen those who have shone forth in obedience and who have not been slothful to remember God as often as they could. Whenever they would stand to pray, immediately they would take hold of their mind and pour forth streams of tears. They were prepared by holy obedience."[93] Thus, we see that the ancient ascetics did not allow themselves vain distractions during their monastic labors, but, while their hands busied with work, their mind exercised in prayer. For this reason, when they came to church or began to do their prayer rule in their cell, their mind and heart would immediately rush to God with no hindrance. On the contrary, whoever during labors and handiwork allowed himself to babble in vain and wander in mind could not deal with his mind when standing at prayer. His mind would constantly break free of his control, constantly turning to those objects that attracted his attention before the time for prayer.

"My son, from your youth up, choose instruction, and you will find wisdom also into old age. Come to her as one who plows and sows, and wait expectantly for her good fruits. For in her work you will labor a little while, then you will quickly eat of her fruit" (Sir 6:18–19). Let us not lose precious, irrevocable time; let us not destroy time by abandoning ourselves to distraction, idle talk, and other pointless pursuits. From the moment we enter the monastery, let us diligently learn the monastic life and in our youth let us cultivate the spiritual field with our true labor, so that in our old age and in our passage into eternity we will rejoice at the abundance of our spiritual gifts, the pledges of our salvation, the pledges of our blessedness in heaven. Amen.

CHAPTER II

The Spirit of a Beginner's Prayer

Introduction: Here we offer a teaching concerning the quality of prayer that is proper to a beginner starting the path of repentance toward the Lord. The most important ideas we present will be discussed separately, so that each will be read with more attention and be more easily held in the memory. Reading them will feed the mind with truth and the heart with humility and can give the soul the necessary directions for your prayerful labors, being a kind of introductory assignment for prayer.

1. Prayer is the raising up of our petitions to God.

2. The foundation of prayer is the fact that man is a fallen creature. He strives to the reception of the blessedness that he had, but lost. Therefore, he prays.

3. Prayer is a refuge of God's great mercy to the human race. The Son of God brought Himself as an atoning, reconciling sacrifice to His Father for the sake of our salvation. On this foundation, if you have decided to begin exercising in prayer, you must cast off doubt and duplicity (see Jas 1:6–8). Do not say to yourself, "I am a sinner. Will God listen to me?" If you are a sinner, then it is to you that the consoling words of the Saviour were spoken: "I have not come to call the righteous, but sinners to repentance" (Matt 9:13).

4. These are the preparatory steps to prayer: a stomach that is not full, the cutting off of earthly cares with the sword of faith, forgiving all offenses with sincerity of heart, gratitude to God for all the sorrowful events in life, abandonment of reverie and absentmindedness, reverent fear, which is so appropriate for the creation when it is allowed to speak with the Creator, according to the unutterable goodness of the Creator toward His creation.

5. The first words of the Saviour to fallen mankind were: "Repent, for the kingdom of heaven is at hand" (Matt 4:17). Therefore, until you enter this kingdom, knock at its doors through repentance and prayer.

6. True prayer is the voice of true repentance. When prayer is not inspired by repentance, then it does not fulfill its calling, and then God will not favor it. However, He will not disdain a "contrite and humble heart" (Ps 50:19).

7. The Saviour of the world calls the poor in spirit "blessed." The poor in spirit are those who have a humble self-assessment, who consider themselves to be fallen creatures who are here on earth as exiles, outside their true homeland (heaven). "Blessed are the poor in spirit," who pray with the profound knowledge of their spiritual poverty, "for theirs is the kingdom of heaven" (Matt 5:3). "Blessed are those who mourn" in their prayers, because of their sense of spiritual poverty, "for they shall be comforted" (Matt 5:4) by the consolation and grace of the Holy Spirit, which consists of Christ's peace and love in Christ to all fellow human beings. When no other human being, even the fiercest enemy, is excluded from the embrace of love of the praying man, then he can be reconciled with even the most difficult events in earthly life.

8. The Lord, as He teaches us to pray, likens the praying soul to a widow who is wronged by an adversary and who constantly petitions a dispassionate and impartial judge (see Luke 18:1–8). Your disposition of soul during prayer should be like this widow. Then, your prayer will be, so to speak, a constant complaint against the sin that does violence against you. Descend deep into yourself; open yourself up through attentive prayer. You will see that you truly are a widow with reference to Christ the Bridegroom, because of the sin abiding in you, so hateful to you, which produces warfare and pain within you, making you a foreigner with respect to God.

9. "I go mourning all the day long" (Ps 37:7), I spent every day of this earthly life in blessed weeping about my sins and shortcomings: "for my loins have been filled with sores, and there is no healing in my flesh" (Ps 37:8). "Loins" here mean the earthly journey in the flesh—the moral state of a person. All the steps of all people on this road are filled with obstacles; their moral state cannot be healed by any personal means or exertions. Only the grace of God can heal us, but it heals only those who acknowledge their sickness. True acknowledgment of one's own sickness is proved by diligent and constant abiding in repentance.

10. "Serve the Lord with fear, and rejoice unto Him with trembling," said the prophet (Ps 2:11). Another prophet says on behalf of God: "upon whom will I show respect, but to the humble and the peaceful and to him who trembles at My words" (Isa 66:2). "He hath regarded the prayer of the humble,

and hath not despised their petition" (Ps 101:18). He is the one who "gives patience to the fainthearted and life to the broken-hearted" (Isa 57:15).

11. Even if someone stands on the very pinnacle of virtues, but prays as though he is not a sinner, his prayer will be rejected by God.[94]

12. "In that day, when I do not sorrow for myself," said a certain blessed practitioner of true prayer, "I consider myself to be in self-delusion."[95]

13. "Even if we undergo many exalted ascetic labors," said St John of the Ladder, "they are not true or fruitful if, at the same time we do not have pain in the heart accompanying repentance."[96]

14. Sorrow of the mind on account of sins is an honored gift of God, and whoever preserves it in his bosom with reverence bears holiness within himself. It replaces all physical ascetic labors when there is no strength to accomplish them.[97] On the contrary, a strong body finds difficulties in the labor of prayer; otherwise the heart will not feel compunction, and his prayer will be powerless and insincere.[98]

15. The sense of repentance preserved a praying person from all snares of the devil. The devil flees ascetics who give off the sweet fragrance of humility, which is born in the heart of the repentant.[99]

16. Let your prayers to the Lord be like a child's speech or a simple child's thought. Do not bring Him your erudition, your wisdom. "Unless you are converted," as though from paganism or Islam or from complexity and duplicity, "and become as little children, you will by no means enter the kingdom of heaven" (Matt 18:3).

17. A child expresses all his desires with crying, and let your prayer also always be accompanied by tears. Not only when speaking the words of prayer, but even during prayerful silence, let your desire for repentance and reconciliation with God, your extreme need for God's mercy, be expressed with tears.

18. The worthiness of a prayer is found only in its quality, not in quantity. Quantity is only praiseworthy when it leads to quality. Quality always leads to quantity; quantity only leads to quality when the praying person prays diligently.[100]

19. The quality of true prayer is found when the mind is attentive during the time of prayer, and the heart sympathizes with the mind.

20. Enclose your mind in the words of prayer that you utter and contain it in attention.[101] Have your eyes closed during prayer.[102] If you do this, you will help the union of the mind with the heart. Utter the words with diligent slowness, and then you will more easily enclose the mind in the words of

the prayer. Not a single word of your prayer will then be uttered without being inspired by attentiveness.

21. The mind, enclosed in the words of prayer, attracts the heart to sympathy with itself. This sympathy of the heart with the mind is expressed by compunction, which is a pious emotion that unites within itself sorrow with quiet, meek consolation.[103]

22. A necessary aspect of prayer is patient waiting.[104] When you feel dryness or insensibility, do not abandon your prayer. For your patient waiting and laboring against the insensibility of the heart, the mercy of God will descent on you in the form of compunction. Compunction is a gift of God that is sent to those who continue steadfastly in prayer (Rom 12:12), who constantly advance in prayer and are led by it to spiritual perfection.

23. The mind that stands before the invisible God in attentive prayer must be itself invisible, since it is the image of the invisible Godhead. That is, the mind must not imagine anything within itself or about itself or before itself. It must be completely without form. In other words, the mind must be completely devoid of fantasies, no matter how much such fantasies might seem blameless or even holy.[105]

24. During prayer, do not seek ecstatic emotions and do not incite your nerves. Do not inflame your blood. On the contrary, you must preserve your heart in profound calm, in which it can be led to a sense of repentance. The warmth of sensuality, the fire of our fallen nature, is rejected by God. Your heart requires purification by tears of repentance and prayer of repentance. When it becomes pure, then God Himself will send down on it His all-holy spiritual fire.[106]

25. Attention during prayer brings the nerves and the blood to a calm state and helps the heart to plunge deeply into repentance and remain in it. The divine fire does not destroy this calm of the heart if it descends to the upper room of the heart, when the disciples of Christ will be gathered there—that is, thoughts and emotions taken from the Gospels. This fire does not burn, does not inflame the heart. On the contrary, it bedews it, cools it, and reconciles the person with all other people and with all circumstances of life. It leads the heart to the unutterable love for God and fellow man.[107]

26. Absentmindedness is a thief of prayer. Whoever prays in a distracted manner feels complete emptiness and dryness within him. Whoever constantly prays distractedly is deprived of all spiritual fruits that usually come from attentive prayer. He makes habitual for himself the state of aridity and

emptiness, and from this state come coldness toward God, despair, darkness of the mind, weakening of faith, and deadness with reference to the eternal spiritual life. All this taken together is an obvious sign that such a prayer is not acceptable to God.

27. Fantasy during prayer is even more dangerous than absentmindedness. Distraction makes prayer fruitless, but fantasy gives rise to false fruits: self-delusion or demonic delusion, according to the Holy Fathers. Imagining objects of the visible world or fantasies of the invisible world invented by the imagination makes the mind, as it were, material, leading it from the divine realm of Spirit and Truth to a country of physicality and falsehood. In this land, the heart begins to sympathize with the mind, not in a spiritual sense of repentance and humility, but with a carnal emotion, a feeling incited by the blood and nerves, an untimely and disorderly pleasure that the sinner has not deserved to receive. This feeling is incorrect and false, because it claims a false love for God. This pernicious and foul love is considered inappropriate in the spiritual experience of the saints, and in actual fact it is only the disorderly emotion of a heart not purified of passions that finds pleasure in vanity and sensuality and that is moved by fantasy and imagination. Such a state is a state of self-delusion. If a person becomes rooted in such a state, then the images that appear to his mind can take on extraordinary vividness and attractiveness. When they appear, the heart begins to immediately inflame and feel impure pleasure, a state that, according to the Holy Scriptures, is adultery of the mind (see Ps 72:27 LXX). The mind thinks that this is a state of grace, a divine state. In such cases, it is close to passing to a state of clear demonic delusion, in which the person loses control over himself and becomes the plaything and laughingstock of the evil spirits. From such "imaginative" prayer, which leads a person to such a state, God turns away with wrath. And then the words of the Scriptures come true: "Let his prayer be turned into sin" (Ps 108:7).

28. Reject all apparently good thoughts and all apparently bright reasonings that come to you during prayer, distracting you from prayer.[108] They come from the realm of falsely named wisdom, and they sit astride vanity, like riders on a horse. Their dark faces are hidden, lest the praying man recognize his enemies in them. But by this they are known as enemies from the camp of the prince of the world—they hate prayer, they distract the mind from prayer, they lead it into prison and grievous slavery, they strip prayer of its meaning and empty the soul. Spiritual wisdom, the knowledge of

God, cooperates with prayer and concentrates the person inside himself, plunging him deep into attention and compunction, bringing down reverent silence, fear, and wonder on the mind, emotions that are born of a sense of the presence and majesty of God. This awareness, in its proper time, can become very strong and make prayer a terrifying judgment seat of God for the one who prays.[109]

29. Attentive prayer, devoid of distraction and fantasy, is the vision of the invisible God, attracting to itself the sight of the mind and the desire of the heart. Then, the mind sees without images and is completely content with this lack of seeing that surpasses all vision. The reason for this blessed lack of vision is the eternal subtlety and unattainability of the Object to which the vision is directed. The invisible Son of righteousness, God Himself, radiates invisible rays that are visible in a palpable sense of the soul. They fill the heart with miraculous calm, faith, courage, meekness, mercy, love for neighbors and for God. By these actions, seen in the inner cell of the heart, the person can admit without a doubt that his prayer has been accepted by God. Then he begins to believe with a living faith and firmly to trust in the Lover and the Beloved. This is the beginning of the revitalization of the soul for God and blessed eternity.[110]

30. The fruits of true prayer are the following: holy peace in the soul, united with quiet, silent joy, devoid of images, self-conceit, and inflamed gushes of emotion; love for others that does not distinguish between good and evil people or worthy and unworthy people, but that mediates for all before God as for himself, as for his own body. From such a love for others, the purest love of God will shine forth.

31. These fruits are the gift of God. They are attracted to the soul by its attentiveness and humility, and they are preserved by faithfulness to God.

32. The soul only then abides in faithfulness to God when it avoids every sinful word, action, and even thought, and when it immediately repents of those sins into which it fell by its weakness.

33. We can prove that we desire to acquire the gift of prayer if we patiently and prayerfully wait at the gates of pure prayer. For patience and constancy, we receive the gift the prayer. The Lord, as the Scripture says, "gives a prayer [grace-filled] to the one praying" (1 Kgdms 2:9) patiently, with only his exertions to sustain him.

34. For the beginning, short and frequent prayers are better than long prayers that occur only infrequently, separated by long stretches of time.[111]

35. Prayer is the best exercise for the mind.

36. Prayer is the head, the source, the mother of all virtues.[112]

37. Be wise in your prayer. Do not ask for anything perishable or vain in your prayer, remembering the command of the Saviour: "Seek first the kingdom of God and its righteousness, and all these things," that is, all the necessities of daily life, "shall be added to you" (Matt 6:33).

38. Whatever you intend to do, whatever you desire, even in the most difficult circumstances of your life, plunge your thoughts down into prayer before God. Ask for whatever you consider necessary and beneficial; however, leave the fulfillment of your petition (or lack thereof) to the will of God in faith and trust in His omnipotence, wisdom, and goodness. He Who prayed in the garden of Gethsemane gave us the best example of such prayer: "Father, if it is Your will, take this cup away from Me; nevertheless not My will, but Yours, be done" (Luke 22:42).

39. Bring to God your humble prayers concerning the virtues that you attempt and all your pious labors. Purify and perfect them by prayer and repentance. Speak of them in your prayer as the righteous Job prayed daily for his children: "Lest my sons consider evil things in their mind against God" (Job 1:5). Hatred is evil; unnoticeably it infiltrates virtues, thereby defiling and poisoning it.

40. Turn away from everything in order to inherit prayer, and, raised up on the cross of self-denial, commit to God your spirit, soul, and body. Then He Himself will give you holy prayer that, according to the teaching of the Apostle Paul and the Universal Church, is the action of the Holy Spirit in man, when the Spirit Himself inhabits man (see Rom 8:26).[113]

Conclusion: Whoever does not strive to exercise attentive prayer, imbued with repentance, the same is devoid of spiritual progress, spiritual fruits, and he is enclosed in the darkness of multifarious self-delusion. Humility is the only altar on which it is permitted to bring a prayerful sacrifice to God. It is the only altar from which prayerful sacrifices are accepted by God.[114] Prayer is the mother of all true, divine virtues. It is impossible to have any success in the spiritual life if you have rejected humility, if you have not taken care to enter the holy union with God through prayer. Exercise in prayer is commanded by the apostle: "Pray without ceasing" (1 Thess 5:17). Exercise in prayer is the command of the Lord Himself, a commandment united with a promise. The Lord invites us, even commands us, to ask, and it will be given, "seek, and you will find; knock, and it will be opened to you" (Matt 7:7). Let prayer "neither slumber nor sleep" (Ps 120:4), until it shows the lover of prayer, the constant practitioner of prayer, the bridal chamber of eternal blessings, until it leads him into heaven. There, constant prayer will transform into a ceaseless sacrifice of praise. This praise will the chosen of God unceasingly utter from the sense of abiding blessedness in eternity, which can sprout here on earth and in time from the seeds of repentance sowed by attentive and zealous prayer. Amen.

CHAPTER 12

The Cell Rule of Prayer

"But you, when you pray, go into your room, and when you have shut your door, pray to your Father who is in the secret place; and your Father who sees in secret will reward you openly" (Matt 6:6). This is the command of the Lord Himself concerning the rule of prayer in the cell.

The Lord, having commanded solitary prayer, very often during His earthly wandering, as we know from the Gospels, abided in prayer Himself. He did not have a place to lay His head, and so, very often, His silent, solitary room was the wordless summit of a hill or a shaded vineyard.

Before His Passion, through which He would buy the salvation of the human race, the Lord prayed in a solitary garden outside Jerusalem in Gethsemane. During this prayer, the God-Man bowed His knees, and from the intensity of His prayerful labor, abundant sweat poured like drops of blood from His face to the earth. The garden of Gethsemane was filled with ancient olive trees. Even during the day, in the light of the sun's rays, it was filled with thick shadows, but when Christ came to pray, it was the middle of the night. No one shared the Lord's prayer with Him. In the distance, His disciples slept, and all around Him nature was resting. To this place came the traitor with torches and an armed crowd. The traitor knew the favorite place and time for Jesus's prayer.

The darkness of night hides objects from curious eyes. The silence of wordlessness does not distract the hearing. In silence in the middle of the night, one can pray with more attention. The Lord chose for His prayer primarily solitude and night. He chose these so that we would not simply obey His command concerning prayer, but so that we could follow His example. Did the Lord Himself have need of prayer? Abiding with us on earth as a man, He was at the same time inseparable from the Father and Spirit as God, having with Them a single divine will and divine authority.

"Go into your room, and when you have shut your door, pray to your Father who is in the secret place." Let not your own left hand know about your prayer! Not your friend, not your family member, not your vanity that lives together with your heart and seeks the slightest opportunity to boast about your prayerful labor, or at least hint at it.

Close the door of your room against all people who come for empty words or to steal your prayer from you. Close the doors of your mind against extraneous thoughts that will come before you to distract you from prayer. Close the doors of your heart against sinful emotions that will try to disturb and defile you, and pray.

Do not dare to bring God your voluble and erudite prayer, invented by you, no matter how powerful or touching they may seem. They are the invention of our fallen reason, and being a defiled sacrifice, they cannot be accepted on the spiritual altar of God. And, admiring the subtle expressions of the prayer you invented and imagining that the subtle action of vanity and sensuality is actually the consolation of the conscience and even divine grace, you will be led far away from true prayer. You will also be led from prayer if you imagine that you are praying a great deal and have already reached some degree of God-pleasing behavior.

The soul that begins its path to God is submerged in a profound ignorance of everything divine and spiritual, though it be rich in the wisdom of this world. Because of this ignorance, it cannot know how much and how it must pray. To help the soul of the beginner in prayer, the Holy Church has established prayer rules. The prayer rule is a collection of several prayers, composed by divinely inspired Holy Fathers, which are appropriate for specific circumstances and times. The purpose of a prayer rule is to give the soul the prayerful thoughts and emotions that it lacks. Not just any such thoughts or emotions, but only the proper, holy, definitively God-pleasing thoughts and emotions. Such thoughts and emotions fill the grace-filled prayers of the Holy Fathers.

For exercise in prayer in the morning, there is a special collection of prayers that is called the "morning rule of prayer." There is another collection of prayers that is called "prayer for the coming night" or "the evening rule." There is also a prayer rule for those who are preparing to commune the Holy Mysteries of Christ. This is called the "rule of preparation for Holy Communion." Those who dedicate a large part of their time to pious exercises read a special group of prayers at three in the afternoon. This is called the "daily rule" or the "monastic rule." Still others read several kathismas of Psalms per day, several chapters from the New Testament, and make prostrations. All this is part of the prayer rule.

Rule! This is an exact name taken from the very action that is effected on the person by prayers. The prayer rule directs the soul in a correct and holy way, teaching it to worship God in spirit and in truth (see John 4:23). On the contrary, the soul that is left to itself cannot walk the correct path of prayer. Because of its damage and darkness by sin, it constantly deviates from the path and sometimes falls into pits by the side of the road—distraction, reverie, and various empty and delusive fantasies of exalted prayerful states invented by vanity and self-love.

The prayer rules preserve the praying man in a salvific disposition of humility and repentance, teaching him to constantly condemn himself, feeding him with compunction, strengthening him with hope in the all-good and all-merciful God, giving him joy in the peace of Christ, love for God and fellow man.

How exalted and profound are the prayers for Holy Communion! What superlative preparation do they give to the one who approaches the Holy Mysteries of Christ! They clean and decorate the house of the soul with wondrous thoughts and emotions, so pleasing to the Lord. Majestically is the greatest mystery of Christianity described and explained in these prayers. In contrast to this loftiness, vividly and truly are the shortcomings of man described, his weakness and unworthiness. From these prayers, the unattainable goodness of God shines like the sun in the sky, for He has willed to intimately unite with man, despite man's worthlessness.

The morning prayers are imbued with energy and the freshness of morning. Whoever has seen the light of the physical sun and the light of the earthly day is taught to desire the vision of the higher, spiritual Light and the endless day of the Sun of righteousness, Christ.

The short time of rest given by sleep at night is an image of the lasting sleep in the darkness of the tomb. And so the evening prayers remind us of our resettlement into eternity. They examine our actions during the course of the day and teach us to offer God a sincere confession of the sins we committed during the day, and our repentance of them.

The prayerful reading of the Akathist to the Sweetest Jesus, in addition to being worthy in its own right, is a superlative preparation for the practice of the Jesus Prayer: *Lord Jesus Christ, Son of God, have mercy on me, a sinner.* This prayer is almost the only exercise of spiritually advanced ascetics who have achieved such simplicity and purity that any multiplicity of thought or words is a burdensome distraction. This Akathist shows with what thoughts the Jesus

Prayer can be accompanied, especially for beginners, for whom the prayer can seem excessively dry. It, in its entire breadth, describes a single petition of a sinner for forgiveness by the Lord Jesus Christ. However, this petition is given various forms, conformable to the infancy of the beginner's mind. Such children are first given soft foods before they are ready for solid food.

In the Akathist to the Mother of God, the incarnation of God the Word and the majesty of the Mother of God are celebrated. For Her giving birth to the incarnate God, "all generations" call her blessed (Luke 1:48). As though on a huge canvas painted with various wondrous colors, shadows, and lines, the great mystery of the incarnation of God the Word is exalted. Any painting is best seen in good lighting, and the extraordinary light of grace illumines the Akathist to the Mother of God. This light acts in many ways—it illumines the mind; it fills the heart with joy and knowledge. The unattainable is understood as though it were fully attainable by the wondrous action of grace on the mind and heart.

Many pious Christians, especially monks, have a very long evening prayer rule, taking advantage of the silence and darkness of the night. In addition to the evening prayer, they add also the reading of kathismas from the Psalter, chapters from the Gospel and the Epistles, as well as Akathists and prostrations with the prayer of Jesus. In those hours in which the blind world abandons itself to boisterous and noisy pleasures, the slaves of Christ weep in the silence of their cells, pouring forth zealous prayer to the Lord. Having spent the night in a vigil of madness, the sons of the world greet the coming day in darkness and despair of the spirit. But the slaves of God meet the day that follows prayerful vigil with joy and energy of spirit, with the knowledge and sense of an extraordinary capability for remembrance of God and all other good deeds.

The Lord bowed His knees during His prayer; you also should not disdain to make prostrations during prayer, especially if you have the energy to pray thus. Prostrating to the face of the earth, according to St Theoleptus,[115] expresses our fall, while the rising up from the earth symbolizes our redemption. Before beginning the evening prayers, it is especially beneficial to do a feasible number of full prostrations. From them, the body will become slightly tired and warmed up, while the heart will be filled with a sense of pious sorrow. Both one and the other help a person read his evening prayers zealously and with attention.

When praying the evening rule and doing prostrations, you should never hurry. You must pray the rule and do the prostrations with the necessary deliberateness and attention. It is better to read fewer prayers and do fewer prostrations, but with attention, than to pray much and do many prostrations in a distracted manner.

Choose a rule for yourself in accordance with your own strength. What the Lord said concerning the Sabbath ("The Sabbath was made for man, and not man for the Sabbath" (Mark 2:27)) can and must be understood to refer to all pious labors, among them the prayer rule.

The prayer rule is for the man, not the man for the prayer rule. It must be appropriate to the strength of a person, for the purpose of helping him progress spiritually. It should not be a burden that cannot be borne, that breaks the body's strength, and that disturbs the soul. All the more so, it should not be a cause of prideful and pernicious self-conceit, harmful condemnation and demeaning of one's fellow man.

A wisely chosen prayer rule that accords to a person's strength and manner of life is a wonderful means for the person who labors for his own salvation. Doing it daily, in the allotted time, makes it habitual, and soon prayer becomes an essential requirement of every day. Whoever has acquired this blessed habit only needs to approach the usual place where he prays his rule, and immediately his soul fills with prayerful disposition. No sooner has he uttered the first word of prayer than his heart is filled with compunction and his mind plunges deep into the inner room of secret prayer.

"I prefer a shorter rule that is always kept rather than a long prayer rule that is quickly abandoned."[116] Any prayer rule that does not correspond to a person's strength ends in the same way—in the ardor of the beginning, the ascetic follows the rule for a certain period of time, though he pays more attention to the quantity than the quality, even at this stage. Then comes exhaustion from a labor surpassing strength, and it gradually forces him to shorten the rule more and more.

Often ascetics, unwisely burdening themselves with an excessively long prayer rule, simply pass from complete fulfillment of the rule to complete abandonment of any rule whatsoever. Whenever an ascetic abandons his rule, or even shortens it alone, he is inevitably filled with confusion. From this confusion later comes spiritual disorder. From disorder comes despair. Intensified despair them gives rise to spiritual paralysis and delirium, and from their actions the unwise ascetic begins to live a wasteful, distracted life, falling with complete indifference to most grievous of sins.

Having chosen for yourself a prayer rule that accords to your strength and spiritual needs, try to diligently and constantly fulfill it. This is necessary to uphold the moral strength of your soul, just as the body's strength needs sustaining by daily, healthy food eaten at appointed hours.

"God will not condemn us on the Day of Judgment for abandoning the Psalms," said St Isaac the Syrian,

> nor for abandoning prayer, but for what follows—the demons' entry into us. The demons, when they find a place, will enter and lock the doors of our eyes. Then they will make us their instruments violently and impurely, with the cruelest of vengeance, forcing us to do everything forbidden by God. And since we abandoned a small thing (the rule, through which we become worthy of the mediation of Christ), we become thralls of the demons, as a certain wise man said, "Whoever does not submit his will to God has submitted it to his adversary." These rules that seem to you so small become walls against those who try to enslave us. The fulfillment of the rule in the cell was wisely established by the founders of the Typicon, inspired from above for the preservation of our life.[117]

The great Fathers who remained in a constant state of prayer thanks to the abundant action of the grace of God never abandoned their prayer rules that they had grown accustomed to perform during their night vigils. We have many proofs of this from their lives. St Anthony the Great, while reading the rule of the ninth hour (the ecclesiastical hour that corresponds to the third hour after noon) was found worthy of a divine revelation. When St Sergius of Radonezh read the Akathist of the Mother of God, the all-pure Virgin appeared to him, accompanied by the apostles Peter and John.

Beloved brother! Submit your freedom to the rule. It will deprive you of sinful freedom, binding you only to those things that will give spiritual freedom, freedom in Christ. These chains will at first seem heavy; later they will become precious to the one bound with them. All the saints of God accepted and bore the easy yoke of the prayer rule. By emulating them, you will also follow the example of the Lord Jesus Christ, Who, having become man and having shown us by His example the model of proper behavior, acted as His Father acted (see John 5:19), said what His Father commanded (see John 12:49), and had as His purpose the fulfillment in all things of the will of the Father (see John 5:30). The will of the Father and the Son and the Holy Spirit is one. With reference to mankind, the will of God is the salvation of mankind. O Most Holy Trinity, our God! Glory to Thee! Amen.

CHAPTER 13

Prayer in Church

Without any doubt, the most exalted and precious of all earthly buildings is the church, the house of God. Though God is present everywhere, in the church, His presence manifests itself in a special way, in a most palpable and beneficial way for man. The manifestation of God is only more palpable and beneficial when man himself becomes the temple of God, the resting place of the Holy Spirit, like the apostles and other saints. But such a state is achieved only very rarely among us Christians. Therefore, leaving for another time the subject of the God-created, reasonable temple of God not made by hands—man—and the worship that must be performed within that temple, let us now speak about the physical church of God, created by the hands of man, and the services that are sung within it, as well as the responsibilities for every Christian to diligently visit this temple of God, and the benefit he receives from attending church services.

The church of God is an earthly heaven. "Standing in the temple of thy glory, we seem to stand in heaven." declares the holy Church in its hymnography.[118] The church is the place of God's communion with man. In it are performed all the sacraments of the Christian Church. The Divine Liturgy and ordinations can only be performed in the church. The other sacraments should also be done only in church, but in extreme cases some may be performed at home, especially the sacraments of Confession and Unction. Day and night the church of God rings with the doxology of God. The church has no place for the words of this world. Everything is holy in the church of God. Even the very walls, the platforms, the air. An angel of God constantly presides over each church; the angels of God and the saints of the Church Triumphant descend into it. One's presence in such a holy place comprises the greatest joy for an earthly wanderer. The holy prophet David, though a king with large and majestic palaces and all possible means for earthly pleasure and enjoyment, examined all and counted its worth in the proper way, saying, "One thing have I desired of the Lord, which I will require; even that I may dwell in the house of the Lord all the days of my life, to behold the fair beauty of the Lord, and to visit His holy temple" (Ps 26:4). The Holy Spirit said this, uttered through the lips of David. Whoever will attend the services in the church of God as often as possible during this earthly life will easily pass into the eternal feast after his soul leaves his body to enter the heavenly, uncreated temple, whose founder is God Himself. In the church, we pray, and we are instructed, and we are purified of our sins, and we communicate with God.

An example of frequent attendance of the Temple of God was provided by the Lord Himself (see John 7:14) and the holy apostles (see Acts 3:1). Christians of all epochs have admitted that frequent attendance at the church of God to be an imperative duty. St Dimitri of Rostov compared church attendance, in all its many services and rites, to a tax paid to a king that a dutiful subject must pay daily.[119] If attendance at every service served in the church is considered by this holy pastor to be an imperative duty of every pious Christian, then how much more so it is imperative for a monk to attend all services! Only the poor receive wavers due to their poverty, and only the sick who cannot leave their cell are allowed to miss the services. The nobles of the court are also exempt from the tax, and spiritually advanced monks are also free of constant church attendance, for they spend their time in spiritual ascetic labors and have already reaped abundant fruits from them, fruits that must be hidden from others. All soldiers and civil servants are exempt from taxation, and in the same way, monks who are busy with obediences during services are also freed from attendance at all services. However, you must pay attention that your obedience or your work (or even your invented sicknesses) do not become a secret justification to avoid prayer. That is a snare of the devil who hates prayer as the mother of all virtues, as the sword that destroys all evil spirits. For the devil uses all possible exertion and means, giving these means all possible good appearance, to distract man from prayer, to disarm him, and then to defeat him or wound him.[120]

There are seven prayer services in a given day (1) Vespers, (2) Compline, (3) The Midnight Office, (4) Matins with first hour, (5) Third hour, (6) Sixth hour, and (7) Ninth hour. They are divided into three groups. [Group one:] The vespers service, which begins every ecclesiastical day, is served together with compline and ninth hour (ninth hour is read before vespers). [Group two:] Matins is served with first hour and the midnight office (The midnight office is read before matins, the first hour afterward). [Group three:] Third and sixth hour are read together with the Typica, which are read after the hours. When matins is combined with vesper or great compline, then the service is called an "all-night vigil." It is served on the eve of great feasts, in honor of the feast. The effect of the all-night vigil on the ascetic is the following: the one who spends the greater part of the night in prayer, with the necessary reverence and attention, feels on the next day a special lightness, freshness, purity of mind, and a capacity for contemplation of God. Therefore, St Isaac the Syrian said, "The sweetness given to ascetics during the day comes from the light of their nightly prayers shining forth on their pure minds."[121] The Divine Liturgy is not included in this daily cycle of services, since it is a special, holy service that celebrates the bloodless divine Sacrifice.

We see a salvific image of proper church attendance in the prayer of the publican (Luke 18:9–14). The publican stood in the back of the church, considering himself unworthy even of raising his eyes to heaven, but beat his chest saying, "God, be merciful to me, a sinner." The publican left the church having attracted to himself the grace of God. And you also, when you come to church, if you have no specific obedience in the church proper, stand in the back in a humble corner or behind a column so that you cannot be distracted and so that your reverence will not be exposed to the ridicule of others. Direct the eyes of your mind to the heart, and your physical eyes to the ground, and pray to God in compunction of heart, not seeing any worthiness in yourself, no virtue, instead admitting yourself to be guilty of a countless multitude of sins, known to you and unknown. We sin a great deal in ignorance because of our limitation and because of the perversion of our nature by sin. The divine Scriptures say that "a contrite and humble heart God shall not despise" (Ps 50:19). You also, if you pray with a sense of your own sinfulness and poverty, you will hear He will pour out on you His abundant mercy. You have some kind of responsibly in the church; then perform it with the greatest reverence and carefulness, as a person who serves God, not man.

Together with the already-mentioned publican, the Gospel tells us that a Pharisee also entered the Temple to pray. As a person with distinction, the Pharisee stood in a prominent place. It is likely that he had a thought—typical to all Pharisees—to instruct the people by his example of pious standing and prayer. He considered vanity to be no danger to him, since he was so advanced in virtue, while a certain amount of hypocrisy was excusable, in view of the benefit to all. What was the prayer of the Pharisee? First of all, he praised God. A good beginning. However, he followed not by listing the blessings of God, but his own merits and glories, so that his beginning should properly have been entirely different. It would have been more correct for the Pharisee to begin by praising himself, not God.

His praise of God was only *pro forma*, as a half-hearted attempt to cover his own pride. This pride, however, manifests itself in the condemnation and debasement of his fellow man, whose conscience was unknown to the Pharisee. The Pharisee failed to guess that the publican's repentant admission of his own sinfulness attracted the mercy of God. The Pharisee, having hypocritically glorified God, said, "I am not like other men—extortioners, unjust, adulterers, or even as this tax collector. I fast twice a week; I give tithes of all that I possess" (Luke 18:11–12). The following is apparent: an ignorance of his own sinfulness, a sense of his own greatness, the subsequent pride that reveals itself through condemnation and humiliation of his fellow man. The prayer of the Pharisee was not accepted by the Lord, Who in conclusion of this parable said, "Everyone who exalts himself will be humbled, and he who humbles himself will be exalted" (Luke 18:14). From this we see that every person who desires God to accept his prayer must bring it with a sense of his own sinfulness and his extreme inadequacies of virtue. He must bring his prayer after first rejecting any knowledge of his own worthiness, being totally worthless before the boundless dignity of God. He must bring it from a heart that has humbled itself before all others, from a heart that has come to love all others, from a heart that has forgiven all others their insults and offenses. "As for me," says the prophet to the Lord in prayer, "by the multitude of Thy mercy I will come into Thine house; in Thy fear will I worship toward Thy holy temple" (Ps 5:8).

Great is the mercy of God to man—the establishment of the cycle of services in God's holy temples. These services were established by the apostles, their holy disciples, and the Holy Fathers of the first centuries of Christianity by inspiration from Heaven.[122] Every Christian can take part in these services, and even the illiterate man can absorb the knowledge, erudition, spiritual poetry of the orators and scribes of Christianity. Through these services, the one who desires can be well trained in the practice of the prayer of the heart, for quantity of prayers leads to quality, as the Fathers said, and so the prolonged monastic services are very capable of helping the ascetic ascend from prayer of the mouth to prayer of the mind and heart. The services of the church contain within themselves the breadth of Christian dogmatic and moral theology. Whoever constantly attends the services and pays attention to the readings and hymnography can instruct himself exactly in all that is necessary for the Orthodox Christian in the field of faith.

Blessed is the monk who always lives near the temple of God! He lives near heaven, near Paradise, near salvation. Let us not reject the salvation that the merciful God gave to us, so to speak, into our very hands. Especially a beginner monk must attend church without fail. In his mature years of exhaustion, when both his years and his sicknesses will confine a monk to his cell, he will then be nourished with that spiritual reserve that he gathered during his years of youth and strength, when he cleaved to the house of God. This spiritual reserve is the prayer of the mind and the heart. May the merciful Lord find us worthy of taking advantage of our monasticism, and before our departure from this earthly life, of already passing to the heavenly realm in our mind and our heart. Only prayer can raise us up to those heights, prayer that is illumined by divine grace. Then, prayer in man becomes already not the prayer of man, but the prayer of the Holy Spirit, who intercedes for the sake of man with "groanings which cannot be uttered" (Rom 8:26). Amen.

CHAPTER 14

Spoken Prayer

Let no person who desires to advance in prayer think lightly of prayer that is uttered aloud attentively, as though that were an unimportant practice, unworthy of respect. If the Holy Fathers speak of the fruitlessness of prayer spoken aloud, but not attended to by the mind, that does not mean that they rejected or diminished the significance of spoken prayer. No! They only required that the mind be attentive. Attentive prayer spoken aloud is also prayer of the mind. Let us first learn attentive spoken prayer, and then it will be easy for us to pray with the mind alone in our silent inner room.

Prayer spoken aloud is indicated by the Holy Scriptures. The Saviour Himself gave us an example of this prayer as well as prayer sung aloud. The evangelist Matthew writes that after the Mystical Supper, "when [Christ and the apostles] had sung a hymn, they went out to the Mount of Olives" (Matt 26:30). The Lord prayed aloud, so that everyone would hear Him, before He resurrected Lazarus, who had been dead for four days (John 11:41–42). Apostles Paul and Silas, while imprisoned, prayed at midnight and glorified God in song. The other prisoners listened to them. In response to their hymnody, "Suddenly there was a great earthquake, so that the foundations of the prison were shaken; and immediately all the doors were opened and everyone's chains were loosed" (Acts 16:26). The prayer of St Hannah, the mother of the prophet Samuel—a prayer often referenced as a model by the Holy Fathers—was not merely mental prayer. Hannah "spoke in her heart; only her lips moved, but her voice was not heard" (1 Kgdms 1:13). Though her prayer was not spoken aloud, being the prayer of the heart, it was also the prayer of the lips. The holy Apostle Paul calls prayer of the lips "the fruit of the lips," and he commands us to "continually offer the sacrifice of praise to God" (Heb 13:15). He also commands that we speak "to one another in psalms and hymns and spiritual songs, singing and making melody in your heart to the Lord" (Eph 5:19). He rebukes inattentiveness in prayer spoken aloud. "For if the trumpet makes an uncertain sound, who will prepare for battle? So likewise you, unless you utter by the tongue words easy to understand, how will it be known what is spoken? For you will be speaking into the air" (1 Cor 14:8–9). Even though these words of the apostle refer specifically to those who prayed and exclaimed the inspiration of the Holy Spirit in foreign tongues, the Holy Fathers have with justification applied them more broadly to all who pray without attention. Whoever prays without attention and therefore does not understand the words he utters aloud—is he any different from someone who speaks a language he does not know?

Citing these words, St Nilus of Sora says that the one who prays with his voice and lips without attention is praying to the air, not to God. "Strange is your desire for God to hear you when you do not hear yourself!" said St Dimitri of Rostov, quoting the words of St Cyprian of Carthage.[123] This is exactly what happens to the person who prays with his voice and lips without attention. Such a person attends to himself too little, allows himself to be distracted so much, wanders off from prayer in his thoughts to such a degree that often he suddenly stops, having forgotten what he was reading or suddenly beginning to read the words from an entirely different prayer, even though the prayer book lies open before his eyes. How could the Holy Fathers fail to rebuke such inattentive prayer, so damaged, even destroyed, by distraction!

"Attention," said St Symeon the New Theologian,

> must be as united and inseparable from prayer as the body is with the soul, the one and the other cannot be divided, cannot exist alone. Attention must anticipate and guard against enemies like a watchman. It is the first to rise against sin, so that the man can resist evil thoughts that approach the heart. After attention comes prayer that immediately destroys and mortifies all evil thoughts that the attention had engaged in preliminary battle (for attention itself is incapable of defeating these thoughts). This warfare waged by attention and prayer determines the life or death of the soul. If we preserve prayer pure through the mediation of attentiveness, then we will prosper. If we do not strive to preserve our prayer pure, but leave it unguarded, then evil thoughts defile it. Then we become useless and are denied spiritual advancement.

Prayer spoken aloud, as any kind of prayer, must inevitably be accompanied by attention. With attentiveness, the benefit of spoken prayer is unquantifiable. Every ascetic must begin from this prayer. First of all, this is the prayer offered by the Holy Church to its children. "The root of monastic life is psalmody," said St Isaac the Syrian.[124] "The Church," said St Peter Damascene, "accepted hymns and various troparia with a good and useful purpose, because of the weakness of our mind, so that we, unwise ones, attracted by the sweetness of psalmody, would praise God as though against our will. Those who can understand and examine the words that they utter are led to compunction. Thus we ascend, as though up a ladder, to good thoughts. As much as we progress in the acquisition of divine thoughts, so much divine desire appears in us and pushes us to come to know the worship of the Father in spirit and truth, according to the command of the Lord."[125]

The mouth and tongue that often exercise in prayer and the reading of the word of God acquire purification, become incapable of idle talk, sinful laughter or mocking, foul, and rotten language. Do you want to succeed in the prayer of the mind and the heart? Learn how to attend to prayer of the lips and the voice. Attentive spoken prayer becomes on its own the prayer of the mind and the heart. Do you want to learn how to quickly and effectively chase away thoughts sown by the enemy of mankind? Chase them away when you are alone in your cell with spoken prayer, uttering the words unhurriedly and with compunction. The air resounds with attentive spoken prayer, and the princes of the air are filled with trembling. Their strength will fail them, and their snares will fall apart and break! The air resounds with attentive spoken prayer, and the holy angels approach the one praying and singing. They join their ranks and take part in the spiritual songs, as some saints of God were found worthy of witnessing, including some of our contemporaries, such as St Seraphim of Sarov. Many great fathers exercised spoken prayer for their entire life, and they abounded with gifts of the Spirit. The reason for their success was that their mind, heart, their entire body and soul were united to their lips and voice. They uttered prayer with their whole soul, with their whole strength, with their whole essence, with the whole man. Thus, the holy Simeon of the Holy Mountain would read the entire Psalter aloud every night. St Isaac the Syrian remembered a certain blessed elder who practiced the prayerful reading of the Psalms. He only had to read one-third of the first kathisma attentively, and after that divine consolation would overcome him with such power that he remained for entire days in holy ecstasy, sensing neither time nor his own self.[126]

St Sergius of Radonezh was visited by the Mother of God, accompanied by the apostles Peter and John, during his reading of the Akathist to the Mother of God. It was said of St Hilarion of Suzdal that when he read the Akathist in church, the words flew out of his mouth as though they were made of fire, with inexplicable power to move those present. The spoken prayer of the saints was inspired with attention and divine grace that joined the powers of man—disunited by sin—into one. Therefore, it breathed such supernatural power and made such a miraculous impression on the listeners. The saints "proclaimed God in the confession of their hearts."[127] They "sang and confessed God unshakably,"[128] that is, without distraction. They sang to God "with understanding" (Ps 46:8).

We must mention that the holy monks of the first times and all who desire to progress in prayer did not practice, or very rarely practiced, singing itself. That which is called "psalmody" in their lives and writings must be understood as meaning unhurried, prolonged reading of Psalms and other prayers. Slow reading is necessary to maintain strict attention and to avoid distraction. Because such slow reading is similar to singing, it was sometimes called "psalmody" (that is, "psalm singing"). It was usually done by heart, for the monks of that time had a rule to memorize the entire Psalter by heart. Reading the Psalms by heart is especially helpful to nurture attentiveness. Such reading is already not reading, strictly speaking, since it is not done from a book, but it is psalmody in the truest sense. It can be performed in a dark cell, with the eyes closed, all of which protects from distraction; while a bright cell, necessary for reading a book, and even looking at a book, can distract and tear the mind away from the heart to external things.

"Some of them sing," says St Symeon the New Theologian, "that is, they pray with the lips."[129] St Gregory of Sinai adds, "Those who sing not at all also do well, if they are spiritually advanced, for these have no need of reading Psalms, but only silence and constant prayer."[130] Reading proper, in the writings of the Holy Fathers, is reading the Holy Scriptures and the works of the Fathers, while when they say "prayer," they mean most often the Jesus Prayer as well as the prayer of the publican and other short prayers that usually take the place of psalmody. But such "prayer" is unattainable for a beginner, and it cannot be explained to him satisfactorily, since it surpasses the reasoning mind and is explained only by blessed experience.

Brothers! Let us be attentive in our spoken prayer, uttered during the church services and in our solitude of the cell. Let us not make our labors or our life in the monastery fruitless by our inattentiveness and our carelessness in the work of God. Carelessness in prayer is pernicious! "Cursed is the man who does the work of the Lord carelessly" (Jer 31:10). The effect of this curse is obvious: the complete fruitlessness and lack of success, even after many years in monasticism. Let us place prayer of the lips, spoken aloud, as the foundation of our prayerful labor, the most important and essential labor of the monk, which all other labors support and uphold. For such prayer, the merciful Lord gives in His time the grace-filled prayer of the mind and heart to the constant, patient, humble ascetic. Amen.

CHAPTER 15

Remembrance of God

"Remembrance is God," according to the Holy Fathers, is a short prayer or even a short spiritual thought to which they have accustomed themselves and to which they try to train their mind, so that it constantly remembers it instead of random thoughts.

Can one replace all thoughts with a single, spiritual, short thought about God? Yes. The holy Apostle Paul said, "I determined not to know anything among you except Jesus Christ and Him crucified" (1 Cor 2:2). Vain, earthly thoughts constantly belabor a person, causing in him a loss of reason, hindering him in the acquisition of beneficial and useful knowledge. On the contrary, a single thought about God, having become habitual to a Christian, enriches him with spiritual reasoning and wisdom. Whoever has acquired Christ within himself by constant remembrance of Him is assured of the divine mysteries, unknown to carnal and emotional men, unknown to earthly wise men, even unattainable for them, for in Christ "are hidden all the treasures of wisdom and knowledge" (Col 2:3). The Christian who has acquired the Lord Jesus Christ within himself becomes the keeper of these treasures.

Remembrance of God is a divine institution. It was commanded by the very incarnate God the Word, confirmed by the Holy Spirit through His messengers (the apostles). "Watch, therefore, and pray always," the Lord said to His disciples (Luke 21:36). He commands this to us as well, who now stand before Him and beg Him to make us worthy of doing His will and being His disciples, Christians not only in name but in life. The Lord said these words, reminding His followers of those moral and physical problems that will fill the earthly wandering of every disciple; those sufferings and fears that will precede death for every one of us, that accompany it, that follow it; those temptations and sorrows that will overcome the world before the coming of the Antichrist and during his lordship; and, finally, the destruction and transformation of the cosmos during the second glorious and terrifying Coming of Christ.

"Watch therefore, and pray always that you may be counted worthy to escape all these things that will come to pass, and to stand before the Son of Man" (Luke 21:36) in the joy of salvation, to "stand" in this joy even after the temporal judgment that will come for every person after his soul leaves his body, as well as on the final judgment during which the chosen will be placed on the right of the Judge, and the rejected on the left (Matt 25:32). "Be serious and watchful in your prayers," said the holy Apostle Peter, repeating the command of the Lord to the faithful. "Be sober, be vigilant; because your adversary the devil walks about like a roaring lion, seeking whom he may devour" (1 Pet 4:7, 5:8).

Repeating and confirming this all-holy, salvific command, the Apostle Paul says, "Pray without ceasing" (1 Thess 5:17). "Be anxious for nothing, but in everything by prayer and supplication, with thanksgiving, let your requests be made known to God" (Phil 4:6). "Continue earnestly in prayer, being vigilant in it with thanksgiving" (Col 4:2). "I desire therefore that the men pray everywhere, lifting up holy hands, without wrath and doubting" (1 Tim 2:8). "But he who is joined to the Lord [through constant prayer] is one spirit with Him" (1 Cor 6:17).

Those who are joined to the Lord and united with the Lord through constant prayer are delivered by the Lord from slavery and service to sin and the devil: "And shall God not avenge His own elect who cry out day and night to Him, though He bears long with them? I tell you that He will avenge them speedily" (Luke 18:7–8). The sign of monastic perfection is constant prayer. "Whoever has achieved this," says St Isaac the Syrian, "has achieved the height of all virtues and has become the dwelling place of the Holy Spirit."[131] Exercise in constant prayer, habituation of oneself in prayer is necessary for every monk who desires to achieve Christian perfection. This is the duty of every monk, laid on him by God's command and his own monastic oath.[132]

Evidently, the holy apostles, having personally received from the Lord the command concerning prayer without ceasing, having passed it on to the faithful, were themselves practitioners of constant prayer. Before the descent of the Holy Spirit, they were all together in one house in prayer and supplication (see Acts 1:14). In this case, "prayer" was those specific prayers that were offered in common, while "supplication" indicates that constant prayerful disposition of their spirit, that is, constant prayer. When the Holy Spirit descended on the apostles, He, having made them temples of God, made them also capable of constant prayer, as the Scriptures say: "My house shall be called House of Prayer for All Nations" (Isa 56:7). St Isaac the Syrian says, "When the Spirit makes His dwelling place in someone, then that person does not cease praying, for the Spirit Himself constantly prays."[133]

The apostles only had only two spiritual labors—prayer and the preaching of the word of God. From prayer they passed to the announcement to mankind of the word of God; from the preaching of the word they returned to prayer. They were in a constant spiritual conversation—either they conversed with God through prayer, or they conversed on behalf of God with mankind. In both kinds of conversations, the same Spirit was active (see Acts 6:2, 4). What can we learn from the example of the apostles? That after obedience— active obedience to the word of God—we must focus all our activity into constant prayer, because constant prayer leads a Christian to the state in which he is capable of accepting the Holy Spirit. When the Lord, Who laid on the apostle various services, made them capable of accepting the Holy Spirit, He commanded them to remain in Jerusalem, the city of peace and silence: "tarry in the city of Jerusalem until you are endued with power from on high" (Luke 24:49).

From the writings of the holy monks we see that remembrance of God was always practiced by monks of the early Church of Christ. St Anthony the Great commanded constant remembrance of the name of our Lord Jesus Christ: "Do not forget the name of our Lord Jesus Christ, but constantly turn your mind to it, contain it in your heart, glorify it with your tongue, saying, 'Lord Jesus Christ, have mercy on me'. Also: 'Lord Jesus Christ, help me'. Also: 'I glorify Thee, my Lord, Jesus Christ.'"[134]

It was not only hesychasts and hermits that practiced constant prayer, but even coenobitic monks. St John of the Ladder speaks about the monks in a coenobium of Alexandria that he visited, saying that they "even during the meals did not cease their prayer of the mind, but through the appointed and customary signs and hand gestures, the blessed reminded each other of the prayer that must be practiced in the soul. They did this not only during the meals, but at every meeting, every convocation."[135] St Isaac, the hesychast of the Egyptian Scetis, told St John Cassian of Rome that his constant prayer is the second verse of Psalm 69: "O God, make speed to save me; O Lord, make haste to help me." Abba Dorotheos, a monk of Abba Serid's monastery in Palestine, taught his disciple, St Dositheos, to constantly practice the remembrance of God by constantly repeating "Lord Jesus Christ, have mercy on me" and "Son of God, help me." St Dositheos prayed either with one prayer or the other. It was given to him in such a form because he was a beginner, so that his mind would not despair at the monotony of a single prayer. When blessed Dositheos became seriously ill and approached his end, his holy instructor reminded him of constant prayer: "Dositheos! Work at your prayer. See that you do not lose it!" When the disease became even more serious, again St Dorotheos said, "Well, Dositheos, how is your prayer? Does it abide?" From this we see that exalted importance given to this instruction by the holy monks.

St Ioannicius the Great constantly repeated this prayer in his mind: "My hope is the Father, my refuge is the Son, my protection is the Holy Spirit. O Holy Trinity, glory to Thee!" (from the evening prayers). A disciple of St Ioannicius, St Eustratius, who is called "the divine" by his hagiographer, acquired constant prayer: "He constantly repeated within himself the prayer, *Lord, have mercy.*"[136] A certain father of the desert in Egypt constantly sat in his cell and plaited rope. He would sigh and say, "What will happen?" Having uttered these words and remained in silence for a time, he repeated, "What will happen?" and shook his head. In this remembrance, he spent all the days of his life, constantly sorrowing about what would happen after his soul would depart from his body. St Isaac the Syrian remembers a certain father who, for the space of forty years, prayed a single prayer: "I, as a person, have sinner. You, as God, forgive me!" Other fathers heard that he would weep while repeating this phrase. He wept, not becoming consoled, and this single prayer, day and night, replaced all other prayer rules for him.[137]

The majority of monks have always practiced the Jesus Prayer for the purpose of remembering God. "Lord Jesus Christ, have mercy on me, a sinner." Sometimes, depending on need, they divided it for beginners into two halves and so would say for a few hours: "Lord Jesus Christ, have mercy on me, a sinner." Then, for the next few hours, they would say, "Son of God, have mercy on me, a sinner." However, it is not wise to often change the words of prayer, because trees that are often replanted never sprout deep roots, as St Gregory of Sinai said.[138] Choosing the Jesus Prayer for remembrance of God is wise, because the name of the Lord Jesus Christ contains within it a special divine power. Furthermore, exercise in the Jesus Prayer naturally inspires thoughts of death, the torments of the aerial spirits, the final judgment of God, the eternal sufferings, and so vividly that the ascetic is moved to weep constantly for himself as for a dead man, already buried and stinking, awaiting the resurrection of the almighty God the Word (see John 11:39, 43, 44).

The benefit of remembrance of God is unquantifiable. It surpasses language, and it is beyond comprehension. Those who have felt it are not capable of fully explaining it. Constant prayer, as the command and gift of God, is inexplicable to human reason and language. A short prayer gathers the mind that, if it is not bound to this remembrance, cannot cease wandering and rushing about all over the place.[139] An ascetic can access his short prayer in any place and in any time, during any task, especially physical tasks. Even while present at the services in church, the ascetic receives benefit by practicing it, not only when the reader is not enunciating the words of the service, but even when everything is easily understood. It helps focus the attention on the words of the service, especially after it has become rooted in the heart and becomes, as it were, essential to the person. Remembrance of God in general, and the Jesus Prayer in particular, serves as a superlative weapon against sinful thoughts. The following words of St John of the Ladder were repeated by many other Holy Fathers: "Defeat the hosts of the enemy by invoking the name of Jesus, for neither in heaven nor on earth will you find a more sure weapon."[140]

Constant prayer leads the ascetic to poverty of spirit. By accustoming oneself to constantly asking God for help, he gradually loses all trust in himself. If he does this successfully, he then acknowledges all success not as his merit, but as God's mercy, concerning which he constantly begs God. Constant prayer guides one to the acquisition of faith, because one who constantly prays begins gradually to sense the presence of God. This sense, little by little, can grow and strengthen to such a degree that the eye of the mind begins to see God in His providence more clearly than the physical eyes see the physical objects of the world. The heart begins to feel the presence of God. Whoever has thus seen God and felt His presence cannot fail to believe in Him with living faith, revealed by deeds. Constant prayer destroys evil through hope in God, leading the ascetic to holy simplicity, curing the mind of its reliance on variety of thought and of its tendency to categorize everything concerning himself and his fellow men.

Instead, it constantly preserves him in simplicity and humility of thought, given by remembrance of God. The one who constantly prays gradually loses his tendency to idle reverie, absentmindedness, vain busyness, and anxiety. The more the holy and humble remembrance of God deepens in his soul and becomes rooted in it, the more he loses all the aforementioned evil tendencies. Finally, he can come to the state of spiritual infancy commanded by the Gospels; he can become mad for the sake of Christ; that is, he can abandon the falsely named wisdom of the world and receive spiritual wisdom from God. Constant prayer destroys curiosity, suspiciousness, and jealousy. From all this, people begin to seem good, and from such a heart, love for one's fellow man eventually arises. The one who constantly prays abides constantly in the Lord.

He knows the Lord as his Lord; he acquires the fear of the Lord; through fear he enters purity, through purity into divine love. The love of God fills its temple with the gifts of the Spirit.

St Isaiah the Solitary said,

> The wise rich man hides his treasures inside his home. The treasure that is revealed for all to see will be stolen by thieves and will be desired by the powerful of the world. So also the humble-minded and virtuous monk hides his virtues, and thereby he does not fill them with the desires of his fallen nature. He rebukes himself every hour and practices secret remembrance of God, as spoken in the Scriptures: "My heart grew hot within me, and while I was thus musing, the fire kindled" (Ps 38:4). What is the fire spoken of here? This is the fire of God: "For our God is a consuming fire" (Heb 12:29). Fire melts wax and dries out the mire of foul impurity, so also with secret remembrance of God, all foul thoughts are dried up and all passions are destroyed in the soul. The mind becomes illumined, thoughts become clear and subtle, and joy pours out into the heart. Secret remembrance of God wounds the demons and drives away evil thoughts. It vivifies the inner man. He who arms himself with remembrance of God is strengthened by God. The angels give him strength. Men glorify him. Secret remembrance and reading make the soul a fortress that is guarded and closed off on all sides, an unshakable pillar, a calm and stormless refuge. It saves the soul, preserving it from vacillation. The demons become distressed and disturbed when a monk arms himself with the secret remembrance of God, which is contained in the Jesus Prayer: *Lord Jesus Christ, Son of God, have mercy on me.* Reading it in silence helps one become practiced in remembrance of God. Secret remembrance is a mirror for the mind, a candle for the conscience. Secret remembrance desiccates lust, tames anger, drives away wrath, takes away sorrow, quiets brazenness, destroys despair. Secret remembrance illumines the mind and casts aside laziness. Secret remembrance gives rise to compunction; from it fear of God becomes rooted in the heart; it inspires tears. Through secret remembrance, a monk acquires un-hypocritical humble-mindedness, reverent moderation, and undisturbed prayer. Secret remembrance is the treasure house of prayer; it drives away thoughts, wounds the demons, purifies the body. Secret remembrance teaches longsuffering and abstinence. It warns of the fires of Gehenna. It preserves the mind without fantasy and brings it instead salvific thoughts of death. Secret remembrance is filled with all good deeds; it is decorated by every virtue, but it is foreign to every evil deed.[141]

St John Cassian said,

Prayer of this short verse (the aforementioned second verse of Psalm 62) should be constant, so that we preserve ourselves from arrogance, and lest temptation tear us down. The practice of this small verse, I repeat, must revolve in your bosom at all times. Do not cease to repeat it, no matter what your task or obedience, even if you are in the middle of traveling. Practice it also as you go to sleep, as you eat food, even as you take care of the essential needs of the body. Such practice of the heart will become for you the most salvific rule, which not only will preserve you unharmed during any attack of the demons, but, having purified you of all physical passions, it will lead you to invisible and heavenly visions. It will raise you to unutterable heights of prayer, known by experience to very few. This short verse will drive sleep away until you, having been formed by these extraordinary words, will learn to practice them also in your sleep. If you awake at night, it will be the first thing that comes to mind. When you wake up in the morning, it will precede all other thoughts. When you get up from your bed, it will occupy you until you begin praying on your knees. It will convey you to every task and labor. It will always keep watch over you. Exercise it according to the command of the lawgiver [that is, Moses, the lawgiver of Israel], while sitting at home or traveling, when lying down to sleep or when getting up from sleep. Write it on the lintels and the doors of your lips. Write it on the doors of your house and in the inner treasure stores of your bosom, so that it, when you lie down, will be a ready psalmody for you. When you stand and begin to work on the correction of all that is necessary for life, it functions as constant prayer.[142]

St John Chrysostom said, "Brothers! I beg you, do not allow yourselves ever to stop fulfilling this rule or even to despise it . . . The monk, whether he eats or drinks, sits or serves, travels or does something else, must constantly cry out: *Lord Jesus Christ, Son of God, have mercy on me!* Then the name of the Lord Jesus, descending into the depths of the heart, will humble the serpent that rules over the pastures of the heart. It will then save and revivify the soul. Constantly abide in the name of the Lord Jesus, so that your heart will swallow the Lord and the Lord will swallow your heart, and so that these two will be one."[143]

A certain brother asked St Philemon, "Father, what is secret remembrance?" The elder answered, "Go, keep vigil over your heart and repeat in your thoughts, with reverence, fear, and trembling: Lord Jesus Christ, have mercy on me."[144]

In the Fathers, sometimes constant prayer or constant remembrance of God is called "instruction." This is because the ascetics, on whose actions the dew of divine grace has descended, have found in this constantly repeated short prayer a profound, spiritual, inexhaustible meaning that constantly attracts and increases attention by its spiritual newness. And so a short verse becomes for them the most expansive of studies, the science of sciences, and practice in it becomes true instruction.

These are the instructions of the Holy Fathers, and this was also their own practice. Not merely all their deeds and words but all their thoughts were consecrated to God. This is the reason for the abundance within them of the gifts of the Spirit. On the contrary, we are careless of our deeds. We do not act according to the commandments of God, but as we like, following the first inclination of our emotions, the first thought that pops into our head. We are even more careless of our words, but as for our thoughts—we pay them no heed whatsoever. They are scattered everywhere; they are all brought as a sacrifice to vanity. Our mind, contrary to the state of mind of the ascetic who wards himself with remembrance, is like a building with four gates, every single one of which is open, before which no guard stands, where anyone may enter and anyone may leave, bringing or taking anything he pleases.

Brothers! Let us cease living such an inattentive and fruitless life! Let us emulate the practice of the Holy Fathers, especially their remembrance of God, in which they held their mind constantly. Young man! Sow with diligence the seeds of virtue; learn with patience and force yourself to all God-pleasing practices and labors; teach yourself to remember God; confine your mind within holy instruction. If you see that it constantly slides away into tangential and vain thoughts, do not despair. Continue your labor with constancy: "Try to return your thought," said St John of the Ladder, "or, rather, to confine your thought in the words of prayer. If it tears itself away because of your youthfulness, lead it back. The mind's natural state is constant movement, but He Who directs all things can give it constancy. If you labor thus constantly, then He Who places the limits to the sea of your mind will come to you and tell your mind in your prayer: 'This far you may come, but no farther!' (Job 38:11)."[145]

On the surface, remembrance seems a strange practice—dry, boring—but in essence it is the most fruitful of labors, the most precious tradition of the Church, the institution of God, a spiritual pearl, the inheritance of the apostles and Holy Fathers, who accepted it and passed it to us by the command of the Holy Spirit. You cannot imagine those riches that you will inherit in the proper time, if you have acquired the habit of constantly remembering God. The eye of the beginner "has not seen, nor ear heard, nor have entered into the heart of man the things which God has prepared for those who love Him" (1 Cor 2:9) not only in the age to come, but even in this life, in which he can foretaste the blessedness of the age to come (see Mark 10:30).

"Prepare yourself," said St John of the Ladder, "by constant prayer, practiced in the secret place of your soul, for your standing in prayer, and you will soon advance."[146] In its own time, remembrance will encompass your entire existence, and you will become as though drunk with it, as though belonging to this world and yet not belonging to it, foreign to it, belonging with the body, but not belonging with your mind and heart. Whoever is drunk on material wine does not remember himself, forgets his sorrow, forgets his ranks, his nobility and dignity. The one who is drunk on divine remembrance becomes cold, emotionless toward all earthly desires and glories, to all material gain and advantages. His thought is always near Christ, Who acts through remembrance as through a sweet fragrance, as "the aroma of life death leading to life" (2 Cor 2:16). Remembrance of God destroys one's sympathy with the world and its passions, and it brings to life within him a sympathy with God, with everything spiritual and holy, with blessed eternity. "For what have I in heaven?" exclaims the one drunk on remembrance. Nothing. "And what have I desired on earth from Thee?" On one thing—that I be constantly united to You through silent prayer. Others desire riches, others glory, but I desire to "cleave unto God, to put in Him [the] trust" in my dispassion.[147]

The words of remembrance must be uttered by a beginner aloud, in a quiet voice, without hurrying, with all possible attention, confining, according to aforementioned advice of St John of the Ladder, his mind to the words of the remembrance. Little by little, his prayer of the lips will become prayer of the mind and then prayer of the heart. But this progression requires many years. One must not seek it before its time; let it happen on its own or, more properly, let God give it to you in His own good time, depending on your spiritual progress and the circumstances of your life. The humble ascetic is content with merely remembering God. This already he considers to be a great benefit of the Creator for His poor and weak creation, man. He admits himself unworthy of grace, never seeking to reveal its effect in himself, knowing from the teaching of the Holy Fathers that such seeking is inspired by vanity, from which come only demonic delusion and perdition, for even such seeking itself is already delusion, since no matter how much one tries to find it, grace comes only by the will of God.[148] Instead, the ascetic should hunger to reveal within himself only his great sinfulness and to acquire the ability to weep for it. He entrusts himself to the will of the all-good and all-merciful God, Who knows to whom it is beneficial to give grace and for whom it is better to withhold it. Many, having received grace, have become careless, high-minded, and self-reliant. The grace given to them served, thanks to their lack of wisdom, only to their greater condemnation. Blessed is pledge of humility in the heart of the monk, according to which he, practicing whatever labor he is assigned, works completely without expectation of reward, hungering and thirsting only to do the will of God. Himself he offers with all faith and simplicity—rejecting his own reasoning, will, authority—to the direction of the merciful Lord, our God, Who desires that all men should be saved and come to a knowledge of the truth. To Him be glory unto the ages of ages. Amen.

CHAPTER 16

The Prayer of the Mind, the Heart, and the Soul

Whoever practices attentive prayer with constancy and reverence, uttering the words of prayer either loudly or in a whisper (depending on need), and confining the mind within the words; whoever during this prayerful labor constantly rejects all thoughts and fantasies, not only the sinful and vain ones, but even the apparently good—to such a person the merciful Lord grants in His time the prayer of the mind, the heart, and the soul.

Brother! It is not beneficial for you to receive the grace-filled prayer of the heart before its time! It is not beneficial for you to sense spiritual sweetness prematurely! If you receive them before their allotted time, before having gained the necessary knowledge of what reverence and what care are needed to preserve this gift of God's grace, you can use it for evil, to the damage and even loss of your soul.[149] Moreover, it is impossible to reveal within oneself the prayer of grace, of the mind and the heart with one's own exertions, because to unite the mind with the heart and the soul—they have been separated by the Fall—is possible only for God. If we force ourselves unwisely to try to reveal those gifts that are sent by God alone with our own exertion, our work will be in vain.

And it would be good if the damage were limited only to a waste of energy and time! Often the prideful seekers after spiritual states of the renewed human nature are subjected to the greatest spiritual sickness that the Holy Fathers call *prelest* (spiritual delusion). This is natural. The very presupposition from which such men begin is a false one. How can the consequences of such a false beginning fail to be false in their own turn? These consequences, which we call spiritual delusion, have different forms and degrees. Spiritual delusion is most often hidden, though sometimes it is obvious to all, and it often places a person in a disrupted state, simultaneously laughable and pitiful. Often it leads to suicide and the final death of the soul.[150] But this demonic delusion, obvious to many in its visible consequences, must also be examined and understood in its very beginning—the false thought that serves as the foundation for all subsequent errors and delusive spiritual states. This false thought of the mind contains the blueprint for the edifice of spiritual delusion, just as the seed already contains the plant that must come from it after it is planted in the earth.

St Isaac the Syrian said,

> The Scriptures say, "The kingdom of God does not come with observation" (Luke 17:20) or with expectation. Those who have labored with such a spiritual hope have been subjected to pride and the fall. But we must establish our heart in the works of repentance and in a life pleasing to God. The gifts of the Lord come on their own, if the temple of the heart will be pure, not defiled. To seek the exalted gifts of God "with observation" is rejected by the Church of God. Those who have endeavored this have been subjected to pride and the fall. Such seeking is not a sign that someone loves God, but rather a sickness of the soul. How can we covet the exalted gifts of God when the divine Paul only boasts of his sorrows and admits that the greatest gift of God is participation in the sufferings of Christ?[151]

Entrust your prayerful labor wholly to God, without Whom even the smallest progress is impossible. Every step toward success in this labor is a gift of God. Reject yourself and give yourself up to God, so that He will do with you as He pleases. After all, He, the all-good One, desires to give you that which has not even occurred to the mind or the heart (see 1 Cor 2:9). He wants to give you such benefits that our fallen mind and heart cannot even imagine. It is impossible for the one who has not acquired purity to have the slightest intimation of the spiritual gifts of God, not by means of imagination, not even by comparison with the most pleasant emotional responses available to man! With simplicity and faith, lay all your trust on God. Do not listen to the falsehood of the evil one, who even in Paradise lied to our forefathers, saying, "you will be like gods" (Gen 3:5). Now he offers you a premature and proud striving to acquire the spiritual gifts of the prayer of the heart, which, I repeat, only God can grant, by Whom all things and all times are predetermined. The place He has predetermined for pure prayer is a vessel purified of all passion, both of body and soul.

Let us work instead on cleaning out our temple (of body and soul) of all idols, of sacrifices to idols, of anything that belongs to worship of idols. As the holy Prophet Elijah gathered all the priests and prophets of Baal near the brook of Kishon and there executed them, so we should plunge ourselves into tears of repentance, and on this blessed stream let us mortify everything that forces our heart to bring sacrifice to sin, all self-justification that we use to excuse all such idolatrous worship of sin. Let us wash the altar and everything that surround it with our tears. Let us double and triple this oblation (as did Elijah), because our spiritual impurity requires most abundant tears to be purified. Let us build an altar from stones in the name of the Lord, these stones being correct perceptions, inspired by the Gospel alone. Let there be no place here for the emotions of the old man, no matter how innocent or refined they may seem (see 3 Kgdms 18). Then the great God will send down His all-holy fire into our hearts and will make our hearts the temple of grace-filled prayer, as He Himself said with His divine lips: "My house shall be called a house of prayer" (Matt 21:13).

At first, let us turn our attention to the passions of the body, to the way we eat and to all the lustful strivings that are stirred up and depend most strongly on excesses in eating. Let us try to wisely organize the state of our body, giving it enough food and sleep so that it would not be exhausted and would remain capable of laboring. But let us give our body so little food that it constantly will carry within itself some deadness, lest it become awake for sin. According to the Fathers, our eating and sleeping depend a great deal on habit. This is why is it very beneficial to train oneself very early to moderate, limited partaking of both food and sleep.[152]

St Isaac the Syrian said the following about fasting and vigil:

Whoever has come to love communion with these two virtues during his entire life has become a confidante of chastity. As the beginning of all evils is the satiation of the stomach and self-weakening by excessive sleep—both of which incite lusts of the flesh—so also the holy way of God and the foundation of all virtues is fasting and vigil and wakefulness in the service of God, while also crucifying the body during the entire night by taking away the sweetness of sleep. Fasting is the enclosure of all virtues, the beginning of labors, the crown of the abstinent, the beauty of virginity and sanctification, the brightness of chastity, the beginning of the Christian path, the mother of prayer, the source of chastity and wisdom, the teacher of silence. It precedes all other good deeds. As the desire for light naturally follows the health of the eyes, so also the desire for prayer follows fasting done with discernment. Whenever someone begins to fast, then from the fast comes a desire to converse with God in the mind. The body of the faster has no desire to remain in bed all night. When the seal of fasting is placed on the lips of a man, then his mind becomes instructed in compunction, his heart pours forth prayer, his face is clothed in sorrow, and all shameful thoughts stand far away from him. No amusements are seen in his eyes. He is an enemy of passionate desires and pointless conversations. It has never been seen that a discerning faster was ever belabored by evil desires. Fasting with discernment is the great temple of all virtues. Whoever is careless about fasting will not succeed in any other virtue. Fasting is a commandment given to our nature from the very beginning, to safeguard it during eating. And it was the breaking of the fast that caused the fall of our created nature. The solution to the problem must return to the source of the problem, and so ascetics only begin to walk toward fear of God when they begin to preserve the law of God.[153]

Whoever eats or sleeps too much will not fail to be defiled by sensual thoughts and emotions. While his soul and body are disturbed by such actions, while the mind still finds sweetness in carnal thoughts, it will not be capable of new and mysterious spiritual movements that are inspired in him by the overshadowing of the Holy Spirit.

As much as fasting is necessary for the one who desires to practice and progress in the prayer of the mind, it is just as important for him to acquire silence or extreme solitude, that is, as much withdrawal as possible from wandering about. If you live in a monastery, leave the monastery walls as little as possible. When you are sent outside the monastery, return as quickly as possible. If you visit a city or a village, guard your senses with extreme attention, lest you see or hear something harmful to your soul, lest you receive an accidental and unforeseen fatal wound. Within the monastery, be familiar with the church, the refectory, and your own cell; go to the cells of other brothers only with a valid reason, and if at all possible, don't go at all. Visit the cell of your spiritual guide and father, if you are so blessed to have a guide in our times, and even so, visit him only at the appropriate times and only when you require his help, never from despair or merely to idly talk. Train yourself to be silent, so that you can be wordless even among people. Speak as little as possible, only according to extreme need. It is very difficult to endure the heavy burden of silence for the one who is used to being distracted; however, anyone who desires to be saved and to progress in the spiritual life must submit himself without fail to this burden and train himself to solitude and silence. After a short time of difficulty, both silence and solitude will become desirable because the fruits of the soul of the wise hesychast will not feign to taste distractions.

St Arsenius the Great, being in the world, prayed that God would instruct Him how to be saved, and he heard a voice that said to him, "Arsenius! Flee all people, and you will be saved." When the saint entered the Egyptian Scetis, in which lived monks who were great in their holiness, he once again begged God, "Teach me how to be saved." He again heard a voice, "Arsenius! Flee, be silent, and be still—these are the roots of dispassion."

St Isaac the Syrian said the following concerning Arsenius the Great:

Silence helps stillness. How is this so? If you live in a large coenobitic monastery, it is impossible to avoid meeting someone. Even the angelic Arsenius could not avoid this, he who loved stillness more than others. It is impossible to avoid meeting the fathers and brothers who live with us; such meetings occur unexpectedly, even when one merely walks to church or to some other place. When the worthily honored saint (Arsenius) saw that he, as one living near a community of people (though this was the Egyptian Scetis, filled only with other monks), found it impossible to avoid meeting with both worldly people and monks who lived in those places, he learned stillness through this grace-filled means—constant silence. If he opened his door by necessity for some, they would only receive the comfort of seeing his face. Any conversation and the need for talk became unnecessary for him.[154]

The same St Isaac said,

Love silence more than all else, for it brings you close to the harvest. The tongue is insufficient to express those benefits that arise from silence. First of all, let us force ourselves to be silent, then from silence is born something that begins to instruct us. May God grant you to sense this something that is born of silence. If you begin to live such a life, I cannot even express the kind of light that will shine forth for you from that quarter. Do not think, brother, that the wondrous Arsenius, as is said of him—when the fathers and brothers entered his cell to see him, he only accepted them and sent them off in silence—acted thus only because he wanted to. He did this because he initially forced himself to act thus. A certain sweetness is born in the heart after a time if you learn this labor, forcing the body to remain in stillness. In such a life, we receive many tears and extraordinary vision.[155]

In his 75th Homily, St Isaac said,

For the duration of a very long time, being the whole time tempted from the right and from the left, and testing myself in different ways through following two ways of living, having suffered countless wounds from the adversary, having been found worthy of great mystical intercession, I, made wise by the grace of God, acquired through many years and by much experience the following experiential knowledge. The foundation of all virtues, the cry of the soul from captivity, the path leading to divine light and life is found in the following two ways of living. First, you must gather yourself in a single place and constantly fast. This means that you must establish for yourself a wise and discerning rule of abstinence of the stomach in a constant place of living from which you do not leave, all the while training and learning about God. From this comes obedience of the senses, from here comes sobriety of the mind, from here comes the taming of the fierce passion that moves in the body, from here comes meekness of thought, from here comes the movement of bright thoughts, from here the desire to do good works, from here exalted and subtle reasoning, from here endless tears at all times and the remembrance of death, from here that pure chastity that stands apart from all fantasy that tempts the mind. The mind becomes quick to see and discern what stands far away (that is, good and evil, even as distant consequences of current action). Then comes the most profound mystical knowledge that the mind conceives by the power of God's word, and through inner movements arising in the soul. Then comes the ability to discern dark spirits from the holy powers, and true vision from vain fantasies. Then comes the fear of wandering in the sea of thoughts, and this fear cuts off sloth and carelessness. Then comes the fire of zeal that destroys all misfortunes and raise you up above all fear. Then comes that fire that despises all lust and roots it out of the thoughts, causing forgetfulness of all memories of the past and everything that belongs to this world and age. In short, from this comes the freedom of the true man, the joy and resurrection of the soul, and its consolation with Christ in the Kingdom of Heaven. If anyone becomes slothful in these two ways of living, let him know that he not only has deprived himself of all the aforementioned blessings, but by despising these two ways of living, he shakes the very foundation of virtue in himself. As these two virtues are the beginning and head of divine labors in the soul, the door and path to Christ (if anyone is capable of remaining in them and enduring in them), so also, on the contrary, if anyone leaves them and walks away from them, he will come to two contrary ways of living, that is, to constant wandering and shameless gluttony. These are the principles of the opposite of what we have spoken of here and they make room in the soul only for passions.

St Isaac continues, "The first of these principles, first of all, unties the senses that have already submitted themselves from the bonds that held them in place." What happens from this? From this comes improper and unexpected adventures that may lead to falling into sin,[156] the rise of powerful waves, a fierce arousal from a vision that takes hold of the body and keeps it imprisoned, eventual relaxation in one's strict manner of thinking, the rise of unfettered thoughts that lead one to perdition, the cooling of one's zeal toward the works of God, and the eventual decline of a love for stillness. Finally, the ascetic abandons his previous way of life, renewing all his forgotten sins and learning new passions, previously unknown, since the constant new encounters with mankind as he moves from country to country unwillingly and variously offer to him new passions for his contemplation. Those passions that were already mortified in the soul by the grace of God and destroyed in the mind by forgetfulness once again begin to come into movement and force the soul to comply. This is what—I do not list everything else in detail—opens up in the monk after he breaks the first proper way of living, that is, from the wandering of the body after rejecting patient endurance in stillness.

What happens after the monk rejects the second way of life (wise fasting)? In other words, what will happen when the man begins to live like swine? What is the life of swine, if not complete freedom given to the stomach, with no rule of limitation? What is it if not constant satiation of the stomach, a disregard of proper times for addressing the needs of the stomach, in contrast to the wise custom of men? What will follow? Heaviness of the head, a significant belaboring of the body with the weakening of the shoulders. From this, it becomes necessary to lessen one's service to God. Laziness appears that does not allow one to do prostrations during the prayer rule, carelessness concerning the common prostrations done in church, a darkening and coolness of the thoughts, a numbing of the mind, lack of reason and an especial darkening of the thoughts, a thick darkness that covers the entire soul, abundant despair in the accomplishment of any work of God, as well as during reading, thanks to the incapability of tasting the sweetness of the word of God, the abandonment of necessary ascetic labors, an unfettered mind that wanders over the entire earth, the accumulation of water in all the members, unclean fantasies at night that offer foul and improper images to the mind, filled with lust and bringing that lust into action in the very soul of the ascetic. The bed of this accursed one, his clothing, his very body are defiled by the abundance of foul emissions that flow from him as from a fountainhead. And this occurs not only at night, but even during the day. The body constantly preys upon filth and defiles the thoughts, so that the person, because of these circumstances, loses hope in maintaining his chastity, for the sweetness of the teasing thoughts acts in his entire body with constant and unendurable burning, and before him enticing images of the mind appear in forms of beauty that irritate him at all times, inducing him to unite with them (that is, with these mental images of beauty). Without a doubt, he does unite with them in his thought and by his desire, because of the darkness of his reasoning mind. This is the same thing that the prophet mentioned: "Surely this was the lawless action of your sister Sodom, namely, arrogance. For in fullness of bread and abundance of wine, she and her daughter lived in self-indulgence" (Ezek 16:49).

A certain wise man also said the following: "If anyone will feed his body to give it pleasure in eating, he will cast his soul into great warfare. If such a person ever comes to himself, desiring to force himself and restrain himself, he will not be able to do this because of the excessive arousal of his bodily movements, because of the forcefulness and power of the enticements and delusions that have enslaved the soul with their desires." Do you see the subtlety of the godless powers? Again the same wise man said, "Gratification of the body, with all its softness and its youthful dampness,[157] becomes the reason for the soul's quick acquisition of passions. Then death will enclose it, and the soul will fall under God's judgment. On the contrary, the soul that constantly remembers its duties abides in freedom. Its cares are lessened, and it does not worry about anything temporal. It cares only reining in the passions and preserving the virtues; it constantly progresses in a life of virtue, filled with joy free of cares, abiding in a refuge with no misfortunes. Gratification of the body not only strengthens the passions and restores them in the soul, but it even uproots the soul from its foundation. In addition, the stomach is aroused to immoderation and countless carnal lusts. It forces man to eat at all the wrong times. The one who is attacked by gluttony does not want to endure even slight hunger (which would allow him to govern himself again), because he is captive to the passions."

All the Holy Fathers write about this in the same manner, but we will not cite them here, lest we leave too large a gap between citations of Scripture.

Having warded our life from the outside by abstinence from excess and from gratification of the body in food and drink, having guarded it by the solitude that depends on us, that is, by constantly remaining in the monastery and by avoiding acquaintances both outside and within the monastery, let us turn our attention to the passions of the soul. Let us attend first of all, according to the command of the Lord, to anger (see Matt 5:22), which has as its foundation pride.[158] Let us forgive our fathers and brothers, those who are near to us and those who are far away, living and departed, all the offenses and insults they inflicted on us, no matter how serious. The Lord commanded us, "And whenever you stand praying, if you have anything against anyone, forgive him, that your Father in heaven may also forgive you your trespasses. But if you do not forgive, neither will your Father in heaven forgive your trespasses" (Mark 11:25–26). First of all, pray for your enemies and bless them (see Matt 5:44), for they are the instruments of divine providence, given to you as recompense for your sins in this short earthly life, lest you receive your deserved retribution in an eternity of hellish suffering. When you act thus, when you come to love your enemies and pray for them to receive all temporal and eternal good things, only then will God descend to help you. Then, you will defeat all your enemies by your prayer, and you will enter into the temple of your mind and heart to worship the Father in spirit and in truth (see John 4:24).

However, if you allow your heart to become hardened with remembrance of offenses, and if you justify your wrath by your pride, then the Lord your God will turn away from you, and you will be abandoned, to be trampled underfoot by Satan. He will trample you with all manner of foul thoughts and emotions, and you will have no strength to oppose him.[159] If the Lord deigns to place dispassion, love, lack of condemnation of others, merciful forgiveness of offenses as the cornerstones of your prayerful labor, then you will defeat your adversaries with especial ease and quickness, and you will acquire pure prayer.

Know that all passions and all fallen spirits are intimately connected with each other. This familiarity, this union, is sin. If you submit yourself to one passion, then you will submit yourself to all other passions as well. If you allow yourself to be captured by a single evil spirit by conversing with the thoughts he inspires in your mind and by enjoying these thoughts or fantasies, then you have allowed yourself to be enslaved by all evil spirits. After your defeat, they will toss you back and forth like a bound captive.[160] This is the teaching of the Holy Fathers, and it is confirmed by experience. If you pay attention to yourself, you will see that when you allow yourself to be defeated by some sin, you will inevitably fall prey to some other sin later, a sin that you never intended to commit. This will continue until you restore your freedom by diligent repentance.

Having placed lack of anger, love, and mercy to others—all commanded by the Gospel—as the cornerstone of your labor of prayer, boldly reject all conversation with thoughts and fantasies. Cut off all thoughts and fantasies with the following words: "I have completely entrusted myself to the will of my God, so I have no need for long conversations with you, or for any suppositions or guesses. 'The Lord is at hand. Be anxious for nothing,' says the Holy Spirit to me, together with all who truly believe in Christ, 'but in everything by prayer and supplication, with thanksgiving, let your requests be made known to God' (Philippians 4:5–6)."

"Be serious," that is, reject satiation and gratification, reject delusive thoughts and fantasies, "and watchful in your prayer, . . . casting your care upon Him, for He cares for you" (1 Pet 4:7, 5:7). "I desire therefore that the men [that is, all Christians who have become perfect in their labor of prayer] pray everywhere, lifting up holy hands" (1 Tim 2:8), minds, and hearts purified of the passions, filled with humility and love, without wrath or contrary thought, that is, devoid of any anger against fellow men, avoiding all coupling with thoughts or finding sweetness in fantasies. Come to hate "every wrong way" (Ps 118:128), and you will hold straight to all the commandments of the Lord. The "wrong way" is conversation with thoughts and fantasies. Whoever has rejected such communication with fantasy can inherit all the commandments of God. He can do the will of God within his heart (see Ps 39:9), constantly uniting with the Lord through prayer, giving his prayer the wings of humility and love. "O ye that love the Lord, hate the thing which is evil," the Holy Spirit exhorts us (Ps 96:10).

It is necessary for the practitioner of prayer to know and see the effect of the passions and the evil spirits on his blood. It is not without reason that the Holy Scriptures say that not only flesh, but "blood cannot inherit the kingdom of God" (1 Cor 15:50). Not only the crude carnal emotions of the old man, but also the subtler emotions, sometimes barely noticeable, arising from the circulation of blood, are condemned by God. All the more, then, this subject needs the attention of the ascetic, since the subtle influence of the passions and the spirits on the blood only then becomes obvious when the heart senses the presence of the Holy Spirit. His presence uncovers all sinful sensations.

Having acquired spiritual perception, the ascetic clearly and suddenly sees the effect of the blood on the soul. He can see in what manner the passions and spirits, acting on the soul through the blood in the subtlest way possible, hold the soul in captivity. Then he will understand and be assured that all effects of the blood on the soul, not only the crude and obvious, but also the more subtle, are an abomination before God. It is a sacrifice that is defiled by sin, unworthy of being placed in the spiritual realm, unworthy of being included among the actions and perceptions of the spirit.

Before the Spirit begins to act in the heart, this subtle effect of the blood remains either completely unclear or little understood; therefore, the incautious ascetic can even mistake it for grace. Proper caution in this case can only be cultivated after a timely purification and renewal by the Spirit. In the meantime, the ascetic should not think that any sensation of the heart is correct, except a sense of repentance, salvific tears for sins that dissipate only with the hope of mercy. God accepts a single sacrifice of the heart, only one sensation of the heart of man's fallen nature: "The sacrifice unto God is a contrite spirit; a contrite and humble heart God shall not despise" (Ps 50:19).

The effect of the blood on the soul is made obvious when we are in the throes of the passion of wrath and wrathful thoughts, especially in people who are easily inclined to anger. A person can come to such a frightful state, when he is aroused by wrath! He loses all mastery over himself. He abandons himself to the lordship of the passion, to the mastery of the spirits who thirst for his destruction and who desire to destroy him, using his own self as their tool. He speaks and acts like a madman. Such an effect of the blood on the soul is obvious also when the blood becomes aroused by carnal passion.

The effect of other passions on the blood is less obvious, but it exists. What is sorrow? What is despair? What is sloth? These are the various actions of sinful thoughts on the blood. Love of money and love of gain also influence the blood. The gratification produced in man by thoughts of enrichment—what else is this, if not the delusive, enticing, sinful agitation of the blood? The spirits of evil, who tirelessly and insatiably thirst for the destruction of man, act on us not only by means of thoughts and fantasies, but by different forms of direct contact, perceived by the flesh, the blood, the heart, the mind. They try to pour their poison into us using all possible ways and means.[161]

We need to be cautious. We need vigilance; we need a clear and exact knowledge of the spiritual path that leads to God. On this path, there are many thieves, robbers, and murderers. Seeing the countless dangers, let us cry out to our Lord and let us beg Him with constant tears to direct us to this narrow and sorrowful path that leads to life. These different ways of inflaming the blood through thoughts and fantasies—they are that fiery sword, given at Adam's expulsion to the fallen Cherubim, which he spins about inside us, prohibiting our entry into God's mystical paradise of spiritual thoughts and perceptions.[162]

We must pay special attention to vanity, whose effect on the blood is very difficult to sense. Vanity almost always acts together with subtle sensuality, giving a person the most refined sinful pleasures. The poison of this pleasure is so subtle that many mistake the pleasure of vanity and sensuality for the consolation of divine grace. Deluded by this pleasure, the ascetic gradually slides into a state of self-delusion, believing his self-delusion to be a state of grace. Finally, he gradually passes completely into the power of the fallen angel who puts on the mask of an angel of light. This ascetic then becomes the instrument, the messenger of the rejected spirits.

Entire books have been written in this state of spiritual delusion. Many such books were praised by the blind world and were read by people (who had not yet purified themselves of passions) with pleasure and exhilaration. This so-called spiritual pleasure is nothing other than the sweetness of subtle vanity, arrogance, and sensuality. The lot of a sinner is not pleasure; his lot is sorrow and repentance. Vanity corrupts the soul, just as carnal lust corrupts both soul and body. Vanity makes the soul incapable of spiritual perceptions, which only begin when all passionate perceptions cease, being cut off by humility. This is why the Holy Fathers offer holy repentance as the universal task of all monks—especially those practicing prayer and desiring to succeed in that labor—for it acts directly against vanity, delivering spiritual poverty to the soul instead. Even after a monk has spent a considerable time practicing repentance, the effect of vanity is still evident on the soul, so similar to the effect of carnal lust.

Passions of the flesh teach one to strive for forbidden union with another body. This passion changes the disposition of the entire soul and body of the one who submits to it, even if the pleasures received are limited to thoughts and fantasies. Vanity leads one to a forbidden union with human glory. When it touches the heart, it brings the blood into a disorderly, enticing agitation. This agitation changes the disposition of man completely, leading him into a union with the evil and dark spirit of the world, thereby separating him from the Spirit of God. Vanity is a kind of fornication with earthly glory.

"It gazes at the essence of things with the eye of lust," said St Isaac the Syrian.[163] Since vanity darkens a person, it makes his approach and union with God difficult, as the Saviour Himself said to the vain Pharisees who sought praise and encouragement from each other and from blind human society:

"How can you believe, who receive honor from one another, and do not seek the honor that comes from the only God?" (John 5:44).

St John of the Ladder and St Nilus of Sora[164] spoke of "prideful zeal" for prematurely seeking that which must come in its own time. We can easily equate this delusional state with the passion of vanity (and its inevitable effect on the blood). Vain thoughts inflame the blood, while vanity, in its own turn, grows and multiplies delusional fantasies and a conceited self-image, a state called by the apostle as being "vainly puffed up by his fleshly mind" (Col 2:18).

From all the aforementioned material, one can understand what is the proper time for the flowering of the prayer of the mind and the heart. Such prayer is most appropriate for a mature age, when all excesses have been tamed in man by the natural flow of time. This is not to say that one cannot practice this prayer in youth, especially if the young person is spiritually ripe and especially if he has a spiritual guide. However, this ripeness does not merely depend on time (either from birth or from one's entry into the monastery). This ripened prayer must come from prolonged preliminary self-examination, not arbitrary self-examination, but done in the Lord Jesus Christ, in the light of the Gospels, which portray the new man and all the many forms of the old man's sicknesses.

One must examine oneself while reading the writings of the Holy Fathers of the Eastern Orthodox Church, who help us use the light of the Gospels without error. The more a person delves deeply into himself and comes to know himself, the more he comes to recognize his passions, the different ways they act on him and attack him. Then he comes to know his weakness; then he can begin to destroy within himself all sinful qualities grafted into his nature by the Fall. Then he can acquire the qualities indicated by the Gospels. And only then will his foundation for the edifice of prayer be completely firm.

He should not rush to lay the foundation; on the contrary, he should take care that his foundation be deep and solid. It is not enough to learn what the passions are, with all their many offshoots, while reading the books of the Fathers. One must read them in the living book of the soul and acquire experiential knowledge concerning them. It is obvious that many years are needed for such exercise to bear fruit, especially in our time, when spiritual knowledge without labor is rare, when every bit of knowledge must be searched in books, considering the proper order and progression of all spiritual knowledge, actions, and states.

Whoever does not work enough on the firmness of his foundation will see many faults in his building, many inconveniences, even significant cracks and other damage. Sometimes, he will even see his building collapse entirely. Brothers! Let us not hurry. Following the advice of the Gospel (see Luke 6:48), let us dig deeply to lay solid, heavy foundation stones for our edifice of prayer. These stones are our habitual fulfillment of the commandments of the Gospel, confirmed by time and prolonged doing.

When the ascetic of Christ, by his own power, takes control of the movements of his blood and weakens its effect on the soul, then, little by little, spiritual perceptions begin to arise in the soul. Subtle, divine thoughts begin to appear in the mind and to attract the mind to examine them more fully, distracting the mind from wandering about everywhere, concentrating the mind within itself.[165] The heart begins to sympathize with the mind through abundant compunction. These spiritual perceptions finally weaken the effect of the blood on the soul; the blood then is free to do its natural service to the body, having ceased to serve (outside its proper function) as the instrument of sin and the demons. The Holy Spirit warms the person spiritually, simultaneously bedewing and cooling the soul, which to this point was only acquainted with the inflammation of the blood.[166] When the noetic Sun of Righteousness appears, the spiritual beasts slink away into their holes, and the ascetic can leave the darkness of bondage, where he was held for so long by sin and the fallen angels. Then he can begin his spiritual work and progress until the evening of his earthly life, until his passage into the eternal life without evening.

The blessed action of the Holy Spirit in man at first showers him with incredible stillness. He becomes dead to the world and the world's vain and sinful pleasures, to any kind of service to the world. The Christian is at peace with all and with everyone, a state deepened by a strange, humble, and exalted spiritual discernment, unknown and unattainable to a carnal or emotional disposition. He begins to feel compassion for all mankind and for every person individually. This compassion then transforms into love. Then he begins to concentrate his attention on prayer. The words of his prayer begin to produce strong, extraordinary impressions on the soul, overwhelming it. Finally, little by little, the heart and the entire soul unite with the mind, and after the soul, the body itself is led into the same union.

Such prayer is called *the prayer of the mind* when it is uttered by an attentive mind with the sympathy of the heart. It is called *the prayer of the heart* when it is uttered with a united mind and heart, when the mind descends into the heart and from its depths utters the words of prayer. It is called *the prayer of the soul* when it is uttered with the entire soul, together with the participation of the body. This prayer is offered by the complete man, when man's entire being becomes, as it were, a single mouth that utters prayer.

In their writings, the Holy Fathers often call these three forms of prayer by a single name, but sometimes they distinguish them. So St Gregory of Sinai said, "Constantly cry out with the mind or the soul." But today, when instruction from living mouths concerning the prayer of the mind, heart, and soul has disastrously diminished, it is very useful to know the differences between them. In some ascetics, the prayer of the mind is more active, in others—the prayer of the heart or the prayer of the soul, depending on the gifts given to each by the Provider of all blessings (both natural and inherent to a state of grace).

Sometimes, a monk utters first one kind of prayer and then another. Such prayer is often accompanied by tears. Then, man partially understands what blessed dispassion is. He begins to feel purity, and from this purity comes a living fear of God that swallows up the crudity of his flesh through a terrifying, previously unknown horror, which is the palpable sense of standing before God. The Christian enters a new life and a new labor, appropriate to his renewed spiritual state. The previous milk is no longer nourishing for him. All his labors flow into a single stream of blessed, constant repentance.

Let those who know understand: I have said what is most necessary for the salvation of the soul. These words are of greatest importance for the true practitioner, though my words are simple. Such a state was expressed by Pimen the Great in answer to the question: "How should an attentive hesychast behave?"

"He should behave as a man who has fallen into a swamp up to his neck, whose neck has a weight pulling it down, and who cries out to God: save me!"[167] Profound sorrow, the weeping of the human spirit inspired to tears by the Spirit of God, is the inseparable fellow-traveler of prayer of the heart. The prayer of the soul is accompanied by a spiritual sense of fear of God, reverence, and compunction. In perfect Christians, both of these sensations eventually transform into love. But even these perceptions belong to the spiritual realm. They are gifts of God, given in their own proper time, impossible to be acquired even by the ascetic if he tries to take them for himself, even if his labor is correct. The prayer of the heart acts most effectively with the invocation of the name of the Lord Jesus. Those who have received the prayer of the heart pray with the soul when they recite the rule and the Psalms.

The prayer of the mind, heart, and soul is commanded by God both in the Old and the New Testaments. "You shall love the Lord your God with all your heart, with all your soul, with all your mind, and with all your strength. This is the first commandment" (Mark 12:30, citing Deut 6:5). Obviously, the fulfillment of the greatest, most exalted commandment is impossible without prayer of the mind, heart, and soul, by which the praying man separates himself from all creation and aspires toward God with his entire being. When in this state of aspiration toward God, the fragmented parts of the ascetic's self suddenly unite, and he sees himself healed by the touch of God. The mind, heart, soul, and body, riven from each by sin, come together in the Lord. Since this union occurs in the Lord and is effected by the Lord, it is simultaneously the union of man with himself and with the Lord. After this union, or at the same time as this union, spiritual gifts are given. Or, rather, the union itself is a gift of the Spirit.

The first spiritual gift produced by the miraculous union is the peace of Christ.[168] After the peace of Christ comes the entire host of Christ's gifts and the fruits of the Holy Spirit, which the apostle lists in the following manner: "Love, joy, peace, longsuffering, kindness, goodness, faithfulness, gentleness, self-control" (Gal 5:22–23). The prayer of a healed, united ascetic who is at peace with himself is devoid of thoughts and demonic fantasies. The fiery sword of the fallen cherubim ceases to act within him. The blood, restrained by power from on high, ceases to be agitated. This sea becomes calm, and the blowing of winds—the fantasies of the demons—has no more effect on it. Prayer that is devoid of thoughts and fantasies is called pure, "un-wandering" prayer.[169] When the ascetic has acquired pure prayer, he begins to devote much time to its practice, often not even noticing this. His entire life, his entire activity is transformed into prayer. The quality of such prayer, as the Fathers say, inevitably leads to quantity. Prayer, once it has encompassed man, gradually changes him, making him spiritual from the union with the Holy Spirit, as the Apostle Paul said, "He who is joined to the Lord is one spirit with Him" (1 Cor 6:17). To this confidant of the Spirit, the mysteries of Christianity are revealed.

The grace-filled world of Christ, into which the ascetic is led by pure prayer, is completely different from a naturally calm, pleasant disposition in man. When this world has come to rest in the heart, it binds all disturbing movement of passions; it removes fear not by removing that which terrifies but through a blessed courage in Christ that does not fear terrifying things. As the Lord said, "Peace I leave with you, My peace I give to you; not as the world gives do I give to you. Let not your heart be troubled, neither let it be afraid" (John 14:27). This peace of Christ is so spiritually powerful that it can destroy every earthly sorrow, every assault of enemies. This power is taken from Christ Himself: "In Me you may have peace. In the world you will have tribulation; but be of good cheer, I have overcome the world" (John 16:33). Called to the ascetic by the prayer of the heart, Christ dispenses spiritual power into the praying heart. This power is called the peace of Christ. It is unattainable for the mind, inexpressible by words, unattainably attained only by blessed experience. "The peace of God, which surpasses all understanding, will guard your hearts and minds through Christ Jesus" (Phil 4:7).

This is the power of the peace of Christ. It surpasses all understanding. This means that it is beyond the comprehension of created minds, both human and angelic (whether holy or fallen). It, as the action of God, in a lordly and divine fashion begins to govern the thoughts and perceptions of the heart. When the peace of Christ appears, all demonic thoughts flee, while human thoughts, together with the heart, submit to its all-holy direction and guidance. From this moment, this peace becomes their king and preserves them, keeping them safe from sin in Christ Jesus. This means that the peace of Christ governs the thoughts by showing them the teachings of the Gospel, illuminating the mind with mystical interpretations of this teaching, while feeding the heart with "daily bread" from heaven that gives life to all who commune of it (see John 6:33).

This holy peace, in its abundant action, brings stillness to the mind and gives a blessed taste of itself to the soul and the body. Then all movement of the blood ceases (in the sense of its influence on the state of the soul); then the silence is great. A certain subtle coolness flows over the person, and he hears mystical instruction. The Christian, held and preserved by holy peace, becomes unapproachable for enemies. He is attached to the sweetness of Christ's peace and, drunk on it, forgets not only the pleasures of sin, but all earthly pleasures, both bodily and emotional.

What a healing draught! What divine medicine! What blessed drunkenness! Truly, what other beginning can there be for the renewal of man, except in this grace-filled sense of peace, by which all the constituent parts of man, fragmented by sin, unite again into one? Without this preliminary gift, without this union of man with himself, can man be capable of any other spiritual, divine state produced by the all-good Holy Spirit? Can a broken vessel hold anything before it is repaired? This sensation of peace in Christ, as all gifts of grace in general, begins to manifest itself first of all during prayer, since this action is the one that best prepares the ascetic, through reverence and attention, to accept the divine peace. Subsequently, having become, as it were, the property of the Christian, this peace constantly accompanies him, constantly arousing him to the prayer offered in the inner room. During prayer, it reveals all spiritual enemies as though from a distance, deflecting and defeating them with its all-powerful right hand.

The holy prophet Isaiah described the greatness of the peace of Christ, its appearance in the chosen nation of God (the New Israel, the Christians), its power to heal the soul, its power to uphold the health of the soul, and the source and giving of this gift by the God-Man in the following prophecy concerning the incarnate Lord: "His name will be called the Angel of Great Counsel, for I shall [give] peace [unto] the rulers [that is, spiritually advanced Christians who have defeated the passions and so are properly called rulers], peace and health by Him. Great shall be His government, and of His peace there is no end. His peace shall be upon the throne of David and over His kingdom, to order and establish it with righteousness and judgment, from that time forward and unto ages of ages. The zeal of the Lord of hosts shall perform this" (Isa 9:5–6).[170] "In His days shall righteousness flourish, and abundance of peace" (Ps 71:7). "The Lord shall bless His people with peace" (Ps 28:11). "The meek shall inherit the earth, and shall be refreshed in the multitude of peace" (Ps 36:11).

As the Holy Spirit declares the Son (see John 16:14) so the action of the Holy Spirit in man, through the peace of Christ, declares that the thoughts of man have entered the all-holy domain of divine righteousness and truth, devoid of error and self-delusion. Only then can man say that his heart has accepted the Gospel: "Mercy and truth are met together, justice and peace have kissed each other" (Ps 84:11). On the other hand, any confusion, even the most refined, no matter how it tries to hide behind self-justification, is a sure sign that the ascetic has left the narrow way of Christ for the wide and easy path to perdition.[171]

Do not condemn an impious man; do not even condemn a confirmed villain, for "to his own master he stands or falls" (Rom 14:4). Do not come to hate the one who slanders you or insults you or robs you. Do not even hate your murderer. They crucify you to the right of the Lord, by the inconceivable dispensation of God's judgments, so that you, with heart-felt understanding and conviction, can say in your prayer to the Lord: "I accept this as what I deserve, according to my deeds. But as for You, O Lord, remember me in Your kingdom." Come to understand that the sufferings sent to you are for your well-being. They are the proof of God's election. Therefore, pray ardently for your benefactors, through whom you receive such gifts, by whose hands you are torn away from the world and become dead to it, on whose hands you are raised up to God.

You must feel compassion for them in equal measure to the compassion that God feels when He sees miserable humanity drowning in sin. God sent His own Son as a Sacrifice to atone for man's enmity against the Creator, knowing that this same creation will, in its majority, mock the Sacrifice and disdain it. Such mercy that rises to love for enemies, that expresses itself in prayers for enemies, leads the ascetic to an experiential knowledge of the truth. The truth is the word of God, the Gospel. The Truth is Christ. Knowledge of the truth leads the soul to divine righteousness, having first purged the soul of the fallen and sin-defiled righteousness of human nature. The peace of Christ is a witness that divine righteousness has entered the soul. The peace of Christ makes man the temple and the priest of the living God: "And His place hath been at Salem [that is, peace], and His tabernacle in Zion. There brake He the power of the bow, the shield, and the sword, and the battle" (Ps 75:3–4).

The greatest teachers of monastic life have been witnesses of this blessed union of man with himself that occurs after the coming of the peace of Christ to his soul. St John of the Ladder said, "*I cried with my whole heart*, that is, with my body, soul, and spirit, *for where are [these] two* united, there is also God in their midst."[172] St Isaiah the Solitary said,

> If you, like the wise virgins, know that your vessel is filled with oil and you can enter the bridal chamber and do not have to remain outside; if you sense that your spirit, soul, and body have blamelessly united and stood undefiled in the day of our Lord Jesus Christ; if the conscience does not accuse or condemn you; if you have become a child, according to the word of the Saviour, who said, "Let the little children come to Me, and do not forbid them; for of such is the kingdom of heaven," (Matthew 19:14)—then truly you have become the bride of Christ. The Holy Spirit has descended on you, though you are still in the body.[173]

St Isaac the Syrian said, "Do not compare those who do miracles, signs, and wonders in the world with those who practice silence in their souls. You must come to love the inaction of stillness more than feeding the hungry in the world and converting the many pagans to the worship of God. It is better for you to release yourself from the bondage to sin than to free slaves from their bondage. It is better for you to reconcile with your soul, bringing the trinity found within you—that is, the body, soul, and spirit—into harmony, than to bring those of different opinions into agreement."[174]

Holy peace is the stillness of mind that is produced by the fulfillment of the commandments of the Gospel, spoken of by St Isaac the Syrian in his 55th

Homily. It was also perceived by Saints Gregory the Theologian and Basil the Great, and when they sensed it, they immediately left for the desert. There, working on their inner man and finally forming him in the image offered by the Gospel, they were granted mystical visions of the Spirit. It is obvious that the stillness of the mind, or the destruction of absentmindedness, is acquired by the mind after its union with the soul. Without this union, it cannot restrain itself from wandering. When the mind, through the action of divine grace, unites with the heart, then it receives prayerful power, spoken of by St Gregory of Sinai: "If Moses did not accept from God the staff of power, then he would not have defeated Pharaoh and Egypt with it. The same is true of the mind. If it will not have in its hand the power of prayer, it will not be able to destroy death and the hosts of enemies."[175]

The spiritual instructions of St Seraphim of Sarov are especially vivid and simple in their description of the teaching concerning the peace of Christ. Everything he said, he took from his own heart-felt, holy experience: "When the mind and the heart unite in prayer and when the thoughts of the soul cease to wander, then the heart becomes warm with spiritual warmth, in which the light of Christ can shine out, filling the inner man entirely with peace and joy."[176]

There is nothing better than the peace of Christ, which ends the warfare against the spirits of the air and the earth. A man's soul becomes wise when the man submerges his mind within himself and practices prayer within his heart. Then the grace of God overshadows him and he is at peace, and even in a state surpassing peace. He is at peace with his conscience. His state surpasses peace also, for the mind contemplates the grace of the Holy Spirit within itself, according to the word of God: "His place hath been in Salem [that is, peace]" (Ps 75:3).

When someone is in such a peaceful disposition, it is as if he eats spiritual nourishment with a spoon. When man comes to such a peaceful disposition, then he can shine the light of knowledge on others. This peace was left by the Lord Jesus Christ as a priceless treasure to His disciples, when He said before his death: "Peace I leave with you, My peace I give to you" (John 14:27). We must concentrate all our strength, desires, and actions to the acquisition of the peace of God, and with the Church, we must constantly cry out: O Lord, Our God! Give us peace!

In every way possible, we must try to preserve this peace of the soul and not be disturbed by the insults of others. We must try to restrain anger and protect the mind and heart from impure thoughts through vigilance. We must endure offenses from others with indifference and train the spirit to believe that all their insults were not meant for us, but for somebody we do not even know. Such a practice can give calm to the heart of man and make him a dwelling place of God Himself.

> We can see how to defeat anger in the life of Paisius the Great. He asked the Lord Jesus Christ, Who appeared to him, to release him from anger. But Christ answered him, "If you want to defeat anger and wrath together, desire nothing, hate no one, humiliate no one."[177] To preserve peace of soul, you must keep despair at bay and try to preserve a joyful disposition, not a sorrowful one. As the wise Sirach said, "For sorrow has destroyed many, and there is no profit in it" (Sirach 30:23). To preserve peace of soul, you must in every way avoid condemnation of others. By your lack of judgment and your silence, you will preserve spiritual peace. When a man is in such a state, he receives divine revelations.[178]

"For the kingdom of God is not eating and drinking, but righteousness and peace and joy in the Holy Spirit. For he who serves Christ in these things is acceptable to God" (Rom 14:17–18).

The peace of Christ is the source of constant grace-filled, spiritual prayer of the mind, heart, soul, uttered by the whole man through the Holy Spirit. The peace of Christ is a constant source of Christ's grace-filled humility, surpassing the mind of man. It would not be a mistake to call such prayer "grace-filled humility," for grace-filled humility is constant prayer. However, we admit that it is necessary to further explain the intimate union of prayer with humility.

What is humility? Abba Dorotheos said, "Humility is divine and unattainable." Is this not the same as "the peace of God, which surpasses all understanding" (Philippians 4:7)? Humility is the mystical action of the divine peace of God, attained only by blessed experience. The Lord Himself teaches us to define humility thus. "Come to Me, all you who labor and are heavy laden, and I will give you rest. Take My yoke upon you and learn from Me, for I am gentle and lowly in heart, and you will find rest for your souls" (Matt 11:28–29). St John of the Ladder, explaining these words of the Saviour, wrote as though from the mouth of the Saviour Himself, "You must learn not from an angel or from a man or from a book but from Me, that is, from My abiding in you, from my illumination and action within you, for I am gentle and lowly in heart and thought, and you will find peace from warfare and rest from passionate thoughts in your souls."[179]

This teaching is a living teaching, filled with grace and experience. Later, in the section concerning humility, St John, having listed the various signs of humility that can be known and understood not only by the one who has such a treasure, but by his neighbors and his friends in the Lord, adds the following: "There are signs that one has obtained this great treasure of humility in his soul (by which he can come to know that he has become a possessor of humility), greater than the ones we have already listed. For all those, except for this one, can be visible to others. You can come to know that you possess true humility only by the multitude of unutterable light and by the indescribable joy of your prayer."

St Isaac the Syrian, when asked about the hallmarks of humility, answered,

> Pride of the soul is its destruction, forcing it to distraction through fantasy and encouraging it to take wing in the clouds of its own thoughts, on which it can wander over all creation. On the contrary, humility gathers the soul in silence. Through humility, the soul focuses in on itself. As the soul is unknown and invisible to the physical eyes, so the humble-minded man is not recognized, though he be in a crowd of people. As the soul is hidden inside the body from the eyes of men and from association with men, so the truly humble-minded man not only does not wish to be seen and understood by men—for he has rejected the world—but he even desires to hide from himself, plunging deep into himself, living and abiding in stillness, completely forgetting his previous thoughts and emotions, becoming as though non-existent, even unknown to his own soul. As much as such a man is hidden, covered, and separated from the world, so much does he completely abide in his Lord.[180]

What is this state, if not the state produced by the grace-filled prayer of the mind, heart, and soul? Can one abide in the Lord other than through the union of prayer? In the same homily, St Isaac also answered the question, "What is prayer?" He said, "Prayer is the abolition and distancing of thoughts from all that is worldly. It is a heart completely turned, toward the hoped-for future."

Thus, are not true prayer and true humility—in their actions and consequences—the same? Prayer is the mother of virtues, the door to all spiritual gifts. Attentive prayer, zealously practiced with endurance and self-coercion, helps one find both the prayer of grace and the humility of grace. Their giver is the Holy Spirit; their giver is Christ. Is it not natural for them to be similar to each other when they have one source? How can such a source fail to be the source of all virtues in general, this wondrous harmony between prayer and humility? They appear suddenly in the Christian whose inner room has been closed for attentive weeping, whose eyes have been shut to the world. Christ Himself enters into such an inner room. "Prayer is the mother of virtues," said St Mark the Ascetic. "It gives birth to them by union with Christ."[181] St John of the Ladder called prayer the mother of virtues and humility the destroyer of passions.[182]

We must further explain and illustrate the union of the mind, soul, and body for those who have not experienced it, so that they can come to know it when it, by God's mercy, begins to be revealed in them. This union is completely obvious, completely perceptible, not some kind of fantastic reverie or something imagined by delusional self-conceit. It can be somewhat explained by contrasting it with the opposite spiritual state, the one that is typical for most of us. This opposite state is the fragmentation of the mind, soul, and body, their lack of harmony in actions with, even direct opposition to, each other. This is the bitter consequence of the fall of our ancestors.[183]

Who does not see this disharmony within himself? Who does not sense this inner warfare and the torture that comes of it? Who does not admit this warfare, this torture, often unbearable, to be our sickness, a sign, a convincing proof of our fall? Our mind prays or we are in a pious frame of mind, but various sinful desires and passions in the heart and the body forcefully drag the mind from its exercise in prayer, for the most part successfully! The very senses of the body, especially vision and hearing, oppose the mind. By giving it constant impressions of the physical world, they lead it to diversion and distraction. When, according to the indescribable mercy of God, the mind begins to unite in prayer with the heart and soul, then the soul—at first gradually and then completely—begins to strive, together with the mind, toward prayer.

Finally, our own perishable body begins also to strive toward prayer, for it was created with an innate desire for God, a desire that was perverted after the Fall into degrading desires. Then the bodily senses become still—the eyes look but don't see; the ears listen but do not hear.[184] Then prayer envelops the whole man. His hands, feet, fingers—indescribably, but obviously and palpably—participate in prayer and are filled with power inexpressible with words. Man, finding himself in a state of Christ's peace and in prayer, becomes unreachable for any sinful thought. This is the same man for whom any battle with sin resulted in immediate defeat.

Now, the soul perceives the approach of the enemy, but the power of prayer that fills it does not allow the enemy to come near and defile the temple of

God. The praying ascetic knows that the enemy is coming, but he does not know with what thought or what kind of sin the enemy approaches. As St John of the Ladder said, "'I did not know the crafty man that turned away from me' (Psalm 100:4), not how he approached, nor why he came, nor how he left. But in such situations, I remain without any perception, for I am united with God now and forever."[185] When the mind is united with the soul, it is very easy to remember God and especially to pray the Jesus Prayer. During this prayer, the bodily senses can remain in complete inaction, and such inaction is conducive to the most profound attentiveness and all the good consequences arising from it.

Reading the Psalms and other prayers is not only possible, but necessary during this union, since the union inspires attentiveness. But since reading the Psalms offers various thoughts to the mind, the mind cannot be as devoid of distraction as with a single, short prayer. One must also strive to unite the mind with the soul during the reading of the Holy Scriptures and the writings of the Fathers. Reading in such a way will be much more fruitful. St John of the Ladder said, "It is required of the mind that during every prayer (and later during any reading that nourishes prayer and that is an offshoot of prayer and the practice of the mind) be an expression of that power that was given to the mind by God. This is why we must be attentive."[186]

Brother! If you have not yet sensed the union of mind, soul, and body, then practice attentive prayer, uniting the prayer of the lips—sometimes spoken, sometimes whispered—with the mind. Act according to the commandments of the Gospel, battling the passions with endurance and long-suffering, never slipping into despair or hopelessness when you are defeated by sinful thoughts or emotions. At the same time, do not allow yourself to be defeated easily. Having fallen down, stand up. If you fall again, stand up again, until you learn how to walk without tripping. The cup of infirmity has its uses; until a proper time, the providence of God allows it, so that the ascetic can be purified of pride, anger, remembrance of evil, condemnation of others, arrogance, and vanity. It is especially important to recognize the action of vanity within yourself and to rein it in. While it acts in you, you will not be able to enter the domain of the spiritual life, for price of entrance is a lack of passionate attachments, which is a gift received after the coming of the peace of Christ.

If you have sensed that your mind has united with the soul and body, that you are no longer fragmented by sin, that you are a united and whole being, that the holy peace of Christ has descended upon you, then preserve this gift of God with all your strength. Let your most important work be prayer and reading of holy books. Let all other work have secondary importance, and remain cold to all the works of the world. Better yet, avoid them outright. This holy peace, this blowing of the Holy Spirit, is subtle, and it immediately departs from the soul that behaves carelessly in His presence, that violates reverence, that destroys faithfulness through falling back into sin, that allows itself to grow slothful. Together with the peace of Christ, the prayer of grace also departs from such an unworthy soul, and the passions break into the soul like ravenous beasts and begin to tear apart the self-betrayed sacrifice that has been abandoned to itself by God (see Ps 103:20–21).

If you eat too much, and especially if you drink too much, holy peace will cease to act within you. If you become angry, you will lose peace for a long time. If you allow yourself to be brazen, it will cease. If you come to love something worldly, if you become infected with a passionate attachment to some thing, to some work of your own hands, or especially if you are infected with an inclination of the heart toward another person, holy peace will immediately leave you. If you allow yourself the sweetness of carnal thoughts, it will leave you for a very, very long time, since peace cannot bear any sinful foulness, especially the passions of the flesh or vanity. You will seek it, but you will not find it.

You will weep at its loss, but it will pay no attention to your weeping, so that you will learn to give the gift of God its proper reverence. Then you will learn to preserve it with the necessary diligence and piety. Come to hate everything that drags you down into distraction, into sin. Crucify yourself on the cross of the commandments of the Gospel, and constantly keep yourself crucified on it. Bravely and boldly reject all sinful thoughts and desires. Cut off all earthly cares; take care only to animate the Gospel within yourself through zealous fulfillment of all the commandments. During prayer, crucify yourself again, crucify yourself on the cross of prayer. Divert all memories from your mind, even the most important ones, all that comes to you during prayer. Disdain them.

Do not theologize, and do not be distracted into the contemplation of brilliant, new, and wonderful thoughts if they suddenly begin to arise in you. The holy silence that descends on the mind during the prayer that perceives God's greatness—this declares God more exaltedly and powerfully than any word. "If you truly pray, then you are a theologian."[187] You have a great treasure! The invisible thieves see this and guess at its price by the loss of their influence over you.[188] They hunger to steal this gift of God from you! They are skilled, rich in both the experience and inventiveness of evil. Be attentive and careful. Develop and preserve the sense of repentance within yourself. Do not admire your own state; instead, look at it as a means to the acquisition of true repentance. Spiritual poverty will preserve the gift of grace within you, and it will encircle you against all the wiles and delusions of the enemy: "a contrite and humble heart God shall not despise" (Ps 50:19). God will not abandon such a heart to the power of the enemy. He will not deprive it of salvation and grace. Amen.

CHAPTER 17

The Jesus Prayer

As I begin to speak of the Jesus Prayer,[189] I call to the aid of my feeble mind the all-good and almighty Jesus. As I begin to speak of the Jesus Prayer, I remember the words of the righteous Simeon concerning the Lord: "Behold, this Child is destined for the fall and rising of many in Israel, and for a sign which will be spoken against" (Luke 2:34). The Lord is the only true sign, a "sign which will be spoken against," a subject of disagreement and argument between those who know him and those who do not. So also the prayer in His all-holy name, being, in the fullest sense, a great and wondrous sign, has become, for some time, a subject of disagreement and argument between those who practice such prayer and those who do not. A certain father fairly remarked that only those who do not know this way of praying reject it. They reject it by prejudice and because of incorrect ideas concerning it.[190]

Paying no attention to the announcements of prejudice and ignorance, with hope in the help and mercy of God, we offer to our beloved fathers and brothers our own small word on the Jesus Prayer, on the basis of the Holy Scriptures, on the basis of the tradition of the Church, on the basis of the writings of the Holy Fathers, who wrote in detail concerning this all-holy and all-powerful prayer. "Let the lying lips be put to silence which disdainfully, and scornfully, speak iniquity against the righteous" and His wondrous name "disdainfully," with a profound ignorance and scorn of the miracles of God. "O Lord, how plentiful is the abundance of Thy goodness, which Thou hast laid up for them that fear Thee, and that Thou hast prepared for them that put their trust in Thee, before the sons of men!" (Ps 30:19–20). "Some put their trust in chariots, and some in horses"—that is, their own vain and carnal mindset—"but we," with the simplicity and faith of children, "will call upon the name of the Lord our God" (Ps 19:8).

The Jesus Prayer is uttered thus: *Lord Jesus Christ, Son of God, have mercy on me, a sinner*. Originally it lacked the final words: a sinner. This word was added to the other words of the prayer later. This word, containing in itself the acknowledgment and confession of sinfulness, is appropriate for us and pleasing to God, who commanded that we cry out in prayer to Him from an acknowledgment and confession of our own sinfulness.[191] For beginners, as a condescension to their weakness, the fathers allowed the prayer to be divided into two halves. At first, you can say: *Lord Jesus Christ, have mercy on me a sinner*; then later you can say: *Son of God, have mercy on me a sinner*. However, this is merely a condescension, not a command or rule that is required to be followed. It is much better to constantly practice a single, whole prayer, not entertaining or distracting the mind with changes or with a desire for change. Whoever finds such change necessary, in his weakness, should not allow these changes to be frequent. For example, you can practice the first half of the prayer before lunch, the second after lunch. While forbidding frequent changes, St Gregory of Sinai said, "Those trees that are frequently replanted do not have deep roots."[192]

Praying by the Jesus Prayer is a divine institution. It was instituted not through a prophet, not by the words of an apostle, not through the mediation of an angel, but it was established by the Son of God and God Himself. After the Mystical Supper, among His many other exalted, parting commands and testaments, the Lord Jesus Christ established the prayer in His name. He gave us this way of praying as a new, unusual, priceless gift. The apostles, at least partially, already knew the power of Jesus's name. They healed incurable diseases by its power, subjected the demons to their authority, defeating, binding, casting them out. The Lord commanded them to use this powerful, wondrous name, promising that it would be especially effective in prayer. "Whatever you ask in My name, that I will do, that the Father may be glorified in the Son. If you ask anything in My name, I will do it" (John 14:13–14). "Most assuredly, I say to you, whatever you ask the Father in My name He will give you. Until now you have asked nothing in My name. Ask, and you will receive, that your joy may be full" (John 16:23–24).

Oh, what a gift! It is the pledge of unending, boundless good things! It has flowed from the lips of the unlimited God, who assumed the limitations of man, who took on a human name—*Saviour*.[193] The name seems limited in appearance, but it expresses the unlimited God, taking from Him its unlimited, divine dignity, its divine qualities and power. O Giver of this priceless, incorruptible gift! How can we, worthless, perishable sinners, accept such a gift? Neither our hands, nor our mind, nor our heart can hold such a gift. You must teach us to know, as much as possible, the greatness of the gift, its significance, the way to accept it, the way to practice it. Otherwise, we will approach the gift sinfully, and we will be subjected to punishments for our ignorance and brazenness. Teach us, so that through our correct understanding and practice of this gift, we may receive from You other gifts, promised by You, known only to You.

In the Gospels, Acts, and Epistles, we see the apostles' unlimited faith in the name of the Lord Jesus and their unlimited reverence for it. By the name of Jesus Christ, they performed astounding miracles. There is no specific event that can teach us exactly how they practiced the prayer of the name of Jesus, but they practiced it constantly. How could they not, when this prayer was given and commanded them by the Lord Himself, when the command was strengthened by a second repetition and confirmation? If the Scriptures remain silent about the specifics of the prayer, then it does so only because this prayer was generally accepted and did not require a special inclusion in the Scriptures because it was universally known and practiced. This fact—of the universality of its practice—is seen clearly in the rule of the Church that replaces all prayer rules for illiterate people with the prayer of Jesus.[194]

The antiquity of this rule is doubtless. Later, it was added to, because more prayers were written in the Church. St Basil the Great wrote a rule of prayer for his flock (which is why some believe that he was the originator of the idea of a "prayer rule"). However, it was not an invention or establishment of the great saint. He merely replaced an oral tradition with a written one, in the same way that he wrote down the liturgy that had existed in Caesarea from the time of the apostles but was not written down, being passed down orally to preserve the holy liturgy from the blasphemy of the pagans.

The monastic prayer rule is most properly expressed by the Jesus Prayer. In such a form it was given generally for all monks of the Orthodox Church. In this form it was given by an angel to St Pachomius the Great for his coenobitic monks. This saint lived in the fourth century; in the rule, the angel spoke of the Jesus Prayer as equally well-known and universally practiced as the Lord's prayer, the fiftieth Psalm, and the Symbol of Faith. St Anthony the Great, a father of the late third, early fourth century, commanded his monks to zealously practice the Jesus Prayer, speaking of it as a prayer that did not require any explanation. The interpretations and explanations of this prayer only began to appear later, because living knowledge concerning it had faded away with time. The Fathers of the thirteenth and fourteenth centuries wrote down a detailed teaching concerning the Jesus Prayer, because at that time its practice had begun to be lost even among monastics.

In the historical records of the Early Church that have survived to our time, the practice of the Jesus Prayer is not mentioned on its own, but only in passing, while describing some other circumstances. Thus, in the life of St Ignatius of Antioch, who was martyred in Rome under the emperor Trajan, we read the following:

> When he was being led to the coliseum to be eaten by beasts, he constantly had on his lips the name of Jesus Christ. The ungodly asked him why he constantly called this name to mind. The saint answered that he, having the name of Jesus Christ inscribed in his heart, only confessed with his lips the One Whom he bore within his heart always. After the saint was eaten by the beasts, his heart was left whole, by God's providence, among his bones. The unfaithful, having found his remains and remembered his words, cut his heart in two, desiring to know if the saint had lied or not. They saw within, on both halves of the heart, the name "Jesus Christ" in gold letters. Thus, the martyr Ignatius was in name and deed a "God-bearer," for he always bore in his heart Christ God Himself, inscribed in his heart by the remembrance of God in his mind, as with a stylus.

The Godbearer was a disciple of the holy apostle and evangelist John the Theologian, and he was found worthy of seeing the Lord Jesus Christ in childhood.

This is that blessed child, whom the Lord placed among the apostles who were arguing about primacy. Christ embraced him and said, "Assuredly, I say to you, unless you are converted and become as little children, you will by no means enter the kingdom of heaven. Therefore whoever humbles himself as this little child is the greatest in the kingdom of heaven" (Matt 18:3–4). Of course, St Ignatius was taught the Jesus Prayer by the holy evangelist, and he practiced it during the blossoming of Christianity, like all other Christians. At that time, all Christians were trained in the practice of the Jesus Prayer, first of all because of the great importance of the prayer, secondly because of the paucity and expensiveness of handwritten books and general illiteracy (the majority of the apostles were illiterate). Finally, it was easily taught and it was effective and powerful. "The name of the Son of God," said the angel to Hermas in the *Shepherd*, "is great and immeasurable. It holds the entire world." Having heard these words, Hermas asked the angel, "If all of creation is held by the Son of God, does He also support those who are called by Him, who bear His name and walk in His commandments?" The angel answered, "He upholds all those who bear His name in their heart. He Himself serves as their foundation and lovingly sustains them, because they are not ashamed to bear His name."

In church history, he read the following account:

A man named Neocorus, a Carthaginian, was a soldier in a Roman cohort that guarded Jerusalem at the time of our Lord Jesus Christ's Passion for the redemption of the human race. Seeing the miracles that occurred at the death and resurrection of the Lord, Neocorus believed in Him and was baptized by the apostles. After he finished his military service, Neocorus returned to Carthage and shared the treasure of faith with his entire family. Among those who accepted Christianity was a certain Callistratus, a grandson of Neocorus. Callistratus, having reached the necessary age, also became a solider. His cohort was filled exclusively with pagans. They noticed that Callistratus did not worship the idols and that at night, in solitude, he prayed for a long time. Once, they listened to his prayer and, having heard that he constantly repeated the name of the Lord Jesus Christ, they denounced him to their commander. Saint Callistratus, confessing Jesus in solitude and in the darkness of night, came to confess him also in the light of day, before all the people. He sealed his confession of Christ with his own blood.[195]

St Hesychius of Jerusalem, a writer of the fifth century, already then complained that the practice of the Jesus Prayer had fallen into decline among the monastics. This decline, with the passage of time, became worse and worse, and for this reason the Holy Fathers tried to uphold the practice by writing about it. One of the last writers of our time who instructed us in this prayer was St Seraphim of Sarov. He himself did not write instructions; they were written from his words by one of his monks. All of St Seraphim's words are anointed by grace. At the present time, the practice of the Jesus Prayer is almost completely lost among monastics. St Hesychius says that the reason for this abandonment is sloth. We must admit that he was right.

The grace-filled power of the Jesus Prayer is found in the very divine name of the God-Man, our Lord Jesus Christ. Though the many proofs from Holy Scripture prove to us the greatness of the name of God, it was especially clearly explained to the Sanhedrin by the Apostle Peter, when the Sanhedrin interrogated the apostle about the authority or power that he used to heal the man lame from birth: "Then Peter, filled with the Holy Spirit, said to them, 'Rulers of the people and elders of Israel: If we this day are judged for a good deed done to a helpless man, by what means he has been made well, let it be known to you all, and to all the people of Israel, that by the name of Jesus Christ of Nazareth, whom you crucified, whom God raised from the dead, by Him this man stands here before you whole. This is the "stone which was rejected by you builders, which has become the chief cornerstone." Nor is there salvation in any other, for there is no other name under heaven given among men by which we must be saved'" (Acts 4:8–12).

This is a witness of the Holy Spirit Himself. The mouth, tongue, and voice of the apostle were merely His instruments. Another instrument of the Holy Spirit, the apostle to the nations, said something similar: "For whoever calls on the name of the Lord shall be saved" (Rom 10:13). "Therefore God also has highly exalted Him and given Him the name which is above every name, that at the name of Jesus every knee should bow, of those in heaven, and of those on earth, and of those under the earth" (Phil 2:9–10).

David, who foresaw the distant future, the forefather of Jesus according to the flesh, declared the greatness of the name of Jesus, having picturesquely described the action of this name, warfare against sin with its help, its power to free the praying man from the bondage of passions and demons, and the grace-filled triumph of those who secure victory by the name of Jesus. Let us listen to the divinely inspired David! With unusual vividness, describing the future founding of the spiritual kingdom of Christ on earth in a thousand years, the Prophet-King said that the dominion of the God-Man will stretch "from sea to sea, and from the rivers unto the world's end. . . . Yea, all the kings of the earth shall fall down before Him, all nations shall do Him service . . . His Name shall be blessed for ever; His Name shall abide before the sun; and all the tribes of the earth shall be blessed in Him; all the nations shall bless Him. And blessed be the Name of His glory for ever, and for ever and ever, and all the earth shall be filled with His glory" (Ps 71:8, 11, 17–19).

The great service of prayer that leads man to the most intimate communion with God appeared on the earth, in the most expansive way possible, from the time of man's reconciliation with God through the God-Man. This service encompassed the entire cosmos. It was established in cities and villages; it flowered in the wild, uninhabitable desert places; it shone forth in dark caves, in crevices, in abysses on the summits of mountains, in the depths of sleepy forests. In this service of prayer, the name of the God-Man received the most important significance, for it is the name of the Saviour of mankind, the Creator of mankind and angels, being the name of the Incarnate God, the Victor over the rebellious slaves and creations—the demons. "The [demons] shall kneel before Him, and His enemies [the fallen angels] shall lick the dust" (Ps 71:9). "O Lord, our Lord, how wonderful is Thy Name in all the world; for Thy majesty is lifted high above the heavens! Out of the mouth of babes and sucklings hast Thou perfected praise, because of Thine enemies, to destroy the enemy, and the avenger" (Ps 8:2–3).

How true! The greatness of the name of Jesus surpasses the understanding of the creatures of heaven and earth. But this understanding is inexplicably accepted by those with child-like simplicity and faith. With the same unselfish disposition, we must also approach the Jesus Prayer and continue practicing it. Constancy and diligence in this prayer must be like a constant striving of an infant for the mother's breast. Then, praying the name of Jesus can bring us total success, the invisible enemies can be destroyed, and the "enemy and the avenger" can be finally overcome. The enemy is called an "avenger" because occasionally (not constantly) he tries, after prayer, to steal everything that was acquired during the time of prayer.[196] For a convincing victory, constant prayer and unending vigil over oneself are needed.

Because of this significance of the Jesus Prayer, David invites all Christians to practice this prayer. "Praise the Lord, ye servants; O praise the Name of the Lord. Blessed be the Name of the Lord, from this time forth and for ever-more. From the rising up of the sun, unto the going down of the same, the Lord's Name is praised" (Ps 112:1–3). "Bring unto the Lord the glory due unto His Name; worship the Lord in His holy court" (Ps 28:2). Pray in such a way that your prayers reveal the majesty of the name of Jesus, and you, with His power, may enter into the uncreated temple of the heart to worship in spirit and truth. Pray diligently and constantly; pray in fear and trembling before the majesty of the name of Jesus, and let those who know Your name by blessed experience "put their trust in Thee," the almighty and all-good Jesus, "for Thou, Lord, hast never forsaken them that seek Thee" (Ps 9:11). Only the one who is poor in spirit, who constantly strives toward the Lord through prayer by means of the constant sense of his poverty of spirit, is capable of reveal-ing within himself the greatness of the name of Jesus. "O let not the meek be turned away" from standing before Thee in prayer, but let him bring his prayer completely to God, not stolen away by distraction, "the poor and needy shall praise Thy name" (Ps 73:21).

"Blessed is the man whose hope is in the Name of the Lord, and hath not had regard unto vanities and lying follies" (Ps 39:5). During his prayer, he will pay no attention to the delusive action of vain cares and passionate attachments that seek to defile and corrupt prayer. The night is especially good for the practice of the Jesus Prayer, for it is silent and dark. At night, the great ascetic of God, David, practiced remembrance of God: "I have remembered Thy name, O Lord," he said. At night, he prepared his soul with divine remembrance, and having reached the proper spiritual disposition, he "kept Thy Law" during the day (Ps 118:55). St Gregory of Sinai advises, citing St John of the Ladder, "At night, dedicate much of your time to prayer, and only a little to psalmody."[197]

In the grievous warfare with the invisible enemies of our salvation, our best weapon is the Jesus Prayer. "All the nations," that is, the demons, "compassed me round about, but in the Name of the Lord have I driven them back. They came about me on every side, but in the Name of the Lord have I driven them back. They came about me like bees on a honeycomb, and burned even as a fire among the thorns, and in the Name of the Lord have I driven them back" (Ps 117:10–12). "By the name of Jesus drive away the enemies, because there is no stronger weapon, not in heaven or on earth."[198] "Through Thee," O Jesus Christ, "will we gore our enemies as with horns, and in Thy Name will we wipe out them that rise up against us. For I will not trust in my bow, and my sword shall not save me; For Thou has saved us from them that afflict us, and hast put them to shame that hate us. We make our boast of God all day long, and in Thy Name we will give thanks forever" (Ps 43:6–9).

The mind, having defeated and routed the enemies of the name of Jesus, joins the ranks of the blessed spirits, enters for true worship of God into the temple of the heart that was closed for it until this moment. The mind sings a new, spiritual song, exclaiming: "I will give thanks unto Thee, O Lord, with my whole heart, and before the angels will I sing praise unto Thee, for Thou hast heard all the words of my mouth. I will worship toward Thy holy temple, and give thanks unto Thy Name, because of Thy mercy and Thy truth, for Thou hast magnified Thy holy Name above all. In whatsoever day I may call upon Thee, quickly hear me; Thou shalt fortify me in my soul by Thy strength" (Ps 137:1–3). The Holy David lists the wondrous actions of the "holy and terrible" Name of Jesus (Ps 110:9). It acts like a medicine that heals in a manner unknown and inconceivable to the sick man, though its effect is obvious because it heals. For the sake of the name of Jesus, practiced by the faithful, help from God descends to him, and he is given forgiveness of sins. For this reason, David, offering to the gaze of God his emptiness and the calamitous state of the soul of every human being produced by a life of sin, begs Him, on behalf of all mankind, for mercy, saying, "Help us, O God our Saviour, for the glory of Thy Name; O Lord, deliver us, and wash away our sins, for Thy Name's sake" (Ps 78:9). For the sake of the name of the Lord, our prayer is heard and salvation is granted. On the foundation of this conviction, David again prays: "O God, in Thy Name save me, and judge me by Thy power. Hear my prayer, O God; hearken unto the words of my mouth" (Ps 53:3–4).

By the power of the name of Jesus, the mind is freed from doubt, the will is strengthened, zeal, and other spiritual qualities are properly oriented. The thoughts and emotions become God-pleasing, belonging to the blameless nature of man, for only such thoughts and emotions are allowed to remain in the soul. The soul has no place for foreign thoughts and emotions, "For God will save Zion, and build the cities of Judah, and they shall dwell there, and have it in possession. The posterity also of Thy servants shall inherit it, and they that love Thy Name shall dwell therein" (Ps 68:36–37). In the name of the Lord Jesus, the soul is given new life, after being mortified by sin. The Lord Jesus Christ is Life (see John 11:25), and His name is living. It gives new life to those who cry out with it to the source of Life, the Lord Jesus Christ. "For Thy Name's sake, O Lord, quicken me by Thy truth" (Ps 142:11). "Thou shalt quicken us, and we shall call upon Thy Name" (Ps 79:19).

When our prayer is heard, animated by the power and effect of the name of Jesus, when divine help will descend to man, when he will be found worthy of forgiveness of sins, when he will be healed and return to his blameless natural state, when his spirit will be restored in its authority—then will follow, in the name of the Lord, the giving of the gifts of grace, spiritual riches and treasures, the pledge of blessed eternity, "For Thou, O God, hast heard my prayers, and hast given an inheritance unto those that fear Thy Name" (Ps 60:6). Then man becomes capable of singing to the Lord "a new song." He is taken out of the ranks of the carnal and emotional, and he is joined to the spiritual who praise the Lord in the "church of the saints." The Holy Spirit, Who until this time has only offered and inspired him to sorrow and repentance, now invites him to "praise His Name in the dance." "Let Israel be glad in her Maker, and let the children of Zion exult in their King. Let them sing praises unto Him with timbrel and psaltery" (Ps 149:1–3). After the renewal of the soul, its powers, brought to a wondrous harmony and agreement, become capable, when touched by the grace of God, of uttering spiritual songs that rise to heaven, to the very throne of God, being pleasing to God.

"O let my heart rejoice to fear Thy Name. I will thank Thee, O Lord my God, with all my heart, and I will praise Thy Name for evermore. For great is Thy mercy toward me, and Thou hast delivered my soul from the nethermost hell" (Ps 85:11–13). "Verily, the righteous shall give thanks unto Thy Name, and the just shall dwell in Thy presence" (Ps 139:14), since, after the driving away of the enemies who inflict distraction, who weaken and defile prayer, the mind enters the darkness of knowing nothing and stands before the very face of God without any obstacle. This noetic darkness is that veil, that cover that hides the face of God. This veil is the unattainability of God for all created minds.

The compunction of the heart then becomes so strong that it is called "confession." The grace-filled action of the Jesus Prayer in spiritually advanced Christians is expressed thus by David: "Bless the Lord, O my soul, and all that is within me bless His holy Name" (Ps 102:1). Exactly! With the abundant action of the Jesus Prayer, all the powers of the soul, even the body itself, take part in prayer. The Holy David, or rather the Holy Spirit through the mouth of David, offers all Christians, without exception, to practice the Jesus Prayer: "Kings of the earth and all peoples, princes and all judges of the world; young men and maidens, old men and children; let them praise the Name of the Lord, for His Name only is exalted" (Ps 148:11–13). A literal reading of the social ranks here listed is fully permissible, but their essential meaning is spiritual. "All people" indicates all Christians. "[P]rinces of the world" are those Christians who have been found worthy of receiving perfection. "Kings" are those who are especially spiritually advanced. "Judges" are those who have not yet acquired full mastery over themselves, but they know the Law of God, they can distinguish good from evil, and, according to the indications and requirements of the Law of God, they can remain in the good, rejecting the evil. "Maidens" are dispassionate hearts that are capable of prayer. "Old men and children" describe the degrees of advancement by means of spiritual labor, which is very different from the advancement given by grace, though the former has its very important role to play. He who has achieved perfection in pious labors is called an elder, while the one who is raised to perfection by grace is a king.

Among the unattainable, miraculous qualities of the name of Jesus, one finds the ability and power to cast out demons. This characteristic is declared by the Lord Himself. He said that "those who believe: in My name they will cast out demons" (Mark 16:17). We must pay special attention to this quality of the Jesus Prayer, because it has an important significance for practitioners of the prayer. First of all, we must say a few words about how demons abide in men. This indwelling is two-fold. The first is perceptible, the second—moral. Satan dwells in a person perceptibly when he inhabits the body of a person in his essence, and from there, tortures the soul and the body of the unfortunate man. In such cases, a man can have a single demon or many demons living inside him. Such a person is called "possessed." In the Gospel, we see that the

Lord healed the demon-possessed, and the apostles did as well, when they cast the demons out by the name of the Lord. Satan's moral indwelling in man occurs when a man becomes the fulfiller of the will of the demons. It was in this sense that "Satan entered" (John 13:27) into Judas Iscariot. In other words, Satan took control of Judas's reason and will and united with him in spirit. All those who do not believe in Christ were and are in such a state, as the holy Apostle Paul told the Christians who had converted from paganism: "And you He made alive, who were dead in trespasses and sins, in which you once walked according to the course of this world, according to the prince of the power of the air, the spirit who now works in the sons of disobedience, among whom also we all once conducted ourselves in the lusts of our flesh, fulfilling the desires of the flesh and of the mind, and were by nature children of wrath, just as the others" (Eph 2:1–3).

All those who have been baptized into Christ, but have been alienated from Him by sins, are also in such a state, to a greater or lesser degree, depending on their sinfulness. This is how the Holy Fathers interpret the words of Christ concerning the return of the demon with seven other demons, fiercer than he, into the house of the soul that the Holy Spirit has abandoned (see the Blessed Theophylact's interpretation of Matthew 12:43–45). The demons who entered in this manner can once again be cast out by the Jesus Prayer, if the practitioner lives in constant and diligent repentance.

Let us undertake this labor, so salvific for us! Let us take care to cast out the spirits that have entered us because of our neglect, by the Jesus Prayer.[199] It has the ability to revive those who have been mortified by sin; it has the ability to cast out demons. "I am the resurrection and the life. He who believes in Me, though he may die, he shall live" (John 11:25). "And these signs will follow those who believe: In My name they will cast out demons" (Mark 16:17). The Jesus Prayer reveals the presence of the demons within man, and it casts them out of man. Moreover, something happens that is similar to the casting out of the demon from the possessed youth after the transfiguration of the Lord. When the youth saw the Lord coming, the spirit "convulsed him, and he fell on the ground and wallowed, foaming at the mouth" (Mark 9:20). When the Lord commanded the spirit to leave the youth, the spirit, from hatred and evil, cried out, convulsed the youth fiercely, and the young man lay as one dead. The power of Satan, dwelling inside man if he lives a distracted, unexamined life, is thrown into confusion at the sound of the name of the Lord Jesus, uttered by the praying man. This power stirs up all the passions in man, and through them brings the entire man into a terrible furor, even producing terrible, strange diseases of the body. In this sense, St John the Prophet said, "For us infirm ones, it only remains to run to the name of Jesus, for the passions, as it is said, are demons, and they are cast out at the utterance of this name."[200]

This means that the actions of the passions and the demons are linked. The demons act by means of the passions. When we experience especial agitation and a roiling of the passions during the practice of the Jesus Prayer, we must not fall to despair or confusion over this. On the contrary, we should be encouraged and prepare ourselves for the coming labor of diligently praying the name of the Lord Jesus, for we have received an obvious sign that this prayer has begun to act within us.

St John Chrysostom says,

> The remembrance of the name of our Lord Jesus Christ incited the enemy to open warfare. For the soul that forces itself to pray the Jesus Prayer can acquire everything through this prayer, both good and evil. First of all, it can see the evil inside its own heart, and then the good. This prayer can force the serpent to act, and this prayer can also subdue him. This prayer can rebuke the sin living within us, and this prayer can uproot it. This prayer can incite all the power of the enemy into action within the heart, and this prayer can defeat it and uproot it little by little. The name of the Lord Jesus Christ, descending into the depth of the heart, overcomes the serpent that rules over its fields, and it saves and gives new life to the soul. Constantly abide in the prayer of the name of Jesus, so that the heart will swallow the Lord, and the Lord will swallow the heart, and so that these two shall be one. However, this work is not accomplished in a single day or even two days, but many years and much time is necessary. We need much time and labor to expel the enemy and for Christ to come and abide in the heart.[201]

It is obvious that St John described the practice, with clear directions on the instrument of this practice, of which St Macarius the Great speaks in his 1st Homily: "Enter, whoever you may be, through the thoughts that constantly grow within you, to the contemplation of your soul, that captive and slave of sin. Examine your thoughts to their very bottom, and investigate the depths of your reasoning, and you will see the nesting, crawling serpent in the abysses of your soul, him who has killed you by poisoning the powers of your soul. The heart is an incalculable abyss. If you destroy the serpent, then you may boast to God in your purity. If not, then humble yourself, praying as an infirm sinner for your secret sins before God."

The same great saint of God said,

> The kingdom of darkness, that is, the evil prince of the spirits who enslaved mankind at the beginning, surrounded and clothed the soul in the power of darkness. This evil master clothed the soul and its entire essence with sin, defiling it completely, making it a prisoner in his kingdom. He did not leave either the thoughts, or the reason, or the body, or any part of the body to be free. He dressed it all in the mantle of darkness. This evil enemy of all mankind defiled and disfigured the soul and body of man; he clothed man in the old man, the defiled, impure, ungodly, insubordinate man who flouts the commandments of God. In other words, he clothed man in sin so that man would no longer see as he would like, but would see everything passionately, hear everything passionately. His feet now strive toward evil deeds, his hands to the works of iniquity, his heart to evil thoughts. But we will pray to God that He disrobes us of the old man, since He alone can take sin from us, since those who captured us and hold us in captivity are stronger than we are, and He promised to free us from this slavery.[202]

Based on this understanding, the Holy Fathers give the following soul-saving instruction to the practitioner of the Jesus Prayer:

> The soul, if it will not sicken very seriously from the tenacity of sin living within him, will never be able to rejoice greatly in the goodness of divine justice. Whoever desires to purify his heart, let him arouse it constantly by the remembrance of the Lord Jesus, having this labor as his only constant instructor. Those who desire to reject their old man should not pray at some times and not others but should constantly abide in prayer by the attention of their mind, though they be physically outside church. Those who intend to purify gold, if they allow the fire in the crucible to go out even for a short time, once again allow the impurities to harden in the gold. In a similar way, those who remember God sometimes, but at other times do not, destroy everything that they acquired by prayer through their sloth. It is proper for the man who loves virtue to constantly destroy the crudity of the heart, so that in such a way evil, little by little, will be burned by the fire of remembrance of good, and the soul will completely return to its natural brightness with great glory. In such a way, the mind, remaining in the heart, purely and constantly prays as the same holy man (Diadochus) said: then prayer will be pure and without demonic delusion, when the mind unites with the heart in prayer.[203]

Let us not fear, practitioners of the Jesus Prayer, neither winds nor storms! Winds are demonic thoughts and images; storms are the agitation of the passions, aroused by those thoughts and images. From the midst of the fiercest storm, with constancy, courage, and weeping, let us cry out to the Lord Jesus Christ. He will forbid the winds and the waves, and we, having come to know the might of Jesus from experience, will offer Him worthy worship: "Truly You are the Son of God" (Matt 14:33). We battle for our salvation. Our eternal faith depends on our victory or our defeat.

"Then," said St Symeon the New Theologian,

> that is, during the practice of the Jesus Prayer, the battle rages. The evil demons attack us with great force; they raise up a storm in our heart through the passions, but by the name of the Lord Jesus Christ they are defeated and cast down, like wax before the face of fire. Still, when they will be cast out and will depart from the heart, they will not cease to battle us, but will disturb the mind through the physical senses. For this reason, the mind does not soon begin to sense calmness and stillness within itself, for the demons, when they do not have the power to confound the mind in its depth, confuse it from without by means of images. Therefore, it is impossible to be completely freed of this warfare, to not be attacked anymore by the evil spirits. This is true of both the perfect and of those who have completely left everything and abide constantly in attentiveness of heart.[204]

At first, the very practice appears to be extraordinarily dry, not promising any fruit. The mind, trying to unite with the heart, at first encounters only impenetrable darkness, the rigidity, and deadness of the heart that does not immediately turn with sympathy to the mind.[205] This should not lead the practitioner to despair or lack of faith. We mention it here to warn and inform the practitioner in advance. The patient and diligent practitioner of the Jesus Prayer will doubtless be content and consoled; he will find joy in the limitless bounty of such spiritual fruits, which his imagination cannot even conjure, in his carnal and emotional state.

In the effects of the Jesus Prayer, there is a proper gradualism. At first, it acts on the mind alone, bringing it to a state of silence and attention. Then, it begins to penetrate into the heart, arousing it from the sleep of death and signifying the revivification of the heart by the appearance of compunction and holy sorrow. Plunging ever deep, little by little the prayer begins to act in all the members of the soul and body, everywhere casting out sin, everywhere destroying the lordship, influence, and poison of the demons. For this reason, during the initial action of the Jesus Prayer, "there is unutterable pain and an indescribable sickness of the soul," as St Gregory of Sinai says. The soul sickens as a woman giving birth, as the Scriptures say: "For the word of God is living and powerful, and sharper than any two-edged sword [that is, Jesus pierces through, as the apostle witnesses] piercing even to the division of soul and spirit, and of joints and marrow, and is a discerner of the thoughts and intents of the heart" (Heb 4:12). It pierces a man, uprooting sinfulness from all the parts of the soul and body.[206]

When the seventy lesser apostles, sent by the Lord to preach, returned to Him after having completed the service laid upon them, they joyfully declared to the Lord: "Lord, even the demons are subject to us in Your name" (Luke 10:17). O, truly this was a worthy joy! How firmly established was this joy! For more than five thousand years, the devil had lorded it over man, enslaving them and making them akin to him through sin. But now, he hears the name of Jesus and submits to the men who were until this moment subject to him. He is bound by the ones that he bound; he is defeated by the ones he defeated.

In answer to the disciples who were rejoicing at the toppling of the authority of the demons over mankind and over their acquiring power over the demons, the Lord said, "Behold, I give you the authority to trample on serpents and scorpions, and over all the power of the enemy, and nothing shall by any means hurt you" (Luke 10:19). The authority is given, and freedom to use this authority is also given, either to defeat the serpent and the scorpions or to disdain this gift and freely submit to them again. The Holy Fathers interpret the "serpents" to mean any obviously sinful endeavors, while "scorpions" are sins that are covered by a mask of blamelessness or even good.

The authority given by the Lord to His seventy disciples is also given to all Christians (see Mark 16:17). Use it, O Christian! Cut off the heads—that is, sinful thoughts before they blossom in the thoughts, fantasy, or perceptions— with the name of Jesus. Destroy within yourself the mastery of the devil over you; destroy all his influence over you; acquire spiritual freedom. The foundation for your labor is the grace of Holy baptism; your weapon is the prayer of the name of Jesus.

The Lord, having given His disciples the power to trample on serpents and scorpions, added the following: "Nevertheless do not rejoice in this, that the spirits are subject to you, but rather rejoice because your names are written in heaven" (Luke 10:20). "Rejoice not so much that the demons submit to you," explains Blessed Theophylact, "but rather rejoice that your names are written in heaven, not with ink, but with divine grace and remembrance of God," that is, through the Jesus Prayer. This is the characteristic of the Jesus Prayer—it raises its practitioner from earth to heaven and includes him in the ranks of the dwellers of heaven. Being in heaven already on earth in mind and heart, through God—this is the most important purpose and fruit of prayer. The defeat and trampling upon enemies that try to counteract this purpose—this is a secondary effect. It should not attract to itself the full attention of the one praying, lest his acknowledgment and contemplation of the victory give entry to thoughts of arrogance and self-conceit. Then, the one who was raised so high will suffer a terrible defeat because of his own victory.

The Gospel continues: "In that hour Jesus rejoiced in the Spirit and said, 'I thank You, Father, Lord of heaven and earth, that You have hidden these things from the wise and prudent and revealed them to babes. Even so, Father, for so it seemed good in Your sight. All things have been delivered to Me by My Father, and no one knows who the Son is except the Father'" (Luke 10:21–22). The Lord rejoiced with the unattainable joy of God at the spiritual progress of man; He declares that the mysteries of the Christian faith are revealed not to the wise and exalted of the world, but to children (in the civic sense, as were the apostles, taken from among the common people, the unlearned, the illiterate). To be a disciple of the Lord, one must become a child and accept His teaching with childlike simplicity and love. To those who have already become disciples, the Lord turns with an explanation of the most mysterious teaching, revealing that the Son, despite assuming humanity, remains above the understanding of all reasoning creatures. Surpassing their understanding is His all-holy name as well. With the simplicity and trusting nature of children, let us accept the teaching concerning the prayer of the name of Jesus; with simplicity and the trustfulness of children, let us begin practicing this prayer. God alone, knowing fully this mystery, will give us this prayer in the degree that is appropriate for us. Let us give joy to God with our labor and progress in this service, which He Himself had commanded and given us.

The Jesus Prayer was universally practiced by the Christians of the first centuries, as we have already mentioned above. It could not have been otherwise. By the name of the Lord Jesus Christ, striking miracles were performed before the face of the entire Christian community, and this inspired the entire Christian community to faith in the boundless power of the name of Jesus. Those who had advanced understood this power from experience. St Barsanuphius the Great expressed himself thus concerning this power, which so abundantly poured forth in the saints of God: "I know one servant of God in our generation who lives in this time and in this blessed place, who can resurrect the dead in the name of our Master Jesus Christ, and cast out demons, and heal incurable diseases, and perform other miracles of equally apostolic degree, as the One Who gave him these gifts testifies of him. But what are all these in comparison with everything that the name of Jesus can do!"[207]

Having before their gaze such miracles, keeping in their memory the testament of the Lord, and having in their heart ardent love for the Lord, the faithful of the Early Church constantly, diligently exercised in the prayer of the name of Jesus with the fiery zeal of the Cherubim and Seraphim. This is the characteristic of love! It constantly thinks of the beloved one; it constantly feels pleasure at the name of the beloved one; it preserves him in the heart, having his name on the mind and the lips. The name of the Lord is above every name. It is the source of sweetness, joy, life. It is Spirit. It gives life. It changes, reorients, deifies. For the illiterate, it replaces the prayer rules and psalmody. The literate, having progressed in the prayer of Jesus, abandon various psalmodies and begin to practice the Jesus Prayer, primarily because of the abundant power and nourishment inherent to it. All this is clear from the writings and instruction of the Holy Fathers.

The Holy Eastern Orthodox Church suggests that all illiterate people pray the Jesus Prayer instead of the appointed rules of prayer. This is not an innovation, but a generally practiced rule. This recommendation, along with other traditions of the Orthodox Church, came to Russia from Greece, and many of the common people, barely literate or completely illiterate, have been nourished by the power of the Jesus Prayer to salvation and eternal life. Many have acquired great spiritual progress. St John Chrysostom, while advising the diligent and constant practice of the Jesus Prayer to all, especially monks, speaks of the practice as general:

> We also have spiritual invocations—the name of our Lord Jesus Christ and the power of the Cross. This invocation not only drives away the dragon from its lair and casts it into the fire, but it even heals from the wounds inflicted by him. If many uttered this invocation and were not healed, this occurred because of their lack of faith, not from the prayer's lack of power. The many who walked behind Christ and crowded around Him did not receive any benefit, but the woman with an issue of blood, having not even touched His body, but only the edge of His clothing, was healed of her flow of blood, which had been of many years' duration. The name of Jesus Christ is frightening for the demons, for the passions of the soul, and for infirmities. Let us protect ourselves with it; let us adorn ourselves with it. The Apostle Paul became great because of it, though he was of one nature with us.[208]

An angel of the Lord gave St Pachomius the Great a rule of prayer for his large community of monastics. The monks who were under the spiritual guidance of St Pachomius had to complete this rule every day, and only the spiritually perfect (that is, those who prayed unceasingly) were freed from this requirement. This rule, given by the angel, consisted of the Trisagion, the Lord's Prayer, the fiftieth Psalm, the Creed, and one hundred Jesus Prayers. In this rule, the Jesus Prayer is spoken of in the same breath as the Lord's prayer; that is, it is assumed to be as generally known and generally practiced as the Lord's prayer. St Barsanuphius the Great said that the monks of the Egyptian Scetis (Wadi El Natrun) spent most of their time practicing the Jesus Prayer. This is also seen in the life of Abba Pambo of the Nitrian mountain, found not far from Scetis, in which his monks lived a life of silence.[209]

Among the many saints mentioned in this essay as practitioners of the Jesus Prayer, St Ignatius the God-bearer lived in Antioch and died in Rome; St Callistratus was born and lived in Carthage; St Pachomius the Great lived in Upper Egypt; the monks of Nitria and Scetis lived in Lower Egypt; St John Chrysostom was from Antioch and lived in Constantinople; St Basil the Great lived in the eastern half of Asia Minor in Cappadocia; St Barsanuphius the Great lived near Jerusalem; St John of the Ladder lived on Sinai and, for a short time, in Lower Egypt, near Alexandria. From this, it is evident that the prayer of the name of Jesus was universal, generally practiced in the Universal Church. Other than these fathers, the following also wrote about the Jesus Prayer: St Hesychius, a fifth-century priest of Jerusalem and a disciple of St Gregory the Theologian (even at this time, he complained that the monks abandoned the Jesus Prayer and vigilance); St Philotheos of Sinai, St Symeon the New Theologian, St Gregory of Sinai, St Theoleptus of Philadelphia, St Gregory Palamas, Saints Kallistos and Ignatius Xanthopoulos, and many others. Most of the writings of these Fathers are collected in a large compendium of ascetic writings called *The Philokalia*.

Russian Fathers who wrote on this subject included St Nilus of Sora, St Dorotheos, St Paisius Velichkovsky, Schema-monk Vasily Polianomerulsky, and St Seraphim of Sarov. All the writings of these fathers are worthy of profound respect because of the depth of their spiritual wisdom and the presence of God's grace in them, but the writings of the Russian fathers, because of their especial vividness and simplicity of language, their closeness to us in time, are more accessible than the writings of the Greek luminaries. In our time, especially the writings of Elder Vasily must and should be acknowledged the best book for anyone who desires to successfully practice the Jesus Prayer.

The elder called his writings an introduction (literally, a "guidebook") to the more exalted writings of the Greek Fathers.

St Nilus of Sora's book is also superlative. One should read it before attempting to read the Greek Fathers. It constantly references them and explains them, preparing the reader for a correct understanding of these profound Holy Fathers who were also often orators, philosophers, and poets. All the works of the Holy Fathers in general concerning the monastic life, especially everything concerning the Jesus Prayer, are a priceless treasure for us, the monks of the last times. During the time of St Nilus of Sora, three hundred years before our time, living vessels of divine grace were very rare, making his times "extremely impoverished," as he himself expressed it. In our own time, they are so rare that one can say without making a mistake that there are *none*. It is considered an extraordinary mercy of God if anyone, having exhausted himself in soul and body in the monastic life, toward the end of this life unexpectedly finds somewhere in the depths a vessel chosen by the impartial God, belittled in the eyes of mankind, upraised and glorified by God. Thus Zosimas found in the uninhabited desert beyond Jordan, completely unexpectedly, the great Mary of Egypt.

Because of this final diminishing of spirit-bearing instructors, the books of the Fathers are the only source to which the soul that thirsts and hungers for the acquisition of essentially necessary knowledge in spiritual labors can turn. These books are the most precious inheritance left by the Holy Fathers to their monastic heirs—us, impoverished ones. These books are crumbs that have fallen to us and that comprise our lot, the crumbs from the feasting table of the Fathers, which is rich in spiritual gifts. It is evident that the greatest number of books about the Jesus Prayer were written at times of greatest impoverishment of that prayer in monastic circles. When St Gregory of Sinai, who lived in the fourteenth century, arrived at Mount Athos, he found, among thousands of monks, only three who had at least some understanding of the Jesus Prayer. The fourteenth and fifteenth centuries contained the greatest number of writings concerning the Jesus Prayer.

"Moved by the mysteries of divine inspiration," said. St Paisius Velichkovsky, "many fathers wrote down the holy teaching, filled with the wisdom of the Holy Spirit, about this divine prayer of the mind, on the foundation of the divine Scriptures of the Old and New Testament. This was allowed by a special providence of God, so that the divine practice of the Jesus Prayer would not be forgotten completely. Many of these books, by God's permission, and because of our sins, were destroyed by the Moslems who overcame the Greek government. Some, by God's providence, were preserved to our time."[210]

The most exalted practice of the prayer of the mind is extraordinarily simple. To be accepted, it requires a childlike simplicity of faith, but we have become so complicated that such a simplicity is impossible, unattainable for us. We want to be intelligent; we want to animate our ego; we cannot endure self-denial; we do not want to act by faith. For this reason, we need instructors who can lead us out of our complexities, out of our cunning, out of our contrivances, out of our vanity and self-conceit, into the breadth and simplicity of faith. For this reason, sometimes a child can acquire extraordinary heights in the practice of this prayer, while a wise man stumbles from the path and falls into the dark abyss of self-delusion.

"In the old times," said St Paisius Velichkovsky,

> the all-holy prayer of the mind shone in many places, wherever there were holy fathers, and there were then many guides for this spiritual labor. For this reason, the Holy Fathers of those time, when writing about it, explained only the unutterable spiritual benefit that came of it, not having any need, as I think, to write about that part of the practice of prayer that is proper to a beginner. They wrote some of this as well, which was clear for those who had an experiential knowledge of the labor, but for those who did not have it, it remained hidden. When some of the Fathers saw that there were fewer and fewer true and un-deluded guides of this practice, then, being inspired by the Spirit of God to preserve the true teaching of the prayer of the mind from complete loss, they wrote down the practices and principles for beginners to enter with the mind into the domain of the heart, where one can truly practice the prayer of the mind without delusion.[211]

We have seen that the holy prophet David invites all people of God, without exception, to pray the name of the Lord, and that by decree, the Holy Church declared that all illiterate people and all who do not know the Holy Scriptures by heart could replace prayer rules and psalmody with the Jesus Prayer. St Simeon of Thessalonica commands and advises bishops, priests, all monks and laypeople to utter this holy prayer at all times, having it like the breath of life.[212]

When a monk is tonsured, he is given a prayer rope with the words: "Accept, brother, the spiritual sword, which is the word of God. Bear it on your lips, mind, and heart, and utter ceaselessly: Lord Jesus Christ, Son of God, have mercy on me." However, St Nilus of Sora instructs that "the remembrance of God, that is, the prayer of the mind, is greater than labors. It is the head of all virtues, as the love of God. Whoever shamelessly and brazenly tries to approach God and speak with Him face to face; whoever forcefully tries to acquire Him, he will easily be killed by the demons if it will be allowed by God, since he sought to acquire Him brazenly and proudly, beyond his own worthiness and dispensation."[213]

If looked at superficially, these words of St Nilus can seem to contradict the commands of the Holy Scriptures, the writings of the Holy Fathers, and the tradition of the Church. However, there is no contradiction; what he speaks of is the Jesus Prayer in its highest form. All Christians must and should practice the Jesus Prayer with the purpose of repentance and calling the Lord's help to themselves, to practice it with fear of God and faith, with the greatest attentiveness to the thoughts and words of the prayer, with compunction of spirit. However, not all are allowed to approach the prayerful worship of the mind, in the hidden room of the heart. The first form of the prayer should be practiced not only by monks living in a monastery, but by laypeople as well. Such attentive prayer can become the prayer of the mind and the heart. If practiced often with the mind alone, in diligent practitioners, the heart will come to sympathize with the mind. In diligent practitioners, such sympathy is expressed with a sense of sorrow and tears that come as a result of compunction.

The second form of the prayer—the prayerful worship of the mind in the heart—requires initial practice in the first form and a successful progress in it. The grace of God by itself, in its own good time, by its own blessing, leads the ascetic of prayer from the first kind of prayer to the second. If it pleases God to leave the ascetic in the first kind of prayer—the prayer of repentance—then let him not seek the second, knowing with conviction that it cannot be seized by human exertion. It is given by God. Remaining in a constant state of repentance is the pledge of salvation. Let us be content with such a state; let us not seek a more exalted spiritual state. Such seeking is a sure sign of pride and self-conceit; such seeking does not lead to advancement, but to stumbling and perdition. St Nilus, on the basis of the teachings of all the Holy Fathers, forbids to prematurely seek the descent of the mind into the heart, to strive for external and inner stillness, to a sense of sweetness, or other exalted prayerful states, which are only revealed when the prayer of repentance will be accepted by God, and the enemies will retreat from the soul. As the Psalmist said, "Away from me, all ye that work iniquity, for the Lord hath heard the voice of my weeping. The Lord has heard my petition; the Lord will receive my prayer" (Ps 6:9–10). Consolation, joy, sweetness, the giving of gifts—all these are the consequences of reconciliation. To seek them before reconciliation is an endeavor full of rashness.

To acquire profound heart-felt prayer requires significant preliminary preparation. This consists of a satisfactory study of the experience of monastic life, while training oneself to live according to the commandments of the Gospel. Holy prayer is founded on a disposition of the soul that is produced by a life lived by the commandments. It abides in such a disposition, and it cannot remain in a soul that lacks such a disposition. This preparation must also consist of the satisfactory study of the New Testament and the Fathers' writings on prayer. The latter is especially important, because due to the lack of spirit-bearing guides, our only instructors in a life of prayer are the writings of the fathers and our own sorrowful prayer before God. Desirable is the prayer of the heart; desirable is the stillness of the heart; desirable is the constant abiding in one's cell and the life in a solitary desert, as especially proper to the development of the prayer and stillness of the heart.

"However, even these good and magnificent endeavors," says St Nilus of Sora, "must be attempted with discernment, in the proper time, after having achieved the necessary level of spiritual progress, as St Basil the Great said: for every good deed must be preceded by discernment. However, without discernment, even a good deed will become an evil one in its untimeliness and lack of moderation. When, with discernment, you determine the right time and measure for good, then you will receive a wondrous gain. And St John of the Ladder, using the words of the Scripture, says, "'To everything there is a season, and a time for every matter under heaven' (Eccl 3:1). And in our own life of holiness, there is a proper time for every task." Then, continuing, St John said, "There is a time for silence, and a time for calm discourse. There is a time for constant prayer, and a time for un-hypocritical service. Let us not be deluded by our proud zeal and seek too early that which must come in its own time. Otherwise, we will not receive anything, even at the allotted time. There is a time to sow words and a time to reap the wheat of unutterable grace."[214]

St Nilus especially forbids rash striving toward an eremitic life. Such striving nearly always appears in people who understand neither themselves, nor the monastic life, and so they fall prey to the greatest obstacles and self-delusion when choosing such a way of life. If monks are forbidden such premature striving toward prayer offered by the mind in the temple of the heart, then how much more is it forbidden to laypeople! There were only a few laypeople in the history of the church who had the profound prayer of the heart—St Andrew the fool for Christ and a few others—but they are an extremely rare exception that can never justify such striving as a rule for all. To include oneself among such exceptional people is nothing other than delusion through self-conceit, a hidden demonic delusion that will eventually reveal itself as open *prelest*.

St Paisius Velichkovsky, in his letter to Elder Theodosius, said, "The writings of the Fathers, especially those that teach true obedience, vigilance of mind, stillness, attentive prayer of the mind, that is, the prayer that is offered by the mind in the heart—these are intended only for monks, not for all Christians in general." The God-bearing fathers, when writing down their teachings concerning such prayer, insist that its beginning and unshakeable foundation is true obedience, from which true humility arises, and only humility can preserve the ascetic in prayer, safe from all delusions that inevitably come to the one who willfully reaches for the unreachable. It is impossible for people in the world to acquire true monastic obedience and the complete cutting off of their own will and reason in all things. How can it be possible for worldly people, without obedience, by their own willfulness, which always leads to demonic delusion, to compel themselves to such an awesome and terrifying work, that is, to such prayer without any guidance? How will they avoid the many different delusions of the enemy that attack the practitioner of prayer in extremely cunning ways? This thing is very frightening—that is, such prayer, not only of the mind, but offered creatively by the mind in the heart—so much so that true ascetics, not only those who are able to cut off their own will, but those who have completely mortified their own will and reason before their fathers, who are themselves true and experienced guides to the practice of this prayer—even they are always in fear and trembling, lest they suffer some kind of delusion during this prayer, even though God preserves them from it for the sake of their true humility, which they have acquired by the grace of God through the aid of their genuine humility. All the more should laypeople fear, living without obedience, if they begin to attempt such a prayer after reading books not intended for them, for there is great danger of them falling into deep demonic delusion that occurs to all who begin the labor of such prayer with self-will, not obedience. The saints have called this prayer the art of arts. Who can learn it without the guidance of an artist, that is, an experienced teacher? This prayer is a spiritual sword, given by God, for the destruction of the enemy of our souls. This prayer has shone forth like the sun, only among monks, especially in the Egyptian desert, in the mountains of Sinai and Nitria, in many places of Palestine, and other places, but not everywhere, as we see from the life of St Gregory of Sinai. He traveled over the entire holy mountain and, having made a diligent search for the practitioners of this prayer, found there not a single person who had even so much as a small understanding about the nature of such prayer.

> This makes it clear: if in such a holy place there was not a single practitioner of the prayer of the mind in the heart, then in many places this prayer was simply unknown to some monastics. And where it was practiced, where it shone forth among monastics like the sun, there the practice of the prayer was preserved as a great and unutterable mystery known only to God and the ones who practiced the prayer. To laypeople, the practice of this prayer was completely unknown. But today, after the Fathers' books were printed, all Christians, not merely the monastics, have come to know about the prayer. Because of this, I fear and tremble that for the aforementioned reason—that is, because of the sinful self-will that leads some to begin the labor of this prayer without a guide—such self-willed laypeople may be subject to demonic delusion. May Christ the Saviour deliver by His grace all who want to be saved.[215]

We consider it our responsibility to present, as much as our infirm mind and experience allow, the teachings of the Holy Fathers concerning the creative practice of the Jesus Prayer, with clear indications which form of the prayer is appropriate for all Christians without exception and beginning monks, and which form is proper only for the spiritually advanced who have been raised up to this advancement by the goodwill of God and the grace of God.

Without any doubt, the first place among all methods must be given to the method offered by St John of the Ladder, as one especially appropriate, completely safe, needed, even necessary for the effectiveness of prayer. This method is appropriate to all Christians who live piously and seek salvation, both laypeople and monks. In *The Ladder*, this great instructor of monastics twice speaks of this method that leads one from earth to Heaven—in his homily on obedience and his homily on prayer. The very fact that he offers this method in his instruction on the obedience of monks living in a communal monastery clearly shows us that this method is necessary for beginner monks. The fact that this same method is offered in a second, more expansive teaching on prayer (after a separate instruction for those practicing silence) consequently shows us that it is also a very effective method for advanced monks and those practicing silence.

We repeat: the great usefulness of this method is found in that it is completely safe, while remaining fully a satisfactory form of prayer. In his homily on prayer, St John of the Ladder says,

> Labor to return, or rather, to enclose your thoughts in the words of the prayer. If it weakens and wanders because of your spiritual infancy, then lead it back. Inconstancy is natural for the mind. Only He Who establishes everything can establish the mind firmly within prayer. If you acquire this practice and will constantly keep to it, then the One Who establishes the limits to your sea will come and say to it during prayer: "This far you may come, but no farther" (Job 38:11). It is impossible to tie down the spirit, but wherever the Creator of the spirit is present, there everything submits to Him. The beginning of prayer is the driving away of thoughts at their very inception; the middle is when the mind abides in the words spoken by the lips or the mind without wandering. The final step of prayer is the ascent of the mind to God.[216]

In his homily on obedience, St John says, "Battle your thoughts constantly, returning the mind to itself when it flies away. God does not require attentive prayer from the beginner. Do not sorrow if your prayer is stolen; instead, be of good cheer and constantly return the mind to itself."[217] Here he offers a method of praying attentively, whether aloud or with the mind alone. The heart cannot help but take part in attentive prayer, as St Mark the Ascetic said, "The mind that prays without distraction constrains the heart."[218]

Thus, whoever prays by this method offered by St John of the Ladder will pray with the lips, the mind, and the heart. He, having succeeded at this prayer, will acquire the prayer of the mind and the heart and will attract to himself the grace of God, as we see from the preceding words of the great teacher of monks. What more should you desire? Nothing. What sort of demonic delusion can there be, if one uses this method to pray? Only one error is possible— finding pleasuring in wandering off mentally. This sin, a completely obvious one, is unavoidable in beginners, but it is capable of immediate healing through returning the mind to the words. It will also be destroyed by the mercy and aid of God in its own time, after constancy in this labor.

One may ask: is it possible that such a great father, who lived at a time when the practice of the Jesus Prayer flourished, says nothing of the prayer of the mind offered in the heart? He does speak of it, but in such a hidden manner that only those who are experienced in the practice of such prayer can understand about what he speaks. This he did, being himself guided by spiritual wisdom, which imbues his entire book. Having expressed the most true and satisfactory teaching concerning prayer, a teaching that is capable of leading the practitioner into a state of grace, St John described everything that happens after the coming of grace only parabolically. "It is one thing," he said, "to turn often to the heart, but it is another thing to be the noetic bishop, prince, and archbishop of the heart who bring spiritual sacrifices to Christ."[219] It is one thing to pray attentively, with the participation of the heart, but it is another thing to descend with the mind into the temple of the heart, and from there to utter mystical prayer filled with the power and grace of God. The second comes from the first.

The attentiveness of the mind during prayer attracts the heart to sympathy. When attentiveness becomes natural to prayer, then the mind can descend into the heart for most profound prayerful worship. All this occurs with the guidance of the grace of God, by its blessing and discretion. Striving to acquire the second before the first not only is pointless, but it can be the cause of great harm. To avoid this harm, *The Ladder* hides these mysteries of prayer from curiosity and frivolity, for the book is intended for the use of all monastics (not just the spiritually advanced). In those blessed times, when vessels of grace were numerous, anyone could rush to them to receive advice in special cases.

Among the monks for whom St John wrote *The Ladder*, the prayer of the mind blossomed under the guidance of experienced, spiritual instruction. The saint also wrote of this tangentially and in a hidden manner in his homily to the pastor.

> First of all, honored father, we need spiritual strength, so that we can lead those whom we desire to lead into the Holy of Holies, to whom we intend to show Christ, Who is present at their mystical and secret feast (especially while they still remain on the threshold of this entrance and when we see that they are burdened and constrained by those who try to prevent their entrance) take them by the hand, like children, and free them from the crowds of their thoughts. If the children are especially naked and infirm, then it is necessary for us to raise them up on our own shoulders and carry them, until they themselves can enter through the doors of the entrance. I know surely that there is usually great constraint and crowding at this entrance. This is why the Psalmist said, "And I sought to understand, but it was too hard for me, until I went into the sanctuary of God" (Ps 72:16–17). This difficulty lasts only until they can enter.[220]

"Whoever desires to see the Lord within himself must seek to purify his heart by the constant remembrance of God. The noetic domain of the one who is pure in heart is within him. The sun shining in that domain is the light of the Holy Trinity. The air that one breathes in that place is the all-holy Spirit. Life, joy, and happiness in that land is Christ, Light of Light of the Father. This is Jerusalem and "the kingdom of God is within [us]," as the Lord said (Luke 17:21). This place is the cloud of the glory of God. Only the pure of heart will enter it, to see the face of their Master, so that their minds will reflect the ray of His light (see St Isaac the Syrian, Homily 8). Try to enter into the hidden room within you, and you will see the room of heaven. They are the same thing. One entrance leads to both. The ladder leading to the kingdom of heaven is within you. It is built mystically in your soul. Submerge yourself in yourself, away from sin, and you will find the steps by which you can climb to heaven."[221]

St Barsanuphius, a monk who achieved the highest degree of spiritual advancement, also led his disciples into the sanctum of the heart through the prayer of grace and the spiritual state produced by it. Among his instructions, we find the following, given to a certain monk who practiced silence:

> May the only sinless God, Who saves those who hope in Him, strengthen your love to serve Him in righteousness and truth for all the days of your life, in the temple and at the altar of the inner man, where spiritual sacrifices are offered to God—gold, frankincense, and myrrh—where the fatted calf is sacrificed, where the pure blood of the blameless Lamb is sprinkled, where the harmonious cries of the holy angels are heard: "then shall they offer young bullocks upon Thine altar" (Ps 50:21). Then—when? When our Lord will come, that Great High Priest who offers and accepts the bloodless Sacrifice. When, in His name, the lame sitting at the beautiful gate will be found worthy of hearing the joyful words: rise up and walk (Acts 3:6). Then the lame man will enter the sacred place, walking and leaping about, and praising God. Then the sleep of sloth and ignorance will cease. Then the slumber of despair and the sleep of the eyes will be taken away. Then the five wise virgins will light their lamps and sing with the bridegroom in the holy bridal chamber. They will cry together, silently, "O taste, and see, that the Lord is good; blessed is the man that trusteth in Him" (Ps 33:9). Then the warfare will cease, as will defilement and all sinful movements. Then the holy peace of the Holy Trinity will reign, then the treasure-house is sealed and remains un-plundered. Pray that you will come to know this and acquire this, and come to rejoice in Christ Jesus, our Lord.[222]

The majestic descriptions of the Fathers inspire the greatest reverence for the prayerful worship of the heart. This reverence and wisdom itself require of us that we reject all premature, self-willed, proud, rash exertions to enter into this mystical sanctum. Reverence and wisdom teach us to remain in attentive prayer, the prayer of repentance, at the doors of the mystical temple. Attention and compunction of spirit—this is that inner room that is given as a refuge to the repentant sinner. It is the threshold of the Holy of Holies. Let us hide there and shut ourselves off from sin. Let all who suffer from moral lameness, all lepers, all blind and withered men, all sinners who are "waiting for the moving of the water" (John 5:3), that is, the mercy and grace of God, gather in this Bethesda. The One Lord Himself, in His own good time, will give healing and entrance into the temple, but only by His unknowable good will.

"I know whom I have chosen" (John 13:18), "You did not choose Me, but I chose you and appointed you that you should go and bear fruit, and that your fruit should remain, that whatever you ask the Father in My name He may give you" (John 15:16).

An extremely good method of learning the Jesus Prayer is offered by the Hieromonk Dorotheos, a Russian ascetic and writer.

> Whoever prays with the lips, but is unmindful of the soul and does not protect the heart, such a person prays to the air, not to God. His work is in vain, for God only listens to the mind and to zeal, not to volubility. One must pray with one's entire zeal—with the soul and mind and heart, with fear of God, with one's entire strength. The prayer of the mind does not allow entrance into the inner room either to absentmindedness or foul thoughts. Do you want to learn how to pray with the mind and heart? I will teach you. Pay diligent attention to my words. Listen to me, my dear one. At first, you must practice the Jesus Prayer aloud, with the lips, tongue, and speech, to yourself alone. When the lips, tongue, and senses become satiated with the prayer uttered aloud, then the spoken prayer ends and begins to be spoken in whisper. After this, one must train the mind to focus in on the feeling of the prayer in the throat. Then the prayer of the mind and the heart can begin to be uttered without constraints, whenever one wishes, constantly rising up, renewing itself, and acting at any time, during any task, in any place.[223]

St Seraphim of Sarov commands the beginner, according to the former custom of the Sarov Hermitage, to pray without ceasing: *Lord Jesus Christ, Son of God, have mercy on me, a sinner.* "During prayer," he says,

> pay attention to yourself, that is, gather your mind and unite it with your soul. At first—for a day, two, or more—practice the prayer with the mind alone, separately, paying attention to every separate word with special attention. When the Lord will warm your heart with the fire of His grace

and will unite you into a single spirit, then the prayer will flow within you without hindrance and will always be with you, giving you joy and nourishing you.[224] This is the meaning of Isaiah's words: "your dew is healing unto them."[225] When you will contain within yourself this spiritual food, that is, converse with the Lord, then why should you visit the cells of your brothers, even if you are invited? Truly, I say to you that idle talk is idle love. If you do not understand yourself, then can you discuss anything else or teach others? Be silent. Be silent always, and always remember the presence of God and His name. Enter no dispute with anyone, but at the same time guard yourself from condemning those who speak much and laugh much. Be in this case both deaf and dumb. No matter what they say about you, let it pass into one ear and out the other. Emulate the example of St. Stephen the New, whose prayer was ceaseless, whose manner was meek, whose lips were silent, whose heart was humble, whose spirit was full of compunction, whose body and soul both were pure, whose virginity was unblemished, whose poverty was true and whose non-acquisitiveness was eremitic. His obedience was without complaint; his labors were full of endurance; his work was zealous. While you sit at meals, do not look around and do not condemn others for how much they eat, but pay attention to yourself and feed your soul with prayer.[226]

The elder, having given such an instruction to a new monk who spent his life in active labors in a community of monastics, and having given him this practice of prayer that is appropriate for an active life, forbids premature, rash striving to the contemplative life and to the prayer appropriate to such a life:

Anyone who desires to live a spiritual life must begin with an active life, and only then can he pass on to the contemplative life. Without the active life, it is impossible to enter the contemplative life. An active life serves to purify us of sinful passions and raises us to a level of active perfection, and by this it lays down a path toward the contemplative life. Only those who have been purified of passions can approach it, only those who have been fully trained in the active life, as we can see from the words of the Scripture: "Blessed are the pure in heart, for they shall see God" (Matt 5:8) and from the words of St Gregory the Theologian, who said that only those who are complete in their experience (in the active life) can approach the contemplation of the heart. One must approach the contemplative life only with fear and trembling, with compunction of heart and with humility, with much testing of oneself by the Holy Scriptures and under the guidance of an experienced elder, if such a one can be found, but never with brazenness and self-will. The audacious and contemptuous one, according to St Gregory of Sinai, who has not approached exalted spiritual states with the necessary worthiness, pridefully tries to force such a state to himself prematurely. Again, if anyone dreams, in his self-delusion, that he is capable of acquiring exalted prayerful states, then his desire is not a true one, but a demonic one. Him will the devil catch in his snares, as his slave.[227]

Thus warning against prideful striving for exalted states of prayer, one can say that the elder asserts the necessity for all monks in general, not in any way excluding beginners and novices, to live an attentive life of constant prayer. It has been noticed, for the most part, that direction that the monk takes upon his entrance into a monastery remains his guiding principle for his entire life.

"The gifts of grace," said St Seraphim, "are given only to those who have the prayer of the mind and who stand vigil over their souls.[228] Those who truly have decided to serve God must exercise the remembrance of God and constant prayer to the Lord Jesus Christ, repeating mentally: *Lord Jesus Christ, Son of God, have mercy on me, a sinner*. Such a practice, together with vigilance to avoid distraction and the maintenance of the peace of the conscience, can bring one near to God and to union with Him. There is no other way we can approach God, according to St Isaac the Syrian, than by ceaseless prayer."[229]

St Seraphim recommends that monks and novices who desire to practice the Jesus Prayer, to more easily avoid distraction and to remain in attentiveness, should stand in church with their eyes closed, only opening them when they will be burdened with a desire to sleep. Then he recommends that they raise their eyes to the holy icons, which will also protect the mind from distraction and inspire it to prayer. The beginner can very easily train himself in the practice of the Jesus Prayer at the long monastic services. Standing during the services, why should he pointlessly and to his own harm wander mentally everywhere? This is impossible to avoid unless the mind be tied to something. Practice the Jesus Prayer. It will hold your mind back from wandering, and you will become more focused, more profound, and you will pay much better attention to the reading and singing in church, at the same time unnoticeably and gradually training yourself in the prayer of the mind.

St Seraphim advises anyone who desires to live an attentive life to not pay attention to rumors, from which the mind becomes filled with idle and vain thoughts and remembrances. He commands to pay no attention to others' business, to not think, judge, or speak of them at all. He commands him to avoid conversations, to act as though he were a wanderer, and to honor any fathers and brothers with a bow in silence, not allowing himself to look at their faces with too much attention,[230] because such gazing will indelibly lead to some kind of impression felt in the soul, which will then lead to distraction, leading the mind away from prayer. In general, the one who leads an attentive life should not look at anything fixedly and should not listen to anything with too much attention. Instead, he should see, but as though not seeing. He should listen in passing, so that the memory and attention would always be free, devoid of the impressions of the world, capable and ready to only accept divine impressions.

It is obvious that the methods offered by Fr Dorotheos and St Seraphim are identical to the one offered by St John of the Ladder. However, St John expressed his method with especial vividness and definitiveness. This father belonged to the ranks of the oldest and greatest teachers of monasticism, and he is admitted as such by the Universal Church. Later holy writers cite him as a trustworthy instructor, a living vessel of the Holy Spirit. On this foundation, we offer his method, trusting in its reliability, for the universal application of our beloved fathers and brothers, not only living in the monasteries, but living in the world—to whomever has a sincere desire to unfeignedly, successfully pray in a God-pleasing manner. This method cannot be avoided. To neglect it would mean to tear attentiveness from prayer, and without attentiveness, prayer is not prayer. It is dead! It is useless blabbing, harmful to the soul, insulting to God. The one who attentively prays inevitably prays by this method, whether more or less. If attention will increase and become stronger during prayer, then inevitably the form of prayer spoken by St John will appear. "Ask with tears," he says, "seek with obedience, and push with long-suffering. For this is the only way that 'every one asks receives, and he who seeks finds, and to him who knocks it will be opened' (Matt 7:8)."[231]

Experience will not fail to show that while using this method, especially in the beginning, one must utter the words with extreme slowness, so that the mind will have time to mold itself to the words. This cannot be achieved through hurried reading. The method of St John is very useful both when praying the Jesus Prayer and when reading the prayer rule, even during the reading of the Psalter and the books of the Fathers. You must learn to read thus, as though reading by syllables—with such a slow pace. Having learned by this method, one can acquire the prayer of the lips, mind, and heart, in the proper measure for anyone leading an active life. St Kallistos, Patriarch of Constantinople, speaks thus concerning prayer:

Ceaseless prayer consists of the constant calling upon the name of God. Whether you are conversing, sitting, walking, working, eating, or doing any other task, you must at all times and in ever place call upon the name of God, according to the command of the Scriptures: "Pray without ceasing" (1 Thess 5:17). Only thus are the attacks of the enemy defeated. You must pray with the heart, praying aloud when you are alone. If anyone is in the marketplace or in the society of others, he should not pray with the lips, but with the mind alone. You should be vigilant over your sight and always look down to guard yourself from distraction and from the snares of the enemy. Perfect prayer is uttered to God without the deviation of the mind into distraction, when all the thoughts and senses of the person are gathered into a single thought of prayer. Prayer and psalmody must be performed not only with the mind, but with the lips as well, as David said, "O Lord, open Thou my lips, and my mouth shall show forth Thy praise" (Ps 50:17). The apostle, showing that the lips are necessary as well, said, "By Him let us continually offer the sacrifice of praise to God, that is, the fruit of our lips giving thanks to His name" (Heb 13:15).[232]

St Barsanuphius the Great, in answer to a hieromonk's question about how to pray, answered,

You must exercise somewhat in psalmody, and somewhat aloud. Time is needed also to test and be vigilant over your thoughts. Whoever has many different kinds of food for lunch eats much and with pleasure, while whoever eats the same food day in and day out not only eats it with not pleasure but sometimes even comes to feel abhorrence for it. The same is true of our spiritual state. In psalmody and prayer of the lips, do not bind yourself, but do as much as the Lord gives you. Do not abandon reading or inner prayer. A little of this, a little of that, and thus you will spend the day, pleasing God. Our perfect Fathers did not have specific rules of prayer, but their entire day was devoted to the fulfillment of their rule. They spent a little time in psalmody, a little time in spoken prayer, a little time in the testing of thoughts, they even spent a little time eating, though they did not worry about it much. Everything they did with the fear of God.[233]

These are the words of a venerable father who was remarkably advanced in the life of prayer. Experience will teach everyone who practices prayer that the utterance of several Jesus Prayers aloud—as well as any prayer—is very useful to hold the mind back from being ravished by distraction. When the enemy presses an especially fierce attack, when the will weakens and the mind darkens, spoken prayer is absolutely necessary. Attentive spoken prayer is also prayer of the mind and of the heart.

Our humble words are not intended to turn away our beloved brothers and fathers from a striving toward more exalted prayerful advancement. On the contrary, we desire this with all our heart. Let all monks be like angels and archangels, who have no rest night or day from the divine love that arouses them to constant and insatiable satiation through glorifying God. It is exactly to ensure the unutterable riches of the prayer of the heart in its own time that we give these warning against acting prematurely, incorrectly, audaciously. What is forbidden is rash, overstimulated striving to reveal within oneself the grace-filled prayer of the heart. This striving is forbidden because its reason is either ignorance or insufficient knowledge and a proud belief of one's capability and worthiness to acquire prayer of grace. This striving is forbidden because the prayer of grace cannot blossom with one's own exertions. This striving is forbidden, for it is a vehement attempt to break down the doors of the mystical temple of God, and it may prevent the goodness of God having mercy on us at some point. It can prevent His making the unworthy worthy, His giving gifts to those not expecting them, those who have condemned themselves to eternal sufferings in the prisons of hell. This gift is given to the humble, to those who belittle themselves before the greatness of the gift. The gift is given to him who has rejected his own will and who has trusted in the will of God. The gift is given to the one who tames and mortifies the flesh and blood in himself, the one who tames and mortifies his carnal mindset concerning the commandments of the Gospel.

Life shines forth commensurate with the degree of the body's mortification. Having come unexpectedly, only by its own desire, it completes and fulfills the mortification begun willingly. Those who are not careful, especially the stubborn, those led by their own self-conceit and self-will, the strivers for exalted states of prayer—these will always be stamped with the seal of rejection, according to the dictates of the spiritual law.[234] Taking this seal off is very difficult, most often impossible. For what reason? Pride and self-conceit that lead to self-delusion, intercourse with demons, and slavery to them do not allow one to see the incorrectness and danger of one's situation. They make it impossible to see either the bitter intercourse with demons or the calamitous, fatal slavery to them. As the Fathers said, "First dress yourself in leaves, and only later, when God commands, you can bring your fruits."[235] First acquire attentive prayer. The one who is purified and prepared by attentive prayer, the one who is educated and bound by the commandments of the Gospel—he will be given the prayer of grace by the all-merciful God in His own good time.

The only teacher of prayer is God Himself, and so true prayer is a gift of God.[236] God gives gradual advancement in prayer to the one who prays in compunction of spirit, constantly, with the fear of God. Attentive and humble prayer gives rise to spiritual activity and warmth that give life to the heart. The revivified heart attracts the mind to itself, becoming the temple of the prayer of grace,[237] the treasure house of spiritual gifts given to it according to its worthiness.

"Labor by the pain of your heart to acquire warmth and prayer, and God will give them to you always. Forgetfulness banishes them; forgetfulness itself comes from sloth."[238] If you want to be delivered from forgetfulness and from imprisonment, first acquire the spiritual fire for yourself. Only its warmth banishes forgetfulness and sloth. And this fire is only acquired by a striving toward God.

> Brother! If you, day and night, do not seek the Lord with pain in your heart, you will not be able to progress. If you, leaving everything else behind, will work at this, then you will acquire it. As the Scriptures say, "Be still, and know . . . " (Ps 45:11) Brother! Petition the goodness of the One Who "desires all men to be saved, and to come unto the knowledge of the truth" (1 Tim 2:4), so that He will give you the spiritual wakefulness that lights this spiritual fire. The Lord, the Master of heaven and earth, came to earth to bring down this fire to earth. I will pray together with you, as much as I am able, for God to give you this wakefulness. He gives grace to all who ask with labor and diligence. When it comes, it will direct you to the truth. It will illumine the eyes, correct the mind, drive away the sleep of paralysis and sloth. It returns the shine to weapons that have become covered with rust in the ground of laziness. It returns brightness to the clothes that have been dirtied in imprisonment by barbarians. It inspires hatred for the foul carrion that comprises the food of captivity. It inspires the desire to be filled with the great Sacrifice brought by our great High Priest. This is that Sacrifice, concerning which it was revealed to the prophet that it purifies sins and takes away iniquities (see Isa 6:7), forgives the sorrowful, gives grace to the humble (see Prov 3:34), appears in the worthy, and through it they will inherit eternal life in the name of the Father, the Son, and the Holy Spirit.[239]

"Spiritual wakefulness or vigilance is a spiritual art that completely delivers a person, with the help of God, from sinful works and passionate thoughts and words, when it is performed for a long time and with great diligence. It is the stillness of the heart; it is the preservation of the mind; it is attention to yourself, devoid of any thought, always, constantly, and endlessly calling Christ Jesus, the Son of God, and God, breathing through Him, and with Him courageously attacking the enemies and confessing to Him."[240] Other Fathers are in agreement with him.[241]

"The first that comes into the heart will restore prayer. When it will rise again and ascend into heaven, then the fire will descend into the upper room of the soul."[242] These words belong to the luminary of Sinai, St John of the Ladder. Evidently, this holy man speaks from his own blessed experience. Something similar occurred with St Maximus the Hut-burner. "I," he said to St Gregory of Sinai,

> from my youth, had a great faith in my Mistress, the Mother of God, and I prayed to her with tears, that she would give me the grace of the prayer of the mind. One time, I came, according to my custom, to Her temple and zealously prayed to her about this. I approached her icon and began to venerate it with reverence, and suddenly I felt that into my breast and heart a warmth descended that did not burn my innards, but on the contrary, sweetened and bedewed me, inspiring my soul to compunction. From this moment, my heart began to remain within itself during prayer and my mind began to be sweetened with the memory of my Jesus and the Mother of God. I had Him, the Lord Jesus, constantly within myself. For this moment, prayer never ceased in my heart.[243]

The prayer of grace appeared suddenly, unexpectedly, as a gift from God. The soul of the saint was prepared to receive this gift by zealous, attentive, humble, constant prayer. Grace-filled prayer did not remain in the saint without its usual consequences, which are completely unknown or uncharacteristic to a carnal or emotional state. The abundant revelation of spiritual fire in the heart, the fire of divine love, was described by St George, the recluse of Zadonsk, from his own experience. But before he received this, he was sent a divine gift of repentance that purified the heart in preparation for love. This gift acted like fire that destroys everything that defiles the courts of the Holy and Powerful Lord,[244] and that brought the body to complete exhaustion.

"The holy and heavenly fire," said St John of the Ladder, "consumes some because of the insufficiency of their purity, while others it, on the contrary, illumines, for they have achieved perfection. The one and the same fire is called a consuming fire and a light that illumines. For this reason, some come out of their prayer as though they were in a heated bath, feeling some relief from defilement and materiality, while others come out shining with light, dressed in the clothing of humility and joy. Those who, after their prayer, sense neither one or the other are still praying bodily, not spiritually."[245]

Spiritual prayer, as here named, is the prayer that is moved by divine grace, while bodily prayer is prayer performed by the person with his own exertion, without the obvious cooperation of grace. Bodily prayer, as St John of the Ladder says, is also necessary to receive the prayer of grace in its own time.[246] What are the signs of the coming of the prayer of grace? It shows its arrival by supernatural tears, and then man enters through the gates of the sanctum of God, into his own heart, into unutterable confession.

Before we begin to describe the method that is offered by the Holy Fathers almost exclusively for those who practice silence (that is, advanced monks), we consider it necessary to prepare the reader somewhat. The writings of the Fathers can be compared to a pharmacy in which many different kinds of medicines are found. However, the sick man, not being well acquainted with the medicinal arts and not having the guidance of a doctor, will have a very difficult time choosing the correct medicine for his particular illness. If in his self-reliance and frivolity, without a good doctor he is unable to choose the correct medicine, then the sick man in a hurry decides for himself and chooses a medicine almost at random, and this choice can be the most unfortunate one. This medicine, beneficial if properly used, can become not only useless, but even harmful if incorrectly taken.

We are in the same situation as this unfortunate sick man, for we have no spirit-bearing guides in relation to the writings of the Holy Fathers concerning the mystical actions of the prayer of the heart and its consequences. The teaching concerning prayer that has come down to us in the books of the Fathers is expressed with satisfactory fullness and clarity, but we, remaining ignorant of the mysteries described by these books (they express, in the greatest detail, the various actions and states of the beginner, the intermediate, and the advanced), we find ourselves in a difficult position of having to choose the actions and states that are most proper for us. Unspeakably fortunate is he who has understood and sensed the degree of this difficulty. Some who had not understood this and had read the words of the Holy Fathers superficially had become superficially acquainted with its offered methods, began to practice methods inappropriate for their degree of spiritual progress, and ended up harming themselves. St Gregory of Sinai, in his work written for an extremely advanced hesychast named Longinus, said, "Silence is one thing, but the common monastic life is something else. Everyone who remains in the life to which he was called will be saved. Therefore, I am afraid to write this down, because of the infirm who will come to see that you live among them. For everyone who attempts a too-difficult labor of prayer because of instruction or hearing from others will perish, as one who has no guide."[247]

The Holy Fathers write that many who have attempted the labor of prayer incorrectly, according to methods for which they had not yet been prepared or were incapable of, fell into self-delusion and even madness. It is not only careless reading of the books of the Fathers without proper understanding that leads to great harm, but even conversations with great saints of God and listening to their preaching can also be harmful, if one is not prepared. This is what happened to the Syrian monk Malpatus. He was a student of St Julian. Malpatus visited St Anthony the Great with his elder, and he heard from him the most exalted teachings concerning the monastic life—everything about self-mortification, the prayer of the mind, purity of soul, and spiritual vision. Not understanding the teaching fully, and being lit on fire by carnal zeal, Malpatus laid on himself the strictest of labors in complete reclusion, with the hope of acquiring that exalted spiritual state of which he heard from the Great Anthony and which he himself saw and perceived in the great Anthony. The consequence of this action was the worst kind of self-delusion. Commensurate with the strength of his labor was the strength of his demonic delusion, and the conceit that enveloped the soul of the unfortunate monk made his soul incapable of repentance and, consequently, healing. Malpatus became the forefather of the Eutychian heresy.[248]

What a tragic event! What a bitter spectacle! A disciple of a great saint, having heard a teaching of the greatest of saints, because of his incorrect application of this teaching to his own life, perished! He perished at a time when, because of the abundance of saints capable of guiding and healing, very few perished from demonic delusion. This example I offer to warn you. Even in the light of countless luminaries, the light of inner monasticism—that is, the mystical, prayerful solitude and stillness of the mind in the heart—was admitted as surrounded by dangers. The more so is this path dangerous during our own time of dark night. All the luminaires of heaven are now covered in dark and thick clouds. One can only travel with extreme care, by feel alone. Studying the Fathers' books, left for us by the providence of God for the moral guidance of contemporary monasticism, is no small labor. To complete it, one needs self-denial, the abandonment of earthly cares—not to mention distractions, amusements, and pleasures—one needs to live by the commandments of the Gospel. One needs purity of mind and heart, for only such a heart can see and understand the spiritual, holy, and mystical teaching of the Spirit concerning the degrees of purification. Whoever has come to know that in our own time the treasure of salvation and Christian perfection is hidden in words uttered by the Holy Spirit or under His influence—that is, in the Scriptures and the writings of the Holy Fathers—let him rejoice spiritually that he has acquired such essentially beneficial knowledge. Let him hide completely from the world in a virtuous life. Let him, for the joy thereof, go and sell everything he has and buy the field in which salvation and perfection are hidden (see Matt 13:44).

To comprehensively study the Scriptures, with the accompanying beginner's method, requires a long time. After this study of the Scriptures, with extreme caution, constantly asking for God's help with prayer and tears, with poverty of spirit, one can attempt those methods that lead to perfection. A certain holy monk told of himself that for twenty years he studied the writings of the Fathers, living the usual life of a monk in a communal monastery. Only after this time did he decide to attempt the contemplative monastic life which he had theoretically studied by reading and, probably (considering the time period of early Egyptian monasticism), from conversations with experienced fathers. Spiritual advancement in the contemplative life by means of reading goes much slower than with the guidance of a spirit-bearing elder. What each holy writer has written comes from his own grace-filled disposition and his own unique life and therefore corresponds to his unique disposition and manner of living.

We must pay especial attention to this point. Let us not get carried away and excited by a book written as with a finger of fire, a book that tells of exalted prayer and spiritual states that are not proper to us. By inflaming the imagination, such reading can harm us by giving us the knowledge and desire for labors that are untimely or even impossible for us. Let us turn to the book of a father who, according to the moderation of his spiritual advancement, was the closest to our own spiritual state. With that in mind, a monk who is only beginning the inner labor of prayer can be offered the instructions of St Seraphim of Sarov, the writings of St Paisius Velichkovsky and his friend, Schemamonk Vasily. The holiness of these people and the correctness of their teachings are not subject to doubt. After studying these books, one can turn to the instructions of St Nilus of Sora. This book is small to look at, but its spiritual depth is extraordinarily great. It is hard to find a question concerning the Jesus Prayer of the mind that is not answered in this book. Everything is written with unusual simplicity, clarity, and completeness. His method for practicing the Jesus Prayer is equally beneficial. However, it should be noted that both his method and the entire book are intended for monks who are already capable of stillness.

St Nilus commands silence of thoughts, all thoughts, sinful or vain thoughts, as well as even seemingly beneficial and spiritual thoughts. Instead of any thoughts, he commands to constantly gaze at the depth of the heart and say: *Lord Jesus Christ, Son of God, have mercy on me.* One can pray standing or sitting or even lying down. Those who are strong in health can pray standing and sitting, while the infirm can pray lying down, because in this prayer is primarily a labor of the spirit, not the body. We must give the body the kind of posture that will give the spirit as much freedom as is necessary for its proper activity. We must remember that here we speak of the labor of monks who have already brought their physical desires into some proper order by their sufficient physical labors, and because of their spiritual success, they can now pass from a physical labor to a spiritual one. St Nilus commands the monk to confine his mind in his heart and to hold the breath as much as possible, to breathe as little as possible. What does this mean? This means that one must pray very quietly. In general, all movements of the blood must be contained, and the soul and body must be kept in a calm position, in a position of silence, reverence, and fear of God.

Without this, the action of the spirit may not begin in us; it appears only when all the movements and upsurges of the blood grow quiet. Experience will soon teach us that to restrain the breath—that is, to breathe slowly and without effort—helps to bring one into a state of stillness and to gather the mind from its wandering. "Many are the virtuous undertakings," said St Nilus,

> but all of them are partial in their importance. However, the prayer of the heart is the source of all good things; it feeds the soul as from a garden. This practice—that is, the vigilance of the mind in the heart, beyond all thoughts—is very difficult for the untrained. It is difficult not only for beginners, but even for those who have long labored, but who have not yet kept and preserved within the heart the sweetness of prayer from the action of grace. From experience, we know that the infirm consider this practice to be very difficult and uncomfortable. Whenever anyone acquires grace, then he prays without difficulty and with love, being consoled by grace. When the *action* of prayer comes, then it attracts the mind to itself, gives it joy, and frees it from distraction.[249]

In order to learn the method offered by St Nilus of Sora, it is very useful to practice it together with the method of St John of the Ladder—that is, to pray without hurrying, very slowly. In the process of offering his method, St Nilus cites many fathers of the Eastern and Universal Church, especially St Gregory of Sinai.

The writings of St Gregory of Sinai, though of great spiritual worth, are not as accessible and clear as the writings of St Nilus of Sora. The reason for this is the style of writing, certain ideas of that time concerning various objects that are now foreign to us, especially the advanced spiritual stage both of the one who wrote the book and the one to whom the book is intended. The method of prayer offered by St Gregory is almost the same as the one offered by St Nilus, who took his teaching concerning prayer both from St Gregory's book and from his own conversations with St Gregory's disciples when he traveled through the East.

> In the morning, says St Gregory, citing the all-wise Solomon, "sow your seed," that is, your prayer, "and in the evening do not withhold your hand," so that the constancy of your prayer, interrupted by distances, does not miss that hour in which it might be heard: "for you do not know which will prosper, either this or that" (Eccl 11:6). From the morning, having sat down on your chair, which should be about the height of a span, bring your mind down from your head into your heart and keep it there, having bowed down in pain, great pain of the chest, shoulders, and neck, and constantly exclaim with your mind or soul: Lord Jesus Christ, have mercy on me. Restrain your breath a little, so that you do not breathe carelessly.[250]

As for the teaching concerning the restraining of the breath, St Gregory cites St Isaiah the Solitary, St John of the Ladder, and St Symeon the New Theologian.

> If we want to find the truth and come to know it without error, then let us try to have a single action of the heart, completely invisible, in no way allowing freedom to the imagination, not allowing fantasy to draw the likeness of some saint or of light, because it is typical of demonic delusion, especially in the beginning of this labor, to delude the mind of the inexperienced through such false imaginings. Let us try to have in the heart a single action of prayer that warms and gives joy to the mind, that ignites the soul to unutterable love of God and man. Then prayer gives rise to considerable humility and compunction, because prayer in beginners is the constantly-moving activity of the Holy Spirit. This action in the beginning is like fire that sprouts from the heart, and in the end it is like sweet-smelling light.[251]

The beginner in this case means the beginner in the labor of hesychasm, not the beginner monk in general. The entire book of St Gregory is intended to instruct advanced hesychasts. Again St Gregory says,

> Some, when giving a teaching concerning prayer, offer a method of praying with the lips, while others suggest praying with the mind alone. I offer the one and the other. Sometimes the mind, being downcast, becomes tired of practicing the prayer, while at other times the lips become exhausted, and so one must pray with both the lips and the mind. However, one must cry out quietly and without confusion, so that the voice does not affect the emotions and attention of the mind, thereby hindering prayer. The mind, having habituated itself to the practice of prayer, will advance and will accept from the Spirit the power to powerfully pray in all the different ways. Then he will not need to pray with the lips and will not even be able to, for he has become completely satisfied with the prayer of the mind.[252]

By thus suggesting that one may pray sometimes with the lips, St Gregory combines his method with the method of St John of the Ladder. In essence, they are one and the same, but St Gregory speaks more specifically of the prayer of those who have achieved a certain level of spiritual progress. The one who diligently practices the method of St John of the Ladder will achieve, given time, that prayerful state of which St Gregory speaks. Prayer, according to the authoritative, practical opinion of St Gregory, must be accompanied especially by patience.

> The monk practicing silence must for the most part sit while practicing the prayer because of the difficulty of this labor, and sometimes he may even lie down on his bed, to give his body some rest. Fulfilling the command to continue earnestly in prayer (Col 4:2) means that you must sit at prayer with patience and not stand up quickly, showing lack of courage because of the physical difficulty of the prayer of the mind and the constant immersion of the mind in the heart. This is what the prophet said: "Agony seizes as a woman giving birth" (Isa 21:3). However, having bowed your head down and gathered your mind in your heart—if your heart has opened for you—call upon the aid of the Lord Jesus. Your shoulders will hurt and your head will often be subjected to aching, but endure with constancy and zeal, searching for the Lord in the heart, for the kingdom of heaven is the inheritance of those who coerce themselves and who take it by force (see Matt 11:12). The Lord indicated that true zeal is revealed in endurance of these and other, similar, pains. Endurance and patient waiting in every endeavor will give rise to many spiritual and physical sicknesses.[253]

The word "sickness" here, more often than not, means not "illness," but compunction of spirit, the sorrow of the spirit, the pain and suffering it feels from a vivid sense of its own sinfulness, from a perception of eternal death, from the knowledge of enslavement by the fallen spirits. The suffering of the spirit is communicated to the heart and body, for they are inextricably linked with the spirit, and by natural necessity, they take part in all spiritual states. In the physically infirm, the compunction of the spirit and its sorrow fully replace physical labors (see Isaac the Syrian, Homily 89). However, those who have a strong constitution will inevitably have to endure constraint of the body. Without this constraint of the body, their hearts will never acquire the blessed sorrow that is born in the infirm from a perception and acknowledgment of their weakness.

> Every endeavor, physical or spiritual, that does not include either pain or difficulty, will never bear fruit, because "the kingdom of heaven suffers violence, and the violent take it by force" (Matt 11:12). This "violence" means physical pain in the body. Many, for the duration of many years, have labored or continue to labor without pain, but since they labor without pain and the warm zeal of the heart, they remain devoid of both purity and the Holy Spirit when they reject the pain of their labors. Those who labor with carelessness and weakness only appear to be laboring, as they think, a great deal, but they do not reap any harvest, being always without constraint. A witness of this is he who said that if all aspects of our life are exalted, but we have no pain in our heart, then our life is erroneous and useless (*The Ladder*, chapter 7). The great Ephraim agrees, saying, "As you work, work with pain in the heart, so that you can cast from yourself the pain of vain labors." If, according to the Prophet Isaiah in chapter 21, our loins are not filled with pain, being exhausted by our labor of fasting, and if we do not suffer, like a woman giving birth, through the painful strengthening of our heart, then we will not give birth to the Spirit of salvation on the field of the heart, as you have heard, but we will only (and this is worthy only of pity and mockery!) boast, imagining that we are *someone* because of our useless desert and our paralyzed hesychasm. During our passage from this life, we will inevitably come to reap our just harvest.[254]

The teaching of St Gregory concerning this pain that must accompany true inner prayer of the hesychast can seem to be strange for a carnal or emotional mindset that is little acquainted with the experience of monastic life. We invite such people to pay attention to the proofs that are acquired by experience.

These proofs provide witness that not only the prayer of the mind, but even attentive reading of the profound works of the Fathers concerning such prayer, produce headaches. The compunction of the heart, due to the revelation by the prayer of one's sinfulness, imprisonment, and spiritual death, is so powerful that it produces pain and a kind of sickness in the body. The existence of such physical pain is unknown to anyone who has no acquaintance with the labor of prayer. When the heart confesses its sinfulness to the Lord, in this calamitous state, the body is crucified. "I am brought into great torment and misery," said David, who was experienced in the labor of prayer, "I go mourning all the day long. For my loins are filled with sores, and there is no healing in my flesh. I was bitter, and utterly humbled; I roared for the very groaning of my heart" (Ps 37:7–9).

In the teaching of St Gregory of Sinai concerning prayer, one notices a particularity that he teaches, which is that the mind must concentrate itself on the heart. This is that labor that is called by the Fathers the artistic work of prayer that is forbidden to all beginning monks and laypeople. Such a method requires extensive preliminary instruction, and even prepared monks must approach such a labor with the greatest reverence, fear of God, and carefulness. Having commanded to focus the mind in the heart, the saint adds: if your heart has been opened. This means that union of the mind with the heart is a gift of divine grace, given in its time, according to God's disposition, but never prematurely, never by the will of the one attempting the labor. The gift of attentive prayer is usually preceded by extraordinary sorrows and spiritual difficulties sent down on our soul to deepen the knowledge of our own poverty and worthlessness.[255] The gift of God is attracted by humility and fidelity to God, expressed by zealous rejection of all sinful thoughts at their very inception. Faithfulness is the cause of purity. To purity and humility are the gifts of the Spirit given.

This creative method of the prayer of the mind is summarized with especial clarity and completeness by blessed Nicephorus, a monk who lived the life of silence on the Holy Mountain of Athos. He correctly calls the labor of prayer the art of arts, the science of sciences, since it gives to the mind and heart knowledge and impressions that flow directly from the Spirit of God, while all other sciences give merely human knowledge and impressions. The prayer of the mind is the highest school of theology.[256]

St Nicephorus said, "This greatest of great endeavors is gained by many (or even all) only by instruction. The rare few, being untutored, by zealous doing and ardency of faith receive this gift from God, but such an exception does not make the rule." For this reason, one must seek an instructor free of spiritual delusion, so that by his guidance we can be taught and instructed amid all the temptations of humiliation and pride that come from the enemy from the right and the left. For our master knows these temptations, having experienced them firsthand. He shows us the noetic path in a trustworthy manner, and we can easily walk this road by his guidance. If we have no guide, we must seek him with all diligence. If, even after an intensive search, we find no true guide, then, having called and prayed to God in compunction of spirit and with tears, in non-acquisitiveness, we must act in the following manner:

> You know that our breathing is composed of air, but we produce our breathing with our heart, nothing else. For it is the instrument of life and physical warmth. The heart pulls air inside you, so that by this inbreathing, you release the warmth inside you, giving you coolness. The servant of this mechanism is the lung, which God created to be rarified, therefore it easily pulls in and expels everything that it contains. In such a way, the heart, attracting coolness to itself by means of breathing and expelling warmth by the same process, inevitably follows the order necessary for the maintenance of life.
>
> So. Sit down, gather your mind, breath in through the nostrils (by which the breath enters the heart) and force your breathing into the quietest possible movement. Force your mind to descend into the heart, together with the breath. When it enters there, then you will be filled with joy and gladness, just as a man who has long been absent from his house cannot contain his joy when he returns to it, for now he again sees his wife and children. In the same way, when the mind unites with the soul, it is filled with unutterable sweetness and joy. Brother! Train your mind to not seek a quick exit from that place, even if at first it is depressed at a sense of inner constraint. When the mind becomes accustomed to its new state, it will no longer love to wander about outside, for the kingdom of Heaven is within us. Examining it there and seeking pure prayer, the mind begins to admit that everything on the outside is abominable and hateful.
>
> If you do enter with your mind into that place of the heart indicated by me, then give thanks to God, and glorify Him, and rejoice, and always persevere in this work. It will teach you everything that you lack in knowledge. You must know that your mind, finding itself in that place, must not be silent or remain slothful, but it must constantly work and learn, never ceasing to utter the words of the prayer: "Lord Jesus Christ, Son of God,

have mercy on me." This prayer, keeping the mind at attention, makes it unassailable by the attacks of the enemy, raising it to daily advancement in love and in godly desires. If, after having worked for a long time, O brother, you still cannot enter the domain of the heart as we have instructed you, then do as follows, and you will find what you seek together with the cooperation of God.

You know that every man's gift of speech is found in his bosom. Inside the bosom, even when the lips are silent, we can speak, converse, pray, sing psalms. To this gift of speech, after having removed from it every thought—you can do this if you desire—offer the invocation of the prayer: "Lord Jesus Christ, Son of God, have mercy on me." And force yourself to utter this inside your bosom instead of any other thought. When you will have done this for some time, then the entrance to the heart will open for you, without any doubt. We know this from our own experience. Then the entire host of virtues will come to you, together with the much-desired and sweet attentiveness in prayer: love, joy, peace, and the others. Through them all your petitions in Christ Jesus, our Lord, will be fulfilled.[257]

Here, first of all, we must pay attention to the spiritual state of the blessed father and the spiritual state that he anticipates in the monk that he instructs. His instruction concerning the stillness of the heart, in cooperation with the stillness of the body, is appropriate for those monks who have been well trained in the rules of communal monastic life, who are capable of battling with contrary thoughts and who know how to be vigilant over their mind. Blessed Nicephorus says to the monk that would follow his instructions: "You know that every man's gift of speech is found in his bosom. Inside the bosom, even when the lips are silent, we can speak, converse, pray, sing psalms." This vivid sense of the gift of speech in the bosom is a gift that only a few monks have. These monks are very advanced, having spent a long time practicing the method of prayer offered by St John of the Ladder. These monks have already acquired considerable attentiveness and have awakened their spirit by this attentive prayer. This awakening of the spirit is what St Nicephorus calls "the gift of speech" that so easily sympathizes with the mind.

People in the more usual spiritual state have a spirit struck down by the Fall, which sleeps a deep sleep, comparable to death. It is not capable of the spiritual exercises indicated here, and it awakens for them only when the mind constantly and forcefully acts to awaken it through the life-giving name of Jesus. The method offered by blessed Nicephorus is superlative. In his exposition of the method, the discerning reader can see that gradualism is necessary to rise up to this method and that its acquisition is a gift of God. This method is explained with even more detail in the works of Saints Kallistos and Ignatius Xanthopoulos, to which we now turn.

St Kallistos Xanthopoulos was a student of St Gregory of Sinai. He was a monk of the Holy Mountain who first learned the monastic life in a community of monks and only later passed to the silent life when he was found to be mature enough for it. He learned the Jesus Prayer while in obedience to the monastery's baker. He also had a good secular education, which is evident in the style of his book. In his later years, St Kallistos was raised to the rank of patriarch of Constantinople. St Ignatius was his closest friend and fellow laborer in the ascetic life. They both acquired great spiritual progress in prayer. Their book is written exclusively for hesychasts. They add to the method of Blessed Nicephorus, saying that it must be practiced with closed lips. They say that a beginner in the hesychastic life must practice the Jesus Prayer according to the method of Blessed Nicephorus, constantly leading the prayer into the heart quietly, using the technique of breathing through the nose, and breathing out just as quietly, having the mouth closed throughout the process.[258]

It is very important to know the significance that the holy guides give to the method that they offer, which, as an external mechanism, can never be confused with the actual work of prayer. In other words, the method itself is not the source of the success of prayer. In the progress of prayer, the power and grace of God are paramount; they accomplish everything. Methods are merely methods, necessary because of our infirmity, but obsolete for those who have already gained spiritual heights. To place all your hope in the method is very dangerous, because it can lead to a superficial, false understanding of prayer that can distract from a spiritual understanding of prayer, which is the only true understanding. False understanding of prayer always leads to fruitless or even harmful exercise in prayer.

"Know this, brother," they say, "that every art and every rule and every various endeavor is foreordained and properly established according to the principle that we cannot yet purely and attentively pray in the heart. When such pure prayer is acquired by the will and grace of our Lord Jesus Christ, then we, leaving behind all the many different methods, unite directly, in a way surpassing expression, with the One who unites alone."[259]

"By abiding in the aforementioned art of pure, attentive prayer of the heart—however, it can be partially impure and not completely devoid of distraction, evidently, because of the thoughts and memories of previous sins that come to battle against you—the laborer acquires the habit of praying without constraint, attentively, purely, and truly, that is, he comes to such a state in which his mind remains within the heart (and is not merely led there by force, trembling with fear, through the mediation of breathing techniques, jumping back out at the first opportunity). In such a state, the mind constantly turns to itself and lovingly remains in the heart and constantly prays."[260]

The labor of the prayer of the mind in the heart "is perfected by the mind through the overshadowing grace of God and through the single-minded (a technical, monastic term), heart-felt, pure, attentive, faithful invocation of the name of our Lord Jesus Christ, not merely from the aforementioned natural breathing technique or from the technique of sitting during the prayer in a quiet and dark place—God forbid! These methods were developed by the divine Fathers only as a means to gather the thoughts from their usual absent-mindedness, to return the mind to itself and to attention."[261]

"Before any other gifts of grace, the laborer receives from the Lord Jesus Christ attention in prayer and the ability to utter His name in the heart with faith. This process is somewhat aided by the natural technique that helps bring the mind down into the heart with the help of breathing through the nose, sitting in a quiet and dark place, and other such things."[262]

These fathers strictly forbid any premature striving to anything that is proper only for more advanced monks. They wanted every monk to follow the established order, according to the rules that were given by divine grace.

> You also, if you desire to learn the hesychasm that leads to Heaven, follow the established laws with wisdom. First of all, come to love obedience, and only then—hesychasm. Just as action is the ascent to vision, so also obedience leads to hesychasm. "Do not remove the eternal landmark which your fathers established" (Prov 22:30 LXX) "Woe to him who is alone when he falls" (Eccl 4:10). Thus, having placed a good foundation to your endeavor, you can, with time, crown the building of the Spirit with a blessed roof. As everything that is begun badly is eventually rejected, so also everything that is prosperously and well begun will be crowned with success, even if sometimes the opposite happens.[263]

In general, it is considered that before you have acquired attentive prayer (not delusive or temporary attention, that is, but constant and effective attentive prayer) it is useful to practice the Jesus Prayer within a community of monastics, aiding this practice with the active fulfillment of the commandments of the Gospel or (which is the same thing) humility. After receiving the gift of attentive prayer, one is allowed to approach hesychasm. This is how Saints Basil the Great and Gregory the Theologian acted. According to St Isaac the Syrian, they first labored in the fulfillment of those commandments that referred to living in human society. Their labor in prayer was, therefore, appropriate for that kind of life. This kind of life began to give their prayer stability and a lack of distraction, and only then did they abandon the communal life and go into the solitude of the desert. There they labored in the prayer of the inner man and eventually gained spiritual vision.[264]

True hesychasm is very difficult in our time, almost impossible. St Seraphim of Sarov, Ignatius of Nikiforov, Nikandr of Babaev, all of whom were monks extremely progressed in the Jesus Prayer, remained only part of the time in total silence, sometimes returning to their monastic communities. The latter in particular never left the monastery to lead an obvious life of silence in solitude, because he was a great hesychast in his soul.

The method of hesychasm that guided St Arsenius the Great was always a superlative one, and now it must be admitted to be the best. This father constantly remained silent, never visited the cells of his fellow monastics, and only received people into his own cell when absolutely necessary. In church, he stood somewhere behind a pillar. He neither wrote nor received letters and in general avoided all intercourse that could distract his attention. His only purpose in life was the preservation of attentiveness.[265] The way of life and hesychasm by which St Arsenius reached great spiritual heights is praised and offered for emulation by St Isaac the Syrian as a very effective, wise, and fruitful method.[266]

In conclusion to our excerpts from the writings of Saints Kallistos and Ignatius Xanthopoulos, we offer their opinion, gained by experience (which is in agreement with the opinion of other Holy Fathers) that to acquire attentive prayer of the heart, much time and labor is needed.

"To constantly pray within the heart," they say, "or to achieve even higher spiritual states, comes about not simply, not accidentally, not after small labors and a short amount of time (though there are rare exceptions to this rule, according to God's disposition), but it requires both a long period of time and no small effort, labors both of the soul and body, a long and protracted period of self-compulsion. Because of the superlative nature of the gifts and grace that we hope to commune of, our labors must be correspondingly difficult, so that, according to the mystical holy teaching, the enemy will be cast out of the pastures of the heart, and Christ will enter into them perceptibly." St Isaac said, "He who desires to see the Lord must endeavor to creatively purify his heart by the remembrance of God, and in this manner, with the brightness of this thoughts, he will see the Lord at all times." And St Barsanuphius, "If the inner labor by God's grace does not help a man, then in vain does he perform bodily labors. The inner work, together with pain in the heart, brings about purity, and purity is true stillness of the heart. Such stillness gives rise to humility, and humility makes man the abode of God. When God enters this abode, then the demons and passions are cast out, and man becomes the temple of God, filled with holiness, filled with illumination, purity, and grace. Blessed is he who sees the Lord in the inner treasure house of the heart, as in a mirror, and who with tears cries out to His goodness." St John of Karpathos: "Much time and labor in prayer is needed in order to find in one's undisturbed disposition of mind a certain Heaven of the heart, where Christ lives, as the apostle said: 'Do you not know yourselves, that Jesus Christ is in you?—unless indeed you are disqualified'" (2 Cor 13:5).[267]

We content ourselves with these quotations from the Holy Fathers, as sufficient to explain the practice of the Jesus Prayer. In other writings of the Fathers, the same teaching is summarized. We consider it necessary to repeat to our beloved fathers and brethren this warning: do not strive to read the writings of the Fathers concerning exalted practices and spiritual states, even if you are curious, even if you find great exaltation in the reading of such texts. Our freedom, in terms of time, must be especially limited. When grace-filled guides were available, then the unhealthy avidity of the beginner was easily spotted and healed. But now there is no one either to heal or even notice such tendency toward delusion. Oftentimes this dangerous avidity is even considered by inexperienced elders to be great spiritual progress, and the enthusiast is encouraged to even greater delusional ardor. This obsession, having acted on the monk and not having been noticed, will continue to act, deviating him ever more from the true path. It would not be remiss to say that the majority of monks are now found in various states of obsession. There are very few who have rejected this dangerous enthusiasm, and there are none who have not at least been subjected to this passion. For this reason, in this time when the books of the Fathers are the only means left to us for guidance in the practice of the Jesus Prayer, we must be especially careful and discerning when we read them, lest we turn this only guidance we have into a means for incorrect action and resulting spiritual disorder.

"Let us search," says St John of the Ladder concerning the choice of a spiritual guide, "not for clairvoyants, but for those who are humble-minded, for they are more appropriate for the illness that has overcome us, in accordance with our own morality. Let them also live close to us."[268] The same must be said about books. We must not choose the most exalted ones, but the ones most appropriate to our own spiritual state. "It is a great evil," said St Isaac the Syrian, "to instruct with exalted teachings someone who is still in the ranks of beginners and is a child in his spiritual development."[269]

When the carnal or emotional man hears a spiritual word, he understands it according to his own state. He perverts and twists this spiritual word and, following it in his own perverted understanding, acquires a false direction and then holds to this false road with obstinacy, as though this road was the one given by a holy word. A certain elder reached Christian perfection, by a special disposition of God, for he acquired the state of stillness, contrary to the usual rules, at an early age. At first, he lived the hesychastic life in Russia's forests (living in a hole in the ground) and then on Mount Athos. After he returned to Russia, he settled in a coenobitic provincial monastery. Many of the brothers, seeing in the elder the obvious signs of holiness, turned to him for advice. The elder instructed them based on his own experience and as a result only harmed the brothers. A certain monk who knew this elder well said to him, "Father! You are speaking to the brethren about actions and states that are inconceivable to their minds, but they, interpreting your words in their own way and acting according to that false interpretation are harming themselves." The elder answered him with holy simplicity: "I see it myself! What am I to do? I consider all to be better than me, and if they ask, I only tell them what I know to be true."

This elder did not know the communal monastic life. It is not only evil that is dangerous for us, but even good can harm us if we do it at the wrong time and in the wrong measure. Thus, for example, not only hunger is dangerous, but also overeating and eating the wrong kind of food, inappropriate to our age or physical state. "Nor do they put new wine into old wineskins, or else the wineskins break, the wine is spilled, and the wineskins are ruined. But they put new wine into new wineskins, and both are preserved" (Matt 9:17). This the Lord said concerning good deeds, which at all costs must correspond to the spiritual state of the doer. Otherwise, they may even destroy the doer and be destroyed; that is, they will be attempted in vain, for the harm and destruction of the soul, contrary to their proper function.

Other than the guides already mentioned, there are other handbooks to learn the proper practice of the Jesus Prayer. We will list the most important ones.

1. Prayer rope (traditional or old believer style). The traditional prayer rope has one hundred knots, while the old believer prayer rope has one hundred notches. Each one represents a single Jesus Prayer, since prayer rules are usually counted in hundreds of Jesus Prayers. One can also count prostrations using a prayer rope. Also, beginner monks use the prayer rope to practice the Jesus Prayer while seated. When attentiveness during prayer increases, then the monk ceases using the prayer rope, for his entire attention is given over to the prayer itself.

2. It is very beneficial to practice the Jesus Prayer together with full prostrations or bows to the waist. These prostrations must be done slowly, with a sense of repentance, as the blessed youth George did, according to the account of St Symeon the New Theologian in his homily on faith (see *The Philokalia*, Part I).

3. In church, or in general, during the practice of the prayer, it is helpful to keep your eyes closed.

4. Hold your left hand on your chest, a little above the left nipple. This simple mechanism will help you sense the aforementioned "power of speech," found in the chest area.

5. The Fathers recommend that a hesychast have a dark cell, with covered windows, to protect the mind from distraction and to help him focus on the heart.

6. A hesychast is recommended to sit on a low chair, first of all because attentive prayer requires physical stillness, and second of all in emulation of the blind poor man in the Gospels, who sat at the wayside and cried out, "Jesus, Son of David, have mercy on me!" (Mark 10:47). He was heard and his request was fulfilled. Furthermore, this low chair is symbolic of the dung heap on which Job sat outside the city when the devil struck him with a terrible illness from head to foot (see Job 2:8). The monk must consider himself to be lame, wounded, torn apart by his own sinfulness, cast out by it from his natural state, subjected to a state contrary to nature. From this calamitous state, he must cry out to the all-merciful and omnipotent Jesus, the Renewer of human nature, "Have mercy on me." A low chair is very useful for the practice of the Jesus Prayer. This is not to say that standing during prayer is rejected. However, since a true hesychast dedicates nearly all his time to prayer, then he sometimes has to practice it sitting,

sometimes even lying down. Especially those who are sick or elderly must avoid excessive bodily labor, lest they waste their energy and lose the ability to practice the labor of their soul. The essence of this practice is in the Lord and in His name. The paralytic was lowered on his bed before the Lord through the roof, and he received healing (Mark 2:4). Healing is attracted by humility and faith.

7. Ascetics of this prayer sometimes have need to help themselves by pouring cold water on themselves or by applying a wet towel to places of increased blood flow. The water should be warm, never frigid, because this kind of water actually encourages the warming of the blood. In general, any task requiring mental concentration has the tendency to increase the body's heat in certain bodily constitutions. St Dorotheos felt this heat when he studied the natural sciences, which is why he cooled himself off with water.[270] This kind of heat will definitely be felt by those who will force themselves especially intensely toward the union of the mind with the heart, using the aforementioned physical techniques and giving them far too much significance (and consequently not giving enough importance to more spiritual methods). Whenever one forces himself physically to do the work of the spirit, the heart begins to warm up. This warmth is a natural result of such labor, and not a spiritual gift. Any physical member of the body, when it is rubbed for a long time, becomes warm. The same occurs with the heart when it is constantly subjected to tension. This warmth is nothing but a physical reaction. It is a carnal warmth, a warmth of the blood, something belonging to the fallen nature.[271]

The inexperienced ascetic, having sensed this warmth, will inevitably think that it is significant in some way. He will find it a pleasant, sweet sensation, and this is the beginning of his self-delusion. Not only must we attach no especial significance to this warmth, but, on the contrary, we must take precautionary measures as soon as it appears. This precaution is necessary for the following reason: this warmth, belonging to the blood, not only passes through the regions of the chest but can very easily spread to the lower regions of the body and bring them into great agitation.

Some people who did not understand this condition fell into confusion, depression, even despair, as is well known from experience. Believing their situation to be calamitous, they came to famous elders, seeking healing in their counsel for their souls, torn apart by bitterness and confusion. These elders, having heard that the invocation of the name of Jesus caused carnal lust to be warmed up within these monks, became afraid of the snares of the devil.

They told these unfortunate ascetics that they had fallen into terrible demonic delusion, and the elders forbade them from further practicing the Jesus Prayer, considering it a source of evil. And these same elders then used these cases as proof of the dangers of the practice of the Jesus Prayer in general. And many believed this condemnation of the holy prayer, because of the respect commanded by these famous elders. Many believed, as though this were a truth confirmed by experience. However, what the elders considered to be terrifying demonic delusion is little more than increased blood flow in the lower regions of the body, produced by an unwisely intense, ignorant application of the physical techniques for the practice of the Jesus Prayer. This physical reaction can be easily remedied in two or three days by the constant application of a towel filled with warm water to the areas of the body that are afflicted.

It is much more dangerous, much closer to demonic delusion, when an ascetic, having sensed this warmth of the blood in the heart or the chest, considers it to be a manifestation of grace, thinking himself to be *something*. In such cases, he begins to invent for himself various spiritual joys, but in actual fact he darkens, deludes, enmeshes, and destroys himself through his self-conceit. The more an ascetic forces and exerts his body, the more will his blood warm up. This is natural! In order to moderate this warmth, in order to prevent it from descending to the lower parts of the body, one must not try to push the mind with especial tension toward the heart. One must not belabor the heart excessively, nor produce heat inside it by the excessive holding of one's breath and pressure applied to the heart. On the contrary, one must hold one's breath gently, leading the mind toward the heart gently. One must strive for the prayer to act in the very top region of the heart, where the power of speech resides, according to the teaching of the Fathers, and where, for this reason, spiritual worship must be offered.

When divine grace will overshadow the labor of prayer and will begin to unite the mind with the heart, then the physical warmth of the blood will completely disappear. Then the prayerful worship will completely change. It will become natural, completely free and easy. Then a different warmth will appear in the heart—a subtle, immaterial, spiritual warmth that produces no carnal agitation. On the contrary, it cools, illumines, bedews, acting like a healing, spiritual anointment of oil, leading one to an unutterable state of love for God and mankind, as St Maximus Kavsokalyvites recounts from his own blessed experience.[272]

I offer the fathers and brethren my humble advice, and I beg you not to reject it: do not coerce yourselves prematurely to reveal within yourselves the action of the prayer of the heart. Prudent caution is so very necessary, especially in our time, when it is nearly impossible to encounter a satisfactory guide for this path, at a time when the ascetic must seek the way into the treasure house of spiritual knowledge himself, by groping in the darkness, guided only by the writings of the Holy Fathers, from which he also must wisely choose the writings most appropriate to his particular case. Instead, live according to the commandments of the Gospel and practice the attentive Jesus Prayer according to the method offered by St John of the Ladder, uniting your prayer with tears, having a single principle and goal for your prayer—repentance.

Then, in a time known only to God, the action of the prayer of the heart will itself open up inside you. Such prayer, produced by the finger of God Himself, is far more preferable to prayer of the heart that is forcibly revealed in the heart through the application of physical techniques. It is better in several ways—it is much greater and more abundant. It is completely free of demonic delusion and other damage, because the one who has received prayer in this manner sees only the mercy of God, the gift of God in his prayer of the heart, while the one who has forcibly acquired it by using physical techniques cannot fail to ascribe great importance to his own labor in gaining the prayer. This is a serious handicap for the narrow path of the spirit, a serious obstacle, a serious hindrance to the further development of spiritual advancement. There is no limit or end to spiritual progress. Even the most insignificant, unnoticed reliance in something other than God Himself can stop spiritual progress completely, because the leader, the feet, the wings of spiritual advancement is faith in God. "Christ is everything for the faithful," said St Mark the Ascetic.[273] Only very few ascetics have reached the heights of spiritual life by relying on physical techniques alone, while a great many have been deranged and harmed. These techniques can be helpful with the guidance of an experienced elder, but if you are guided only by books, it is very dangerous, because of the ease with which you may fall, because of your ignorance and lack of wisdom, into demonic delusion and other spiritual and physical disorders.

For this reason, some people, seeing the harmful consequences of such an unwise practice of the Jesus Prayer, combined with a superficial and muddled understanding of the prayer, have ascribed spiritual harm not to ignorance or rashness, but to the all-holy Jesus Prayer itself. Is there anything more sorrowful, more calamitous than such blasphemy, such delusion?

The Holy Fathers, in their instructions concerning prayer of the heart, were not specific concerning in what part of the heart the prayer must be attempted, likely because during their times, no such instruction was needed.

St Nicephorus speaks of the "power of speech" in the chest as a generally known fact. It is difficult for an expert in some subject to foresee and anticipate all questions that may arise from complete ignorance. Where ignorance sees darkness, knowledge sees nothing unclear. In subsequent times, these unspecific writings of the Fathers concerning the heart have been a source of confusion and incorrect practice of the Jesus Prayer in those who, having no elder, did not satisfactorily examine the writings of the Fathers. Some of these decided to practice the creative prayer of the heart only on the foundation of quickly obtained, superficial knowledge, and they placed all their reliance on the physical techniques for the acquisition of spiritual prayer. A detailed examination of this subject has, therefore, become necessary.

The human heart looks like an elongated sac, widening at the top, tapering at the bottom. Its upper half, located opposite the left nipple, is firmly attached, while its lower half, descending to the bottom of the ribcage, is free. When it fluctuates, that is what we call the beating of the heart. Many, having no idea of the structure of the heart, believe the heart to be in that place where they physically feel a beat. Obstinately approaching the practice of the prayer of the heart, they direct their breathing toward the heart, but to the part of the heart that most quickly leads to carnal agitation. When they do this, their heartbeat intensifies, and they believe this purely physical reaction to be a spiritually advanced state, leading them to demonic delusion.

Schemamonk Vasily and St Paisius Velichkovsky wrote that among their contemporaries, many came to harm by misusing the physical techniques.[274] Subsequently, other examples of such spiritual disorder appeared often; they continue to appear in our own time, even though the desire to practice the Jesus Prayer has lessened to an extreme. It is impossible not to encounter this spiritual delusion, for it is the inevitable consequence of ignorance, self-will, conceit, premature and prideful zeal, and the complete diminishment of experienced elders. Schemamonk Vasily, citing St Theophylact and other Fathers, affirmed that the three powers of the soul—the intellectual, incensive, and desiring powers—are physically located in the following manner.

The intellectual power (the spirit of man) is found in upper part of the heart. The middle part of the heart houses the desiring power (the will), and the lower part of the heart houses the desiring power (as well as the physical senses). Whoever tries to inflame the lower part of the heart, inciting it to action, activates the desiring power of the soul. This part of the heart is closest to the genital region of the body, and by its nature it activates those regions of the body. So whoever incorrectly uses the breathing techniques of the Jesus

Prayer powerfully activates carnal lust in a purely physical manner. What a strange phenomenon! On the surface, it seems that the ascetic is praying, but his prayer only gives rise to sexual desire, which should be mortified by the practice of prayer. Then the ignorant one who incorrectly applied the physical techniques ascribes to the Jesus Prayer that which should instead be ascribed to his own ignorance!

The prayer of the heart is produced by the union of the mind with the spirit, two parts that were sundered by the Fall and are united by the grace of redemption. The conscience, humility, meekness, love for God and man, and other such qualities are focused in the spirit of man (the intellectual power). These are the qualities that must be united in prayer with the mind. All the ascetic's attention must be focused on this. This union is accomplished by the finger of God, Who alone is capable of healing the wound of the Fall. The practitioner of the prayer proves the sincerity of his will to receive this healing by constantly abiding in the prayer, by confining his mind to the words of prayer, by living externally and internally by the commandments of the Gospel, all of which make the spirit capable of union with the praying mind. At the same time, a creative direction of the mind toward the upper part of the heart, the seat of the intellectual power of the soul, can help somewhat. But any excessive pressure in the use of this physical technique (as one that incites physical warmth) is harmful. The warmth of the body and the blood has no place in prayer.

The diligent practice of the Jesus Prayer in particular, and remembrance of God in general, is especially abhorrent to the devil, because it helps us to abide in constant union with God (leading to salvation) and to constantly repel the attacks of the enemy. Therefore, whoever practices the Jesus Prayer will be subjected to extraordinary persecution by the devil. "What our adversary desires and labors for most of all," says St Macarius the Great, "is to distract our mind from remembrance of God and from love for Him, and for this he uses the pleasures of the world, distracting one from the true good to ostensible, insubstantial benefits."[275] For this reason, whoever has consecrated himself to true service to God by the constant practice of the Jesus Prayer must especially guard himself from distraction of the thoughts. He must in no way allow himself any "idle talking of the mind," so to speak. Instead, paying no attention at all to thoughts and desires that appear in the mind, he must constantly return his mind to the prayer of the name of Jesus, as to a refuge, believing that Jesus will sleeplessly care for that servant of His who constantly abides near Him through constant remembrance of Him.

"The evil demons," says St Nilus of Sinai, "at night try to disturb the spiritual practitioner directly, but during the day they do this through people, surrounding him by slander, attacks, and misfortunes."[276] This order in the demonic warfare is soon made obvious to any practitioner of the prayer. The demons tempt by thoughts and by desires of the mind, by remembrance of the most necessary objects, by apparently spiritual contemplation, by inciting "busyness," and by inspiring fear and other manifestations of lack of faith.[277] A sense of confusion is always a true sign of the approach of the fallen spirits, with their multifarious demonic warfare, even if the form in which they approach you appears righteous.[278] To ascetics living in solitude and practicing intense prayer, the demons appear in the form of monsters, seductive objects, or even as bright angels, martyrs, saints, or Christ Himself. One must not fear the threat of the demons, but one must be suspicious of all such apparitions. In such cases, which, for all that, are very rare, our first responsibility is to run to God, throwing ourselves completely to His will and asking Him for help. We should pay no attention to the visions and never converse with them, considering ourselves to be too weak for any encounter with the spirits of enmity and too unworthy for any converse with the holy angels.

The true, God-pleasing ascetic of prayer will be subjected to extraordinary sorrows and persecution from his own brethren and people in general. As we already mentioned, the main instigators here are the demons. They use as their instruments both those people whose will has become one with the will of the demons and those who do not understand the demonic warfare and become unwilling tools in the hands of the demons. The demons also use those who, though they understand the cunning of the enemy, are insufficiently attentive and careful of themselves, and so allow themselves to be fooled by the demons. The most striking and horrifying example of the degree to which man can come to hate God, the word of God, the Spirit of God when he merges the disposition of his spirit with the disposition of demons, is seen in the Jewish chief priests, elders, scribes, and Pharisees, who committed the worst of human crimes—deicide.

St Symeon the New Theologian says that by the suggestion of the demons, monks that lead a hypocritical life, who envy true zealots of piety, use any means they can find to upset them and even to cast them out of the monastery.[279] Even well-intentioned monks who lead a superficial life and have no understanding of a spiritual life can be tempted by true spiritual practitioners, finding their behavior to be strange. They can come to condemn and slander them, even insulting them and oppressing them in various ways. The great practitioner of the Jesus Prayer, St Seraphim of Sarov, endured much unpleasantness as a result of the ignorance and carnal mindset of his fellow monks, because those who read the Law of God carnally try to fulfill it only with external deeds, without the labor of the mind, "understanding neither what they saw nor the things which they affirm" (1 Tim 1:7).

"He who travels the path of the inner, contemplative life," St Seraphim instructs and consoles, drawing upon his own spiritual experience, "must never waver or abandon it only because people, who have attached themselves to the external and sensual, pierce us to the very heart with their contrary opinions and in every possible way try to distract us from following the inner path, laying various obstacles in our way. We must not waver at any obstacles in our path, always strengthening ourselves in such cases with the word of God: 'do not be afraid of their terror; nor be troubled. Sanctify the Lord Himself [by the remembrance in the heart of His divine Name], and He shall be your fear' (Isa 8:12–13) for God is with us."[280]

When St Gregory of Sinai—the providence of God used him as an instrument of the revival among monastics of the practice of the Jesus Prayer—came to Mount Athos and began to convey his God-given knowledge to pious, zealous, and wise ascetics who only had a carnal understanding of worship, they at first opposed him. This is how strange the teaching of spiritual labor is for those who have no understanding of it or no conception of its existence. Such monks tend to give excessive significance to physical asceticism. The prayer of the mind is even more bizarre to a carnal or emotional mindset, especially when it is infected with pride or the poison of heresy. Then the hatred of the human spirit that has entered communion with Satan is expressed as raving fury directed at the very Spirit of God.

In order to explain this and in general to come to understand how wrongly the carnal and emotional mindset understands everything spiritual, how it perverts it to fit its own darkness and fallenness (this in spite of all earthly erudition), we will here summarize in short the slanders and blasphemies of the Latin monk Barlaam (and some other Western writers) concerning the Jesus Prayer. In his *Ecclesiastical History*, Bishop Innocent writes that Barlaam, a monk of Calabria, arrived in the fifteenth century in Seloignes, a city of the Eastern Greek empire. Here, in order to act for the Western Church, but under the cover of Orthodoxy, he rejected Catholicism. Having written a few works proving the orthodoxy of the Eastern Church, he earned the praise and trust of the Byzantine emperor. Knowing that Greek monasticism was the most important bulwark of the Church, Barlaam wanted to weaken it with the hopes of destroying it and weakening the entire Church.

With this purpose in mind, he expressed the desire to live the strictest monastic life and cunningly convinced a certain desert dweller of Athos to reveal to him the creative practice of the Jesus Prayer. Having received what he desired, and having only superficially understood the teaching, Barlaam assumed that the breathing techniques that the Fathers (as we have already learned) considered only a means were in actual fact the entire essence of the practice of the Jesus Prayer. Therefore, he concluded that the spiritual visions of spiritually advanced monks were phantoms seen only by the physical eyes. He told this to the emperor, maintaining that the practice of the Jesus Prayer was a dangerous delusion. A council was called in Constantinople.

St Gregory Palamas, an Athonite monk and a great practitioner of the prayer of the mind, entered the fray against Barlaam, and with the power of God's grace, he defeated him. Barlaam and his blasphemies were anathematized. He returned to Calabria and to Catholicism, but he left behind him among many Greeks (who were only superficial Christians) who trusted in his teachings. He also brought his teaching into the West, where his blasphemies and preposterous calumnies were accepted as confessions of the truth.[281] The historian Claude Fleury, describing Barlaam's actions, like Barlaam, also placed undue emphasis on the physical techniques of prayer, perverting the meaning of the Jesus Prayer. Fleury copied out passages describing the breathing techniques from St Symeon the New Theologian's homily on the three forms of prayer, found in *The Philokalia*. Using these passages, he maintained that Symeon taught that a monk, having sat in the corner of his cell, must direct his eyes and thoughts to the middle of his stomach, that is, to his belly button, holding the breath, even with the nose, etc. It would be hard to believe that the well-educated and wise Fleury would have written such nonsense, if it were not so obviously written in the pages of his history.

Bergier, another very educated and intelligent writer, says that the Greek monk-contemplatives, because of the intensity of their concentration, had become mad and fallen into fanaticism (that is, demonic delusion). In order to reach a state of ecstasy, he says that they directed their eyes at their belly button, holding their breath; then they imagined that they saw a sparkling light, and so on.[282] By perverting the form of prayer used by the practitioners of the Jesus Prayer in the Eastern Church and by blaspheming against them, the Latins did not stop at this blasphemy against the work of the Holy Spirit. We will leave the slander and blasphemy of heretics to the judgment of God; with a sense of sorrow, not condemnation, let us turn away our gaze from their ridiculous words, and let us listen to what our own blessed practitioner of prayer, St Seraphim of Sarov, has said about the vision of the light of Christ.

> To accept and see the light of Christ *in the heart*, one must as much as possible distract oneself from any visible objects, having first purified the soul with repentance, good deeds, and faith in the One Crucified for us. We must close our physical eyes, plunge the mind into the depths of the heart, and there to cry out the name of our Lord Jesus Christ. Then, as much as he is zealous and ardent in spirit, the man will find sweetness in the utterance of the name, which will arouse in him the desire to seek even greater illumination. When after such exercise the mind will fully descend to the heart, then the light of Christ will shine forth, illumining the temple of the soul with divine light, as the Prophet Malachi said, "But to you who fear My name the Sun of Righteousness shall arise with healing in His wings" (Mal 3:20 LXX). This light is at the same time life according to the word of the Gospel: "In Him was life, and the life was the light of men." (John 1:4)[283]

From this it is evident, contrary to the slander of the Calabrian monk Barlaam and other Latins, that this light is not material, but spiritual. It opens the spiritual eyes; it is contemplated by them, even though it also can act on the physical eyes, as occurred with the holy Apostle Paul (Acts 9). St Macarius the Great gave a detailed and especially clear summary of the teaching concerning the divine light in his Homily 7. He also said, "It is the essential radiance of the power of the Holy Spirit within the soul, and through it all knowledge is opened, and God is truly known by the worthy and beloved soul."[284]

All the Holy Fathers of the Eastern Church agree with this holy witness, for they have experientially come to know Christian perfection and have expressed it in their writings, as much as is possible to express inexpressible mysteries in material terms. It is very useful to know that the fruit of pure, attentive prayer is the renewal of human nature, that the renewed nature is provided and adorned with gifts of divine grace. However, any striving to prematurely acquire these gifts, a striving that chooses self-will over God's good will concerning us, is extremely dangerous and leads only to demonic delusion. For this reason, all the Fathers speak very briefly of the gifts of grace, speaking instead in great detail about the process of acquiring pure prayer, which naturally leads to the acquisition of such gifts. The labor of prayer requires diligent study, while gifts of grace appear of their own accord, as the natural qualities of a renewed human nature, when this nature, having been purified by repentance, will be sanctified by the overshadowing of the Spirit.

St Paisius Velichkovsky, who lived at the end of the eighteenth century, wrote a short work on prayer of the mind as a refutation of the blasphemies uttered against the prayer by a certain falsely wise philosopher-monk who lived in the Western Cherkas, a contemporary of St Paisius.

"In our days," says St Paisius in a letter to elder Theodosius,

> a certain monk, a so-called wise philosopher, having seen that some zealots of the prayer fell into delusion (as a result of their self-will and ignorant guidance by elders who were not experienced in the practice of the prayer) did not blame the self-will and inexperience of the elders, but blasphemed the holy prayer itself. He rose up, aroused by the devil, so belligerently, that he greatly surpassed even the ancient, thrice-accursed heretics Barlaam and Akindinos, who blasphemed this prayer. Having no fear of God or shame before men, he uttered horrifying and shameful blasphemies against this holy prayer, against those who practice it zealously, words that are unbearable for the ears of a chaste person. Moreover, he has begun such terrible persecutions against the zealots of this prayer that some of them, abandoning everything, have fled to our country to lead a God-pleasing eremitic life. Others, being weaker in mind, have come to such madness from the vile words of the philosopher, that they have thrown the books of the Fathers in their possession, as we have heard, into the river, after having tied them to a brick. So successful has his blasphemy been that some elders have forbidden the reading of the books of the Fathers at the pain of retracting their blessing to those who do read them. The philosopher, not contenting himself with such verbal blasphemy, intended to outline these blasphemies in writing, when God struck him with His punishment. He lost his sight, which prevented his intention from coming to fruition.

In general, a carnal or emotional mindset, no matter how rich it may be with the wisdom of the world, gazes wildly and unkindly at the prayer of the mind. This prayer is a means for the union of the human spirit with the Spirit of God, and so it is especially strange and hateful to those whose spirits are favorably disposed to hosts of the fallen angels, rejected and at war with God, who do not acknowledge their own fallenness, who proclaim and uphold their fallen state as the most progressed of states. "For the message of the cross," proclaimed by the mouth of the apostles to all mankind, "is foolishness to those who are perishing." It remains foolishness when it is proclaimed by the mind to the heart and to the entire old man through prayer, but for the ones who are being saved, "it is the power of God" (1 Cor 1:18). The Greeks, who did not know

Christianity, and the Greeks who turned back to paganism from Christianity, "seek," according to their disposition, "after wisdom" in the prayer of the heart, but they only find "foolishness." However, true Christians, infirm and insignificant to the naked eye because of the labor of prayer, find "Christ the power of God and the wisdom of God. Because the foolishness of God is wiser than men, and the weakness of God is stronger than men" (1 Cor 1:22–25).

It is not surprising that the educated of our own time, having no understanding of the prayer of the mind according to the tradition of the Orthodox Church, but having only read about it in the works of Western writings, have repeated the blasphemies and absurdities of these writers.[285] The spiritual friend of St Paisius Velichkovsky reminds him of other monks who rejected the practice of the Jesus Prayer for three reasons. First of all, they considered this practice only proper for the saints and dispassionate monks. Secondly, they recognized the almost complete lack of spiritual guides of this practice. Thirdly, they were afraid of falling into demonic delusion. The unfairness of these reasons has already been examined by us in another volume.[286] Here it is sufficient to say that those who reject the Jesus Prayer for these reasons only practice spoken prayer, but they do not progress at all, even in this prayer. Because they reject the experiential knowledge of the prayer of the mind, they cannot achieve the necessary attentiveness even in their spoken prayer, because such attentiveness is given primarily by the prayer of the mind. Psalmody sung aloud, without attention, in the midst of considerable distractions that are unavoidable for the practitioners of purely physical prayer who disdain the prayer of the mind, act very weekly on the soul, superficially, giving only the fruits appropriate to the labor. Very often, when such prayer is practiced constantly and in great quantity, it leads to self-conceit with all its attendant consequences.

"Many," says Schemamonk Vasily,

not having experiential knowledge of the prayer of the mind, sinfully judge that this prayer belongs only to those who are already holy and dispassionate. For this reason, practicing only psalmody, the singing of troparia and canons, they remain only in this, their external worship. They do not understand that such sung worship is given to us by the Fathers for a time, because of the infirmity and infancy of our mind, so that we, learning little by little, can ascend the ladder of the prayer of the mind, not remain to the end of our days in merely external prayer. What is more juvenile than being satisfied with smug self-conceit at having read aloud our prayers? We think that we are doing something great, consoling ourselves with mere quantity, but we are only feeding our inner Pharisee![287]

"Let everyone who names the name of Christ depart from iniquity," advises the apostle (2 Tim 2:19). This bequest, which refers to all Christians, especially refers to those who intend to practice the constant prayer of the name of the Lord Jesus. The most pure name of Jesus does not endure to remain in the midst of impurity. It requires that all impurity be cast out and rejected by the spiritual vessel. Entering into the vessel according to the measure of its purity, the name, of its own accord, begins to act on the vessel and to perform further purification, for which the exertion of man is not sufficient, and which is required to make the vessel a worthy dwelling place of the spiritual, all-holy treasure. Let us avoid all excess or even satiety in food, being moderate and even abstinent in eating and drinking. Let us stop seeking the pleasure of delicious food and drink. Let us give our body rest with sufficient sleep, but not excessive. Let us reject idle talk, laughing, jokes, blasphemy. Let us cease our unnecessary exits from our cell to visit our brothers. Let us not allow our brothers to visit our own cell, even if they do it in so-called love, instead covering their desire for empty conversation and diversions that empty the soul. Let us reject fantasy and pointless reverie that arises in us as a result of our lack of faith, because of our irrational "busyness," because of our vanity, remembrance of evils, irritability, and other passions.

With fullness of faith, let us commit all things to the care of the Lord, and let us replace our volubility of thought, our empty woolgathering, with constant prayer to the Lord Jesus. If we are still surrounded by enemies, let us cry out with strong groaning and sorrow to the King of kings, as the oppressed and insulted from the common people cry out to the king. If we have already been admitted to the inner chamber of the King, then let us bring our petition to Him and ask His mercy with surpassing gentleness and humility, from the very depths of our soul. Such prayer is especially strong. It is completely spiritual; it is expressed directly to the very ears of the King, to His very heart.

The necessary, essential condition for progress in the Jesus Prayer is living according to the commandments of the Lord Jesus. "Abide in My love" (John 15:9), He said to His disciples. What does it mean to abide in love for the Lord? It means to constantly remember Him, constantly abide in union with Him by the spirit. The former is dead without the latter, and it cannot even be realized. "If you keep My commandments, you will abide in My love, just as I have kept My Father's commandments and abide in His love" (John 15:10). If we constantly fulfill the commandments of the Lord, then in our spirit we will unite with Him. If we unite with Him in spirit, then we will strive toward Him with our entire being. We will constantly think of Him. Direct all your actions, all your behavior according to the commandments of the Lord Jesus. Direct your words, thoughts, senses according to them, and you will come to know the characteristics of Christ. Having sensed within yourself these character-istics by divine grace, and from this perception having come to understand them by experience, you will find imperishable sweetness that does not belong to this world and this age. This is a gentle sweetness, but a strong one that destroys any inclination of the heart to earthly pleasures.

Having delighted in the characteristics of Jesus, you will come to love Him and you will desire that He will abide in you completely. Without Him, you will consider yourself to be perishing and lost. Then you will constantly cry out from the fullness of conviction, with your entire soul: "Lord Jesus Christ, Son of God, have mercy on me, a sinner." The Jesus Prayer will replace all other prayers. After all, can all those other prayers fit within themselves or express a thought more expansive than the forgiveness of sins by Jesus? Make this the only goal of your life—to do the will of Jesus in all situations, no mat-ter how seemingly insignificant or trivial, and try to act only in a way that would please Jesus, and then all your deeds will be equally worthy of heaven. Come to love the will of Jesus more than the desires of your flesh, more than the calmness and comfort of your body, more than your life, more than your soul. Read the Gospel as often as possible, and study in it the will of your Lord and Saviour. Do not leave unattended the shortest line from the Gospel, even the seemingly least important commandment. Rein in and mortify all move-ments that come from your fallen human nature, not only the sinful ones, but even the ones that seem good. These so-called virtues are often very well developed in pagans and heretics, but they are distinct from the evangelical virtue, as the West is far from the East. Let everything proper to the old man fall silent inside you!

Let Jesus alone act within you by His most holy commandments; let all your thoughts and perceptions flow from these commandments. If you will live in such a way, then the Jesus Prayer will not fail to blossom within you, though you live in the deep desert or in the midst of the cares of a monastic community, because the place where the prayer settles and finds its rest is the mind and the heart renewed by the knowledge, taste, and fulfillment of the "good and acceptable and perfect will of God" (Rom 12:2). A life lived by the commandments of the Gospel is the only true source of spiritual progress,

accessible to everyone who desires sincerely to progress spiritually, no matter what social status the unknowable providence of God wills to place him
in.

The practice of the Jesus Prayer by its very nature requires constant vigilance over oneself. St Seraphim said, "Reverent prudence is here needed for
the reason that this sea, that is, the heart with all its thoughts and desires that
must be purified by attentiveness, is 'great and wide . . ., wherein are things
creeping innumerable, both small and great beasts' (Ps 103:25). In other words,
there are many vain, incorrect, and impure thoughts in the mind, the offspring
of the evil spirits."[288]

We must constantly watch over ourselves lest sin sidles up to us and devas-
tates the soul. Even this is not enough: we must constantly examine our mind
and heart, so that they will abide in the will of Jesus and will follow His holy
commands, so that our carnal mindset will in no way supplant our spiritual
mindset through vile cunning, so that we never become entranced with any
warmth of the blood, so that we will as much as possible constantly mortify
the flesh, remaining in a kind of gentle breeze, a coolness (see 3 Kgdms 19:12).
When we begin to perceive this gentle coolness, then from it we will more
clearly see the will of God, and we will do it more freely. When the will of God
will be more easily understood, then the hunger and thirst for divine righteousness is aroused with especial power within the ascetic. Then he, in a profound acknowledgment of his poverty and in sorrow, with renewed fervor tries
to uncover this righteousness with himself through the most attentive, most
reverent prayer.

"This divine prayer," said St Paisius Velichkovsky, "is the greatest of all
monastic labors, the height of perfection, as the Fathers say, the source of
virtues, the subtlest, invisible action of the mind in the depths of the heart.
Correspondingly, the invisible enemy places inviable, subtle snares, barely perceptible to the mind, of multifarious delusions and fantasies."[289]

To try to lay a new foundation for the Jesus Prayer other than the one already
laid is impossible, for the foundation is our Lord Himself, Jesus Christ, the
God-Man, who has ineffably clothed the limitless nature of God in the limited
nature of man, and from the limited nature of man, He revealed the actions
of the unlimited God. Because of our spiritual infancy, the Holy Fathers offer
us certain techniques, as we have already said, to better train ourselves in the
Jesus Prayer. These techniques are nothing other than techniques, and they
are not anything special. We must not pay too much attention to them, nor
should we ascribe too much importance to them. All the power and action

of the Jesus Prayer flows from the worshiped and almighty name of Jesus, for "there is no other name under heaven given among men by which we must be saved" (Acts 4:12). In order to acquire this ability in ourselves, we must be remade according to the commandments of the Gospel. The Lord Himself said, "Not everyone who says to Me, 'Lord, Lord,' shall enter the kingdom of heaven," both the One that awaits us after our blessed repose and the One that is revealed in us during our earthly life, "but he who does the will of My Father in heaven" (Matt 7:21).

For the advanced, such external methods are not necessary. Even in the midst of crowds, they remain in stillness. All obstacles to spiritual advancement are within us, only within us! If something acts on us from without as a hindrance, and then this only serves as a rebuke to our infirm will, our double-mindedness, our sin-damaged nature. We would need no external methods if we lived as we should live. Our life is lax; our will is precarious, worthless, and so we need external techniques, just as those with pained legs need crutches and a staff. The merciful fathers, seeing that I desire to practice the Jesus Prayer, and also seeing that I am completely alive to the world, that it acts powerfully on me through my senses, advise me to pray in a solitary, dark cell, so that in such a way my senses will come into inactivity, so that my conversation with the world will cease, so that my descent into myself will be ameliorated. They advise me to sit during my prayer on a low stool, so that my body will have the placement of a pauper who asks for alms, and so that I will better sense the poverty of my soul. When I am present at a service in church and pray the Jesus Prayer during the service, the fathers advise me to close my eyes to better protect myself against distraction, because my vision is alive to all that is material, and no sooner do I open my eyes than immediately the objects I see begin to imprint themselves on my inner eye and distract me from prayer. There are many other external methods found by practitioners of prayer to help the body accomplish a spiritual labor. These methods can be used beneficially, but their use must differ according to the spiritual and physical qualities of each person. Some mechanisms that are very beneficial for a certain ascetic can be useless or even harmful for another. The advanced reject all external techniques, just as the man healed from lameness throws away his crutches, just as a child who has grown up throws away his swaddling clothes, as the scaffolding is taken down from a house that is already built.

For every person and for all people, it is useful to begin the training in the prayer of the name of Jesus by speaking the Jesus Prayer aloud with the mind confined to the words of the prayer. This confining of the mind to the words of the prayer expresses the strictest attention to these words, without which the prayer would be like a body without a soul. Let us leave it to the Lord Himself to transform our attentive spoken prayer into the prayer of the mind, heart, and soul. He will do this without fail when he sees us at least somewhat purified, educated, refined, prepared by a life lived according to the commandments of the Gospel. A wise parent will not give a sharp sword to his infant child. The child is not in any state to use the sword against an enemy, and he will only play with the dangerous weapon, quickly and easily piercing himself with it. The child in spiritual development is not capable of accepting spiritual gifts. He would use them not for the glory of God, not for his benefit or the benefit of his neighbors, not to fight off invisible enemies. Instead, he will use them to defeat himself, for he will imagine himself to be someone great, becoming filled with evil pride, evil contempt of others.

Even when we lack these spiritual gifts, filled as we are by foul passions, we are still proud and exalt ourselves. We do not cease to condemn and belittle our fellow men, who are in all senses better than we! What would happen if we were entrusted with some spiritual treasure, some spiritual gift that separates one from his brothers and shows him to be a chosen one of God? Would this not be the cause of frightening spiritual sickness for us? Let us try to become perfect in humility, which consists of an especially blessed disposition of the heart and appears in the heart from the fulfillment of the commandments of the Gospel. Humility is the only altar on which we are allowed by the spiritual law to bring the sacrifice of prayer. From this altar table, our sacrifice of prayer can ascend to God and appear before His face. Humility is the only vessel into which the hand of God places His gifts of grace.

Let us practice the Jesus Prayer without expectation of gain, with simplicity and firmness of intention, our only purpose being repentance, with faith in God, with complete fidelity to the will of God, with trust in the wisdom, goodness, omnipotence of His holy will. If we choose physical techniques to aid prayer, let us try to use them with all possible prudence and discernment, never getting carried away with them merely because of our curiosity or our unwise and unchecked zeal, which seems like virtue to the inexperienced but is called proud brazenness and mad elation by the Holy Fathers. Let us primarily turn to the simplest and most humble methods, since they are safest.

We repeat: all physical techniques must be considered nothing other than means that have become useful to us because of our infirmity. Let us not put any reliance in them, nor on the quantity of our prayers, lest our exclusive trust in God be stolen from us, lest we end up essentially relying on ourselves or on something material and vain. Let us not seek the sweetness of spiritual vision. We are sinners. We are unworthy of spiritual sweetness and visions. We are not capable of receiving them because of our old man. By attentive prayer, let us seek to turn the gaze of our minds within, so that our sinfulness will be revealed to us. When we uncover it, let us stand mentally before our Lord Jesus Christ as members of the hosts of the lepers, the blind, deaf, lame, paralyzed, possessed, and let us begin our sorrowful groan of prayer from the poverty of our spirit, from a heart broken by pain at our sinfulness. May this cry be limitlessly fruitful! May every loquacity and grandiloquence be revealed as incapable of expressing this cry of the soul! Because of its inexpressibility and profusion, let it flow constantly, becoming streamlined into a short prayer of expansive meaning: *Lord Jesus Christ, Son of God, have mercy on me, a sinner.* Amen.

CHAPTER 18

A Wanderer

From where do You come?[290] Where is Your usual home? Where were You until this moment? Why have You left me alone until now, an orphan, in poverty, in terrible death? Having come to know You, I now acknowledge that such was my state without You. How terrible it was! I stood at the threshold of dark hell. I was cast down into a deep abyss from where is no escape. Do not abandon me! I cannot be without You! If you will leave me, again I will stand before the gates of hell, again I will be cast into the abyss, again I will be in unbearable and inexpressible tribulation.

You approach! I do not see the manner of Your approach; I see it, not with my physical eyes, but with my perception. You give me no time or ability to reflect—who are You? Unexpectedly you appear in the soul, invisible and unattainable! You appear with inexpressible quietness and subtlety, together with the might and power of the Creator, because You transform the entire man. You change, transform, recreate, renew the mind, the heart, and the body! You—the Strong Man—enter into the house, tie down the strong one, steal the vessels of the house, but not for perdition—for salvation! Both the house and the vessels were previously Yours. You arranged them for Yourself, but they gave themselves into bitter imprisonment to the predator. Until now they— my mind, my soul, my body—were under the authority of an evil master, and they acted under his influence. You come. From this moment, they are at Your disposal, and they begin to act under Your holy, blessed influence. What shall I call You? How shall speak of You to my brothers?

What name shall I give to the Wanderer Who has come to rest under the roof of my soul, under a dilapidated roof, a roof that has come to complete disrepair, open to all gusting winds, rain, and snow, barely good enough to be used as a barn for animals? What have You found in my heart, filled as it is with various sinful thoughts that enter under my roof without hindrance and find there, as in a food trough for swine, the tasty food of passionate feelings?

It seems to me that I know my Guest! But, gazing at my own impurity, I fear to utter His name. A single irreverent utterance of the great and all-holy name can be condemned! How much more frightening is the actual presence of the One Who is named! But You are here! Your limitless goodness has led You to this foul sinner, so that the sinner, having come to know the worth and calling of man, having tasted by his own experience, having seen with his senses, "that the Lord is good" (Ps 33:9), abandoned the path of lawlessness, abandoned the swamp of foul-smelling passions that he so loved before, began to labor at the acquisition of purity through repentance, became Your temple and abode.

How will I name this Wanderer that soars within me? How will I name this wondrous Guest who came to console me in my exile, to heal me of my fatal illness, to pull me out of my dark abyss, to lead me to the fruitful field of the Lord, to set me on the paths of righteousness and holiness, to take away the impenetrable veil that until this moment covered my eyes, separating me from majestic eternity and my God? How will I name this Teacher Who announces to me the teaching about God, a teaching at once new and ancient, a divine, not human teaching?

Will I name Him light? I do not see the light, but it illumines my mind and heart beyond any word, beyond any earthly teaching, without words, with unutterable quickness, in a kind of strange—how will I express the inexpressible?—touch to my mind or by action within my very mind? Will I name Him fire? But He does not burn; on the contrary, He bedews pleasantly and cools. He is a certain "gentle breeze" (3 Kgdms 19:12), but from Him, as from fire, all passions, all sinful thoughts flee. He does not utter a single word; He does not speak, but at the same time He does speak, teach, sing forth wondrously, mysteriously, with unutterable gentleness, subtlety, changing, renewing the mind and heart that listen to Him in silence in the cell of the soul. He has no form or image, nothing in Him of the material. He is completely immaterial, invisible, extremely subtle.

Suddenly, unexpectedly, with unspeakable gentleness He appears in the mind, the heart, gradually pouring out into the entire soul, into the whole body, taking control of them, casting out of them all that is sinful, ceasing the action of the flesh in the blood, uniting all the parts of man that were riven, making our nature whole, our nature that had been torn apart by a terrible fall, just as a potter's vessel shatters from a fall. Who, seeing this recreation, will not recognize the hand of the Creator, the only One who has the power to form and reform?

Until this moment I speak only of the act, not naming the One Who acts. I fear to name Him! Look at me, brothers! Examine what is happening with me! Will you tell me what is occurring within me? Will you tell me Who is doing this to me? I feel, I sense within myself the presence of the Wanderer. From where has He come and how has He appeared within me? I do not know. Having appeared, He remains invisible, completely unfathomable. But He is present, because He acts within me, because He owns me, though He has not destroyed my free will, leading it to His will by the unutterable holiness of His will. With an invisible hand He took my mind, took my heart, took my soul, took my body. No sooner have they felt His hands than they came back to life! A new perception, a new movement appeared within them—perceptions and movements of the spirit! I did not know these perceptions and movements until this moment; I did not even know or guess at their existence. They appeared, and from their appearance the perceptions and movements of the flesh and emotions have either hidden themselves or been bound. They appeared like life, and my previous state has disappeared like death. From the touch of this Hand, my entire being, my mind, heart, and body have united, have become something whole and one. Then they plunged into God and remain there while that invisible, unfathomable, almighty Hand holds them there. What sort of feeling envelops me there? My entire being is surrounded by a profound, mystical silence, beyond all thought, beyond all silence, beyond all physical movements produced by the blood. My entire being simultaneously celebrates the Sabbath of rest and acts, under the direction of the Holy Spirit. This direction is inexpressible with words.

I am like a drunk man. I forget everything, being fed by unknown, imperishable food. I find myself completely beyond everything sensual, in the domain of the immaterial, in the domain that is above not only materiality, but is above all thought, all understanding. I do not even feel my body. My eyes see and do not see; seeing, they see nothing. My ears hear and do not hear. All my members are drunk, and I am reeling on my feet. I try to hold onto something with my hands, lest I fell, or I lie on my bed, as though in a sickness without sickness, in paralysis that comes from an excess of strength. This cup of the Lord, the cup of the Spirit, "how strong it is!" (Ps 22:5).

Thus I spend days, weeks! Time contracts . . . This wondrous silence embraces my mind, heart, soul, and they strive with their entire strength to God. They have become lost, so to speak, in the eternal movement toward the boundless. This silence is at the same time conversation, but without words, without any variety, without thoughts, surpassing all thought. The Wanderer

Who does all this has an unusual voice and speech, for He speaks, and I listen, without words or sounds. I seek in the Scriptures for a passage that would speak of such wonders, so that I can come to know this wondrous Wanderer, and unwillingly I stop before the words of the Saviour: "The wind blows where it wishes, and you hear the sound of it, but cannot tell where it comes from and where it goes. So is everyone who is born of the Spirit" (John 3:8). How am I to characterize this action within me? It reconciles and unites man with himself, and then with God. It is impossible to fail to recognize in this action the blowing of the grace-filled peace of God, "surpasses all understanding, will guard your hearts and minds through Christ Jesus" (Phil 4:7). This peace renews man by the Holy Spirit. Truly! Through this action, the mind and heart become evangelical, become Christ's. Man sees the Gospel inscribed within himself, on the tablets of his soul, by the hand of the Spirit.

The divine Wanderer walks away, hides just as unnoticeably as he came and appeared to me. But He leaves in my entire being the sweet smell of immortality—as immaterial as He is immaterial—a spiritual, enlivening sweet smell perceptible to the new senses that He planted in me or resurrected within me. Enlivened, fed by this sweet fragrance, I write and relate this word of life to my brethren. When this sweet fragrance will fade, when the foul smell of deathly passions once again spreads through my soul, then my word will be without life, infected by foulness and corruption!

If anyone, hearing a great word concerning the action of the Spirit from the mouth of a sinner, begins to waver in unbelief, confused in thought, imagining that this action of the Spirit is actually a demonic delusion, let him reject such a blasphemous thought! No, no! These are not the actions and characteristics of delusion! Tell me, is it typical of the devil, the enemy, the killer of man to become man's physician? Is it typical of the devil to unite the parts and powers of man, which have been riven by sin, to lead them away from slavery to sin to freedom, to lead them out of a state of enmity, internecine warfare, into a holy state of peace in the Lord? Is it typical of the devil to pull man out of the deep abyss of ignorance of God and to give instead a living, experienced knowledge of God that no longer needs any external proofs? Is it typical for the devil to preach and describe the Redeemer in detail, to preach and explain the approach toward the Redeemer by repentance? Is it typical of the devil to restore in man the fallen image, to make orderly the disordered likeness? Is it typical for him to offer a foretaste of spiritual poverty and, at the same time, resurrection, renewal, union with God? Is it typical of the devil to raise man to the heights of theology, upon which man is like nothing, without thought, without desire, completely submerged into wondrous silence? This silence is the dissolution of all the strength of the merely human nature that has rushed forward toward God and, so to speak, has disappeared before the infinite greatness of God (see Job 42:6). Demonic delusion acts differently from God, Who is the boundless Lord of men, Who was and now is their Creator. He Who created and recreates—does He not remain the Creator? And so, listen, my most beloved brother, listen and hear how the actions of delusion differ from the actions of God!

When demonic delusion approaches man—either by thought or by fantasy or by subtle pride or by visions visible to the physical eyes or by voices heard by the physical ears—it always approaches not as a boundless master, but as a seducer, seeking sympathy in the person, and from this agreement, asserting power over him. Its action, whether manifested from within or without a man, always comes from outside a man. That is, man can reject it. Delusion always announces itself originally with a certain confusion of the heart; only those whom it already controls have no doubt when it approaches. Delusion never unites man, riven by sin, into a single whole. Delusion never stops the enticement produced by the movement of blood, never instructs the ascetic to repent, and never diminishes him in his own eyes. On the contrary, it inspires fantasy; it warms the blood; it offers man a kind of tasteless, poisonous pleasure. It subtly flatters him, inspiring conceit, founding in the soul the idol of the ego.

Divine action is immaterial. It is not seen or heard. It is not expected; it is impossible to imagine. It does not lend itself to any comparison with experiences of this age. It comes and acts mystically. At first, it shows man his sin, always increasing man's sense of sinfulness, constantly holding his terrible sin before his eyes, leading the soul to self-condemnation. It reveals to us the depth of our fall, this terrible, dark, profound abyss of perdition into which our race has fallen through the sin of our forefather. Then, little by little, it gives increased attention and compunction to the heart during prayer. Having prepared the vessel in this manner, suddenly, unexpectedly, immaterially, God touches the riven parts of man, and they unite into a whole. How does He touch? I cannot explain it: I saw nothing; I heard nothing; but I see myself changed. Suddenly, I felt myself to be so from the action of the self-governing Lord. The Creator acted in this re-creation, just as He acted in my creation.

Tell me. The body of Adam, molded from clay, when it lay on the ground, still not enlivened with a soul before the Creator, could it have any understanding of life, any sense of it? When he was suddenly given life and a soul, could he first reflect: should I take the soul or accept it? Created Adam suddenly sensed himself to be living, thinking, desiring! With the same kind of suddenness is man recreated. The Creator was and is the unlimited Master. He acts as He wills, supernaturally, surpassing all thought, all perception, eternally, subtly, completely spiritually, immaterially.

And yet you are still racked with doubts! You look at me and, seeing before you such a terrible sinner, you unwillingly ask: is it possible that in this sinner, in whom the passions rage so obviously and strongly, the Holy Spirit acts directly? This is a fair question. And I am brought to confusion and terror by it! I am enticed, I sin, I fornicate with sin, I betray my God, I sell Him for the abominable price of sin. And despite my constant betrayal, despite my treacherous, faithless behavior, He remains immutable. Incapable of evil, He awaits my repentance with longsuffering, and He uses all means possible to attract me to repentance and self-correction. You have heard what the Son of God says in the Gospel? "Those who are well have no need of a physician, but those who are sick . . . For I did not come to call the righteous, but sinners, to repentance" (Matt 9:12–13). This is what the Saviour said; this is how He acted. He reclined at table with publicans, sinners, and He led them through conversion to faith and virtue to spiritual relations with Abraham and the other righteous men. Do you wonder, and are you amazed at the endless goodness of the Son of God? Know that the all-holy Spirit is equally good. He equally thirsts for the salvation of man. He is equally meek, milk, long-suffering, greatly merciful, for He is one of Three consubstantial Persons of the Holy Trinity, Who are indivisibly and unconfusedly the One Divine Essence, having a single nature.

Even sin attracts the Holy Spirit to man! Any sin that is not actualized by deed, but that is seen within the person, admitted, and mourned over—this attracts the Spirit! The more man examines his sins, the more he plunges into deep sorrow over his sinfulness, the more pleasant and more accessible he is for the Holy Spirit, Who, like a physician, approaches only those who admit their sickness; on the contrary, He turns away from those who seek to enrich themselves with their vain self-opinion. Gaze at your sin; plumb the depths of your sinfulness! Reject yourself, do not "count [your] life dear to [yourself]" (Acts 20:24). Plunge deeply into the vision of your sins, into sorrow for them! Then, in the proper time, you will see yourself recreated by the unfathomable, and all the more inexplicable action of the Holy Spirit. He will come to you when you do not expect Him. He will act within you when you will admit yourself to be completely unworthy of Him!

But if you secretly desire grace—beware! You are in a dangerous position! Such expectation is proof of a secret sense of self-worth, and this, in turn, is proof of hidden arrogance, in which is pride. Pride quickly leads to demonic delusion. Delusion easily attaches itself to pride. This delusion is a turning aside from truth and from the One who cooperates with the truth—the Holy Spirit. It is a deviation to falsehood and to the ones who cooperate with falsehood—the rejected spirits. Demonic delusion already exists as a seed in arrogance; it already exists in a sense of self-worth, even in the very expectation of receiving gifts of grace. These are its original manifestations, a kind of bud, flower, embryo—the first signs of a healthy fruit. From such false understanding comes false perception. False understanding and perception produce self-delusion. To this self-delusion is added the active, delusive influence of the demons. The demons are lords of the domain of falsehood. He who willingly submits himself to the demons willingly enters into bondage. As one darkened and deluded by falsehood, which he admitted to be truth, he loses mastery over himself, without even noticing it! Such a state is the state of demonic delusion. We enter this state; we are cast into it, for our pride and self-love. "He who loves his life will lose it, and he who hates his life in this world will keep it for eternal life" (John 12:25). Amen.

CHAPTER 19

A Mystical Interpretation of Psalm 99

"Obe joyful unto God, all the earth!" (Ps 99:1). Here, man is called "the earth." This name is given to man by his Creator, God. God said to Adam, "For dust you are" (Gen 3:19). Though I am a being with a soul, I am still earth. I am ensouled with a dead soul. My dead soul, during the time of the earthly life, is buried in the earth, that is, imprisoned in a passionate body as in a prison, bound, enslaved to it. After the separation from the body, it descends into the bowels of the earth. My soul must be given life if it is to be saved.

For dust to come to life and "be joyful unto God," one must initially destroy its inner disunion, produced by the Fall. Dust must unite with itself, within itself. Only "all the earth" can "be joyful unto God." Only a whole, united with itself, that is, the entire being of man, guided by the mind that is not stolen or shaken in prayer by foreign thoughts, can strive with all its powers toward God. Only "all my bones" (Ps 34:10) can turn with a living word of true prayer toward God. These "bones" are what Scripture calls all the constituent parts of man, collected and recreated by the Lord, united into one among themselves, united into one with the Lord. Then man will understand, from the personal inner experience of his soul that he has come to life spiritually, that before this he was imprisoned, in bonds, in death.

Inspired by this blessed experience, St Ephraim said,

Your grace has multiplied within me, O Lord, and it has satisfied my hunger and thirst, it has enlightened my darkened mind, it has gathered my wandering thoughts, and it has filled my heart. Now I worship, bow down, pray, and beseech You, confessing my weakness. For the sake of Your love for mankind, weaken now within me the waves of Your grace and preserve it as an advance for my sake, so that I may again receive it in that terrifying day (the Second Coming or the day of my death). Do not be angry with me, O Lover of mankind! I cannot bear to be without it, and so, having rejected

269

all doubt, I turn to You with prayer. Your grace has multiplied without me above all measure, and my tongue has cleaved to the roof of my mouth, having no means of expressing these riches. My mind is confused, unable to bear the multitude of grace's waves. O Image and Radiance of the all-blessed Father! Calm the waves of grace within me today, because it burns my members and heart. Calm it here, so that there You can give it to me again. Save me, Master, and make me worthy of Your kingdom. Do not remember my iniquities, nor become angry with the brazenness of my prayer. Grant me that which I ask and enter within me as into a mansion (see John 14:23), with Your blessed Father, in the day of His revelation. O Christ! Allow me this prayer, for You alone are the Giver of life. Hide my iniquities from my friends! Accept these my tears! Let my sorrow be brought before You![291]

These words are the words of one who has become spiritually drunk with the mercy of God. This is the joy that the Psalmist speaks of.

"Serve the Lord with gladness, and come in before Him with joy" (Ps 99:2). As long as prayer is stolen by foreign thoughts, as long as the labor of prayer is accomplished with difficulty, with sorrow, with coercion and violence of oneself, the one praying will not be permitted before the face of God. When prayer begins to be uttered with the entire being, then the labor will be filled with spiritual sweetness. This sweetness will inspire the ascetic to labor further, giving him encouragement, strength, firmness in the labor. Then the labor of prayer becomes the most important, constant, exclusive labor of the ascetic. In inexpressible joy, the practitioners of constant prayer enter with their spirit before the invisible face of God and stand before the face of God. They stand before His face because extraneous thoughts and fantasies, which can become an impenetrable veil separating man from God, are absent. There is no obstacle to vision! But God, inexplicably seen with the pure heart, remains invisible. "No one has seen God at any time" (John 1:18) because of the eternal subtlety, spirituality of His Essence. The perfection of God's Essence is the reason for His unapproachability not only for the vision of creatures, but even for the understanding. His Essence is the "thick darkness . . . under His feet," the darkness that is His "hiding-place." "He bowed the heavens also, and came down . . . He mounted upon the Cherubim, and did fly; He came flying upon the wings of the wind" (Ps 17:10–12). This bowing down of the heavens and His descent are God's willing self-diminishing, His accommodation of His own omnipotence and unutterable goodness to the qualities of His own creatures. It is as if He diminishes Himself, descending from the height of His perfection to make His all-holy energy perceptible to the Cherubim and those human beings who have become like the Cherubim, capable of bearing God. The energy of the Spirit of God is likened to the movement of wind or flying on the wings of the wind to show that this energy is immaterial, completely spiritual.

Joy and gladness are proper to that soul that has begun to feel the return of life, that has felt its release from imprisonment to sin and the fallen spirits, that has felt the overshadowing of divine grace, that has felt that by the energy of this grace, it now stands before the presence of God, raised up into the blameless and blessed service to God. This joy and gladness are so powerful that the Holy Spirit invites the one who has experienced them to cry out in joy. How can one not cry out with joy after being freed, revivified, given wings, after having ascended from earth to heaven? This crying out is natural to the spirit of man. It is powerful, but spiritual; the flesh and blood have no part, cannot have any part, in this joy. Their self-willed activity is put aside. They bend their necks to submission to the active grace of God, becoming instruments for the true labor, no longer distracting man into incorrect states and actions.

"Know ye, that the Lord, He is our God; it is He that hath made us, and not we ourselves, for we are His people, and the sheep of His pasture" (Ps 99:3). Whoever prays with impure prayer has a dead knowledge of God, as though He were an unknowable and invisible God. However, when this same person is freed from distraction and slavery to his thoughts, he is allowed before the invisible presence of God. Then he knows God with living knowledge, a knowledge of experience. He comes to know God as God.[292] Then man, having turned the gaze of the mind inward to himself, sees himself to be a creature, not a self-generating being, as people falsely imagine themselves to be, being in the midst of darkness and self-delusion. Then he places himself in the proper reference toward God, the place of a creature before a Creator, admitting himself to be required to reverently submit to the will of God and to do it with all zeal. The pasture of God is His will, revealed for His sheep in the Sacred Scripture and in His ineffable judgments.

"Enter into His gates with thanksgiving, and into His courts with praise; be thankful unto Him, and praise His Name" (Ps 99:4). The means to acquire access to the presence of God is humility. Humility is the gate to God, the entrance into the courts of God, into the uncreated palace and temple of God, the temple of the heart, within which God settles after the sacrament of baptism. The gates of God belong only to God. They are His gates; they open up only by His hand. Before they can be opened, God grants confession,

confession of the heart, confession from the whole soul. This confession is
the result of humility. This confession is man's expression of self-consciousness before God. This self-consciousness only appears when our eyes are
opened to ourselves by the touch of grace on the eyes of the soul. The mind
casts off the blindness that has until this moment darkened it and deprived
it of proper, God-pleasing self-consciousness. We confess, confess from the
fullness of conviction, the conviction with which the Creed must be confessed. This is the conviction that we are fallen creatures, burdened both by
the sinfulness that belongs to human nature in general and the sinfulness
that belongs to us as individuals. We praise the justice of God that has cast
out our iniquitous race from Paradise to earth, that has cursed all mankind to
labor and suffering, that punishes every person with individual punishments
for his personal sins.

After this confession, undistracted prayer appears. It is a gift of God. The
right hand of this gift takes the praying man from the midst of the distractions that surround and captivate him, and he is presented, without any distraction, before the presence of God in the uncreated temple of God in the
heart. From this utter humility and from utter submission to the will of God,
pure, holy prayer is born. It cannot arise in any other way, or as a result of
any other actions, just as grapes only grow on a vine, not some other tree.
This prayer is also called singing, because the prayer of the spirit is a holy,
mystical song that glorifies God. The great Paul said, "Be filled with the Spirit,
speaking to one another in psalms and hymns and spiritual songs, singing
and making melody in your heart to the Lord" (Eph 5:18–19). Or, as we read
in the morning prayers, "Illumine the eyes of my heart, open my lips to the
instruction of Your words, to understand Your commandments, to do Your
will, to glorify You in song with the confession of the heart, and to proclaim
Your all-holy name!"

"For the Lord is gracious, His mercy is everlasting, and His truth even from
generation to generation" (Ps 99:5). After coming to know and confessing the
justice of God, after admitting the judgments of God to be just, the ascetic of
prayer comes to know the limitless mercy of God, which is inextricable from
His justice. In this union of God's goodness with His justice, His all-holy truth
is revealed: "Mercy and truth are met together, justice and peace have kissed
each other" (Ps 84:11). Into this prayer of the man who prays purely, spiritual
sweetness flows forth from a perception of God's goodness. This sweetness
submerges the spirit of man into the depths of humility, at the same time raising him from earth to heaven. Such a man of prayer is the solitary hesychast.

This hesychast remains constantly in the presence of God by the action of God within him. He remains outside the world, above all thoughts concerning the passing world, above all sympathy with the passing world. The heart, having come to life by spiritual perception for God and everything that belongs to God, dies for the world, dies for everything that is hostile to God and foreign to God. In this death is life; in this perishing is salvation. Amen.

CHAPTER 20

Salvation and Christian Perfection

Many speak of salvation, and many desire to be saved. But if one asks them what is this salvation, they have a difficult time answering. It would not be a problem if this difficulty would end the matter. But no, the harmful consequences arising from this are significant. Ignorance of what leads to salvation gives all our actions in this arena of virtue a certain ambiguity, even wrongness. To all appearances, we perform many good deeds; but in essence, we do very little for our salvation. Why is this so? The answer is simple. We do not know what our salvation consists of.

To know what our salvation consists of, we must first know what our fall consists of, because salvation is only necessary for the fallen. Therefore, whoever seeks salvation must admit, by necessity, that he is fallen. Otherwise, why is he seeking salvation? Our fall occurred through the destruction of our communion with God and through our entering communion with the fallen and rejected spirits. Our salvation consists of destroying this communion with Satan and restoring communion with God.[293]

Part 1

The entire race of man is lost, in a fallen state. We were deprived of communion with God in our very root and source—in our forefathers, thanks to their willing sin. They were created without blemish, having no part with sin and corruption. From their very creation, they were communicants of the Holy Spirit. Having received existence, inherent to humanity, they also received supernatural life from their union with the Divine nature. Having willingly rejected submission to God, having willfully submitted themselves to the devil, they lost their communion with God, their freedom and dignity, having abandoned themselves to submission and slavery to the fallen spirits. They willingly rejected life; they called death down on themselves; they willfully destroyed the wholeness given them when they acted well and instead poisoned themselves with sin.[294] As the source of the human race, they passed on, and do not cease to pass on, that infection, that perdition, that death to all mankind. Adam, created by the all-holy image and likeness of God, was supposed to produce a correspondingly holy progeny. Instead, he defiled the image, destroyed the likeness, and produced descendants according to a defiled image, a destroyed likeness. The Sacred Scripture, which witnessed that man was created in the image of God (see Gen 1:27), already deprives the children of Adam of the same image. Scripture says that they were born in Adam's image (see Gen 5:3); that is, they were the same as Adam became after the Fall. Because of the loss of likeness, the image became perverted.[295] On behalf of every person who enters life after the Fall, Scripture utters a bitter confession: "For behold, I was conceived in wickedness, and in sins did my mother bear me" (Ps 50:7). Man became an enemy of God, his own Creator (see Rom 5:10).

God, in His unutterable goodness, once again called the race of man to communion with Himself. This He accomplished by means of the most miraculous, inconceivable events. One of His Three Hypostases, the all-holy Word, accepted humanity and was conceived in the womb of the All-pure Virgin by the grace of the Holy Spirit. He set aside from Himself the usual form of human conception from the seed of man, for this was a conception that was infected with sin. Thus, in the human race, a blameless Man appeared, unblemished like the Forefather, Adam. This sinless Man was a communicant of the Divine Essence, similar to Adam, but in an incomparably greater way, for the first-created was a man made holy by grace, but the Incarnate God became the God-Man. He took upon Himself all the sins of mankind. He could do this, because, being a man, He was also the all-powerful, all-perfect God. Having taken all mankind's sins on Himself, He brought Himself as an atoning Sacrifice to the justice of God for the sake of sinful mankind. He redeemed mankind, for He could do this.

The unlimited and endless Holy One redeemed the many (though limited) sins of man by His suffering and death. Truly did the Sacred Scripture declare concerning Him: "Behold! The Lamb of God who takes away the sin of the world!" (John 1:29). The God-Man substituted Himself for the whole world and every human being individually. All virtues, both social and individual, that flow from the fallen human nature have lost their significance after the incarnation of God. They have all been replaced by the great Deed of God: "I believe in Him Whom God sent" [a paraphrase of John 6:29]. This great Deed of God is our salvation, as the Lord Himself witnessed: "And this is eternal life [that is, salvation], that they may know You, the only true God, and Jesus Christ whom You have sent" (John 17:3).

All the virtues of a Christian must flow from Christ, from the human nature renewed by Him, not from fallen nature. Our fall does not consist in the destruction of good from our nature—this is an exclusive quality of the fallen angels—but in the intermixing of our natural good with unnatural evil. Therefore, our fallen nature has good deeds and virtues associated with it directly. These virtues are performed by pagans, Muslims, and all others who are strangers to Christ. These good deeds and virtues are defiled by the contamination of evil, and so are unworthy of God and actually hinder communion with Him. Thus, they counteract our salvation. Let us, therefore, reject this so-called good or, better yet, this great evil! Let us reject the actions of our fallen heart! Let us dedicate ourselves to a life commanded by our faith in Christ! Let us cease to live a life directed by our fallen reason, enticed by our fallen heart! Let us begin to lead a life according to the directions of the commandments of the Gospel, according to the requirements of the will of God. If we live like this, we will be saved.

Those who ascribe great significance to the good deeds of our fallen nature fall into a terrible, dangerous sin. Without realizing it, they belittle and even reject Christ. We often hear this question from them: "Why will not pagans, Muslims, Lutherans, and all others who are either obvious or secret enemies of Christianity, be saved? There are many among them that are extremely virtuous." Evidently, such questions and rebuttals come from complete ignorance of what the fall and salvation of man consist of. Evidently, such questions and rebuttals belittle Christ, for in them is expressed the following idea: the Redemption and, by extension, the Redeemer, were not necessary for mankind, because people can save themselves by their own means. In short, such questions and rebuttals reject Christianity outright.

The virtues of fallen human nature (such as the laws of the Old Testament) had their worth before the coming of Christ. They led humanity to a state, capable of accepting the Saviour. The God-Man Himself said concerning His coming, "The light has come into the world, and men loved darkness rather than light, because their deeds were evil. For everyone practicing evil hates the light and does not come to the light, lest his deeds should be exposed. But he who does the truth comes to the light, that his deeds may be clearly seen, that they have been done in God" (John 3:19–21). It is natural for those who have come to love sin to reject Christ, for Christ commands sinners to abandon the sin that they love so much. It is natural for lovers of virtue to come and join themselves to Christ, for the fullness of the good that they love is Christ Himself.

"In truth I perceive that God shows no partiality. But in every nation whoever fears Him and works righteousness is accepted by Him" (Acts 10:34–35). The holy Apostle Peter uttered these words on the occasion of God's call to convert the pagan centurion, Cornelius, to the faith. Striving toward true virtue prepared and made Cornelius capable of accepting salvation. This is how we can understand the expression "is accepted by Him," as explained by St John Chrysostom, for the context given by St Luke in the Book of Acts offers the same interpretation. Cornelius, though a pagan, had left his idols and prayed zealously to the One True God. He also gave abundant alms. Once, during prayer, an angel of God appeared to him and said, "About the ninth hour of the day he saw clearly in a vision an angel of God coming in and saying to him, 'Cornelius! . . . Your prayers and your alms have come up for a memorial before God. Now send men to Joppa, and send for Simon whose surname is Peter . . . He will tell you what you must do'" (Acts 10:3–6). The prayers and alms of Cornelius were so powerful that the merciful Lord looked upon them; however, they, by themselves, did not ensure salvation for Cornelius. They made him capable of believing in Christ, but only faith in Christ gave Cornelius salvation. This is a very fitting valuation of the good that belongs our fallen nature! Such virtue only has worthy when it brings one to Christ. When it is content with itself and leads a person away from Christ, then it becomes the worst evil, depriving us of the salvation given by Christ (for it cannot give salvation by itself).

The Old Testament is similar in this respect to natural virtue. To deviate from the Law before the coming of Christ was a departure from God; however, a desire to remain in the Law after the coming of Christ became deviation from God (see Gal 5:4). The Old Testament was a servant of salvation, preparing mankind for Christ, the Only One Who gives salvation. However, for the Jews who wanted to remain always with the Old Testament, it became the instrument of their own perdition. The soul-destroying sin of the Jews was the following: they, acting in pride and self-delusion, gave the covenant of God a different meaning than the one given by God. For the sake of the Old Testament—the mere shadow of the truth—they rejected the New Testament. For the sake of a shadow, they rejected the object that cast the shadow. For the sake of temporary guidance toward salvation, they rejected salvation itself. They rejected the redemption and the Redeemer.

Equally soul-destroying is the sin of those who, blinded by their pride and self-conceit, ascribe unnecessary importance to their own good deeds, the deeds of their fallen nature. "'A thief and a robber is he,' said St Macarius the Great, who 'does not enter the sheepfold by the door, but climbs up some other way' (John 10:1), and the same is the one who justifies himself without Christ's justification. All the saints, leaving aside their own truths, sought the truth of God and there found holy love, hidden from nature."[296] Nature, being corrupted by the Fall, has a corrupted kind of truth. "We are all become as unclean, and all our righteousness is like a filthy rag" (Isa 64:5 LXX). "From the feet all the way to the head, there is no soundness in" fallen man (Isa 1:6). "The evil that has struck us down, according to the interpretation of the Fathers, is not partial, but covering the entire body and entire soul, overwhelming all its powers."[297]

There is nothing pure left in our nature, nothing left undamaged, nothing uninfected by sin. We can do nothing of ourselves without the contamination of evil. When water mixes with wine or vinegar, every drop ceases to taste like water. So also our nature, being infected by evil, contains impurity in every manifestation of its activity. All our inheritance, all our dignity, resides exclusively in the Redeemer.[298] "A man is not justified by the works of the law but by faith in Jesus Christ" (Gal 2:16). To receive the Redeemer with living faith, one must completely reject one's life (see Luke 14:26), that is, not only his sinfulness, but even the righteousness of the fallen nature. Striving to preserve for yourself the righteousness of the fallen nature, corrupted by sin, is an active rejection of the Redeemer. "You have become estranged from Christ, you who attempt to be justified by law; you have fallen from grace" (Gal 5:4). "If righteousness comes through the law, then Christ died in vain" (Gal 2:21).

This means that a frame of mind that admits the worth of personal human righteousness before God after the coming of Christ is a form of blasphemy that perverts such a frame of mind entirely. Such a frame of mind does not consider Christ necessary for salvation; it is no different than a complete rejection of Christ. The Lord said to the Pharisees who were proud of their own righteousness: "If you were blind, you would have no sin; but now you say, 'We see.' Therefore your sin remains" (John 9:41). "For I did not come to call the righteous, but sinners, to repentance" (Matt 9:13).

This means that those who do not admit their sins to be sins, or their righteousness to be merely useless rags, defiled and ripped apart because of communion with sin and Satan, are strangers of the Redeemer. Perhaps they confess Him with their lips, but with their actions, and in their spirit, they reject Him. The holy Apostle Paul, himself a blameless Pharisee in terms of the natural law and the Law of Moses, considered his righteousness to be "loss for the excellence of the knowledge of Christ Jesus my Lord." He rejected His own righteousness, considering it "as rubbish, that I may gain Christ and be found in Him, not having my own righteousness, which is from the law, but that which is through faith in Christ, the righteousness which is from God by faith" (Phil 3:8–9). "We seek to be justified by Christ, we ourselves also are found sinners" (Gal 2:17), for there is no possibility of approaching Christ and becoming assimilated to Him without first sincerely admitting yourself to be a sinner, a lost sinner, having no personal justification, no personal dignity.

"Therefore by the deeds of the law no flesh will be justified in His sight, for by the law is the knowledge of sin. But now the righteousness of God apart from the law is revealed, being witnessed by the Law and the Prophets, even the righteousness of God, through faith in Jesus Christ, to all and on all who believe. For there is no difference; for all have sinned and fall short of the glory of God, being justified freely by His grace through the redemption that is in Christ Jesus" (Rom 3:20–24).

According to the immutable law of asceticism, an abundant acknowledgment and perception of one's sinfulness, given by the grace of God, comes before all other gifts of grace. It prepares the soul for accepting these gifts. The soul is incapable of receiving them, if it will not first come to the blessed state of poverty of spirit. "When the mind sees all its sins, in number like the sand of the sea, that serves as a sign of the beginning of the illumination of his soul, a sign of its health."[299] Having come to this state, St Tikhon of Zadonsk said, "We come to know our sins—this is the beginning of repentance.[300] Let us repent, admit ourselves to be nothing. The more worthless the ascetics of Christ admit themselves, the more God, for He is good and merciful, makes them worthy.[301] What belongs to us? Only weakness, corruption, darkness, evil, sins."[302] Let us beware of this death-bearing delusion! Let us fear to reject Christ! Let us fear the definite loss of salvation for assimilating such false thoughts, so hostile to faith!

In our time, care is needed, for now the preaching of the exaltedness of the virtues and success of fallen mankind is spreading with especial insistence. These preachers have a clear goal—to attract all to the doing of such virtues and such successes. Mocking the all-holy goodness of Christianity, this preaching tries to inspire disdain and hatred for Christianity.

The works of salvation are the works of faith, the works of the New Testament. These deeds are performed not by human knowledge, not by human will, but by the will of the all-holy God, revealed to us in the commandments of the Gospel. The Christian who desires to inherit salvation must perform the following actions:

1. Come to believe in God as God commanded us to believe in Him, that is, accept the teaching about God that God Himself revealed. We must accept Christianity, which is preserved in all purity and fullness only in the Orthodox Church, planted by the God-Man in the East, spread from the East to the rest of the world, but to this moment only remaining in fullness in the East, which has preserved the God-given Christian teaching without perversion, without changes, and without the contamination of human and demonic teachings. "But without faith it is impossible to please Him, for he who comes to God must believe that He is, and that He is a rewarder of those who diligently seek Him" (Heb 11:6). The teaching of Christianity is declared by universal preaching and is received by faith. Since it is a divine teaching, a teaching revealed by God, surpassing all human reasoning, it cannot be accepted without the sympathy of the heart, by faith. Faith, by its very nature, is capable of accepting by the heart that which is inconceivable to the mind and cannot be understood by the usual means of reasoning. "He who believes and is baptized will be saved; but he who does not believe will be condemned" (Mark 16:16).

2. The one who has come to believe must repent in his previous willful, sinful life and to firmly decide to lead a God-pleasing life. "As obedient children, not conforming yourselves to the former lusts, as in your ignorance; but as He who called you is holy, you also be holy in all your conduct" (1 Pet 1:14–15). It is impossible to have communion with God, nor remain in such communion, if you remain and abide willingly in a sinful life. The New Testament commands all who approach God to repent as the first condition of access to God. John the Forerunner of the Lord began his preaching with a call to repent, saying to rejected mankind, once again called to communion with God: "Repent, for the kingdom of heaven is at hand!" (Matt 3:2). The God-Man Himself began preaching with the same words: "From that time Jesus began to preach and to say, 'Repent, for the kingdom of heaven is at hand'" (Matt 4:17). The Word of God commanded His holy apostles to begin their preaching with the same words, having first sent them "to the lost sheep of the house of Israel," who were wallowing in perdition, despite their gift (though a prototypical one) of communion

with God. God the Word commanded: "As you go, preach, saying, 'Repent, for the kingdom of heaven is at hand'" (Matt 10:7). The call to faith and repentance is a divine call. Obedience to such a call is necessary for salvation; it is the fulfillment of the all-holy will of God.

3. Having believed in God, having rejected a sinful life for communion with God, we then enter this communion through the first Christian sacrament—holy baptism. Baptism is birth into the divine life. It is impossible to begin a natural life without being born in the natural way; likewise, it is impossible to begin communicating with God—this is our only true life and our salvation—without first entering Christianity through holy baptism. This is a divine institution. By baptism, we enter into "regeneration" (Titus 3:5), that is, a new, holy life that was given to Adam at his creation, but was lost by him at the Fall, and returned to us by our Lord Jesus Christ. "Most assuredly, I say to you, unless one is born again, he cannot see the kingdom of God . . . Most assuredly, I say to you, unless one is born of water and the Spirit, he cannot enter the kingdom of God" (John 3:3, 5). Being born physically, we count our ancestry from our forefather according to the flesh, Adam, who gave us life, but with it eternal death. Through holy baptism, we pass into the spiritual inheritance of the God-Man, Who, according to the prophet, is "Wonderful, Counselor, Mighty God, Everlasting Father, Prince of Peace" (Isa 9:6 (NKJV)). He, giving birth to us in spirit, destroys within us the seed of death that was planted in us by our physical birth, and He gives us eternal life, salvation, blessedness in God. St John the Theologian said this concerning those who believed in God and have been reborn by holy baptism: "But as many as received Him, to them He gave the right to become children of God, to those who believe in His name: who were born, not of blood, nor of the will of the flesh, nor of the will of man, but of God" (John 1:12–13). Holy Baptism, having made us children of God, restores our freedom, given us at our creation, lost by us in the Fall. It restores our strength of will, leaving it to our decision either to remain children of God or to reject that sonship.[303] Thus in Paradise it was left to the choice of the forefathers—to remain eternally in blessedness, or to lose it. "Therefore we must give the more earnest heed to the things we have heard, lest we drift away" (Heb 2:1). Holy baptism is sealed by another sacrament that follows it immediately in time, holy unction. It is proper to call this sacrament a seal, just as it is correct to call holy baptism a condition, a covenant between God and man. The seal that endorses this condition is holy unction.

4. Remaining a son to God—sonship being a gift of holy baptism—is accomplished by a life lived according to the commandments of the Gospel. Loss of sonship is the result of deviation from a life lived according to the Gospel commandments. Both of these truths are witness by the Lord Himself: "If you keep My commandments, you will abide in My love . . . If anyone does not abide in Me, he is cast out as a branch and is withered; and they gather them and throw them into the fire, and they are burned" (John 15:10, 6). To be saved, the one baptized into Christ must life according to the commandments of Christ.

5. The God-Man, having given birth to us for salvation by holy baptism, leads us into an intimate union with Himself by another great, ineffable sacrament—the Holy Eucharist. Through the Eucharist, we are united and our body and blood is intertwined with the Body and Blood of the God-Man.[304] "He who eats My flesh and drinks My blood abides in Me, and I in him. Whoever eats My flesh and drinks My blood has eternal life, and I will raise him up at the last day. Most assuredly, I say to you, unless you eat the flesh of the Son of Man and drink His blood, you have no life in you" (John 6:56, 54, 53). The God-Man, through this sacrament, completely separated us from our relationship with the old Adam and led us into the most intimate relation, union with Himself. How can those who are one with the God-Man fail to be saved? "Wherever the body is, there the eagles will be gathered together" (Luke 17:37). These eagles are nourished by this body, as the Holy Gospel witnesses. By a worthy and frequent reception of this spiritual food that has come down from heaven and has given life to the world, we become spiritual eagles, rising up from the depths of our fleshly state to the heights of the spiritual state. We will fly up to the place where the God-Man raised His human nature and body, being of old in God the Father by His divine Essence, and sit on the right of the Father in His human nature after He redeemed mankind.

6. To give strength to our weakness, to heal the wounds of sin received after holy baptism, to uphold the holiness by which we were sealed in holy baptism, God gave us the sacrament of Confession. By this sacrament, the state given by holy baptism is renewed and restored. We must run to confession as often as possible; the soul of that person who has the custom of confessing his sins often is held back from sinning by the reminder of his imminent confession. On the contrary, those who do not confess sin frequently may find it more difficult to deter sin which cannot be hidden in the twilight.[305]

Part II

The Gospel speaks of two blessed states—the state of salvation and the state of Christian perfection. A certain rich and noble Jewish youth fell at the God-Man's feet and asked Him to tell him what he should do to inherit eternal life, salvation. To a Jew, that is, to one who believed in God correctly, the Lord answered, "If you want to enter into life, keep the commandments" (Matt 19:17). When the youth asked which commandments these were, the Lord indicated a certain commandment that defined how the faithful related, in a way pleasing to God, to their fellow man, without directly referencing the command to love God, for this command would have been known to any Jew and, at least externally, practiced by all of them. The moral and religious sickness of the Jew, by the time of the coming of Christ, had changed.

This disease changed in its external form, remaining in essence the same as it was before—the striving to deviate from God. The Jews never expressed that irresistible inclination to idol worship that so plagued both the spiritual and civil welfare of mankind for millennia, though they were constantly tempted by it, beginning with the Exodus from Egypt and ending with the Babylonian captivity. Satan never managed to entice them to worship him through the worship of idols. He prepared another snare for them, another fatal abyss, more effective, incomparably deeper and darker than idol worship.

Satan was content to leave the Jews as servants of the One True God, but only superficially. Moreover, he enticed them to an intense, incorrect respect for the rituals of the Law and the elders' interpretations of the Law, while he managed to steal their respect for the commandments of God. He led them into the minutest and subtlest study of the letter of the law of God, but at the same time, he stole from them the study of the Law of God in life. He used this knowledge of the letter of the Law as a means to lead them into the worst kind of pride, the most horrifying arrogance. They, calling themselves, and presenting themselves to others, as children of God, in actual fact were the enemies of God and the children of the devil (see John 8:44). Under the pretense of faithfulness to God, they rejected God. Under the pretense of preserving communion with God, they rejected communion with God. They became infected with Satanic hatred for God, and they confirmed this hatred by the worst of sins—deicide.[306]

All this happened because they abandoned the God-pleasing life! All this happened because they abandoned the kind of relation with their fellow man that God commanded, and which always leads to the death of communion with God, which remains only as a superficial reality. For this reason, when the Saviour was asked by the young man about salvation, He told him to love his fellow man as God commanded. So every Orthodox Christian, if he wishes to pass from a slothful life to an attentive life, if he wishes to labor at his salvation, he must at first pay attention to his relations with his fellow man. In these interactions, he must correct everything that needs correction, and he must offer God sincere repentance for everything that is already beyond correction. Then, he must predetermine how he will begin to act in all things in a way that pleases God.

The publican Zacchaeus, being converted by the Lord, said, "Look, Lord, I give half of my goods to the poor; and if I have taken anything from anyone by false accusation, I restore fourfold" (Luke 19:8). And he heard the most joyful words from the all-good and almighty Lord, who remains today just as good and just as almighty as then: "Today salvation has come to this house, because he also is a son of Abraham; for the Son of Man has come to seek and to save that which was lost" (Luke 19:9–10). The Lord admitted Zacchaeus to be a son of Abraham only after he made a firm commitment to live a God-pleasing life. It follows, therefore, that before this conversion, he was not a son of Abraham, even though he was his physical descendant. In the same way, as long as a Christian continues to live a sinful life, contrary to the commandments of the Gospel, he is not actually a Christian at all, even though he has the right to be called so, for he has been joined to the Christian race by holy baptism. But what is the use of confession in words, while you reject in deed?

"And then I will declare to them," that is, those who disdain to fulfill the commandments of the Gospel, "I never knew you; depart from Me, you who practice lawlessness!" (Matt 7:23). To be saved, it is necessary to fulfill all the commands of the Gospel, which are only preserved in their necessary fullness in the One, Holy, Orthodox Church.

The aforementioned youth, having heard the Lord's answer (that he must live according to the commandments to be saved), answered, "'All these things I have kept from my youth. What do I still lack?' Jesus said to him, 'If you want to be perfect, go, sell what you have and give to the poor, and you will have treasure in heaven; and come, take up the cross, and follow Me'" (Matt 19:20–21). It is possible to be saved while still retaining your riches, living a life in the world. However, if you seek perfection, you must first reject the world. Salvation is necessary for all; the search for perfection is given to those who desire it. The model of Christian perfection is evident in the holy apostles, as Apostle Paul witnessed concerning them and himself, saying, "Therefore let us, as many as are mature, have this mind" (Phil 3:15), that Christian perfection, being a life in God, is the endless field of spiritual progress, as infinite as God is infinite (see Phil 3:12, 20).

"This perfection, this always-growing perfection of the perfect, as expressed to me by one who had tasted of it, so illumines the mind and casts out of it all that is material, that after entering into this heavenly field, the ascetic, more often than not, ascends from this life according to flesh, in a state of spiritual drunkenness, to heaven in vision (and there he remains). The Psalmist, also probably speaking from experience, explained it thus: 'God's mighty in the land are very high exalted' (Ps 46:10)."[307]

He who was raised up to the third heaven, and who remained there in his heart's perceptions and thoughts, said, "Our citizenship is in heaven" (Phil 3:20). Perfection consists of the clear communion of the Holy Spirit, Who, having entered into the Christian, bears all his desires and all his thoughts with Him into eternity. David confessed such a state of his own soul: "The Spirit of the Lord spoke by me, and His word was on my tongue" (2 Kgdms 23:2). David could truly say, inspired by the Holy Spirit: "How amiable are Thy dwellings, O Lord of hosts! My soul desireth and longeth for the courts of the Lord; my heart and my flesh have rejoiced in the living God" (Ps 83:2–3). "Like as the hart panteth after the water-brooks, so longeth my soul after Thee, O God. My soul hath thirsted for the mighty living God; when shall I come and appear before God's face?" (Ps 41:2–3). "Woe is me, for my wandering hath been prolonged" (Ps 119:5).

It is not natural for a person, in his usual state, to have such an ardent desire to pass into eternity. It is only natural for a Spirit-bearing man, as the Spirit-bearing Paul said concerning himself: "For to me, to live is Christ, and to die is gain . . . For I am hard-pressed between the two, having a desire to depart and be with Christ, which is far better" (Phil 1:21, 23). St Isaac the Syrian said,

> When a merchant has finished his business and received his money, he hurries to return home. Likewise, a monk, until he has not completed his work in the field of salvation, does not yet want to leave his body. However, when he has sensed in his soul that his work is done and that he has received the pledge, then he begins to desire the coming age . . . The mind, having acquired the wisdom of the Spirit, is like a man who has found a ship at sea. When he boards this ship, he immediately sails on it from the sea of the passing world to the island that belongs to the future life. The perception of the coming age in this life is like a small island in the sea—the one who has landed on this island will no longer want to labor in the waves of the fantasy of this age.[308]

St Macarius the Great vividly describes Christian perfection in the following manner:

Man must, so to speak, walk twelve steps, and then achieve perfection. If
anyone has reached this stage, then he has come to perfection. Again, when
grace begins to act more weakly, he descends one step and stands on the
eleventh. Another who is rich and abundant with grace always, day and
night, remains on the twelfth step of perfection, being free and pure of
everything, always exalted to the heights. If this supernatural state, revealed
today to man, experienced by him personally, remained with him always,
then he would be incapable of taking up any service to the Word, nor to do
any kind of labors, nor to hear that in some situations he must worry about
himself and the coming day. Instead, he would just sit in a corner, exalted,
and as though drunk. For this reason, the full measure of perfection is not
given to man, so that he can have care for his brothers and labor in the service of the Word. But the wall is already destroyed, and death is defeated.
This we must understand in the following manner: just as in some places,
even when lit by a candle, a certain dark power and thick air dampen the
light, so also the spiritual light is found under a kind of veil. For this reason,
he who is within this spiritual light must confess himself not yet perfect or
freed completely from sin. The wall that separated him from God has been,
so to speak, torn down, but only partially, and not completely or forever,
because sometimes grace guides and strengthens a man in abundance, and
sometimes it weakens and lessens, in accordance with what is most beneficial for the man. Who has achieved in this life the perfect state and come to
know the world to come experientially? I have not seen a single person who
has completely acquired Christian perfection, who has become completely
free of any sin. Though some are at peace in grace, some pierce through to
mysteries and revelations, some taste unutterable sweetness in grace; however, sin still remains in them . . . I have yet to see anyone completely free,
for even I have reached the height of perfection sometimes, and I have come
to know that here is not a single person who is fully perfect.[309]

For this reason, as we have seen, St John of the Ladder and like him many
Holy Fathers have called human perfection within Christianity "an incomplete completeness," as the holy Apostle Paul also said, "Not that I have already
attained, or am already perfected; but I press on, that I may lay hold of that for
which Christ Jesus has also laid hold of me. Brethren, I do not count myself
to have apprehended; but one thing I do, forgetting those things which are

behind and reaching forward to those things which are ahead, I press toward the goal for the prize of the upward call of God [that is, Christian perfection] in Christ Jesus" (Phil 3:12–14).

Christian perfection is a gift of God, not the fruit of human labor. The labor itself only proves how actual and sincere is our desire to receive the gift. The labor that reins in and tames the passions makes human nature capable of accepting the gift. It depends on the person to clean and decorate (and even this with God's help) the house in anticipation of God, but God's coming into this house depends entirely on God's good will.[310] Non-acquisitiveness and rejection from the world are absolute conditions for the acquisition of perfection. The mind and heart must be completely directed to God. All obstacles, all sources of distraction must be removed. "Whoever of you does not forsake all that he has cannot be My disciple" (Luke 14:33). Trusting in the passing goods of this world must be replaced with complete trust in God, while the good themselves but be replaced by the promise of God, Who said, "Therefore do not worry, saying, 'What shall we eat?' or 'What shall we drink?' or 'What shall we wear?' For after all these things the Gentiles seek. For your heavenly Father knows that you need all these things. But seek first the kingdom of God and His righteousness, and all these things shall be added to you" (Matt 6:31–33).

In the midst of deprivation, in the midst of difficult circumstances—into which, apparently, a Christian willingly places himself, having rejected all riches and benefits given by the world—he is actually placing himself in the best possible situation for grace to work with him. The world never places its followers in such an advantageous position, which is explained by St Paul thus:

> But in all things we commend ourselves as ministers of God: in much patience, in tribulations, in needs, in distresses, in stripes, in imprisonments, in tumults, in labors, in sleeplessness, in fastings; by purity, by knowledge, by longsuffering, by kindness, by the Holy Spirit, by sincere love, by the word of truth, by the power of God, by the armor of righteousness on the right hand and on the left, by honor and dishonor, by evil report and good report; as deceivers, and yet true; as unknown, and yet well known; as dying, and behold we live; as chastened, and yet not killed; as sorrowful, yet always rejoicing; as poor, yet making many rich; as having nothing, and yet possessing all things.

This is the state in which all the holy apostles lived, having left everything behind and following in the footsteps of the Lord (see Matt 19:27). They had no material riches, but they gave to the whole world which was drowning in perdition, priceless spiritual riches—the knowledge of God and salvation. They had no material riches, but the cosmos belonged to them. In every city, in every village that they visited, God's providence prepared for them a refuge and the necessary sustenance. "All who were possessors of lands or houses sold them, and brought the proceeds of the things that were sold, and laid them at the apostles' feet" (Acts 4:34–35).

This was also the state of the holy martyrs. Before going to the place of their testing, they would usually free all their slaves and give all their money to the poor.[311] Having severed any connection with the world, they took off their own clothing (that is, their body), which was conceived in sin, and they put on the robes of the Holy Spirit, putting on the very Lord Jesus Christ Himself. They transformed their earthly clothing, their body, into spiritual clothing, their corruptible into incorruptible, their sinful to holy, their earthly to heavenly. The sufferings of the holy martyrs had a special character—they suffered not as the children of the old Adam, but as the members of Christ. The holy martyr Felicitas was pregnant when she was imprisoned into a dark and dank prison for her confession of faith. In the prison, her labor pains started. During the birth, which was difficult, Felicitas could not stop herself from crying out. When one of the guards heard her, he said, "You are screaming like this now; how badly will you scream when you are given to the beasts to be eaten?" She answered, "I am suffering now, but during the tortures, Another will suffer in my stead, for now I suffer for Him."[312]

Martyrdom was by no means a human invention or the result merely of human will—it was a gift of God given to mankind, and so it was supernatural, as the holy Apostle Paul said, "For to you it has been granted on behalf of Christ, not only to believe in Him, but also to suffer for His sake" (Phil 1:29).

Like martyrdom, monasticism is also a gift of God. Monasticism is a supernatural labor. It is the same as martyrdom, in essence, only appearing as something else, something nebulous, to a superficial, ignorant glance. Like martyrdom, monasticism requires preliminary and complete rejection of the world. Just as martyrdom begins with various tortures of the body, and ends with the death of the body, so also the labor of monasticism begins with the cutting off of one's own will and mindset, rejection of all physical pleasures, and it ends with the death of the soul and body to sin, and their coming back to life for God. Having stood against sin even to death, having bought victory over sin by never sparing the body even during the most intense, supernatural labors, many monks have easily passed from the monastic labor to the labor of martyrdom, in the sense of the similarity between these two labors. (Both of them require rejection of the world and the self.)

Just as martyrdom is never understood by the proud who serves the corruption of the world—he even considers it nothing but rabble-rousing—so also monasticism is equally inexplicable to him. Martyrs began to find abundance of gracious gifts, depending on the degree of their physical suffering. The same is true of monastics. The grace of God revealed its activity commensurate with the degree of their mortification for sin. This grace increases as much as the holy deadness of the monks increases. The labor of any monk is supernatural. It must without fail be accomplished by victory over the bestial tendencies of the body, which have, after the Fall, become natural to every person. The asceticism of some holy monks seems even more incomprehensible in its supernaturalism than martyrdom. All we need to do to be assured of this is to read the lives of Mark the Athonite, St Onuphrius the Great, St Mary of Egypt, and others. Why then do martyrdom and monasticism seem madness and absurdity to the slaves of sin and the world? Evidently, because such people only accept the virtue of fallen nature to be virtuous. They do not understand or even know Christianity.

To acquire perfection, after giving away our money to the poor, we must take up our cross (see Mark 8:34). Abandonment of material goods must be followed by rejection of the self, which is, in essence, the bearing of the cross, or the willing and constant submission to sorrows of a dual nature, which make up a cross, as it were, fashioned from two types of wood that are connected to each other and intertwined with each other. These two kinds of sorrows are as follows: the first is everything that is allowed by divine providence for our spiritual formation, while the second are the sorrows we must willingly lay on ourselves to rein in and mortify our passions, for the mortification of our fallen human nature.

St Paul says the following concerning the sorrows sent by divine providence: "For whom the Lord loves He chastens, and scourges every son whom He receives. If you endure chastening, God deals with you as with sons; for what son is there whom a father does not chasten? But if you are without chastening, of which all have become partakers [that is, true servants of God], then you are illegitimate and not sons. Furthermore, we have had human fathers who corrected us, and we paid them respect. Shall we not much more readily be in subjection to the Father of spirits and live?" (Heb 12:6–9).

The holy Apostle Paul raises us to a spiritual understanding of sorrows and comforts all who have been subjected to them with the following words:

> Beloved, do not think it strange concerning the fiery trial which is to try you, as though some strange thing happened to you; but rejoice to the extent that you partake of Christ's sufferings, that when His glory is revealed, you may also be glad with exceeding joy. If you are reproached for the name of Christ, blessed are you, for the Spirit of glory and of God rests upon you. On their part He is blasphemed, but on your part He is glorified. But let none of you suffer as a murderer, a thief, an evildoer, or as a busybody in other people's matters. Yet if anyone suffers as a Christian, let him not be ashamed, but let him glorify God in this matter. For the time has come for judgment to begin at the house of God; and if it begins with us first, what will be the end of those who do not obey the gospel of God? Now "If the righteous one is scarcely saved, where will the ungodly and the sinner appear?" Therefore let those who suffer according to the will of God commit their souls to Him in doing good, as to a faithful Creator. (1 Pet 4:12–19)

According to the instruction of St Paul, sorrows permitted by providence must be accepted with the greatest submissiveness before God, just as he himself accepted all temptations allowed by God for his instruction: "I take pleasure in infirmities, in reproaches, in needs, in persecutions, in distresses, for Christ's sake. For when I am weak, then I am strong" (2 Cor 12:10). According to the instruction of St Peter, when sorrows come, we must trust completely in the all-holy will of God and, with especial vigilance, firmly hold to the commandments of God, from which the enemy tries to distract us by thoughts of sorrow, hopelessness, complaining, anger, even blasphemy. Cast "all your care upon Him, for He cares for you" (1 Pet 5:7). We must "count it all joy when [we] fall into various trials" (Jas 1:2), because these temptations are the sign of God's calling, a sign of being chosen, a sign of sonship. From the midst of sorrows, let us glorify God, as the righteous, long-suffering Job glorified Him from the midst of many different calamities that surrounded him from all sides (see Job 2:10). Let us thank God in the midst of sorrows, for they will fill the heart of the grateful one with spiritual consolation and the power of endurance. This gratitude is commanded by God Himself. "In everything give thanks; for this is the will of God in Christ Jesus for you" (1 Thess 5:18).

St Peter Damascene said,

> Parents who love their children, being incited by love, threaten the children who allow themselves to act unwisely with the intention of helping

them lead a good life. In the same way, God allows temptations like a rod that turns the worthy away from the devil's evil council. "He who spares the rod hates his son, but he who loves him instructs [disciplines] him with care" (Prov 13:26 LXX). It is better to run to God with endurance rather than fall away from him because of the fear of calamities, falling instead into the clutches of the devil, incurring eternal abandonment and the pain associated with it. One of the two will inevitably occur with us. Either we must endure the former, which is temporary, or be subjected to the second, eternal, sufferings. However, neither the one, nor the other touches the righteous, because they, loving the events that seem to us to be misfortunes, instead rejoice at them, greeting all temptations as godsends, as times for the acquisition of spiritual gain, and they remain unwounded. The man who has been struck by an arrow, but not fatally, will not die. Only he whose wound is fatal will die. Was Job harmed by his temptations? On the contrary, did they not crown him? Were the apostles and martyrs terrified by tortures? They rejoiced, said the Scriptures, "So they departed from the presence of the council, rejoicing that they were counted worthy to suffer shame for His name" (Acts 5:41). The more a victor is attacked, the more laurels he wins, the more joy he feels from his victories. When he hears the sound of the trumpet, he does not fear, as though it were a voice uttering a curse. On the contrary, he rejoices from the foretaste of the laurels and the reward. Nothing so ensures an easy victory as courage with faith! Nothing so ensures a quick defeat as self-love and fear that are born of unbelief.[313]

The Lord promised sorrows to His followers for the duration of their earthly wandering. He promised an earthly life like His own, spent in deprivations and persecutions, but at the same time, He charged that they remain courageous and hopeful. "If the world hates you, you know that it hated Me before it hated you. If you were of the world, the world would love its own. Yet because you are not of the world, but I chose you out of the world, therefore the world hates you" (John 15:18). "In the world you will have tribulation; but be of good cheer, I have overcome the world" (John 16:33). No sorrow, no temptation will be capable of overcoming or defeating you, if you will believe in Me and remain in Me through the fulfillment of my commandments.

"God is faithful, who will not allow you to be tempted beyond what you are able, but with the temptation will also make the way of escape, that you may be able to bear it" (1 Cor 10:13). Also, the Holy Spirit witnesses in another place: "Many are the troubles of the righteous, but the Lord delivereth them out of all. The Lord keepeth all their bones; not one of them shall be broken"

(Ps 33:20–21). Let us believe the promises of God; let us not fear the stormy sea of sorrows, and we will successfully sail over it, protected by the invisible, but almighty right hand of God.

The second kind of cross consists of willing spiritual labors, established and commanded by God, by which the sinful desires of the body, and, consequently, the soul, are reined in. Concerning this, St Paul said, "I discipline my body and bring it into subjection, lest, when I have preached to others, I myself should become disqualified" (1 Cor 9:27). The Apostle Peter said: "Since Christ suffered for us in the flesh, arm yourselves also with the same mind, for he who has suffered in the flesh has ceased from sin" (1 Pet 4:1). "Those who are Christ's have crucified the flesh with its passions and desires" (Gal 5:24). The flesh that is not crucified, but rather fattened and consoled by abundant food, pleasures, and rest, cannot help but sympathize with sin, cannot help but find pleasure in it, cannot help but be incapable of accepting the Holy Spirit, cannot help but be devoid of God, even hostile to Him. "Now she who is really a widow, and left alone," in other words, whoever has truly rejected the world, died for it, separated himself from all things and all people for the sake of serving God, "trusts in God and continues in supplications and prayers night and day. But she who lives in pleasure" in spite of leaving the world externally and giving away all her money to the poor, "is dead while she lives" (1 Tim 5:5–6), because "he who sows to his flesh will of the flesh reap corruption, but he who sows to the Spirit will of the Spirit reap everlasting life" (Gal 6:8).

The crucifixion of the flesh is of utmost importance to the ascetic of Christ! It is necessary to submit to the easy yoke of labors for the sake of reining in the bestial strivings of our flesh, but not to waste the body's health and strength, which are necessary for the ascetic life. "We have learned to be murderers of the passions, but not the body."[314] Even for those weak in body and sick, it is very harmful to break one's asceticism, for it will only make the sickness worse, not strengthen the body. A wise moderation is especially capable of upholding and preserving the body's powers and health, both in people with strong constitutions and sick, weak people.

After giving away one's money to the poor and cutting off all ties with the world, the first task for an ascetic of Christ must be removing himself from the midst of temptations by going to a monastery. Such departure from the world wipes away all previously acquired sinful impressions, and the possibility of being tempted anew is greatly reduced. The true servant of God is invited to such solitude by the Holy Spirit Himself: "Come out from among them and be separate, says the Lord. Do not touch what is unclean, and I will receive you. I will be a Father to you, and you shall be My sons and daughters" (2 Cor 6:17–18). Even in the holy monastery, it is necessary to protect yourself from harmful acquaintances, from walking about, visiting the cells of your brothers or receiving them in your own, so that the soul will become ready for the word of God being sowed in it, to bring spiritual harvest at the proper time. Even the physical fields are prepared for better harvests by harrowing with metal instruments that pull all harmful weeds from the ground.

St Simeon the Studite commanded his disciple, St Symeon the New Theologian, when he entered the monastery: "Pay attention, child, if you want to be saved, do not converse during church services and do not visit the cells of others. Do not have a free manner of discourse. Preserve your mind, so that it does not wander here and there, but gaze constantly on your sins and on the eternal sufferings" (from his life). In the cell, you must only have the things you cannot do without, as simple as possible. Excessive or beautiful things immediately cause the heart's inclination toward them, and then the mind will be distracted and begin to fantasize and wander, and this is very harmful.

The second labor is moderate fasting. Fasting for beginners is entirely determined by the monastery's refectory. In the refectory, one must only eat what is necessary, never allowing yourself to be full. In general, this means that you should eat as much as you need for your body to be able to fulfill all your obediences. The traditions of the Fathers and the laws of the monastery forbid any eating outside the refectory. Those monks whom God brings to a hesychastic life, to a life of constant labor in prayer and contemplation of God, must only eat once a day.[315] Such a monk should never be full and only content himself with the food either allowed by monastics or sent by God. Such freedom requires strict vigilance, because it is easy to find reason to eat too much or too selectively. True pleasure awaits us in the coming age. In this age, the path to the age to come, we should forbid ourselves any pleasures, contenting ourselves only with natural needs, not the desires of the passions. Solitude and fasting—these are the essential aspects of monastic life, and from them monks received their name in ancient times: "monachos," from the Greek "monos," meaning "one" or "solitary." Monks have also always been known by the name "fasters."

The third labor is vigil. The beginner monk only begins to labor in vigil properly when he never misses a church service. For a hesychast, the labor of vigil is especially important. Active remembrance, even a foretaste, of death and the impartial Judgment of God that follows death—these are the most effective ways of succeeding at this labor. The monk seeks to anticipate the dread standing before the Judge through reverent standing at prayer, as though standing directly before the presence and gaze of God Himself. He hopes to ask and receive the forgiveness of his sins, so that, after the departure of his soul from the body, he could travel the way from earth to heaven with no fear. Therefore, he always stands before the doors of God's mercy during his cell rule of solitary prayer. He knocks at these doors with tears, with his heavy groaning, his humble words, flowing from the depths of a heart that is in pain from acknowledging its sinfulness.

The more the spiritual perception of the fear of God increases, the more will the monk stand vigil at prayer. However, in the beginning, he will have to force himself to this labor, for without this self-constraint, no final and complete victory over the passions is possible. He must approach the state commanded by the Lord:

> Let your waist be girded and your lamps burning; and you yourselves be like men who wait for their master, when he will return from the wedding, that when he comes and knocks they may open to him immediately. Blessed are those servants whom the master, when he comes, will find watching. Assuredly, I say to you that he will gird himself and have them sit down to eat, and will come and serve them. And if he should come in the second watch, or come in the third watch, and find them so, blessed are those servants. But know this, that if the master of the house had known what hour the thief would come, he would have watched and not allowed his house to be broken into. Therefore you also be ready, for the Son of Man is coming at an hour you do not expect. (Luke 12:35–40)

Such a state is given by the fear of God. Those who have begun to fear God begin to live on earth like sojourners at an inn, every moment expecting the time to leave. The time of the earthly life shortens before their very eyes when boundless and majestic eternity opens up before them. The thought that they can be called by the Lord unexpectedly inspired them to remain constantly vigilant, on a constant watch against sin, which constantly attacks. They spend their nights as they do their days, taking rest in sleep only as needed, never allowing themselves to deeply fall into sin and become soft because of it. They lie down on their hard beds already dressed and girded, so that they can get up as soon as necessary. The labor of vigil must correspond to the physical strength of a person. It, just like solitude and fasting, becomes stronger with the ascetic's gradual passing from a carnal or emotional to a spiritual state of grace. The spiritual man, though he is weak in body, can endure an incomparably greater labor than a strong carnal or emotional man. The former is aroused to labor by the grace of God and encounters fewer obstacles from his flesh, and he is usually capable of setting aside his weakness when he enters into such a state.

To make a physical cross, you need two connected crossbars. To make a spiritual cross, you also need two spiritual crossbars. The first is sorrows undertaken willingly, that is, ascetic labors that crucify the flesh and keep it in such a state of crucifixion. The second is external sorrows that rein in and humble the spirit of man that is constantly inclined toward pride because of its damage by the Fall. The connection of these sorrows creates that cross that we are commanded to take up and with which we are to follow Christ. Without this cross, emulation of Christ is impossible.

Those who have not crucified their flesh, who have not reined in their sinful desires and inclinations, those who take pleasure in sensual perceptions and thoughts cannot unite with Christ, for they are in communion, through the pleasures and enticements of sin, to Satan. "So then, those who are in the flesh," that is, those who live a carnal life, feeding their body, consoling it, softening it, "cannot please God" (Rom 8:8). "For those who live according to the flesh set their minds on the things of the flesh" (Rom 8:5). In other words, those who lead a carnal life always have a carnal mindset. They do not remember or care for eternity; they have a false reference to the earthly life, consider it eternal, acting only for it. They highly value passing, earthly honors and privileges. They cannot assimilate the New Testament to themselves; they cannot reject the fallen nature; instead they develop it, honoring its so-called worth and success.

"For to be carnally minded is death, but to be spiritually minded is life and peace. Because the carnal mind is enmity against God; for it is not subject to the law of God, nor indeed can be" (Rom 8:6–7). It is not natural, not even possible for a carnal mindset to submit itself in holiness. We will receive no benefit if we abandon our riches and leave the world for the monastery if we continue to satisfy the capricious desires of our flesh, if we do not raise it to the cross, depriving it of excess and pleasure, leaving only what is necessary to survive. The first command given by God to man was the commandment concerning fasting. It was given in Paradise, and it was confirmed by the Gospel. After it was broken, holy Paradise could not prevent man's death. After man broke the law, even the redemption of the God-Man does not leave us impervious to perdition.

"For many walk, of whom I have told you often, and now tell you even weeping, that they are the enemies of the cross of Christ: whose end is destruction, whose god is their belly, and whose glory is in their shame—who set their mind on earthly things" (Phil 3:18–19). As the Apostle instructed the Christians thus, he begged them to emulate his own life (see Phil 3:17), which he lived "in weariness and toil, in sleeplessness often, in hunger and thirst, in fastings often, in cold and nakedness" (2 Cor 11:27).

Fasting is the foundation of all monastic labors; without it, it is impossible to preserve solitude, to rein in the tongue, to lead a sober, attentive life, to succeed in prayer and vigil, to acquire the remembrance of death, to see the multitude of one's own sins. The monk who disdains fasting shakes the foundation of the edifice of his virtues. The edifice will not stand if the builder will not wake up and take care to shore up the foundations in time.

St John of the Ladder said, "The lord of the demon is the fallen daystar, and the beginning of passions is overeating.[316] Do not lead yourself into delusion! You will not free yourself from Pharaoh, and you will not see the heavenly Passover if you will not constantly taste the bitter herbs and unleavened bread. The bitter herbs are forcing yourself to fast and labor, while the unleavened bread is a humble mindset. Let these words come true in your own life: 'But when [the demons] trouble me, I put on sackcloth, and humbled my soul with fasting, and my prayer shall turn into mine own bosom' (Ps 34:13)."[317] If you gave an oath to Christ to go by the straight and narrow path, then constrain your stomach. If you console and broaden it, then you are breaking your oath. Be attentive and hear these words: "Broad and easy is the path of gluttony, for it leads to the passion of lust, and many are those who walk this way. The narrow and strait path is the way of fasting that leads to a pure life, and there are few who walk this way."[318]

What does it mean to "follow Christ" (see Matt 19:21) after giving away your money and taking up the cross? To follow Christ means to live your earthly life only for heaven, just as the God-Man lived His own life. Those who live piously in the midst of the world, following the commandments of the Gospel, are likened in their virtuous lifestyle and spiritual disposition to the Son of God. However, those who have rejected the world and have crucified their flesh through asceticism, who have attracted the grace of the Holy Spirit into themselves because of the mortification of their flesh for sin[319]—these receive a special likeness to the God-Man. They are "led by the Spirit of God, [and] . . . are sons of God" (Rom 8:14) by grace, having likened themselves to the image of the Heavenly Man, the second Adam, the God-Man.[320]

It is not the word, not a superficial knowledge according to the letter (which has no significance with God), that witnesses to them that they are children of God. The all-holy God Himself witnesses to this, having entered into them perceptibly for them and having united with them in spirit.[321] "And if children, then heirs—heirs of God and joint heirs with Christ" (Rom 8:17). From where can such glory come for the impoverished, fallen creature that is man? Only from living faith in Christ, our God, Creator, and Saviour. Such living faith has taught the chosen ones of God not only to accept the Redeemer with their heart, but to confess Him with their life by rejecting the world and by taking up an even heavier cross, make up of both willing and unwilling sorrows, and by exactly fulfilling the "good and acceptable and perfect will of God" (Rom 12:2). "If indeed we suffer with Him," says the apostle to the hosts of Christ's ascetics, "we may also be glorified together" (Rom 8:17). Having compared the eternal, heavenly glory prepared for those who suffer for Christ with the temporary sufferings of this age, St Paul says, "For I consider that the sufferings of this present time are not worthy to be compared with the glory which shall be revealed in us" (Rom 8:18).

These sorrows mean nothing! Our almighty and all-good Establisher of Labors has laid such spiritual consolation into these sorrows that for the sake of Christ sorrows become in themselves a source of joy. "These physical sufferings," said great martyr Eustace in his final prayer to God (see his life), "are joys for Your servant." Monastic sorrows have the same quality. In their heart, a source of spiritual sweetness and joy pours and bubbles forth, a sacrifice of firstfruits in time for the sake of blessedness in eternity. The cross is an instrument of victory, the honorable sign of a Christian. "God forbid that I should boast except in the cross of our Lord Jesus Christ, by whom the world has been crucified to me, and I to the world" (Gal 6:14).

The union between the human body and spirit is worthy of profound examination and wonder. A man's way of thinking, his heart's perceptions depend a great deal on the state of his body. "When the stomach is constrained," said St John of the Ladder, "the heart is humbled. When the stomach is satiated, then thoughts become infected with pride."[322]

"There is no other way for the soul to come to humility," said St Pimen the Great, "except by lessening food for the body." An abbot of a certain coenobium asked St Pimen, "Why do I not have the fear of God?"

"How can you perceive in yourself the fear of God," he answered, "when your stomach is filled with pies and cheeses?"[323] When the body is satiated, the heart cannot help but give rise to lustful sensations, while the mind will breed lustful thoughts and fantasies that by their power and enticement are capable of changing the most resolute good intention and to turn it to taking pleasure from sin. This is why St John of the Ladder said, "He who pleases his own stomach and at the same time desires to defeat the spirit of lust is like someone who tries to put out a fire using oil."[324] St Isaac the Syrian said, "Come to love shabby clothes in order to bring low the thoughts that arise inside you, that is, the arrogance of the heart. Whoever loves the sparkle of wealth cannot acquire humble thoughts, because the 'inner heart is impressed according to the external image.'"[325] "The holy Apostle Paul, listing the works of the flesh, put especial stress on 'hatred, contentions, jealousies, outbursts of wrath, selfish ambitions, dissensions, heresies' (Gal 5:20), that is, on the failings of the human spirit. For what reason? For the following: these kinds of sins expose the carnal mindset of a person, and a carnal mindset exposes a life lived by the flesh, a rejection of the Cross of Christ."[326] From church history we know that all heresiarchs were subject to this fate.

I, the much-suffering Ignatius, have written this to incite myself and to instruct others to live the ascetic life. I have noticed that those subjects of spiritual study that I write down on paper are most beneficial to my own learning and sometimes are useful also for my beloved brothers, because of the contemporaneity of their style. If anyone reads these words, let him forgive my shortcomings in knowledge and word! If anyone reads these words and finds in them something useful for his soul, then I beg him to pay attention to these impoverished words and to examine himself carefully in the light of the ideas here summarized.

It is absolutely necessary for all Christians, lay or monastic, to fulfill the command of the Saviour with all diligence: "For whoever desires to save his life will lose it, but whoever loses his life for My sake and the gospel's will save it" (Mark 8:35). "He who loves his life will lose it, and he who hates his life in this world will keep it for eternal life" (John 12:25). What does it mean to love your life? It means to love fallen nature, its characteristics, defiled by the Fall, its falsely named wisdom, its desires and enticements, its "truth." What does it mean to save your life in this world? It means to develop the characteristics of fallen nature, to follow your own reason and your own will, to create your own righteousness from the so-called good deeds of fallen nature.

What does it mean to lose your life for the sake of Christ and the Gospel? What does it mean to hate your life? It means to admit and know the Fall and the disorder of your nature by sin. It means to come to hate the state produced in us by the Fall and to mortify it by rejecting all actions stemming from our own reason, our own will, our own desires. It means to forcibly assimilate the reason and will of the nature renewed by Christ. It means to guide our actions according to the all-holy teaching of God and by His all-holy will, revealed to us by God Himself in the Gospels. Fallen nature is hostile to God. Following the reasonings and enticements of our fallen nature is a striving toward sure, eternal damnation. For this reason, the holy desert-dwelling fathers, the guides of monastics and all Christians uttered so many terrifying rebukes against following one's own will and reason.

St Pimen the Great said, "The will of man is a wall of metal between God and man, a stone that strikes at the will of God. If man abandons it, then he can say, 'By my God I shall leap over a wall. As for my God, His way is undefiled' (Ps 17:30–31). If our self-will is further aided by self-justification, then the person becomes corrupt and is lost."[327]

Self-justification in this sense is an acknowledgment that our actions according to our own will are fair or even righteous. This is a clear sign of spiritual disorder and a deviation from the path to salvation. Abba Dorotheos said, "I know of no other reason for a monk's fall than following the will and desires of his own heart. They say: for this or for that reason this man fell. But I say that I know no other reason for falls than this. Have you seen any one fall? Know: he followed himself." Then Abba Dorotheos continues by telling that when he was in the monastery of Abba Serid, he was guided by the instruction of the Spirit-bearing elder, John, completely rejecting his own understandings and his heart's inclinations. When the learned and intelligent Dorotheos had some kind of personal thought concerning a spiritual matter, he said to himself, "Anathema to yourself and your own reasoning and your knowledge!"[328] What a model of blessed hatred for his own life, hatred commanded by the Saviour of our souls and bodies! What a model of blessed loss of life for the sake of Christ and the Gospel for the salvation of life. What a model of the saints' way of dealing with their own fallen nature!

Brothers, let us follow the teaching of Christ! Let us follow the life, actions, way of thinking of the holy ones of God! Let us not fail, for the sake of our salvation, to reject our fallen nature! For the sake of true self-love, let us reject the delusive love for self, our pride! For the sake of our striving toward salvation (by following the commandments of the Gospel), let us cast aside all actions dictated by the laws of our fallen nature, so beloved by the world, so hostile to God! Let us come to hate our so-called good deeds that arise from our falsely named wisdom, from the excitation of blood, from the emotions of the heart, no matter how these thoughts and emotions seem to be exalted, blameless, holy. Such "virtues" are only capable of developing self-conceit, pride, self-delusion within us, so harmful for our salvation. They do not illumine the eyes of the soul, as the commands of the Lord do (see Ps 18:9 LXX). On the contrary, they worsen the blindness of the soul; they make this blindness irreparable.

Those who do such "good deeds" will go to the eternal torments, for they did the works of fallen nature, the good deeds that are always mixed with evil, the defiled virtues, from which the Lord turns away His all-holy gaze, as from a Satanic abomination. To fulfill the good deeds of fallen nature, one does not need to be a Christian, for they belong to mankind at large. Wherever the virtues of fallen nature are fulfilled, amid the applause of the world, the Saviour of the world is excluded, rejected.

The works of faith, the works of salvation, the fulfillment of the commandments of the Gospel belong only to Christians. St Mark the Ascetic said the following concerning the true kind of virtue: "The good cannot be believed or acted upon, save in Christ Jesus and in the Holy Spirit."[329] The fulfillment of the commandments of the Gospel leads a person into true knowledge of God and knowledge of self, to true love for himself and his fellow man and for God. Such virtue leads man to communion with God that develops more and more depending on the zeal and exactness with which the commandments of the Gospel are fulfilled. Communion with God, given to a Christian even during the time of his earthly wandering, is the pledge of heavenly and eternal blessedness.

This pledge witnesses to its own faithfulness. It witnesses so clearly and powerfully that many have decided to subject themselves to the greatest sorrows to preserve this pledge. They have preferred it to the entire temporal life. Pitiful, bitter is that blindness with which the world disdainfully looks on the deeds of the Christian faith, judging and condemning them irrationally, to its own peril. How insignificant do the deeds of faith appear to the world compared to the loud and picturesque deeds of the world! What sort of a good deed, to all appearances, is the admission of personal sinfulness, for which the mercy of God was poured down on the publican? (see Luke 18:10–14). What sort of a good deed, to all appearances, is humility, by which the worst sinners are reconciled with God and have inherited eternal blessedness? What sort of a good deed is the confession of Christ, a confession expressed by few, simple words? And by whom? By a condemned thief! These few, simple words led the thief into Paradise, accomplished that which all the most brilliant virtues of mankind could never and will never do.

"For the message of the cross is foolishness to those who are perishing," and equally foolish do they consider a life lived by the Gospel, "but to us who are being saved," both the message of the cross and a life according to the Gospel are "the power of God" (1 Cor 1:18) that heals and saves our souls (Luke 6:19).

The Holy Fathers of all times constantly expressed their relationship to the revealed teaching of God by the words "I believe." In contemporary society, which considers itself primarily educated and Christian, the expression of the heart's relationship to Divine Revelation is most often expressed in the phrase, "I think." From where did these words come? From ignorance of Christianity. It is a sorrowful spectacle when a son of the Eastern Church intellectualizes about the Christian faith outside the bounds of the teaching of his own Church, contrary to the divine teaching. He intellectualizes with self-will, ignorance, and blasphemy. Is not such a way of thinking a rejection of the Church, of Christianity? Let us fear our own ignorance that leads us into eternal damnation. Let us learn Christianity. Let us come to love obedience to the Holy Church, beloved to all who have knowledge of the faith of Christ. Let us become zealous doers of the commandments of the Gospel; let us do them as bound slaves (see Luke 17:10) who must do their duty, but who constantly fail at doing it, or do it unsatisfactorily and are humbled. Let the Gospel guide us to good deeds, not the inflammation of the blood and nerves. Let us learn to do good deeds with humility, without overexcitement that always leads to (and works together with) vanity, arrogance, or pride. When the Lord pours into us the holy coolness of humility, all the activity of the waves of the heart's emotions will cease. Then we will come to know that all excitation accomplishes is the most exalted and bombastic of human vices and is no more than flesh and blood. "I say, brethren, that flesh and blood cannot inherit the kingdom of God" (1 Cor 15:50).

Be saved, O my beloved brothers, be saved! "Be saved from this perverse generation" (Acts 2:40), said the Apostle Peter to those Jews from whose ranks—generally so hostile to Christianity—some were inclined to accept Christianity. "By seeking salvation, he will save his own soul," said the ancient great monks concerning the true Christians of the last times.[330] This means that salvation for the last Christians will be very difficult because of the great increase of sinful temptations and thanks to a general deviation of mankind toward sin. To be saved, we need extraordinary exertion; we need extraordinary striving;

we need extraordinary diligence and self-preservation, extraordinary wisdom, extraordinary endurance. But our almighty Master and Commander, our Life, our Strength, our Salvation, the Lord Jesus Christ, Who warned us that "in the world you will have tribulation," has also encouraged us: "but be of good cheer, I have overcome the world" (John 16:33), "and lo, I am with you always, even to the end of the age. Amen" (Matt 28:20).

PART
II

CHAPTER 21

The Various States of Human Nature in Relation to Good and Evil

I Introduction

The ascetic of Christ, in order to fairly judge concerning himself and to correctly relate to himself, must absolutely understand his own nature correctly. A true thought is the source of all good things, but a false thought is the source of erroneous action and its inevitable fruits. If we do not see our asceticism crowned with spiritual crowns, or if we see it crowned, instead, with the fruits of self-delusion, then we must know that the reason for this was a false direction, a false starting point for our spiritual activity. Alas! Often the gaze of the mind is struck by a sorrowful spectacle that inspired bitter tears in the heart. What can be more tragic than seeing an ascetic who spent his entire life in the bosom of his monastery, constantly serving God, constantly laboring, seeing, with an impartial gaze directed within, that he has no spiritual fruits? Instead, he sees within himself the increased activity of various passions that, when he first entered monasticism, were very weak, almost inactive! What can be more tragic than seeing the monks' conversion and correction become at a certain age and state more and more difficult? It is a great and blessed event when we glorify Christ within ourselves. It is a terrible tragedy when we develop within ourselves the fallen ego, leading to estrangement from God both in time and in eternity.

II The Three States

To avoid this great tragedy—estrangement from God both in time and eternity—let us begin our journey on correct and holy paths. To achieve a correct Christian lifestyle, let us clearly examine human nature in its three states—the state after creation, the state after the Fall, and the state after the redemption.[331] Only then can a Christian's life be correct, salvific, and God-pleasing: when he acts, or tries to act, only according to the laws of human nature that are renewed by Christ.

III Human Nature after the Creation of Man

In the first state, human nature was completely foreign to evil. In this state, only complete good lived and acted. Mankind had no experiential knowledge of evil. He only knew that evil existed and also that an experiential knowledge of that evil would be harmful to him (see Gen 2:9, 17; 3:2). Our theoretical, superficial knowledge of evil could not have any negative influence on human nature, for it was dead knowledge in relation to both the internal and external activity of man, equal to ignorance. The fall of man occurred through an active, experiential knowledge of evil, in assimilating the evil to himself. In the same way, a theoretical knowledge of poison does not kill; on the contrary, it cautions against death by poisoning. A practical knowledge of poison, that is, drinking it, leads to death.

IV Human Nature after the Fall

In fallen human nature, good is intermingled with evil. The evil that entered man merged and became confused with the natural good of man to such a degree that man's natural goodness can never act without contamination of evil. Man was poisoned by the incitement of sin. In other words, he came to know evil by experience. This poison of experience penetrated into all the members of his body, into all the powers and characteristics of the soul. The body, the heart, and the mind are all struck down by the sickness of sin. Perniciously flattering himself and deluding himself, fallen man considers his reason to be healthy. A healthy mind is what man had before the Fall; after the Fall, all people, without exception, have a false reasoning, which must be rejected if they are to be saved (see 1 Tim 6:20–21). "The light of mine eyes, even that is gone from me" (Ps 37:11). This is what Scriptures say about the wisdom of our fallen nature.

While perniciously flattering themselves and deluding themselves, people still believe their hearts to be good. No, it was good before the Fall, but after the Fall, its good was mixed with evil, and for salvation, it must be rejected as defiled. God, the Knower of hearts, has called all men evil (see Luke 11:13). Everything in man has become disordered because of the infection of sin.

Everything acts incorrectly, everything acts under the influence of evil and self-delusion. This is how his will acts, this is how all his heart's perceptions act, this is how all his thoughts act. It is futile and useless for mankind to call their faculties good, noble, or exalted! Our fall is profound. Very few people consider themselves to be fallen creatures in need of a Saviour. Most of us look at our fallen state as a completely triumphant state, and we even spend all our energy to make this fallen state more established and well developed.

To separate the contamination of evil from the natural good in man has become impossible through man's own exertions. Evil has pierced to the very principle of humanity. Man is conceived in sin and born in iniquity (see Ps 50:7). From the moment of birth, man cannot engage in a single thought, word, or emotion, not even for the shortest of minutes, without there being at least a small amount of evil intermingled with the good. The Holy Scriptures witness to this concerning fallen mankind: "There is none righteous, no, not one; . . . They have all turned aside; They have together become unprofitable; There is none who does good, no, not one" (Romans 3:10–12). Indicating his own fallen nature, the holy Apostle Paul said, "For I know that in me (that is, in my flesh) nothing good dwells; for to will is present with me, but how to per-form what is good I do not find" (Rom 7:18). Here, by "flesh," the apostle means not the physical body of a person, but the carnal state of man at large—his mind, heart, and body. Even in the Old Testament, man is called by the word *flesh*: "My Spirit shall not remain with these people forever, for they are flesh" (Gen 6:3). In this carnal state, sin and eternal death reside, as though it were their own body.

The Apostle Paul calls the carnal state "this body of death" (Romans 7:24) and the "body of sin" (Rom 6:6). This state is called flesh, body, the body of death, and sin for the following reason: in this state, the mind and the heart, which should be striving toward the spiritual and holy, instead are nailed down only to the material and sinful. They live in matter and sin. The human body of the Apostle Paul, as everyone knows, was the temple of the Holy Spirit. It was pierced through with divine grace and from it flowed the action of the divine grace (see Acts 19:12). These expressions, which so faithfully describe the carnal state into which human nature was plunged after the Fall, cannot in any way be associated with St Paul: "So then, those who are in the flesh can-not please God" (Romans 8:8), "that the body of sin might be done away with" (Rom 6:6). "Who will deliver me from this body of death?" (Rom 7:24).

The Apostle is very good at describing this confusion of good and evil in fallen man when man is left to his own devices. When he tries to do good, evil of necessity sneaks in and perverts the good, casting down the thoughts that futilely try to serve God truly in the spiritual temple.

> For we know that the law is spiritual, but I am carnal, sold under sin. For what I am doing, I do not understand. For what I will to do, that I do not practice; but what I hate, that I do. If, then, I do what I will not to do, I agree with the law that it is good. But now, it is no longer I who do it, but sin that dwells in me. For I know that in me (that is, in my flesh) nothing good dwells; for to will is present with me, but how to perform what is good I do not find. For the good that I will to do, I do not do; but the evil I will not to do, that I practice. Now if I do what I will not to do, it is no longer I who do it, but sin that dwells in me. I find then a law, that evil is present with me, the one who wills to do good. For I delight in the law of God according to the inward man. But I see another law in my members, warring against the law of my mind, and bringing me into captivity to the law of sin which is in my members. O wretched man that I am! Who will deliver me from this body of death? I thank God—through Jesus Christ our Lord! So then, with the mind I myself serve the law of God, but with the flesh the law of sin. (Romans 7:14–25)[332]

Again, the word *flesh* here means the carnal state that describes all attempts by the human mind to fulfill the will of God while in a fallen state, until man is renewed by the Spirit. The Spirit, having entered into man, then frees him from slavery to sin (see Rom 8:14), destroying the body of sin (see Rom 6:6), that is, the carnal, fallen state of human nature. This is how we must also understand these words of the apostle: "flesh and blood cannot inherit the kingdom of God" (1 Cor 15:50). Here, "flesh and blood" mean the thoughts and perceptions arising in the fallen nature that keep a person stuck in his carnal state, both in mind, heart, and body. This state is called "the old man" (see Eph 4:22), whom the apostle commands us to cast off and to put on "the new man, which was created according to God, in true righteousness and holiness" (Eph 4:24). He said the same thing to the Romans: "But put on the Lord Jesus Christ, and make no provision for the flesh, to fulfill its lusts" (Rom 13:14), and to the Corinthians: "We shall also bear the image of the heavenly Man" (1 Cor 15:49).

It is well known that the Apostle Paul was himself renewed by the Spirit and had put on Christ. Illumined by the Spirit, and moved by love for his fellow man, he uttered—on behalf of fallen man, who tries to tear apart the chains of sin—a confession of the state produced by the Fall, a state in which man, forced by the evil living within him, cannot help but to do evil, even if he wants to do good.[333] Such a vision of the Fall of man is a gift of God's grace.

In the society of fallen human beings, some people are called "good." They are called this incorrectly, relatively speaking. In such a society, the person who does the least amount of evil is called good, while the person who does the least amount of good is called evil. However, an evil person can become so adept at evil, that his entire activity becomes a constant stream of evil-doing. In the strictest sense, there is no good person. There is no person, in his fallen state, who is capable of doing pure good, untainted by evil. As the word of God says, "No one is good but One, that is, God" (Matt 19:17). The same word of God calls, as we have already said, all men evil (see Luke 11:13). The Old Testament righteous were called righteous only in comparison with other people, but not compared to God (see Rom 4:2–3, Job 1:8). If compared to God, all fallen mankind, without exception, is unworthy of God. All the deeds of human nature, tainted by the Fall, have become unpleasing to God, since they are defiled by the impurity of sin that cannot be filtered out. Only faith in the promised Redeemer—a faith proven by the works of faith—joined the Old Testament saints to God, being for them a justification (see Rom 4:2–8, Gal 2:18–26). Only faith gave them hope for salvation, a hope of eventually coming out of the prisons of hades into which all souls, without exception, were cast down after their departure from the body, until the Incarnate God destroyed the gates of hell.

It is not enough that sin through the Fall has become almost natural to man. It has become so natural that the Scriptures have called sin the "life of man" (see Rom 8:2) and have called rejection of sin a rejection of self (see Matt 16:24). Fallen man has accepted into himself Satan, who has deluded him. Man has become the abode of Satan.

St Macarius the Great said, "In a certain way, the very enemy who fights and ensnares us is found within us, abiding in us."[334] This is not in any way my own personal judgment on the matter or an invented fantasy, but knowledge gained by experience, received by those who, as St Macarius also says in the same homily (chapter 5), have committed themselves sincerely to the Lord and firmly abide in prayer and unshakably battle against the enemy that attacks them.

Such experiential knowledge of the fall of human nature is not accessible for a Christian who lives in the midst of the world, tied down by cares, torn away from self-contemplation by constant diversions. We do not direct our words to such a Christian. Let him earn his salvation by doing good deeds in the bosom of the Orthodox Church, especially by alms and chastity. We direct our words to the monks who have committed themselves to serve God, who desire to see within themselves the kingdom of God revealed in power and glory. The immutable spiritual law of asceticism requires that man first tear asunder the bonds of materiality by which he is bound from without, and then to attempt tearing apart those bonds with which the spirits of evil bind him in the depth of his mind and heart.

St Macarius the Great said,

> After man broke the commandment and was exiled from Eden, he found himself tied in two ways and by two kinds of bonds. In this world, he is bound by the objects of the world, and love for the world (that is, love for carnal passions and desires, for riches and glory, for created things, for one's wife and children, for relatives, for the fatherland, for places, for clothes, for all visible things that the word of God commands him to reject by his own will, for he has become enslaved to them all by his own will). Having been freed from all this, man can then fulfill the will of God completely. The human soul is bound, imprisoned inside itself, surrounded by walls and chained with dark bonds to such a degree by the spirits of evil, that it cannot love God, believe in Him, or revere Him, no matter how much it would like to.[335]

Later in the same homily, St Macarius, that great guide of monastics, teaches us that only those who have cast off themselves the chains of the world and have committed themselves to a true and exclusive service to God can uncover within themselves their own bondage, slavery, eternal death. On the contrary, whoever does not start with the casting off of these bonds that have been placed on him by his materiality—that is, by the visible world and the earthly temporal life with its provisions and relationships—will never come to know or even notice his imprisonment. He will never see the spirits of evil acting within him. He remains forever a stranger to himself. Nourishing within himself his inmost passions, not only does he not know them, but very often he thinks their desires are the desires of righteousness, and their actions are the actions of the grace of God or the consolation of his conscience. In the monastic life, physical, ascetic labors, no matter how great they may be, cannot of themselves reveal the inner bonds or the inner calamity. For this, spiritual asceticism is required. Physical labors that are not accompanied by spiritual asceticism are more dangerous than helpful. They can become the cause of an extraordinary strengthening of the passions of the soul—vanity, hypocrisy, cunning, pride, hatred, envy, arrogance. "If the inner work, done in the Lord," said St Barsanuphius the Great, "cannot help a man, then he labors externally in vain."[336]

The following spiritual exercises can help reveal an ascetic's inner imprisonment and serve as a reason to begin battling the thoughts and emotions:

1. True obedience. With obedience, a beginner ascetic, cutting off his will and his own reason for the sake of God and to fulfill the will and reason of a spiritually advanced guide who has himself acquired total obedience to God, will inevitably inspire the fallen angel to battle, thereby revealing his presence within the young monastic. If the ascetic will not be deluded by the evil and cunning representations of the evil one who will try to distract him from obedience with many different excuses, and if he will remain steadfast in his labor, he will arouse the invisible enemy to envy and fierce warfare. Then, the enemy will not fail to incite various sinful fantasies, thoughts, sensations, enticements inside the ascetic. By doing so, however, he will reveal the extraordinarily great breadth of evil that hides in the depths of the heart, though it appeared previously not to exist at all.

2. Reading, studying, and fulfilling the commandments of the Gospel. These, cutting off active sin, mostly destroy sin in the very mind and heart as well. Fulfillment of these commandments or, more correctly, striving to fulfill these commandments will of necessity rebuke the sin that abides in us. It will also incite a fierce internal battle against the spirits of evil.

3. Dishonor and other sorrows also reveal sin hiding in the depths of the soul. Sorrow at being dishonored is called a testing for this reason, because it reveals the hidden state of the heart. Naturally, in the person who is still under the authority of sin, dishonor reveals the sin that lives in the depth of the soul through the resulting sorrowful state of the soul, the thoughts of complaining, the anger, the self-justification, the desire for revenge, the hatred. A sudden increased activity of these passions in the soul or an extraordinary intensity of such thoughts or fantasies is a definite sign that our fallen, proud spirit is acting up.

4. Attentive prayer, especially the Jesus Prayer, with exertion will unite the heart with the mind, will uncover the serpent that nests in the depth of the heart, and, wounding him, will cause it to move. St Kallistos and St Ignatius Xanthopoulos, in their book on stillness and prayer, offer the following quote of St John Chrysostom:

> I pray you, brethren, never to break or disdain the rule of prayer. I have heard some fathers who said that the monk who broke or disdained the rule was no longer a monk. He must—whether he eats or drinks, whether he is in his cell or performing an obedience or traveling, or doing anything

else—constantly cry out, "Lord Jesus Christ, Son of God, have mercy on me," so that the constantly remembered name of our Lord Jesus Christ would cause the enemy to war against him. For the soul that exerts itself thus can find anything, both good and evil. At first it will see the evil in the depths of its heart, and later the goodness that is hidden in it (that is, the grace of God that was planted inside him during his baptism.[337]

Such a state of inner warfare must be endured cheerfully, as St Macarius the Great instructs. The ascetic must have undoubting faith and trust in the Lord, together with great endurance, awaiting help and the gift of inner freedom from the Lord.[338]

Those who are still subject to the power of the passions err very seriously when they require dispassion of themselves. Such incorrect expectations, which come from an incorrect self-assessment, lead them into extraordinary distress when the sin that lives in them begins to show itself. They begin to despair and lose hope. They think, in their incorrect view of themselves, that the manifestation of sin is something unusual, something that occurs outside the normal pattern of things. But in actual fact, the manifestation of sin in the thoughts, perceptions, words, and deeds (here we do not speak of deadly or willful sins, but temptations of the devil) is a logical, natural, necessary step.

"If the passions attack us," said Abba Dorotheos,

> then we must not be distressed by this. To be upset that the passions attack us is the work of ignorance and pride, and it only happens because we do not know our spiritual state and avoid working on it, as the Fathers have said. Therefore, we do not progress spiritually, because we do not understand our own measure, and we have no patience in the labors we undertake, but instead hope to acquire virtues without labor. Why is the passionate man surprised when the passion attacks him? Why is he confused by this? You have acquired this passion, you have it within you, and you are surprised? You have accepted its pledges into your heart, and now you say, "Why is it attacking me?" Better for you to endure, labor, and pray to God.[339]

Whoever sees the sin within himself, thanks to this vision, will spend the entire day of his earthly life in sorrow for his own sinfulness, prayerfully showing himself and his calamitous state to the Lord, groaning in the pain of his heart:

> Mine eyes are ever toward the Lord, for He shall pluck my feet out of the net. Be charitable unto me, and have mercy on me, for I am only-begotten and poor. The sorrows of my heart are enlarged; O bring Thou me out of my

troubles. Deliver my soul from the sword, and my only-begotten from the hand of the dog. For what profit is it to a man if he gains the whole world, and loses his own soul? Or what will a man give in exchange for his soul? Save me from the lion's mouth, and my lowliness also from the horns of the unicorns, because my adversary the devil walks about like a roaring lion, seeking whom he may devour. Look upon my humbleness and my hardship, and forgive all my sins. Consider mine enemies, how many they are, and they bear a tyrannous hate against me. O keep my soul, as You kept the soul of your slave, Job, and deliver me; let me not be confounded, for I waited upon Thee, O Lord.[340]

Whoever lives by this rule, without any doubt, will be found worthy to say in his time: "With hope did I wait for the Lord, and He heard me, and heeded my prayer. And he brought me up out of the horrible pit, and out of the miry clay, and set my feet upon the rock, and ordered my steps. And He hath put a new song in my mouth, even a hymn unto our God" (Ps 39:2–4). He Who gave a promise to those who hope in Him and never ceased to trust in Him does not lie, even if we suffer for a long time and intensely because of the violence of our sin. He Who gave the promise will definitely honor it. "And shall God not avenge His own elect who cry out day and night to Him, though He bears long with them? I tell you that He will avenge them speedily" (Luke 18:7–8). Here in the expression "bearing long," we must understand God's allowing temptations to befall man for his own benefit for a certain amount of time, whether from his own sin or from the fallen angels.

"The prince of the world," said St Macarius the Great,

is a rod of chastisement for those who are infants in the spirit, a whip that wounds. However, as we have said before, he only prepares a greater glory and honor by tempting them and warring against them . . . Through him, the great work of our salvation is accomplished, as somewhere it is written: "Evil, having an evil intention, unwittingly aids the good." For the good souls that have good intentions, even the apparently sorrowful eventually turn to the good, as the apostle himself witnessed: "And we know that all things work together for good to those who love God, to those who are the called according to His purpose" (Romans 8:28). This rod of chastisement is allowed to act only with this purpose: that, thanks to him, all the vessels in a hot stove be tested, and the good ones become harder, while the useless would only reveal their capability of being destroyed, unable to bear the heat of the fire. He, that is the devil, being the creation and the slave of God, does not test as much as he thinks is necessary. He does not attack to the degree in which he would like, but only as much God's will allows and permits him. God, exactly knowing the state of all and the endurance of everyone, sends each as much as he can bear to be tested. "God is faithful, who will not allow you to be tempted beyond what you are able, but with the temptation will also make the way of escape, that you may be able to bear it" (1 Corinthians 10:13). Whoever seeks the door and knocks on it, whoever keeps asking until the end, will receive what he asks.[341]

The reason God allows an ascetic to be tested by the spirits of evil and sin is found in the necessity for man to come to know his own fallenness exactly and definitively. Without this, he will not be able to know and accept the Redeemer as he should. It is necessary to come to know one's fallen nature, its inclinations, its natural activity, so that later, having accepted the grace of the Holy Spirit given by the Redeemer, we will not use it to harm ourselves, nor will we ascribe its action to ourselves, but will instead become its worthy vessel and instrument.

St Gregory of Sinai said,

If man will not be abandoned and defeated and overcome, if he will not be subjected to every passion and thought, defeated by the evil spirits, he will never find any help from his deeds, or from God, or from anyone else. For this reason he despairs, being tempted from all sides, for he is unable to come to compunction of spirit, to consider himself the least of all, the slave of all, even more worthless than the demons, since he is defeated and tormented by them. This is a punitive humiliation, allowed by providence, after which God gives another gift, an exalted one, which is divine power, acting through God and accomplished by Him in all. Man sees this power within himself like a weapon, and with this weapon, he performs God's miracles.[342]

This is how we explain that wondrous reality of the saints of God. They, being vessels of the Holy Spirit, also saw, admitted, confessed themselves to be the worst sinners, worthy of all punishments, both temporary and eternal. They completely knew and studied their own fallen nature, in which there was nothing that had not been undefiled, and so everything good that they did through the grace of God that had entered into them, they ascribed not to their own actions, but to the grace, with complete conviction. They constantly feared lest some thought or emotion would arise from the fallen nature that would offend the Holy Spirit.[343]

A quick passage from the state of warfare to the state of spiritual freedom does not benefit man. St Macarius the Great said,

> Often souls who became communicants of divine grace, who were filled with heavenly sweetness and who found pleasure in the stillness of the spirit, but who were not proven, not tested by sorrows dealt by the evil spirits, remained in spiritual infancy, and so to speak, were unworthy of the kingdom of Heaven. "But if you are without chastening, of which all have become partakers, then you are illegitimate and not sons" (Hebrews 12:8). Therefore, temptations and sorrows are sent to man for his benefit, so that the soul, tested by them, would become stronger and more worthy before its Lord. If it will endure to the end with hope in the Lord, then it will not fail to receive the benefits promised by the Holy Spirit, and complete freedom from the venom of the passions.[344]

For this reason, except for some very rare exceptions (these are always due to a special divine dispensation), ascetics of Christ spend the majority of their time on earth in warfare with sin, in bondage to unmerciful Pharaoh. After leaving Egypt—the land of making brinks and overeating meat, which are images of a carnal state—the servants of the true God plundered the Egyptians; that is, they bore away with them the riches of an active mind, which they acquired in the battle with sin and the evil spirits. This is the divine dispensation concerning the immutable spiritual law.[345]

St Isaac the Syrian tells the following story:

> There was a recluse, a justly-honored elder. Once, I came to him because my sorrow at being tempted was oppressing me. The elder was sick at that time, supine on his bed. I greeted him, sat near him, and said, "Father, pray for me, for I am very sorrowful because of the temptations of the demons." He opened his eyes, looked at me attentively and said, "My son, you are young. God will not allow you to be tempted." I answered him, "Yes, I am young, but I am tested with the temptations of strong men." He said again, "If that is so, then God wants to make you wise." I said, "How can God make me wise when every day I foretaste my death?" Again, he said, "God loves you. Be silent. God will give you His grace." And he added, "Know, my son, that I battled with demons for thirty years. For the first twenty years, I never felt any lessening of the warfare. In my twenty-fifth year, I began to sense some peace. After more time passed, the consolation increased. At the end of the thirtieth year, the consolation was so firm (before, it would come and leave

again), that now I don't even know the measure of my own consolation."
This is the kind of consolation that comes from a much-laboring and prolonged action.[346]

Having laid our trust in our almighty and all-good God, let us try—by living
a true monastic life, through the clouds, smoke, and storm of constantly arising
thoughts—to descend to our soul, captive and deadened by sin, foul-smelling,
without comeliness, lying in the tomb of the fallen. There, in the abyss of our
heart, we will see the serpent who killed our soul.[347]

A profound and exact knowledge of the fall of man is extremely important
for an ascetic of Christ. Only with such knowledge, as though from the depths
of hell, can he prayerfully, in true compunction of spirit, cry out to the Lord,
as the holy Symeon, the New Theologian instructs, "God and Lord of all! You
have authority over all creation and all souls. You alone can heal me. Hear the
prayer of this accursed one, and kill the serpent who nests within me, by the
power of the all-holy and life-giving Spirit."[348]

In the state of the Fall, sin and the devil have so much control over man
that he has no possibility of countering them, but unwillingly is enticed by
them,[349] not in mortal sin, as we have already said, but most often into sins
of the thoughts. Ardent ascetics very rarely allow this internal disturbance to
manifest itself, either in action or even in word.

V Human Nature after the Redemption

Human nature was renewed by the redemption. The God-Man renewed it by
Himself and in Himself. This new nature, renewed by the Lord, is engrafted,
so to speak to fallen nature through baptism. Baptism, without destroying
human nature, does destroy its state of fallenness. Without actually making
the nature something else, it changes its state, having united human nature to
the divine nature.[350]

Baptism is both a death and a resurrection, both a burial and a birth.

In the baptismal font, the human nature that was damaged by sin is buried
and dies. From the font, renewed human nature arises. The sin of the old Adam
is plunged into the font, and from the font arises a son of the New Adam. This
the Lord Himself witnessed, saying, "Most assuredly, I say to you, unless one is
born of water and the Spirit, he cannot enter the kingdom of God. That which
is born of the flesh is flesh, and that which is born of the Spirit is spirit" (John
3:5–6). From these words, it becomes obvious that the Holy Spirit accepts the
carnal man into the font. This is man as he became after the Fall. Then, the

Spirit leads the same man from the font, but he has become spiritual, for the Spirit killed in him the sinful, carnal state, giving rise to a spiritual one. In baptism, man is forgiven his ancestral sin, received from his forefathers, as well as all of his own personal sins committed before baptism. During baptism, man is given spiritual freedom.[351] He is no longer a slave of sin, but he can willingly choose good or evil. During baptism, Satan, who lives in every person of the fallen nature, is cast out of man. The baptized man is given a choice to remain a temple of God and be free from Satan or to throw God aside and once again become the abode of Satan.[352] During baptism, the baptized puts on Christ.[353]

During baptism, all people receive equality, because the dignity of every Christian is equal, for this dignity is Christ Himself. This dignity is endlessly great, and in it all earthly differences between people are destroyed (see Gal 3:28). These differences, being worthless, are not removed by Christ during the earthly life. By remaining, they more vividly reveal their worthlessness. Like a body, when the soul has left it, is admitted to be dead, even though it has not yet decomposed. In baptism, abundant grace of the Holy Spirit pours out on the person. This is the grace that left Adam in paradise, because he followed his own sinful reason and the will of the fallen angel. Grace once again approaches the one who has been redeemed by the blood of the God-Man, the one who is being reconciled with God, the one who rejects his own reason and will, the one who has buried the desires of fallen nature in the baptismal font.

"Christ, being wholly God," said St Mark the Ascetic, "gave the one being baptized the complete grace of the Holy Spirit that appears not because of our own exertions, but is revealed and manifested to us commensurate with our fulfillment of the commandments."[354] The baptized man, in doing good with the help of his renewed human nature, develops within himself the grace of the all-holy Spirit, received during baptism, which, being unchangeable in itself, shines brightly in the person the more good he does. In the same way, the ray of the sun shines more brightly when there are fewer clouds, but a cloudy sky does not affect the shining of the ray of the sun itself. On the contrary, if someone does evil after baptism, acting according to fallen nature, bringing it back to life, a man loses his spiritual freedom more or less. Sin once again receives authority over man. The devil once again enters man, becoming his master and guide. Though he was delivered from bitter and heavy imprisonments by the almighty right hand of God, he once again is found in chains, in prison, in captivity, in hell, and by his own will.

This is the calamity that befalls every person, more or less, depending on the kind of sin he allows himself and depending on how habitual is his life in sin. A sin that lives within man and forces him to act according to its will is called a passion. Passions do not always reveal themselves obviously. A passion can live secretly in a person and slowly kill him. His spiritual freedom then is completely lost if the baptized man allows himself to lead a life according to the reason and will of fallen nature, because the baptized person had rejected his nature and had promised to model himself in all actions, words, thought, and perceptions on the will and reason of the Lord Jesus Christ, that is, according to the commandments and teaching of the Gospel. To follow one's own fallen nature, to follow its reason and will, is an active rejection of Christ and the renewal He gave in baptism. The rejuvenation of fallen nature is a complete return to eternal death, a complete development of it within the self. Why did the Jews and the Greeks perish, and why do they continue to perish? From their love for fallen nature. Some insist on the dignity of the righteousness of fallen nature, its virtue, while others insist on its reason. Both become strangers to Christ, the only Truth, the only treasure house of reason (see Col 2:3, Rom 5:19). It is impossible for the one who has not rejected his own nature, who has not admitted it to be in all senses defiled because of the Fall, to approach and unite with Christ, or, having been united, to remain in this union.

The mercy of God beautifully revealed many of the mystical teachings of Christianity through visible Nature. The revivification of all plants in spring is an image of the resurrection of people. The actions of certain natural medicines that first intensify the symptoms of the disease, and only afterward heal it, serve as an image of spiritual asceticism, which first uncovers in the person his secret passions, forcing them into action, and later, little by little, destroys them.[355] The effect of baptism over man is comparable.

Let us go into the garden and see what the gardener is doing with the apple trees to help them bring sweet fruit. Every apple tree that has grown from a seed, taken even from the sweetest apple, will only bring forth sour, bitter, or even harmful fruits. Therefore, every apple tree that grows from a seed is called wild. Our fallen nature is like a wild apple tree. It can only bring forth bitter, harmful fruit, that is, virtues intermixed with evil and poisoned by evil, which destroys the person who considers this so-called virtue, which has become wholly evil from the addition of evil, to be a good worthy of man and God.

In order to turn a wild apple tree into a domesticated one, the gardener cuts off all its branches without mercy, leaving only the trunk of the tree. To this trunk, he then grafts a branch from a domesticated apple tree. This graft then becomes one with the trunk and the root and begins to spread its own branches in all directions. New branches replaced the chopped-off ones. A natural tree is replaced with one that has been worked with artifice. The engrafted tree, however, is held in place by the wild trunk, and it drinks water from the earth through the wild roots. In a word, the life of the engrafted tree is one with the life of the wild tree. Such a tree begins to bear superlative fruits, which at the same time belong to the wild tree and are completely different from its natural fruit produced in a "wild" state.

Later, for the rest of the life of the tree, the gardener carefully watches for any growths from the original, wild tree, because they will again bear a sour fruit, which, attracting the sap of the tree, and transferring it from the engrafted branches, will dry up and destroy the superlative fruit. To preserve the worth, health, and strength of the apple tree, it is necessary for all the branches to come only from the engrafted, new part of the tree.

Something similar to this engrafting of a good tree to a wild apple tree occurs during the sacrament of baptism with the baptized person. Something like the gardener's actions to preserve the health of the newly engrafted tree must also be done in the life of the baptized person. In baptism, our essence is not cut off, even though it was conceived in sins and was borne in iniquities. Rather, the body of sin is cut off; the carnal and emotional state of nature is cut off, the state that is capable of only producing good mixed with evil. To the essence, to the life, to the being of man the human nature renewed by the God-Man is engrafted. All the thoughts, emotions, words, and deeds of a baptized Christian must belong to the renewed nature, as St Mark the Ascetic said: "Good cannot be believed in or acted upon except in Christ Jesus and through the Holy Spirit."[356] The baptized Christian must never allow fallen nature to act again within him. He must immediately reject every inclination and urge of fallen nature, even if they seem on the surface to be good. He must only fulfill the commandments of the Gospel in his thoughts, emotions, words, and deeds. If he lives thus, the promises of the Lord to the apostles will be his as well:

> Abide in Me, and I in you. As the branch cannot bear fruit of itself, unless it abides in the vine, neither can you, unless you abide in Me. I am the vine, you are the branches. He who abides in Me, and I in him, bears much fruit; for without Me you can do nothing. If anyone does not abide in Me, he is cast out as a branch and is withered; and they gather them and throw them into the fire, and they are burned. If you abide in Me, and My words abide in you, you will ask what you desire, and it shall be done for you . . . If you keep My commandments, you will abide in My love, just as I have kept My Father's commandments and abide in His love. (John 15:4–10)

What can be more clear or definite than this? Only he who abides by all the commandments of the Gospel, given by God, with all diligence, can abide in love for God. Not the kind of love that is natural to fallen nature, but the love that is a gift of the Holy Spirit, which pours out on the man who is renewed by the action of the Holy Spirit (see Rom 5:5), the love that united man with God. Whoever disdains the commandments, whoever follows the urging of fallen nature destroys love and tears asunder the union.

Having called together the people and His disciples, the Lord declared to them: "Whoever desires to come after Me, let him deny himself, and take up his cross, and follow Me. For whoever desires to save his life will lose it, but whoever loses his life for My sake and the gospel's will save it" (Mark 8:34-35).

It is obvious that here what is expected of us is not rejection of existence, but rejection of fallen nature and its will, reason, and righteousness. Sin and the state of the Fall are so natural to us, have so become intertwined with our existence, that rejecting them has become the same as rejecting ourselves or even losing our life. To save our life, we must absolutely lose our life. To save ourselves, we must absolutely reject ourselves, our fallen ego that refuses to admit the reality of the Fall. While this ego exists, Christ will not bring us any benefit. "If anyone comes to Me and does not hate . . . his own life also, he cannot be My disciple" (Luke 14:26). "And he who does not take his cross and follow after Me is not worthy of Me. He who finds his life will lose it, and he who loses his life for My sake will find it" (Matt 10:38-39).

The Lord commanded the loss of one's life not only for His sake, but for the sake of the Gospel, explaining the latter by the former. The loss of one's life for the sake of the Lord is the rejection of the reason, righteousness, and will of fallen nature for the sake of fulfilling the will and righteousness of God, as expressed in the Gospels, for the sake of emulating the reason of God that shines forth from the Gospels. All who force themselves to fulfill the teaching of the Gospels know from experience how opposed and hostile to the Gospel are the reason, righteousness, and will of fallen human nature. Any reconciliation or agreement between the fallen and renewed natures is impossible.

Rejecting fallen human nature is an inevitable, even palpable necessity of salvation. Only he who constantly studies the Gospel and tries to bring it to life within himself by his actions can accomplish this rejection. The Gospel is the teaching of Christ. The teaching of Christ, as the teaching of God, has the force of law. Exact fulfillment of the law uttered by God, our Creator and Redeemer, is the absolute duty of the creatures who have been redeemed. A perfunctory study and fulfillment of the law is no better than a rejection of the Law-giver.

The holy Apostle Paul said, "For as many of you as were baptized into Christ have put on Christ" (Gal 3:27). This means that whoever has been baptized into Christ has received in baptism itself a gift of the Holy Spirit that is active in him—a living perception of Christ, a sense of His qualities. But the freedom to choose willingly either the old or the new is never taken away from the baptized; just Adam in paradise had the freedom to live by the command of God or to break it. The apostle says to those who have believed and are baptized: "The night is far spent, the day is at hand. Therefore let us cast off the works of darkness, and let us put on the armor of light. Let us walk properly, as in the day, not in revelry and drunkenness, not in lewdness and lust, not in strife and envy. But put on the Lord Jesus Christ, and make no provision for the flesh, to fulfill its lusts" (Rom 13:12–14).

Having the freedom to choose, the baptized Christian is invited by the Holy Spirit to uphold union with the Redeemer, to uphold within himself this renewed nature, to uphold the spiritual state given by baptism, to abstain from pleasing the desires of the flesh, that is, following the way of carnal lust and its emotional mindset. These words of the Apostle Paul have the same meaning: "The first man was of the earth, made of dust; the second Man is the Lord from heaven. As was the man of dust, so also are those who are made of dust; and as is the heavenly Man, so also are those who are heavenly. And as we have borne the image of the man of dust" for we are all born in ancestral sin, together with all the consequences of the Fall that have become natural to our fall, all the weaknesses that were revealed in Adam after his fall, "we shall also bear the image of the heavenly Man" (1 Cor 15:47–49) thanks to our baptism, which gives us this image. If we diligently do the commandments of the Gospel, they will preserve in us this image, in all its divine wholeness, perfection, and refinement.

To put on the image of the Heavenly Man, to put on the Lord Jesus Christ, to always bear in the body the death of the Lord Jesus Christ (see 2 Cor 6:10) means nothing other than constantly killing within ourselves the carnal state by constantly abiding in the commandments of the Gospel. This is how the holy Apostle Paul put on the God-Man and remained in union with Him, and for this reason he could with boldness say concerning himself: "It is no longer I who live, but Christ lives in me" (Gal 2:20). He also requires the same of all the faithful! "Do you not know yourselves, that Jesus Christ is in you?—unless indeed you are disqualified" (2 Cor 13:5). This is a fair requirement and a fair rebuke! By holy baptism, the fallen nature of every human being is cut off, and the nature renewed by the God-Man is engrafted to him. For this reason, baptism is called by the Holy Scriptures "the washing of regeneration" (Titus 3:5), while life after baptism is called "the regeneration" (Matt 19:28). Every baptized Christian must reveal and develop renewed human nature within himself. Thereby he will reveal the Lord Jesus Christ living, speaking, and acting within him. The Christian who does not do this "is disqualified."

The Apostle Paul gives an especially exact and detailed explanation of the sacrament of baptism:

> Or do you not know that as many of us as were baptized into Christ Jesus were baptized into His death? Therefore we were buried with Him through baptism into death, that just as Christ was raised from the dead by the glory of the Father, even so we also should walk in newness of life. For if we have been united together in the likeness of His death, certainly we also shall be in the likeness of His resurrection, knowing this, that our old man was crucified with Him, that the body of sin might be done away with, that we should no longer be slaves of sin. For he who has died has been freed from sin. Now if we died with Christ, we believe that we shall also live with Him, knowing that Christ, having been raised from the dead, dies no more. Death no longer has dominion over Him. For the death that He died, He died to sin once for all; but the life that He lives, He lives to God. Likewise you also, reckon yourselves to be dead indeed to sin, but alive to God in Christ Jesus our Lord. Therefore do not let sin reign in your mortal body, that you should obey it in its lusts. And do not present your members as instruments of unrighteousness to sin, but present yourselves to God as being alive from the dead, and your members as instruments of righteousness to God. (Romans 6:3–13)

From this excerpt, we can clearly see that baptism is at the same time death and resurrection. After the forefathers died, death immediately struck their soul, and the Holy Spirit immediately abandoned their souls. Since He was the only true life of the soul and body, immediately evil entered into the soul, being the only true death for the soul and body. The warning of the Creator was fulfilled to the letter: "Of the tree of the knowledge of good and evil you shall not eat, for in the day that you eat of it you shall surely die" (Gen 2:17). In a single moment, death made the spiritual man carnal and emotional. It made the holy one a sinner. It made the incorruptible into corruptible. It communicated weakness, sickness, impure desires to the body. It finally struck down the bodies of the forefathers after several centuries had passed.[357]

Holy baptism, on the contrary, communicates resurrection to the soul and transforms the carnal and sinful man into a spiritual and holy man. It destroys the body of sin, that is, the carnal state of man. It purifies not only the soul of man, but even his body, giving him the ability to resurrect with glory, while the resurrection itself will occur later, in the time appointed by God. As a long period of time passed from the appearance of death in man (invisible to the physical eyes) to the actual moment of his soul's departure from the body (visible to the physical eyes), so also there is a divinely appointed period of time between the appearance of resurrection in the body and the actual resurrection of the body through the reunion of the body and soul. What the soul is to the body, so the Holy Spirit is for the whole man, that is, for his body and soul. Just as the body dies the death of all animals when the soul leaves the body, so also the whole man, both soul and body, dies to the true life, to God, when the Holy Spirit abandons him. As the body resurrects when the soul returns to it, so also the whole man, body and soul, resurrects spiritually when the Holy Spirit returns to him. This rejuvenation and resurrection of man are accomplished by the sacrament of baptism. Through holy baptism, the son of the first Adam is rejuvenated and resurrected, but not in the state of incorruption and holiness in which Adam was created. He comes back to life; he resurrects in a state incomparably greater, in a state given to mankind by God Who became Man. Baptized Christians, renewed by baptism, do not put on the original, incorrupt image of the first man, but they put on the image of the Heavenly Man, the God-Man.[358] The second image is as much greater than the first as the God-Man surpasses Adam in holiness.

The transformation produced by holy baptism in man is completely obvious, perceptible; however, this change remains unknown to the greater part of Christians. We are baptized in childhood, and from childhood we abandon ourselves to tasks that belong only to the passing world and fallen nature. And so we darken within ourselves the spiritual gift given by holy baptism, just as the shining of the sun is darkened by thick clouds. But the gift is not destroyed. It continues to remain within us for the entirety of our earthly life, just as the sun is not destroyed by being covered by clouds. As soon as the baptized Christian abandons the life of fallen nature and begins to wash away his sins with tears of repentance, as soon as he crucifies his flesh with its passions and lusts, as soon as he enters the field of the New Man—the gift of the Spirit once again begins to reveal its presence in the baptized Christian. Then it also begins to develop and prevail in the person. Purification by repentance is a consequence and action of the grace that was planted in baptism. Repentance is a renewal, a return of the state given by baptism.³⁵⁹ Those who have been purified by repentance can have an experiential understanding of the transformation wrought in man by holy baptism.

St John Chrysostom said, "When we are baptized, then the soul, purified by the Spirit, shines brighter than the sun, and we not only see the glory of God, but from it we borrow a certain measure of radiance. As pure silver reflects the sun when facing it, not because of its nature, but because of the sun's rays, so also the soul, being purified and made brighter than silver, takes a ray of the Spirit's glory and pours it forth together with the Spirt."³⁶⁰

Though there is no direct, factual description of this transformation of the baptized in the book of Acts—in the early Church this transformation would have been a universally known fact, and this transformation was evident to all through the gifts of the Holy Spirit that most often manifested themselves immediately after baptism—there are certain events that have preserved the proofs of this transformation for posterity. Thus, when the eunuch of the Ethiopian queen was baptized and came out of the water, the Holy Spirit immediately descended on him. The eunuch, no longer in need of a guide, since his guide became the Spirit Himself, continued with joy into his distant country, even though he only just found out about the Lord Jesus Christ from a short conversation with the Apostle Philip (see Acts 8:39).

The conversion of Cornelius was even more wondrous. The Holy Spirit descended on him and the other pagans who were with him and believed in the Lord, and they began to speak in foreign tongues that they had no way of knowing, proclaiming the greatness of God Whom they did not know until this very moment (see Acts 10:44–46). Even though the Spirit had already descended on them, the holy Apostle Peter commanded they be baptized in water, according to the unchangeable requirement of the sacrament.

Ecclesiastical history has also preserved for us the following incredibly important event. The Roman Emperor Diocletian, who conducted the bloodiest campaign of persecution against the Christians, spent most of the year AD 304 in Rome. He came to the capital to celebrate his victories over the Persians. Among the many diversions that the emperor enjoyed was a visit to the theater. A certain Genesius, a comic actor, had great success with the public. Once, when he acted in the theater in the presence of the emperor and a great number of people, he pretended to be sick, lay down on his bed, and said, "Oh, my friends! I feel very sick. I would like you all to console me." The other actors answered, "How can we console you? Shall we caress you with an adze, so that you will feel better?"

"Foolish people," he answered, "I want to die a Christian."

"Why?"

"So that in this great day God will accept me as the prodigal son."

Immediately they sent for a "priest" and an "exorcist." These actors came up to the bed and said to Genesius, "Our son, why did you call us?"

He answered, "Because I want to receive mercy from Jesus Christ and to be reborn for the forgiveness of my sins."

They "baptized" him and then dressed him in white clothing, in mockery of the Christian rite. Then "soldiers" came and took him and presented him before Diocletian, as though to be interrogated, just like the martyrs in the arena.

Genesius said,

O Emperor and your entire court! You wise men of this city! Hear me. Whenever I would only hear the name "Christian," I would always feel great abhorrence for this name. I would shower those who confessed this name with curses. I even hated my friends and relatives if they converted. I despised this faith to such a degree that I studied its sacraments in detail to mock them before you on the stage. But when the water touched my naked body, when my lips spoke the words "I believe in Christ," I saw a hand coming down from Heaven. Surrounding this hand were radiant angels. They read aloud all my sins committed from childhood, as from a book, and then they washed them away with the same water in which I was baptized in your presence. Then they showed me the book. It was empty and white as snow. And so, great emperor and people, you, who have reviled the Christian sacraments, must come to believe, as I now do, that Jesus Christ is the true Lord. He is the Light of Truth and through Him you can receive forgiveness.

Diocletian, angered by these words, ordered that Genesius be beaten with rods, and then he committed him to the prefect Plautia for tortures until he should again sacrifice to the idols. He was raked with metal claws and burned with torches for a long time. While he was being tortured, he cried out, "There is no other King, save the One I saw! I honor Him and serve Him! Even if you were to deprive me of life a thousand times for serving him, I will still always belong to Him! Tortures will not tear away the confession of Jesus Christ from my lips, nor out of my heart. I am heartily ashamed of my previous error, of the abhorrence that I used to have for this holy name. I am sorry that I became his follower so late." Eventually, Genesius was beheaded.[361]

At the funeral oration of his father Gregory, the bishop of Nazianzus, who was baptized as a mature man, St Gregory the Theologian says the following:

He was approaching that regeneration by water and the Spirit, by which we confess to God the formation and completion of the Christ-like man, and the transformation and reformation from the earthy to the Spirit. He was approaching the laver with warm desire and bright hope, after all the purgation possible, and a far greater purification of soul and body than that of the men who were to receive the tables from Moses. Their purification extended only to their dress, and a slight restriction of the belly, and a temporary continence. The whole of his past life had been a preparation for the enlightenment, and a preliminary purification making sure the gift, in order that perfection might be entrusted to purity, and that the blessing might incur no risk in a soul which was confident in its possession of grace. And as he was ascending out of the water, there flashed around him a light and a glory worthy of the disposition with which he approached the gift of faith; this was manifest even to some others, who for the time concealed the wonder, from fear of speaking of a sight which each one thought had been only his own, but shortly afterwards communicated it to one another. To the baptizer and initiator, however, it was so clear and visible, that he could not even hold back the mystery, but publicly cried out that he was anointing with the Spirit his own successor.[362]

St Gregory the Theologian here calls Holy Baptism "regeneration by the water and Spirit," illumination, purification, a gift, a perfection acquired by virtue, an offering of faith, a mystery. In his oration on baptism he elaborated, "And as Christ the Giver of [baptism] is called by many various names, so too is this Gift, whether it is from the exceeding gladness of its nature (as those who are very fond of a thing take pleasure in using its name), or that the great variety of its benefits has reacted for us upon its names. We call it, the Gift, the Grace, Baptism, Unction, Illumination, the Clothing of Immortality, the Laver of Regeneration, the Seal, and everything that is honorable."[363] Further in the same oration, he says, "To know the power of this mystery is already an illumination!" This is how St Gregory the Theologian understood this sacrament, having been baptized in a mature age, having come to know from his own experience and the experience of the saints of his time, that unutterable transformation, that complete regeneration, that new life that those who are baptized worthily perceptibly sense from the sacrament of baptism. This transformation occurs with those who prepare themselves for baptism in the proper way and therefore perceive and come to know its total power.

As we have seen, St Gregory mentioned the miracle that occurred when his father walked out of the baptismal font. His friend, St Basil the Great, the archbishop of Caesaria in Cappadocia, had a similarly perceptible experience of the sacrament, as we read in his life.[364]

One must prepare diligently before accepting holy baptism. This preparation is the immutable condition for the mystery bearing abundant fruit, for it serves for the salvation of the man, not his greater condemnation. This we say to explain the importance of the sacrament and especially to instruct those who approach baptism as adults, not as children (which is the usual age that we are baptized in our time). Preparation for holy baptism is true repentance. True repentance is the inherent condition for baptism to be accepted in the proper manner, for the salvation of the soul. Such repentance consists of admission of one's sins as sins, in confessions, in abandonment of a sinful life.

Or expressed otherwise: repentance is an admission of one's fallen state, an admission of the necessity of the Redeemer. Repentance is a condemnation of one's own fallen nature and a rejection of it for the sake of renewed nature. It is necessary for our vessel—here I call the mind, heart, and body of man the vessel of God's grace—to be purified for the acceptance and preservation of the spiritual gift given by holy baptism. This vessel must not only be purified, but examined diligently, lest there be some defect, such as a crack, so that the defect can be mended carefully. If the defects are not mended, then the living water[365] poured into the vessel by Holy Baptism will not remain in the vessel. It will seep out, a disaster for the vessel! These cracks are sinful habits. Our inner Jerusalem must everywhere be warded, as by walls, with good habits and customs. Only then can our fallen nature be brought as a sacrifice and a whole burnt offering in the font of baptism. Then renewed nature, given by baptism, will become a worthy altar from which to offer sacrifices and whole burnt offerings pleasing to God (see Ps 50:20–21).

Without such preliminary preparation, what kind of benefit can we receive from baptism? What benefit can we receive from baptism if we, being baptized in mature years, in no way understand its significance? What benefit can we receive from baptism when we, being baptized in childhood, remain subsequently completely ignorant of the gift we received? But the gift is priceless, and not only that, we have also accepted a terrifying duty; our responsibilities are just as eternal and immeasurable as the gift itself.

What benefit can we receive from baptism if we do not understand that we are fallen or even do not admit that our nature is imprisoned in a state of bitter bondage to sin? If we consider the contaminated good that we do from our fallen nature to be grace-filled virtue? If we consider this so-called virtue of fallen nature to be refined and noble? If we strive stubbornly to do this so-called virtue, never noticing that it only feeds and develops our self-love, only distancing us more and more from God, only strengthening and sealing our fall and falling away from God? What benefit can we receive from baptism when we do not even consider mortal sins to be sins, such as fornication with all its many offshoots, instead calling it "enjoyment of life"? When we do not remember that our nature was renewed by baptism? When we completely neglect living according to the laws of renewed nature, instead showering it with insults and mockery?

St John, the Forerunner of the Lord, whose baptism was a washing of repentance, but did not give entry to the kingdom of heaven, required that everyone who approached his baptism confessed his sins. St John did not himself need this confession of sins,[366] but he cared for the spiritual benefit of those who accepted baptism from him. Truly, how can a person enter the field of repentance without first confessing his sins? How will he understand the relative seriousness of various sins and the means of repenting of them, if an experienced spiritual guide will not tell him? How, without a spiritual father, will he come to know of spiritual weapons and the means of using them against sinful thoughts and perceptions, sinful habits, and passions that have become rooted inside him from frequent repetition? Confession of sins is necessary to feel the proper remorse for previously committed sins, as well as to protect oneself in the future from falling to the same sins. Confession of sins has always been accepted by the Church of Christ as an indispensable requirement for repentance. All who wished to be baptized had to confess their sins, so that holy baptism would be accepted and preserved as it should be, as is proper for such a great sacrament that can never be repeated. Finally, repentance is a divine institution and a gift of God to fallen mankind.

"Repent, for the kingdom of heaven is at hand" (Matt 3:2), said the holy Forerunner to those who came to him and accepted from him the baptism of repentance. The heavenly kingdom, as the Forerunner later explained, was signified in his preaching by the sacrament of New Testament baptism. To accept the coming kingdom of heaven, man must repent. The Saviour of the world also required repentance of people before He could give them the gift of salvation through holy baptism, to make people capable of accepting the heavenly, spiritual gift. "Repent, for the kingdom of heaven is at hand," he said (Matt 4:17). "The time is fulfilled, and the kingdom of God is at hand. Repent, and believe in the gospel" (Mark 1:15).

Everything has already been done for you! No work is required of you, no labor, no addition to the gift! All that God seeks from you is purification by repentance, because it is impossible to entrust the priceless, all-holy, spiritual treasure to those who are impure and have no intention of becoming pure.

When He sent the disciples to preach, the God-Man commanded them to preach repentance because of the imminent coming of the heavenly kingdom (see Matt 10:7). The Apostle Paul said concerning himself that he, while wandering over the face of the earth, preached repentance to all, Jews and Greeks alike, and through repentance, conversion to God and faith in our Lord Jesus Christ (Acts 20:21). When thousands of Jews believed in the Saviour in Jerusalem after Peter's preaching on Pentecost, they asked him and the other apostles: "'Men and brethren, what shall we do?' Then Peter said to them, 'Repent, and let every one of you be baptized in the name of Jesus Christ for the remission of sins; and you shall receive the gift of the Holy Spirit'" (Acts 2:37–38).

Everywhere we see repentance as the only entrance, the only ladder, the only threshold to faith, the Gospel, the kingdom of heaven, God, all the Christian sacraments, including holy baptism, that new birth of man into Christianity. Rejection of the former sinful life is absolutely necessary, as is a firm conviction to lead a life according to the commandments of the Gospel, so that the gifts of the Holy Spirit, given in baptism, can be worthily accepted and preserved. The pastors of the early Church of the first centuries took all possible care to prepare those who approached baptism—at that time nearly everyone was baptized only in mature years—so that they would have a complete understanding of the nature of the spiritual gift they were receiving.[367]

Even today's pastors have a holy obligation to give an exact and detailed interpretation of holy baptism to those who have already been baptized in their childhood and therefore have no experiential knowledge of the sacrament. They received the gift; they will have to answer for how they used it! A timely preparation for giving this account to God is necessary, extremely necessary! A perfunctory or ignorant use of this gift will lead to the worst possible consequences. Whoever does not use the gift according to the desires and commands of the Gift-giver; whoever will not develop within himself the grace of baptism actively, living by the commandments of the Gospel; whoever will hide the gifted talent in the ground, that is, will bury the grace of baptism as in a tomb; whoever will destroy in himself all the activity of grace, having given himself completely to earthly cares and pleasure—this person will lose the grace of baptism at the Judgment of Christ. The unworthy possessor of the gift will be cast out "into the outer darkness. There will be weeping and gnashing of teeth" (Matt 25:30). To have a proper understanding of the importance of holy baptism, you must lead a God-pleasing, evangelical life. Only such a life can clearly and adequately explain the mysteries of Christianity to a Christian.[368]

Baptism is a sacrament that cannot be repeated. "I confess one baptism for the remission of sins," declares the holy Creed. As being born into the physical life can only be done once, so also the second birth into regeneration—baptism—can only be done once. Various diseases that attack a person after birth and threaten his physical life can be treated by various medicines that give support to the force of life that is given by natural birth. In a similar way, when various sins committed after baptism attack and disorder the spiritual life of a person, the healing is found in repentance, whose effectiveness is based on the grace of the Holy Spirit that was planted in man by holy baptism. Its effectiveness is further ensured by the development of this grace that is crushed and suffocated by sins.

"Christ," said St Mark the Ascetic,

> as perfect God, gave the baptized the perfect grace of the Holy Spirit, which does not require anything of us, but is revealed to us and is manifested as much as we live according to the commandments. He gives us more grace so that we can achieve the "unity of the faith and of the knowledge of the Son of God, to a perfect man, to the measure of the stature of the fullness of Christ" (Ephesians 4:13). [This "unity of faith" refers to the absorption of a Christian's entire life by faith; moreover, all his actions will then be an expression of spiritual intellect, that is, the Gospel.] Therefore, whatever we bring Him after our regeneration [that is, baptism], it will still be all His and by Him planted within us [by the sacrament of baptism].[369]

VI The Renewal of Redeemed Human Nature by Repentance

Those who desire to acquire an experiential knowledge of holy baptism, who desire to reveal the secret mystery and priceless spiritual gift placed by the unutterable goodness of God into the spiritual treasure-house, who desire to see their nature in a state of renewal and regeneration, who desire to perceive and see Christ within themselves, can achieve all of this by repentance. Only repentance, proper and seemly for a Christian, can correspond to the gift that he desires to reveal in himself. True repentance corresponds to baptism. Only baptism, by the unutterable goodness of God, can give man the gift of God, but only through repentance can the Christian who has allowed himself to live by the promptings of fallen nature, who has brought death back to life within him, who has killed life within himself, receive the gift again from the goodness of God.

In baptism we are born of water and the Spirit, and in repentance we are regenerated by tears and the Spirit. Repentance is the never-ending crying of a child to God concerning a lost gift, with the hope of once again receiving that gift. "I have not kept my own vineyard" (Song 1:6 LXX) exclaims the soul in terrible sorrow, for it has descended from nature renewed by baptism back into the domain of fallen nature. It has lost its freedom; it is ruled by sin. "Tell me . . . where you shepherd your flock" (Song 1:7 LXX). "There are no spiritual perceptions or thoughts within me! The entire flock of my emotions and thoughts are useless! They are goats, for they are a mixture of good with evil! They are mine, because they are born from my fallen nature! I have lost all the qualities of my nature, renewed by baptism!"

St Isaac the Syrian was once asked what thoughts should occupy an ascetic of Christ in his solitude. He answered,

> You ask me about thoughts? The one thought that should constantly occupy a person in his cell to help him mortify himself to the world, that is, to sin? Does an assiduous and sober-minded person need to ask how he should act when he is alone with himself? What else can occupy the mind of a monk in his cell other than sorrow? Does his sorrow leave him any chance to turn to any other kinds of thoughts? What other thoughts can be better than this? The very place of a monk, his solitude, his life are like living in a tomb, devoid of any human joys. It teaches him that sorrow is his sole occupation. The very significance of his name calls him and incites him to tears. He is called the mourner, that is, one who is filled with bitterness in his heart. All the saints have left this earthly life in tears. If the saints wept, their eyes constantly filled with tears, until the very moment of their passage from this life, then who should not weep?
>
> Consolation for a monk flows from his tears. If even the perfect and victorious wept here, then how can the wounded ever bear to cease weeping? Does the one who has a dead body lying next to him, who sees himself as that body killed by sins, have any need of instruction about what sort of thoughts should inspire his tears? Your soul is killed with sins; your most priceless treasure is struck down to death. Is it possible that you should

cease to cry for it? If we enter stillness and abide in it with endurance, then we can abide in weeping. Therefore, let us constantly pray with the mind to the Lord, so that He will send us tears. If this gift of grace will be given us, this greatest and most exalted of all gifts, then we, thanks to this gift, will become pure. When we acquire purity, then this purity will not be taken away from us until we leave this life.[370]

Evidently, such tears can only arise in a person who has a clear understanding of his own fallen nature and state, so far from the nature renewed by baptism. Only such a person can bewail bitterly and cry constantly, for he has understood the worth of what he has lost.

"Godly sorrow is a constant and inculcated sense of pain in the heart. This sorrow constantly, deliriously seeks that for which it thirsts, with inner tension it runs after that of which it has been deprived, and it weeps bitterly in its wake."[371] This painful sense of sorrow must become the definition of a repentant Christian. To abandon this sorrow is a sign of self-delusion and error. Only a humility that emulates Christ's can calm the weeper; only love in Christ can console him, can wipe away his tears, and can illumine his face and heart with the light of heavenly joy. Sacrifices and whole burnt offerings from fallen nature are not acceptable. The only God-pleasing sacrifice that fallen nature can offer is a heart broken by compunction (see Ps 50:18–19).

When one stops living according to the commandments of the Gospel and reverts to the condition of fallen nature, one ceases to live a life proper to renewed nature. In a similar way, a return to the state proper to renewed nature from a state of fallenness also occurs when we decidedly and completely take up a life proper to the teachings and testament of the God-Man. When we enter this arena, our inner warfare is revealed, because, before repentance, living according to our own fallen will and reason deprived us of our spiritual freedom, abandoning us to imprisonment to sin and the devil.

He who repents exerts himself to live by the commandments of the Gospel, while sin and the devil, having received authority given to them freely by his previous life, try to keep the prisoner captive, in chains, in prison. An experiential knowledge of this imprisonment through the palpable perception of the imprisonment and the violence of the evil one, an experiential knowledge of spiritual death through a perception of that death—these serve to strengthen and consolidate the penitent's tears.

"This battle," says St Mark the Ascetic, "is an internecine battle. It is not a battle with external enemies. It is not our brethren against whom we must battle. It is within us, and no other person can help us in this warfare. We have only helper—Christ, Who is hidden within us mystically by holy baptism. He is unconquerable and He cannot be destroyed. He will strengthen us if we will forcefully fulfill His commandments."[372]

Here the holy ascetic does not reject the guidance of spiritually experienced elders. God forbid! He advises to always rush to the counsel of one's spiritual fathers and brothers (see his 1st Homily). In this passage, however, he wants to show that our invisible victory in the inner warfare depends exclusively on our own will and the action of grace planted within us in baptism, conforming to our will, which is revealed and proved by how well we fulfill the commandments of the Gospel (which express the unattainable will of God for man). For this reason, some ascetics, though they receive abundant and constant guidance from spiritual elders, bear very poor fruits, while others, having heard only a short instruction, in a short period of time reveal prompt spiritual progress through the spiritual gifts given them in baptism. "Know this to be true," said St Isaac the Syrian, "that every good that acts within you mentally and secretly came about as a result of the intercession before God of your baptism and your faith, by which our Lord Jesus Christ called you to do good in His name."[373] You were not called to do the so-called good deeds of fallen nature.

Whoever repents in such a manner is helped by the judgments of God, as the holy prophet David said: "Thy judgments shall help me" (Ps 118:175). God's providence sends many different sorrows to the penitent. "For whom the Lord loves He chastens, and scourges every son whom He receives" (Heb 12:6). Endurance of sorrows with gratitude to God, together with the admission that we are worthy of the sorrows, and an admission that this particular sorrow is exactly the salvific medicine needed for our personal salvation—these are the signs of true repentance.[374]

"He who does not know the judgments of God," says St Mark the Ascetic, "travels a path between dangerous rapids, and any wind will immediately cause him to crash." Whoever battles the sorrows sent to him does not know that he is actually opposing the command of God, while whoever accepts them with true wisdom, according to the Scriptures will say: "With hope I wait for the Lord" (Ps 39:2). He who has come to know this truth does not oppose sorrows; he knows that they bring man to fear of God. His previous sins, being remembered merely as a mental image, can actually bring harm, defiling the one who has hope for good. When the mind, by rejecting itself, by simplicity of thought acquires hope, then the enemy, under the pretense of confession, brings to mind vivid images of previous sins (especially carnal ones). He reawakens the passions that the grace of God has erased by forgetfulness and harms the man. In such cases, even a firm mind that abhors the passions can become darkened, being disturbed by the remembrance of committed sins. If he is, on the contrary, still dark and sensual, then inevitably he will begin to passionately converse with the thoughts that come, so that the remembrance becomes not confession, but a mental repetition of the previously committed sins.

> If you wish to bring to God a blameless confession, then do not call to mind the images of previous sins, but courageously endure all the sorrows that come upon you as a result of these sins. Sorrows come as retribution for previous sins, the heaviness of each retribution depending on the heaviness of the sin. He who is wise and knows the truth confesses to God not by calling to mind his committed sins, but by enduring the sorrows that come as a result of those sins. If he rejects suffering and dishonor, he will not bring repentance even if he does other good deeds, for vanity and lack of suffering serve sin, even when the ascetic does good deeds.[375]

"The way of God is a daily cross. The man who is especially graced by the providence of God is known by how constantly God sends him sorrows."[376] "[God's] strength is made perfect in [the] weakness" of fallen human nature (2 Cor 12:9), when this nature is crushed into dust by the Cross of Christ. On the contrary, fallen human nature can only flourish in the abundance of means granted it by fallen human society: in education, in riches, and in honors. These are the foundation and the means of flourishing of fallen nature. When it flourishes thus, fallen nature accepts worship from blinded, miserable humanity, as the whore of Babylon did (Rev 18:19), entering a state of adultery that results from rejecting Christ and the Holy Spirit (sometimes even without actual words of rejection, for this rejection is one of essence, activity, life). After the God-Man renewed our nature, any return of a man to his fallen nature is adultery, treason against God.

The grace of holy baptism raises a Christian, through repentance, to spiritual freedom. This is the freedom that he had when he left the baptismal font. Like a sick man after prolonged treatment, he begins to feel within himself that freshness and strength that he had before his sickness, when he was still healthy. The primary reason for the renewal of his strength is not the treatment, but the vitality that was planted into his nature by the Creator. The treatment only helped his vital force to fight the sickness, to defeat and reject the sickness, which is nothing other than a disorder of the activity of that vital force. Repentance requires some measure of time, depending on circumstances, and especially depending on the will of divine providence that guides us. We can see this vividly in the lives of many of God's saints who passed from a state of sinfulness to a state of holiness by repentance. St Mary of Egypt told St Zosimas that she battled her thoughts and desires, which had the strength of fierce animals, for seventeen years.[377]

Because we neglect to preserve this precious gift given in baptism (by living according to the iniquitous law of our fallen nature), the authority of sin begins to assert itself in us unwittingly. Without even noticing it, we lose our spiritual freedom. Our grievous bondage remains invisible to many of us. Instead, we pretend that this state is the most satisfactory freedom. Our state of bondage and slavery is only revealed to us when we begin to fulfill the commandments of the Gospel. Then, our fallen intellect stubbornly rises up against the mind of Christ, and our heart wildly, hostilely considers the fulfillment of the will of Christ as though it were a capital sentence. Then, we come to know through experience how bitterly we have lost our freedom, how horribly we have fallen. Then we see the profound depth of our fall that reaches all the way down to the abysses of hell.

However, we must not despair and grow apathetic from such knowledge. We must bravely and decidedly commit ourselves to repentance, as to an all-powerful physician, who has the authority and power from God to treat and heal all sins, no matter how grievous or numerous, no matter how habitual our sins have become. Christ gave Himself to us and even entered into us through holy baptism; then He hid Himself in us when we did not show our desire for Him to live in us and direct us. Christ will inevitably reveal Himself within us if we prove our desire for Him to abide in us through our sincere repentance. "Behold, I stand at the door and knock. If anyone hears My voice and opens the door, I will come in to him and dine with him, and he with Me. To him who overcomes I will grant to sit with Me on My throne, as I also overcame and sat down with My Father on His throne" (Rev 3:20–21). The voice of Christ is the Gospel.

St Macarius the Great describes the proper order through which a repenting sinner rises up to holiness through repentance in the following manner: "He who desires to approach the Lord and be found worthy of eternal life, to become the abode of God, worthy of the Holy Spirit, to receive a chance to blamelessly and purely bear the fruits of the Spirit according to the commandments of the Lord, must begin thus. First, he must firmly believe in the Lord and completely commit himself to His commandments. He must reject the world completely, so that his mind will not be busy with any thoughts of the physical objects of the world but will instead remain constantly in prayer, never coming to despair at the long expectation of the coming of the Lord and His help. Instead, he must have his mind constantly directed to the Lord. Later, he must constantly train himself to do all good deeds and to fulfill all the Lord's commandments, even if his heart does not desire this because of the sin that still resides in him. He must force himself to be humble before all men, to consider himself the least and worst of all. He must not seek honor or glory or praise for himself from anyone, as it is written in the Gospel. Instead, he must always keep the Lord and His commandments before his gaze, seeking to please Him alone. He must train himself also to be meek, even if his heart opposes it. As the Lord said, 'Learn from Me, for I am gentle and lowly in heart, and you will find rest for your souls.'" (Matt 11:29)

He must also be merciful, compassionate, co-suffering, good, forcing himself to be thus. As the Lord said, "Therefore be merciful, just as your Father also is merciful" (Luke 6:36). And also: "If you love Me, keep My commandments" (John 14:15). Force yourselves, for "the violent [that is, those who coerce themselves] take [the kingdom of heaven] by force" (Matt 11:12). And "Strive to enter through the narrow gate" (Luke 13:24). He must always keep the humility of the Lord, His life, His behavior before his gaze. He must keep them always in his memory, as a model for emulation, never allowing these thoughts to be stolen by forgetfulness.

As much as he is able, he must force himself to pray constantly, constantly asking with constant faith for the Lord to come and make him into His abode (see John 14:23), so that He will instruct him in all His commandments, confirm him in them, to make his soul a fitting home for Jesus Christ. When he will act thus, coercing himself despite the opposition of his heart, training himself to accomplish all good deeds and to remember the Lord always, forcing himself to always expect Him in much goodness and love—then the Lord, seeing his disposition and his zeal, seeing how he forces himself constantly to remember the Lord and to do all good deeds, to be humble-minded, meek, and loving, how he submits his heart to the yoke of Christ, coercing his heart to only do good deeds, then, I say, the Lord will pour His mercy on him at the appointed time. He will deliver him from his enemies and from the sin living inside him, and He will fill him with the Holy Spirit. In this way, the ascetic will, without difficulty or self-coercion, fulfill the commands of the Lord truly then and always.

> It would be even more correct to say that the Lord Himself will fulfill His commands within the man, revealing spiritual fruits, while the man will only offer the fruits in purity as sacrifices. But before this can happen, everyone

who approaches the Lord (as we have already said) must force himself to the good, in spite of the opposition of his heart, in constant expectation with undoubting faith in the goodness of God. We must coerce ourselves forcefully to be merciful to all others, to have a man-loving heart, to have humility before all, to have long-suffering before all, to not sorrow in soul during exiles and dishonors, never to complain. As it is written, "Beloved, do not avenge yourselves" (Romans 12:19). We must force ourselves to pray, especially when we have not received the gift of prayer from the Holy Spirit. When God sees how we labor and coerce ourselves to do good, He will give us the true prayer of Christ, an abyss of mercy, true love for man. In short, He will give all spiritual gifts.[378]

We see that many sinners, having offered repentance, reached the highest levels of Christian perfection. They restored within themselves the gift of baptism, not only to the degree to which it was given, but developing it greatly as a result of living by the commandments of the Gospel. Having acquired and returned spiritual freedom to themselves, they did not stop there. They were not content with this merely, but they did not cease the repentance and spiritual sorrow that had returned them this freedom. They came to know their weakness and tendency toward sloth from experience. They saw how fickle man is (see Isaac the Syrian, Homily 1), and this constantly incited them to further tears. "Do not boast about tomorrow" (Prov 27:1), they say to themselves daily. Because of their new-found purity, it was revealed to them that "Thy commandment is exceeding broad" (Ps 118:96). Compared with the limitless breadth of the command of the boundless Lord, their fulfillment of the commandment was admittedly insufficient. They even called and admitted their fulfillment of the commandments of the Gospel to be profanation of the commandments.[379] They washed away their virtues with their tears, as though they were sins. No sinner weeps for his most grievous sins as these slaves of Christ bemoaned their virtues. "The heaven is not pure in His sight" (Job 15:15). In other words, even the pure, holy angels have limited purity, and compared with the all-perfect purity of God, they are impure. So also all holy people are impure before Him, even though they are already in heaven while living on earth (see Phil 3:20).

For this reason, they weep and continue to offer repentance, plunging ever deeper into their repentance. "For I know of nothing against myself, yet I am not justified by this; but He who judges me is the Lord" (1 Cor 4:4). Despite his great spiritual gifts, despite the super-abundant grace of God that resided in the apostle, he said with complete sincerity: "Christ Jesus came into the world to save sinners, of whom I am chief" (1 Tim 1:15).

These are the means to increase the grace of baptism to boundless measure, inconceivable and implausible to the human mind in its fallen state:

1. Living by the commandments of the Gospel
2. Contemplating our own fallen nature
3. Contemplating the endless greatness and perfection of God
4. Comparing human nature—worthless in its limitations—with the limitless nature of God
5. Contemplating the consequences of Adam's sin and the consequences of our own sinfulness
6. Sorrowing over our calamitous spiritual state and that of all mankind
7. Enduring all personal troubles patiently.

The increase of the holy spiritual gift given by baptism is just as boundless as the gift given by God from His divine nature is boundless (see 2 Pet 1:4). This cultivation of the gift will overwhelm the entire being of a Christian. When we see this spiritual cultivation in the chosen vessels of God, then the effect of holy baptism on man, expressed by Christ in the parables of the Gospel, becomes completely obvious.

"The kingdom of heaven is like a mustard seed, which a man took and sowed in his field, which indeed is the least of all the seeds; but when it is grown it is greater than the herbs and becomes a tree, so that the birds of the air come and nest in its branches" (Matt 13:31–32). This is a likening filled with divine humble-mindedness.[380] The Son of God "made Himself of no reputation, taking the form of a bondservant, and coming in the likeness of men" (Phil 2:7). In this "form" He willed to be included not among the hosts of the powerful, glorious, and rich of the world, but the hosts of poor and suffering. As the prophet said, "He has no form or beauty . . . He was dishonored and not esteemed" (Isa 53:2–3). "His soul was delivered over to. He was considered among the lawless" (Isa 53:12), being crucified between two thieves, as though He were the worst and most dangerous of the criminals. His all-holy, life-giving, divine commandment He called "least" (Matt 5:19), in that simple, artless form that they were offered. He added, however, that breaking even a single of these "least" commandments could be the reason for eternal perdition.[381]

Thus, Christ likened the grace of baptism to the smallest of earthly seeds. And truly, what can be simpler and more ordinary, to all appearances, than holy baptism? It is typical for people to wash in water, to plunge into it. A sacrament in which the body and soul are washed clean of sinful impurity is associated with an everyday action.[382] The death and burial of man are replaced by a momentary submersion in water. Invisibly for the physical eyes, the Holy Spirit descends and recreates fallen man. The circumstances of the temporary life remain the same as before for the baptized man, but only externally.

Externally, the gift given by baptism is so invisible that it can easily be compared to a single, tiny mustard seed.[383] This gift is priceless. It grows and develops by the doing of the commandments, and then its greatness will supersede all the other gifts that the generous hand of the Creator gifted man in abundance, and it will make man the temple of heavenly thoughts, sensations, revelations, and states natural only to the inhabitants of heaven. "The kingdom of heaven is like leaven, which a woman took and hid in three measures of meal till it was all leavened" (Matt 13:33). How humbly and yet how truly is the spiritual Gift given by baptism called leaven (that is, yeast). Everyone who accepts holy baptism is betrothed to Christ, is united with Christ, and therefore with all fairness can be called (figuratively) His bride. This bride (that is, the woman of the parable) hides, that is, preserves and develops, the gift of grace by living a life according to the Gospel in her mind, heart, and body (see 1 Thess 5:23), until the gift imbues, fills, and envelops the entire man.

Would you like to see not only a soul, but a human body that is filled and permeated with the gift of grace given in baptism? Then turn your gaze to Paul, whose handkerchiefs had the power to heal (see Acts 19:12), who was not harmed by the bite of a poisonous snake (see Acts 28:5). Look at St Mary of Egypt, who levitated from the ground while praying, who walked on the surface of the Jordan as though it were dry land, who traveled a thirty-day journey in the space of a single hour. Look at St Mark of Trache (celebrated on April 5), who raised a mountain from its foundations and cast it into the sea with his voice alone. Look at St Ioannicius the Great who, like a spirit, was invisible to those whom he did not want to meet, even though he stood next to them. Look at the bodies of ascetics that lie incorrupt for many centuries, refusing to heed the law of corruption, universal for all mankind. Instead, they pour forth streams of healing, streams of sweet-smelling fragrance, streams of life.

St Sisoes the Great, who had especially abundant gifts of the Holy Spirit, said, "Spiritual gifts are natural for the person into whom God has entered by the grace of Holy Baptism and by the continued life according to the commandments."[384] This he uttered from his own experience. Is not the same truth witnessed by the Holy Scriptures? "For as many of you as were baptized into Christ have put on Christ" (Gal 3:27). For those who have put on Christ, who have Christ abiding within them, the gifts of the Spirit are natural, for wherever Christ is, there also are the Father and the Spirit.

VII Renewed Human Nature and Evil

The following question naturally arises: what is the relationship of renewed man to evil? He cannot fail to have exact knowledge of evil. But we have seen that Adam's blameless human nature in the state immediately following creation had no sooner gained experiential knowledge of evil, than it died because of it. Therefore, it is vitally important to understand how renewed human nature must relate to the experiential knowledge of evil. We answer: the purity of the heart, a spiritual state proper to renewed nature, is called by the Gospel the kind of "blessedness" that gives one a vision of God (see Matt 5:8). It appears in the soul after the blessedness of mercy and flows naturally from this blessedness.

It is well known that the evangelical beatitudes represent spiritual states that reveal themselves in a Christian when he lives by the commandments of the Gospel. Each state of blessedness reveals itself in step-by-step fashion, one after another. Each state gives rise to the state that follows.[385] After rejecting our own righteousness as nothing but defiled evil, from the midst of sorrow over our fallen state, from the midst of meekness (that contentment with all sorrows, both visible and invisible), we begin to sense in our soul the hunger and thirst of God's righteousness. The righteousness of God is found in mercy, where the Gospel commands us to seek it:

> But I say to you, love your enemies, bless those who curse you, do good to those who hate you, and pray for those who spitefully use you and persecute you, that you may be sons of your Father in heaven; for He makes His sun rise on the evil and on the good, and sends rain on the just and on the unjust. For if you love those who love you, what reward have you? Do not even the tax collectors do the same? And if you greet your brethren only, what do you do more than others? Do not even the tax collectors do so? Therefore you shall be perfect, just as your Father in heaven is perfect. (Matthew 5:44–48)

The perfection of Christian, and therefore universally human, virtue in renewed nature is found in a grace-filled mercy that emulates God's own mercy. It is produced in a Christian only by the development of the divine grace given in baptism and cultivated by a life governed by the commandments. Such mercy gives rise to spiritual purity. Purity is fed by mercy; it lives by mercy. St Isaac the Syrian was once asked, "What is purity?" He answered, "Purity is a heart that is filled with mercy for all creatures." When further asked: "What is a merciful heart?" the great teacher of monastics said the following:

> It is a heart burning for all creatures, for men, birds, beasts, demons—in a word, for all creation. By recalling them, the eyes of a merciful person shed tears in abundance because of the strong and vehement mercy that grips such a person's heart. From constant endurance, his heart has become the heart of a child, and he cannot be indifferent when he hears or sees any harm or even any minor grief that disturbs creation. Therefore, he hourly offers prayer with tears for the irrational beasts, for the enemies of the truth, even for his own enemies, that they be preserved and purified. He even prays for the creatures that slither on their bellies, out of the great mercy that moves abundantly in his heart in God's likeness.[386]

Out of the great mercy that St Isaac felt in his own heart, he cried out, "In the day that you will suffer with someone else—no matter how that person suffers, whether in body or in thought, when he is good or evil—consider yourself a martyr and look at yourself as one who has suffered for Christ, as one who has been found worthy of being a confessor. Remember that Christ died for sinners, not for the righteous. See how great it is to sorrow for the evil and to go good to sinners! It is greater than doing the same for the righteous. Even the apostle recalls this and is amazed at it" (see Romans 5:6–8).[387]

When comparing the righteousness of fallen human nature with divine righteousness, which is found in grace-filled, spiritual mercy, St Isaac calls the latter worship of God, and the former worship of idols.[388]

Apostle Paul speaks of the acquisition of this mercy thus: "Therefore, as the elect of God, holy and beloved, put on tender mercies, kindness, humility, meekness, longsuffering; bearing with one another, and forgiving one another, if anyone has a complaint against another; even as Christ forgave you, so you also must do" (Col 3:12–13).

St Macarius the Great said, "Grace so strongly pacifies all the powers of the heart that the soul, from great joy (mercy), becomes like a gentle child, and man then no longer condemns Greeks, Jews, sinners, laypeople, but with a purified eye, the inner man gazes at all and rejoices over the whole world and desires to honor and love to the utmost both Greeks and Jews."[389] St Isaac also said, "Purity of heart sees God; it shines and blossoms in a soul not because of human learning, but when one ceases to see the evil of man."[390] When a man ceases to see evil in his neighbor, then his relationships with his fellow man will be entirely swallowed up in his mercy for all.

Is it possible that such blindness for the failings of others is actually a blindness of the mind or a kind of admission of evil as good? No. On the contrary, the blindness of the mind, not seeing sins and evil, admitting evil to be good—all this is what unrepentant sinners do when they justify their own sin. The saints of God, illumined by the Spirit of God, know evil in every detail. They know evil's snares and its venom. They, thanks to this knowledge given by the Spirit, especially carefully guard themselves from experiential knowledge of sins, that is, actually sinning in deed.

"We know that whoever is born of God does not sin; but he who has been born of God keeps himself, and the wicked one does not touch him" (1 John 5:18). With the help of grace-filled mercy, which is how true Christians relate to all fellow human beings, Christians remain strangers to the sinfulness of their neighbors, which can only be infectious to them if they condemn the sinner, ruining their joyful, holy state of peace. "The peace of God, which surpasses all understanding" (Phil 4:7), which abides in the saints of God, immediately reveals any approaching thought of the evil one, no matter what mask of righteousness the thought might try to put on.

In his homily[391] on spiritual discernment of thoughts, passions, and virtues, St John of the Ladder says that such discernment appears from a clean conscience and a pure heart. For beginners in the spiritual life, this discernment takes the form of knowing their fallenness and their own personal sinfulness. In intermediates in the spiritual life, this discernment differentiates true good from natural good and from evil (both open evil and evil hiding under a mask of good). Finally, in the perfect, this discernment is spiritual wisdom that shines forth from the Holy Spirit. It sees the way evil acts in other people. Thus, the Apostle Peter was able to say to Simon Magus: "For I see that you are poisoned by bitterness and bound by iniquity" (Acts 8:23).

In his introduction to the homily on holy stillness, St John of the Ladder says that the holy ones of God have an exact and specific knowledge of sin by the revelation of the Holy Spirit.[392] The beginning of the illumination of the soul and a sign of the soul's health consists of the mind beginning to see its own sins, which are in number like the sand in the sea, as St Peter Damascene says.[393] This father calls the vision of one's own fallenness and sinfulness nothing less than spiritual vision that opens up within him from the action of grace in the person who lives by the commandments of Christ.[394] The Holy Church commanded its children to prayerfully ask of God a great gift—"to see my failings and not condemn my brother."[395]

Fallen nature is struck with blindness of the mind. It cannot see how it has fallen; it cannot see its own sins; it cannot see that it is an exile on earth.

Instead, it disposes of earthly things as though they were eternal, as though the soul itself lives only for the earth. Fallen nature not only cruelly condemns and judges the sins of other people, but from its own fearfully disordered state, it even invents new sins for its neighbor that he never committed. It is tempted by the most exalted Christian virtues, perverting their importance according to its own so-called wisdom and its heart's hatred.

On the contrary, renewed nature has a grace-given knowledge and vision of evil. This vision not only does not destroy the wholeness of good in man, but it even serves to inspire man to a stricter protection of self against coming to know evil experientially. Renewed nature knows that such knowledge kills. Renewed nature sees and knows the evil in itself, in other men, and in demons, but it remains undefiled by evil, because its vision and knowledge don't belong to him, strictly speaking, since they were not acquired by his own exertions, but given by God. One can compare one's experiential knowledge of evil through the Fall with the knowledge of illnesses by the sick. The knowledge of evil found in renewed man is the knowledge that physicians have concerning diseases. The sick know sicknesses by experience, but they do not understand the causes or treatment of the disease. The physicians, though they do not experience the sickness, know it far better than the sick, for they understand the causes and the means to treat it.

VIII Conclusion

Having written down, as much as my meager talents allow, the various states of human nature and its relationship with evil, to whom shall I turn with the conclusion of my impoverished words? These words are, after all, an accusation against my own failings. Therefore, I will end by exhorting myself, as is proper for any such writing. I will take the exhortation from one of the Fathers of the Church. If any of my fellow men find it appropriate for themselves, let them accept this with love.

> You have remembered that nobility that you accepted in baptism by grace, but rejected willingly for the passions of the world. You have desired to restore this nobility with a good will. Such a desire you have proven with action, having come to this holy school, having put on the honorable robes of repentance and having given an oath to remain in the monastery until you die. You have made a second covenant with God. The first covenant was made when you entered this world. The second, when you began to approach the end of this life. Then, you were accepted by Christ for the sake of piety. Now, you are joined to Christ by repentance. Then, you

received grace; now, you confess your debt. Then, being a child, you did not perceive the honor given to you, though later on, when you were older, you understood the greatness of the gift, and you shut your mouth to any self-justification. Now, after your knowledge has developed enough, you begin to understand the meaning of your oath. Take care that you do not neglect this promise to repent. Take care that you be not rejected and cast out, like some broken vessel, into the outer darkness, where "there will be weeping and gnashing of teeth" (Matthew 22:13). There is no other way to return to salvation, save by the way of repentance.[396]

"Therefore, as the Holy Spirit says: 'Today, if you will hear His voice, do not harden your hearts as in the rebellion, in the day of trial in the wilderness, where your fathers tested Me, tried Me, and saw My works forty years. Therefore I was angry with that generation, and said, "They always go astray in their heart, and they have not known My ways." So I swore in My wrath, "They shall not enter My rest."' Beware, brethren, lest there be in any of you an evil heart of unbelief in departing from the living God; but exhort one another daily, while it is called "Today," lest any of you be hardened through the deceitfulness of sin. For we have become partakers of Christ if we hold the beginning of our confidence[397] steadfast to the end." (Heb 3:7–14).

"Seeing then that we have a great High Priest who has passed through the heavens, Jesus the Son of God, let us hold fast our confession. For we do not have a High Priest who cannot sympathize with our weaknesses, but was in all points tempted as we are, yet without sin. Let us therefore come boldly to the throne of grace, that we may obtain mercy and find grace to help in time of need" (Heb 4:14–16). Amen.

A Short Biography of Bishop Ignatius (Brianchaninov)

The future Saint Ignatius was born on April 15/28, 1807, in the village of Pokrovskoye in the Vologda region of Russia. His given name at birth was Dimitry Alexandrovitch Brianchaninov. Of noble birth, his father was a wealthy provincial landowner. In due course the young Dimity was sent to study at the Pioneer Military Academy in St Petersburg to be educated as a military officer.

Even before entering the academy Dimitry had aspired to the monastic life, but his family did not support these plans. Nevertheless, as a student he was able to find some time to devote to prayer and the inner life and to find other students with similar aspirations. Remaining obedient to his parents he remained diligent in his studies, winning the praise of his teacher and coming to the attention of the Grand Duke Nicholas Pavlovich, the future Tsar Nicholas I.

After graduating from the academy he took up his first commission in the army but soon became seriously ill. This made it possible for him to request an honorable discharge and having made a full recovery to at last embrace the monastic life. He was duly tonsured as a monk in 1831 and given the name Ignatius. His spiritual father was the revered Elder Leonid of Optina. Shortly after his tonsure he was ordained as a priest.

Meanwhile, his absence from the army had come to the attention of Tsar Nicholas. As soon as he was able to locate Fr Ignatius in his small monastery near Vologda he ordered him back to the capital. So, at the age of only twenty-six, Fr Ignatius was made an Archimandrite and appointed as head of the St Sergius monastery in St Petersburg. He served faithfully in that capacity for the next twenty-four years.

In 1857 he was ordained to the episcopacy, serving as Bishop of Stavropol and the Caucasus. This period of his life lasted for only four years, after which he withdrew into seclusion at the Nicolo-Babaevsky monastery in the Kostroma region of Russia. Here he was able to devote the remaining six years of his life to spiritual writing and correspondence with his numerous spiritual children. He composed five volumes of *Ascetical Works*, the fifth of which, *The Arena*, has been translated into English.

Bishop Ignatius reposed on April 30/May 13, 1867. The Russian Orthodox Church canonized him at their local council in 1988 and his relics now reside at the Tolga monastery in the Yaroslavl region of Russia.

Notes

All references to source material in the original text were to the classic Russian language editions. The author followed a Russian cultural practice where one is not necessarily expected to provide all background detail and source material. Unless otherwise indicated, the quotations and their citations have been translated from the original text.

Chapter 1

    1. According to the interpretation of St Pimen the Great (see the *Skete Patericon*).

    2. Homily 38 [of St Isaac the Syrian].

Chapter 2

    3. Gratitude to God is part of the inner work of the monk and consists of thanking and glorifying God for all that occurs—both the pleasant and the sorrowful. This work was commanded to the apostle by the Lord himself. "In everything give thanks; for this is the will of God in Christ Jesus for you" (1 Thess 5:18). This work of gratitude is described with especial power in the *Answers of St Barsanuphius the Great*. [In English it may be referred to as St Barsanuphius the Great and St John the Prophet, *Directions for the Spiritual Life, or Guidance toward Spiritual Life*.]

    4. St Ephraim the Syrian, a Church Father of the fourth century, wrote a literary version of the story of the wondrous Joseph in the style of the time, which is read in church, according to the Typicon, on matins of Great and Holy Tuesday.

    5. See especially the "Beneficial chapters" of St Gregory of Sinai in part 1 of *The Philokalia*. This is a generally accepted opinion among the Fathers of the Church. [In English *The Philokalia*, Volume 1, trans. E. Kadloubovsky and G. E. H. Palmer (London: Faber and Faber, 1983).]

    6. Porro ab Aegiptiis didicimus, quod in linqua eorum resonet: Salvator mundi, S. Hieronimi. Liber de nominibus hebraicis.

    7. *Notes on the Book of Genesis* by St Philaret of Moscow.

    8. *Notes on the Book of Genesis* by St Philaret of Moscow.

Chapter 3

    9. St John Cassian, "On Anger," in *The Philokalia,* Part IV [In English *The Philokalia*, Volume 4, trans. E. Kadloubovsky and G. E. H. Palmer (London: Faber and Faber, 1999).]

Chapter 4

    10. *The Ladder.* Homily 28, chapter 45. [Available in English translation as: *The Ladder of Divine Ascent*, trans. Archimandrite Lazarus (London: Faber and Faber, 1959).]

11. Isaiah 50:11, as interpreted by St Barsanuphius the Great in his 158th Answer. [In English it may be referred to as St Barsanuphius the Great and St John the Prophet, *Directions for the Spiritual Life, or Guidance toward Spiritual Life.*]

12. As quoted by Saint-Patriarch of Constantinople Kallistos and St Ignatios of Xanthopoulos in *The Philokalia*, Part II, chapter 5.

13. St Kallistos and St Ignatius Xanthopoulous. *The Philokalia*, Part II, chapter 6.

14. Homily 72 [of St Isaac the Syrian].

15. Homily 5 [of St Isaac the Syrian].

16. Homily 2 [of St Isaac the Syrian].

17. Homily 49 [of St Isaac the Syrian].

18. See Matthew 5:22, 25–26, 29.

19. See Matthew 6:15.

20. See Luke 12:16–20.

21. See 1 Thessalonians 4:16 and John 5:28.

22. See St Nilus of Sora's seventh sermon.

23. See 1 Corinthians 4:4.

24. *Apophthegmata* [The Apophthegmata Patrum is the Sayings of the Fathers].

25. Homily 1 [of St Isaac the Syrian].

26. *Apophthegmata.*

27. Cassianus lib. IV. De instititutis, renuntiantiam, cap. 39.

28. Cassianus lib. IV. De instititutis, renuntiantiam, cap. 35.

29. Abba Dorotheos. *Instruction 4: On the Fear of God.*

30. St Macarius the Great. Homily *37, chapters 2, 3.*

31. See Matthew 13:44.

32. [This quote is possibly a compilation of various homilies of St Isaac the Syrian.]

33. *The Rule for Holy Communion: Canons, Order of Preparation, and Prayers after Holy Communion* (Jordanville, NY: Holy Trinity Monastery, 2017), 83.

34. St Symeon the New Theologian, Homily 2.

35. The letters of St George the Recluse of Zadonsk. Part 2, letter 37, 1860.

36. Homily 55 [of St Isaac the Syrian].

Chapter 5

37. See also Genesis 32:28. Both Jacob and Israel are names for the nation of Israel in this case. In a spiritual sense, Israel indicates Christians who have reached a significant level of spiritual success.

38. See Psalm 17:12.

39. Abba Dorotheos. *Instruction 11.*

40. See John 13:2–27.

41. [It appears that St Ignatius is noting a play on words. In the Slavonicized Russian of the Russian ecclesiastical world of the nineteenth century, the word "dukh" could mean either spirit or wind. The play on words, then, is deliberate, if we consider that in the first sentence of the paragraph the judgments of God are a "wind" and in the second, they are "the Spirit."]

42. "The angels," says St John of Damascus in his *Exposition of the Orthodox Faith* (book 2, chapter 3, "On Angels"), "are called bodiless and immaterial only in comparison with us. Compared to God, the only One who is incomparable, everything is crude and material, including the angels."

43. See Romans 9, for example.

44. See St John of Damascus. *Exposition of the Orthodox Faith.* Book 2, chapter 3, "On Angels."

45. The Skete Paterikon.

46. St John of Damascus. *Exposition of the Orthodox Faith.* Book 2, chapter 3, "On Chapters."

47. St John of Damascus. Book 4, chapter 13.

48. It should be noted that all this refers to carnal people in whom the soul is not vivified by the action of God's grace. Those who have been renewed by this action do have a more clear understanding of their soul.

49. Descartes and his followers consider the soul to be a substance completely opposed to the body, not having anything in common with the body, not having any reference to space and time. We Christians only admit God alone to be independent of space and time.

50. See also St John of Damascus, *Exposition of the Orthodox Faith,* Book 4, chapter 13.

51. See Genesis 2:5–6.

52. See Genesis 3:16.

53. See Genesis 3:16–19.

54. See Revelation 22:11, 15.

55. See Genesis 2:7, 22, 3:1–11; Psalm 118:125, 89:13, 89:16, 37; and others.

56. See Romans 5:10.

57. See Theophylact of Bulgaria's interpretation of Luke 14:17. [In English: *The Explanation of the Holy Gospel According to St Luke: Vol. 3* by the Blessed Theophylact (Manchester, MO: Chrysostom Press, 1997).]

58. Interestingly, the armies of the Emperor of Rome, the lord of the earth, were about twelve legions. Evidently, Christ's intention here is to describe an army that is more numerous even than the greatest army on earth.

59. See Hebrews 12:8.

60. This is especially vivid in the book of Job. The righteous man at first listed his virtues and described them in a beautiful, realistic way. However, when he was purified and perfected by his many sorrows, then his self-opinion changed. He saw himself as though disappearing before the majesty of God. He admitted himself to be no more than earth and ashes.

Chapter 6

61. A certain brother asked St Sisoes the Great to give him a word for his benefit. The elder answered that a monk must be lower than the idols. When the brother asked what that meant, the elder answered, "The Scriptures describe the idols as having mouths, but not speaking, having ears, but not hearing, having eyes, but not seeing. This is how a monk should be. And since idols are filth, so the monk must consider himself to be less than filth" (*Apophthegmata*, letter "C").

62. See Colossians 2:8.

Chapter 7

63. See Hebrews 10:22.

64. See Isaac the Syrian. Homily 55.

65. See *The Imitation of Christ*, book 3, chapter 2. In the section we quote here, the warming of the heart in self-delusion is so vividly and picturesquely described that we consider it not excessive to bring to the attention of the reader the text itself:

"Speak, Lord, for Thy servant heareth." "I am Thy servant. Give me understanding that I may know Thine ordinances . . . Incline my heart to Thine ordinances. . . . Let Thy speech distil as the dew." The children of Israel once said to Moses: "Speak thou to us and we will hear thee: let not the Lord speak to us, lest we die." Not so, Lord, not so do I pray. Rather with Samuel the prophet I entreat humbly and earnestly: "Speak, Lord, for Thy servant heareth." Do not let Moses or any of the prophets speak to me; but You speak, O Lord God, Who inspired and enlightened all the prophets; for You alone, without them, can instruct me perfectly, whereas they, without You, can do nothing. They, indeed, utter fine words, but they cannot impart the spirit. They do indeed speak beautifully, but if You remain silent they cannot inflame the heart. They deliver the message; You lay bare the sense. They place before us mysteries, but You unlock their meaning. They proclaim commandments; You help us to keep them. They point out the way; You give strength for the journey. They work only outwardly; You instruct and enlighten our hearts. They water the exterior; You give the increase. They cry out words; You give understanding to the hearer. Let not Moses speak to me, therefore, but You, the Lord my God, everlasting truth, speak lest I die and prove barren if I am merely given outward advice and am not inflamed within; lest the word heard and not kept, known and not loved, believed and not obeyed, rise up in judgment against me. Speak, therefore, Lord, for Your servant listens. "Thou hast the words of eternal life."

The brazenness of this pomposity and prattle inspire and sorrow in a soul raised by the teachings of the Orthodox Church. There is no room for repentance here! There is no compunction of the spirit! This is a direct rushing toward the most intimate and close union with God! This, in general, is the spirit of the ascetic writings of the West. One of them, expressing his incorrect understanding of the merits of the Mother of God, ends his ecstatic circumlocution with the following words: "So, let us throw ourselves into the embrace of the Mother of God!" The Holy Eastern Church offers an opposed disposition of spirit: "If we did not have Your holy saints as intercessors and Your own goodness to have mercy of us, how would we have dared, O Saviour, to sing to You Who are constantly praised by the angels?" (Troparion on Great Compline). In another hymn, we heard, "To the Mother of God we diligently approach, we who are sinful and humble, and we fall down before her, calling in penitence from the depth of our soul: O Mistress, help us, have mercy on us, save us, for we are perishing from the multitude of our sins. Do not turn away from your servants, for we have no other hope but you" (Penitential Canon to the Mother of God). This Western state of self-delusion and demonic *prelest* is not understandable to those who were not raised in spiritual ascesis within the tradition of the Orthodox Church. Such people are inclined to consider this calamitous spiritual state as the most correct and gracious state. The translator of the *Imitation* into Russian from Latin included an instruction to the reader at the end of his edition. Indicating the section quoted above, this vivid portrait of self-delusion and *prelest*, he recommends that the reader warm himself up in emulation of this section before every spiritual reading. Evidently, such a disposition gives anyone the freedom to explain the Holy Scriptures as one wishes and removes from the reader the requirement to follow the interpretations of the Holy Fathers and the Church. This is an essential dogma of Protestantism.

66. St Gregory of Sinai. "On Self-delusion." *The Philokalia,* Part I. St Kallistos and St Ignatius Xanthopoulos. *The Philokalia*, Part II, chapter 73.

67. St Isaac the Syrian. Homily 36.

68. St Isaac the Syrian. *Homily 21.*

Chapter 8

69. See the *Chronicle* of St Dimitri of Rostov.

Chapter 9

70. St Macarius the Great. Homily 4, chapter 9.

71. St Macarius the Great. Homily 8, chapter 6.

72. St Macarius the Great. Homily 37, chapters 2, 4.

73. Experiential proof of this is seen in the holy martyr Arian. He, while a pagan hegemon, covered himself in the blood of many holy martyrs, but later he believed in Christ, and he imprinted

his faith in his heart by a triumphant confession of faith and his own martyrdom. (See the sufferings of the holy Martyr Philemon from December 14, and the martyrs Timothy and Mavra on May 3 from *The Lives of the Saints* of Dimitri of Rostov.)

74. St John of the Ladder. *The Ladder*, Homily 26.

Chapter 10

75. Homily 4 [St Mark the Ascetic].
76. St Mark the Ascetic. Homily 4.
77. St Macarius the Great. Homily 3, chapter 1.
78. *The Ladder*. Heading of Homily 28.
79. Ecclesiastes 11:9 according to the Slavonic (LXX), not the English (Masoretic).
80. [The citation from St Symeon the New Theologian is missing.]
81. "On the Three Kinds of Prayer." *The Philokalia*, Part IV, chapter 1.
82. Nicophorus the Monk. His homily in *The Philokalia*, Part II, chapter 18.
83. *The Philokalia*, Part II.
84. *St Nilus of Sora*. Homily 2.
85. *The Venerable Seraphim of Sarov*. Instruction 11.
86. *The Venerable Seraphim of Sarov*. Instruction 4, according to the 1844 Russian edition.
87. *The Ladder*. Homily 28, chapter 46.
88. Homily 2 [St Nilus of Sora].
89. Homily of Nicephorus the Monk. *The Philokalia*, Part II.
90. "On Abba Philemon." *The Philokalia*, Part IV.
91. "On the third form of attention and prayer." *The Philokalia*, Part I.
92. St John of the Ladder. *The Ladder*, Homily 4, chapter 2.
93. St John of the Ladder. *The Ladder*, Homily 28, chapter 31.

Chapter 11

94. St Isaac the Syrian. Homily 55.
95. These words were uttered by Hieroschemamonk Athanasius, a hesychast living in the tower of the Svensk Monastery of diocese of Orel, to a certain pilgrim who visited him in 1829.
96. *The Ladder*. Homily 7, chapter 64.
97. St Isaac the Syrian. Homily 89.
98. St Isaac the Syrian. Homily 11.
99. St Gregory of Sinai. "On Spiritual Delusion and Many Other Subjects." *The Philokalia*, Part I. "When the devil sees someone who lives in his tears, he does not remain there, for where the tears are, repentance soon comes, which he fears."
100. St Meletios of Galicia. "A Poem about Prayer."
101. *The Ladder*. Homily 28, chapter 17.
102. According to the advice of St Seraphim of Sarov in his 11th instruction.
103. St Mark the Ascetic. "On Those Who Think to Be Saved by Deeds." *The Philokalia*, Part I, chapter 34.
104. St Gregory of Sinai. "How a Hesychast Must Sit and Pray." *The Philokalia*, Part I.
105. St Kallistos and St Ignatius. "On Hesychasm and Prayer." *The Philokalia*, Part II.
106. *The Ladder*. Homily 28, chapter 45.
107. St Maximos Kavsokalyvites. "Conversation with St Gregory of Sinai." *The Philokalia*, Part I.
108. *The Ladder*. Homily 28, chapter 59.
109. *The Ladder*. Homily 28, chapter 59.

110. St Meletios of Galicia. "A Poem about Prayer."

111. St Dimitri of Rostov. *The Inner Man*. Part 1, chapter 4.

112. St Macarius the Great. Homily 3, chapter 1. This was also said by many other Fathers of the church.

113. St Isaac the Syrian says in his Homily 21, "Whoever has acquired constant prayer has reached the pinnacle of virtue and has become the habitation of the Holy Spirit."

114. The opinion of St Pimen the Great in the *Apophthegmata*.

Chapter 12

115. *The Philokalia*, Part II.

116. St Matoes. *Apophthegmata*, letter "M."

117. Homily 17 [St Isaac the Syrian].

Chapter 13

118. *The Unabbreviated Horologion or Book of the Hours* The Unabbreviated Horologion or Book of the Hours (Jordanville, NY: Holy Trinity Monastery, 1997), 84.

119. St Dimitri of Rostov. *Written Works*. "The Inner Man."

120. St Macarius the Great. Homily 1, chapter 3.

121. Homily 40 [St Isaac the Syrian].

122. The life of St Ignatius the God-bearer from St Dimitri of Rostov's *The Lives of the Saints*.

Chapter 14

123. "The Inner Man." Chapter 3 [St Dimitri of Rostov].

124. Homily 40 [St Isaac the Syrian].

125. "Concerning the Third Vision." *The Philokalia*, Part III.

126. Homily 31 [St Isaac the Syrian].

127. [As witnessed in the first morning prayer of St Macarius the Great: O God, cleanse me, a sinner, for I have never done anything good in Thy sight; but deliver me from the evil one, and let Thy will be done in me, that I may open mine unworthy mouth without condemnation and praise Thy holy name: of the Father and of the Son and of the Holy Spirit, now and ever and unto the ages of ages. Amen. *Prayer Book* (Jordanville, NY: Holy Trinity Publications, 2005), 15.]

128. [See Prayer VI of St Basil. *Prayer Book* (Jordanville, NY: Holy Trinity Publications, 2005), 19.]

129. "Homily on the Three Forms of Prayer." *The Philokalia*, Part I.

130. Fifteen Chapters on Hesychasm. *The Philokalia*, Part I, chapter 8.

Chapter 15

131. Homily 12 [St Isaac the Syrian].

132. According to the rite of tonsure in the small schema, the abbot, as he gives the new monk his prayer rope, commands him to pray the Jesus prayer constantly. By accepting the prayer rope, the new monk gives an oath to fulfill this command of his master.

133. Homily 21 [St Isaac the Syrian].

134. Antonio Magni Opera. PG 40: 1080.

135. *The Ladder*. Homily 4, chapter 17.

136. *The Lives of the Saints*, January 9.

137. Homily 55 [St Isaac the Syrian].

138. "Fifteen Chapters on Hesychasm." *The Philokalia*, Part I, chapter 2.

139. St Isaac the Syrian. Homily 72.

140. *The Ladder.* Homily 21, chapter 7.

141. *Apophthegmata.* "Letter H."

142. Cassiani callatio 10, cap. 10.

143. quoted by St Xanthopoulos. *The Philokalia*, Part II, chapter 21.

144. "Concerning Abba Philemon." *The Philokalia*, Part IV.

145. *The Ladder.* Homily 28, chapter 17.

146. *The Ladder.* Homily 28, chapter 31.

147. *The Ladder.* Homily 28, chapter 5, citing Psalm: 72:25, 28.

148. St Isaac the Syrian. Homily 55.

Chapter 16

149. St Isaac the Syrian. Homily 5: "We must not seek great things before their time lest we lose the gift of God because of the quickness with which we receive it. Everything that is easily gained is easily lost. Everything that is gained with pain in the heart is preserved diligently."

150. St Symeon the New Theologian. "On the First Form of Attention and Prayer." *The Philokalia*, Part I. See also Ignatius Brianchaninov, *The Field; Cultivating Salvation* (Jordanville, NY: Holy Trinity Monastery, 2016), the sections concerning the Jesus Prayer and the conversation of the elder and his disciple, pages 183 and 236.

151. St Isaac the Syrian. Homily 55.

152. See the life of St Dositheos from the book of instructions by Abba Dorotheos.

153. Homily 21 [St Isaac the Syrian].

154. Homily 21 [St Isaac the Syrian].

155. Homily 21 [St Isaac the Syrian].

156. Experience shows that any meeting with women, with debauched society, and with any other temptations exercises incomparably stronger force on a monk than on a layman who is always surrounded by temptations. The more attentive and strict the life of a monk, the more disastrous the effect. The passions within him were mortified by fasting, and so they attack with insane fierceness when the monk ceases to be watchful. If the awakened passion does not immediately kill him, it can still inflict a horrible wound. Healing this wound can require many years, bloody labors, and more than anything—a special mercy of God.

157. In the ascetic tradition, excessive water in the body is associated with sexual desire. Hence, "youthful dampness" is a euphemism for a tendency toward lustful thoughts.

158. St Mark the Ascetic. "Epistle to Monk Nicholas."

159. St Mark the Ascetic. "On Fasting and Humility."

160. St Isaiah the Solitary. Homily 8, chapter 1. This monk, who had come to understand himself profoundly, said, "Sometimes I see myself like a horse that runs around without a rider." Whoever finds this horse, sits on him, and when that rider gest off, another seizes the horse and also sits on him."

161. St John of Karpathos. *The Philokalia*, Part IV, chapter 87.

162. This original interpretation of the cherubim-guarding Paradise is taken from St Macarius the Great (Homily 37, chapter 5) and St Mark the Ascetic (Homily 6).

163. Homily 56 [St Isaac the Syrian].

164. Homily 11 [St Isaac the Syrian].

165. "Before all other spiritual gifts, the Lord gives the mind a lack of wandering." St Kallistos and St Xanthopoulos. *The Philokalia*, Part II, chapter 24.

166. See the conversation between St Maximus the Hut Burner and St Gregory of Sinai. *The Philokalia*, Part I.

167. *Apophthegmata.*

168. St Barsanuphius the Great. Answer 184.

169. St Isaac the Syrian. Homily 15.

170. [Famously, this passage diverges greatly in the LXX and Masoretic texts. I have amended the translation slightly from what is normally printed in English Bibles to better fit the Russian version—NK.]

171. *Guidance toward the Spiritual Life* of St Barsanuphius the Great and John the Prophet. Answer 59.

172. *The Ladder.* Homily 29, chapter 61, quoting Psalm 118:145 and Matthew 18:20.

173. Homily 19 [St Isaiah the Solitary].

174. Homily 56 [St Isaac the Syrian].

175. *The Philokalia*, Part I, chapter 114.

176. Instruction 11: "On Prayer."

177. From the life of St Paisius the Great, June 19.

178. Instruction 3, 4. "On the Peace of Soul and Preserving It."

179. *The Ladder.* Homily 25, chapter 3.

180. Homily 48 [St Isaac the Syrian].

181. "To those who would think to be justified by deeds." Chapter 35.

182. *The Ladder.* Homily 25, 28.

183. St Symeon the New Theologian calls such a state of our nature its "tearing apart" in his 3rd Homily.

184. St Symeon the New Theologian. Homily 10.

185. *The Ladder.* Homily 29, chapter 10.

186. *The Ladder.* Homily 28, chapter 38.

187. St Nilus of Sinai. *Chapters on Prayer.* Chapter 61.

188. "When the Lord turned again the captivity of Zion, then were we like unto them that are comforted. Then was our mouth filled with joy, and our tongue with merry-making; then shall they say among the nations, the Lord hath done great things for them" (Ps 125:1–2). In the Psalter, the "nations" are often understood figuratively as the demons. In other words, the ascetic will only be delivered from slavery to the demons when his mind ceases to be distracted by their offered thoughts and fantasies, when he begins to pray with pure prayer, always united with spiritual consolation. This deliverance is obvious to the demons: "Then shall they say among the nations, the Lord hath done great things for them."

Chapter 17

189. [Note: There is a lengthy article on the Jesus Prayer in *The Field*, the first volume of St Ignatius's collected works. Since this particular essay has its unique features, it was considered not excessive to include it in this second volume. There are some repetitions, of course, but we must say that they are only repetitions of salvific truths, and this is not without benefit. "For me to write the same things to you is not tedious, but for you it is safe" (Phil 3:1)—NK.]

190. Schemamonk Vasily Volianomerul'skii, whose works were published in the nineteenth century together with Paisius Velichkovsky.

191. St Nilus of Sora. Homily 2.

192. "Fifteen Chapters on Stillness." *The Philokalia*, Part I, chapter 2.

193. "Jesus" means "Saviour" in Hebrew.

194. See the Psalter with additions.

195. *The Lives of the Saints*. September 27.

196. St Nilus of Sora. Homily 9.

197. "Very Useful Chapters on How to Sing." *The Philokalia*, Part I.

198. St John of the Ladder. *The Ladder*. Homily 21, chapter 7.

199. St Gregory of Sinai. "On Breathing." *The Philokalia*, Part I, chapter 3.

200. *The Answers of St Barsanuphius and St John*. Answer 301.

201. Quoted by St Kallistos and St Igantius Xanthopoulos. *The Philokalia*, Part II, chapter 49.

202. Homily 2, chapters 1, 2 [St John of the Ladder].

203. St Kallistos and St Ignatius Xanthopoulos. *The Philokalia*, Part I, chapter 56.

204. "On the third kind of attentiveness." *The Philokalia*, Part IV, chapter 1.

205. *The Philokalia*, Part I.

206. "How to Find the Active Life." *The Philokalia*, Part I, chapter 4.

207. Answer 181 [St Barsanuphius the Great].

208. Homily 8 on the Epistle to the Romans [St John Chrysostom].

209. Answer 74. St Gregory of Sinai, "15 Chapters on Stillness." *The Philokalia*, Part I, chapter 4.

210. "Chapters on the Prayer of the Mind." Chapter 1.

211. "Chapters on the Prayer of the Mind." Chapter 4.

212. Quoted by Elder Vasily in his introduction to the books of St Gregory of Sinai.

213. St Nilus of Sora, Homily 11.

214. Homily 11 [St Nilus of Sora].

215. The writings and life of St Paisius Velichkovsky, published in Russian by the Optina Hermitage in 1847.

216. *The Ladder*. Homily 28, chapters 17, 19.

217. *The Ladder*. Homily 4, chapter 93.

218. "To Those Who Think to Be Justified by Deeds." *The Philokalia*, Part I, chapter 34.

219. *The Ladder*. Homily 28, chapter 51.

220. *The Ladder*. Chapter 14.

221. *The Ladder*. Homily 2.

222. Answer 115 [St Barsanuphius the Great].

223. Instruction 32 [Hieromonk Dorotheos].

224. Very few fathers instruct one to unite the mind with the heart soon after the beginning of the prayerful labor. Usually, many years must pass between the beginning of the labor and the union of the mind with the heart through grace. We must prove the sincerity of our intentions through constancy and long-suffering.

225. [This is a direct translation of the Slavonic (LXX). The English reading differs (Masoretic)—NK.]

226. Instruction 32 [St Seraphim of Sarov *The Spiritual Instructions*].

227. Instruction 29 [St Seraphim of Sarov *The Spiritual Instructions*].

228. Instruction 4 [St Seraphim of Sarov *The Spiritual Instructions*].

229. Instruction 11 [St Seraphim of Sarov *The Spiritual Instructions*].

230. Instruction 6 [St Seraphim of Sarov *The Spiritual Instructions*].

231. *The Ladder*. Homily 28, chapter 56.

232. *The Philokalia*, Part IV.

233. Answer 177 [St Barsanuphius the Great].

234. See Matthew 22:12–13.

235. St Barsanuphius the Great and John the Prophet, answer 325.

236. *The Ladder*. Homily 28, chapter 64.

237. St Kallistos and St Ignatius Xanthopoulos. *The Philokalia,* Part II, chapter 5, Instruction 5 of St Seraphim of Sarov.

238. St Barsanuphius and St John the Prophet, Answer 264, 274. These answers were given to Abba Dorotheos, who by the blessing of these fathers practiced constant remembrance of God, that is, the Jesus Prayer of the mind. The Fathers commanded the Abba not to weaken in this labor, but to sow with hope. Answer 263.

239. Answer 111 [St Barsanuphius and St John the Prophet].

240. St Hesychius of Jerusalem. "On Vigilance." *The Philokalia*, Part II, chapters 1, 3, 5.

241. See also Blessed Nicephoros. "On Vigilance and the Preservation of the Heart." *The Philokalia*, Part II. St Symeon the New Theologian. "On the Third Form of Prayer." *The Philokalia*, Part I.

242. *The Ladder*. Homily 28, chapter 45.

243. *The Philokalia*, Part I.

244. See St Isaac the Syrian. Homily 68.

245. *The Ladder*. Homily 28, chapter 51.

246. *The Ladder*. Homily 28, chapters 16, 21, 27.

247. "On How One Must Sing." *The Philokalia*, Part I.

248. St Isaac the Syrian. Homily 55.

249. Homily 2 [St Nilus of Sora].

250. "15 Chapters on Stillness." Chapters 2, 8 [St Gregory of Sinai, "On Stillness and Prayer" found in *The Philokalia*].

251. "Instruction in Silence and Prayer. How to Acquire Action in Prayer."

252. "On Silence: How to Speak the Prayer."

253. "How a Hesychast Must Sit and Practice the Prayer."

254. "On Silence and the Two Forms of Prayer. In 15 chapters." Chapter 14.

255. See St Isaac the Syrian. Homily 78.

256. St Nilus of Sinai. "On prayer." *The Philokalia*, Part IV, chapter 61.

257. *The Philokalia*, Part II.

258. See chapters 19, 45 of their book. [*The Philokalia*].

259. See chapter 38 [*The Philokalia*].

260. See chapter 53 [*The Philokalia*].

261. See chapter 24 [*The Philokalia*].

262. See the heading of chapter 24 [*The Philokalia*].

263. chapter 14 [*The Philokalia*].

264. See St Isaac the Syrian. Homily 55.

265. *Apophthegmata*.

266. Homily 41 [St Isaac the Syrian].

267. Chapter 52 [*The Philokalia*].

268. *The Ladder*. Homily 4, chapter 141.

269. Homily 74 [St Isaac the Syrian].

270. See his Instruction 10 [St Dorotheos].

271. See St Kallistos. "The Model of Attention in Prayer." *The Philokalia*, Part IV.

272. *The Philokalia*, Part I.

273. "Concerning the Spiritual Law." *The Philokalia*, Part I, chapter 4.

274. A letter of St Paisius to Elder Theodosius, published in *Optina Hermitage* (1847).

275. Homily 1, chapter 3. Homily 2, chapter 15 [St Macarius the Great].

276. "On Prayer." *The Philokalia*, Part IV, chapter 139.

277. "On Prayer." *The Philokalia*, Part IV, chapters 9, 10, and others

278. "On Prayer." *The Philokalia*, Part IV, chapters 91, 100. *The Philokalia*, Part II, chapter 73.

279. See *The Philokalia*, Part I, chapter 13.

280. Instruction 29 [St Seraphim].

281. "The Schism of Barlaam," Part 2 of Bishop Innocent's *Ecclesiastical History*.

282. *Dictionnaire Thologique par Bergier.* Volume *IV.* Hesichistes.

283. Instruction 12 [St Seraphim of Sarov].

284. Homily 12, chapter 43 [St Macarius the Great].

285. See, for example, the *Encyclopedic Dictionary* of Starchevky, under "Hesychasts."

286. [See "On Humility: A Conversation between an Elder and His Disciple," in *The Field; Cultivating Salvation*, by Ignatius Brianchaninov (Jordanville, NY: Holy Trinity Monastery, 2016), 174.]

287. Introduction to the book of St Gregory of Sinai.

288. Instruction 5.

289. *The Scroll.* Chapter 4.

Chapter 18

290. A note concerning the title of the essay: this essay is taken from the experiences of a certain monk who practiced the prayer of the mind and reached the spiritual drunkenness of which St Isaac the Syrian speaks in his Homily 55. This drunkenness is a spiritual perception, as the same St Isaac explained in his Homily 38: "Spiritual wisdom is a perception of Eternal Life, and Life Eternal is a divine perception, that is, gifted by the Holy Spirit." St Macarius speaks of spiritual perceptions in his Homily 7, as does St Symeon the New Theologian in his 1st Homily. St Gregory of Sinai and St Nilus of Sora call it the prayerful action of grace. The title "wanderer" is also used by St Macarius in his 4th Homily.

Chapter 19

291. Homily 58, according to the Slavonic translation. St John of the Ladder cites these words in *The Ladder*: "Who has become worthy of this dispassion of the Syrian before the coming glory? The glorious one among the prophets, David, said to the Lord: 'O spare me, that I may recover my strength' (Ps 38:14). The ascetic of the Lord cried out, spare within me the waves of Your grace" (Homily 29, chapter 8). A young monk named Zechariah reached a similar state. He was given a special, perceptible grace of the Holy Spirit because of his humility. St John of the Ladder also says, "The fire that descends into the heart restores prayer. When it stands up and ascends into heaven, then the fire descends into the upper room of the soul" (Homily 27, chapter 45).

292. St Mark the Ascetic, *On the Spiritual Laws*. Chapters 13, 14.

Chapter 20

293. See the text for the service of baptism. [The Order of Holy Baptism, trans. Laurence Campbell (Jordanville, NY: Holy Trinity Monastery, 2006).]

294. St Gregory Palamas's letter to the nun Xenia.

295. If you are interested in the distinction between the image and likeness of God, read the works of St Dimitri of Rostov (*The Chronicle*, volume 4).

296. Homily 31, chapter 4. Homily 31, chapter 4 [St Macarius the Great].

297. Abba Dorotheus. Homily 1. "On Rejecting the World."

298. St Mark the Ascetic. "On the Spiritual Laws," chapter 4.

299. St Peter of Damascus. *The Philokalia*, Part III. Book 1, chapter 2.

300. Collected letters, volume 15, letter 73 [St Tikhon the Bishop of Voronezh and Wonderworker of Zadonsk].

301. Collected letters, volume 15, letter 70.

302. Collected letters, volume 15, letter 11.

303. Abba Dorotheos. Instruction 1.

304. St John Chrysostom, as quoted by St Kallistos and St Ignatius Xanthopoulous in chapter 92 of their work on prayer and hesychasm. *The Philokalia*, Part II.

305. *The Ladder*. Homily 4, chapter 53.

306. The Gospel is filled with the Lord's rebukes of their evil ways, especially in chapter 23 of Matthew and in chapter 8 of John. ·

307. St John of the Ladder. *The Ladder*. Homily 29, chapter 5.

308. Homily 85 [St Isaac the Syrian].

309. Homily 8, chapters 4, 5 [St Macarius the Great].

310. See John 14:32.

311. E.g. the lives of Great martyrs Dimitri of Thessalonica and George.

312. Histoire du Christianisme par Fleury. Livre 5, chapter 17.

313. *The Philokalia*, Part III. Book 1. "For without humble-mindedness it is impossible to be saved."

314. St Pimen the Great. *Apophthegmata Patrum*.

315. This is the advice of St Peter Damascene. "The necessary and abundant work of the seven bodily actions." *The Philokalia*, Part III, Book 1.

316. *The Ladder*. Homily 14, chapter 30.

317. *The Ladder*. Homily 14, chapter 52.

318. *The Ladder*. Homily 14, chapter 29.

319. See Romans 8:10.

320. See 1 Corinthians 15:47–49.

321. See Romans 8:16.

322. *The Ladder*. Homily 14, chapter 22.

323. *Apophthegmata Patrum*.

324. *The Ladder*. Homily 14, chapter 21.

325. *The Ladder*. Homily 14, chapter 21.

326. St Simeon the Fool for Christ revealed the reason for Origen's errors and perdition was the rejection of the Cross of Christ.

327. *Apophthegmata Patrum*.

328. Instruction on how not to trust your own reason.

329. "On the Spiritual Law" [St Mark the Ascetic].

330. St Pambo in *Apophthegmata Patrum*.

Chapter 21

331. The Holy Fathers call the first state the "natural state," the second, the "sub-natural state," and the third, "supernatural." See St Isaac the Syrian, Homily 4, Abba Dorotheos and others.

332. St Peter Damascene, summarizing the spiritual visions of grace given to the mind of the ascetic of Christ when he is purified, mentions that one of these visions is the vision of man's fall. See "On the eight spiritual visions."

333. Abba Dorotheos, Instruction 1.

334. Homily 4, chapter 16. This becomes clear when we read the exorcism read before the sacrament of baptism. Fallen man has literally become the abode not only of sin, but of Satan. By the sacrament of baptism, Satan is cast out of man, but through a slothful and sinful life, Satan can reenter the baptized Christian, as we will describe in more detail later [St Macarius the Great].

335. Homily 21, chapter 1 [St Macarius the Great].

336. Answer 210 [St Barsanuphius the Great].

337. *The Philokalia*, Part II, chapter 49.

338. Homily 21, chapters 3, 4 [St Macarius the Great].

339. Instruction 13, how to endure temptations. Our own Russian ascetic, St Seraphim of Sarov, said, "You must be kind to your soul in its weakness and infirmity. You must endure your insufficiencies, as you must endure them in others. But at the same time you must not grow lazy, but push yourself to get better. Have you eaten too much or done some other wrong of this nature, typical of human weakness? So you did it. Do not be distressed by this and do not add harm to harm, but courageously inspire yourself to correction, all the while striving to preserve the peace of the soul, according to the words of the apostle: 'Happy is he who does not condemn himself in what he approves' (Romans 14:22)."

340. A free-form prayer taken from various Scriptural references, including Psalm 24:15–20, 21:21–22, Matthew 16:16, 1 Peter 5:8, and Job 2:6.

341. Homily 4, chapters 6–8 [St Macarius the Great].

342. *The Philokalia*, Part I, chapter 117.

343. St Macarius the Great, Homily 27, chapters 4, 5, 18.

344. Homily 7, chapter 14 [St Macarius the Great].

345. See Exodus 3:21–22.

346. Homily 31. Here the word *action* is used to indicate spiritual labor, because the Fathers most often use this word to indicate the labor of the thoughts and the heart. The word *labor* usually refers only to physical asceticism (see also St Barsanuphius the Great, Answer 210).

347. Homily 1, chapter 1.

348. *The Philokalia*, Part I. "43 chapters on theology."

349. Abba Dorotheos, Instruction 1.

350. See 2 Peter 1:4.

351. The Lord freed us by holy baptism, having given us forgiveness of sins and the ability to do good if we desire it. He gave us the strength not to be forced to incline to evil, for whoever is subject to sin, is distracted and oppressed by sin, as it is said in Scripture, that ever man is tied with the bonds of his own sin (see Prov 5:22). Abba Dorotheos said the following in his first instruction: "Baptism does not take away our free will. It gives us freedom, so that the devil no longer can do violence to us when we do not allow him. After baptism, it is given to our will to live either in the commandments of Christ, the Master and God into Whom we were baptized, to walk in the way He commanded, or to return through evil actions to our enemy and adversary, the devil" (see also St Symeon the New Theologian, *The Philokalia*, Part I, chapter 109).

352. See Matthew 12:43–45.

By baptism, the evil spirit is cast out, and so it travels about seeking other souls, but in them, it finds no rest, for rest for the demon is only found in distressing the baptized by evil actions. The unbaptized belong to them from the beginning (conception), and so he returns to the baptized man with seven other spirits. Just as there are seven gifts of the Spirit, so also there are seven evil spirits. When the devil returns to the baptized and finds him slothful, that is, not living that active life that wards off the enemy, then, having entered into him again, he wars against him even more fiercely than before. Whoever has been washed clean by baptism but has been again defiled later has no hope for a second baptism. His only hope is much-laboring repentance.

This is Blessed Theophylact's explanation of the Gospel passage.

353. See Galatians 3:27.

354. Homily 3. "On Baptism" [St Mark the Ascetic].

355. "'When sinners spring up as the grass, and when all the workers of wickedness do flourish, it is so they may be consumed for ever and ever' (Psalm 91:8). These 'sinners' are the passionate thoughts, who like grass are weak and have no strength. So, when passionate thoughts only arise in the soul, then they flourish, that is, become revealed, as workers of wickedness. They will be consumed forever and ever, for when the passions become obvious to the ascetic, then they become destroyed by the ascetics. Pay attention to the pattern: first passionate thoughts arise, thereby revealing their flourishing, and only afterwards will they be destroyed" (Abba Dorotheos. Instruction 13, *On the Endurance of Temptations*).

356. "On the Spiritual Law," chapter 2 [St Mark the Ascetic].

357. See St Macarius the Great. Homily 7, chapter 26.

358. "Through baptism, the Christian is transformed in mind, word, and deed, and, according to the strength given him, becomes the same as the One Who gave birth to him" (20th moral canon of St Basil the Great).

359. St Mark the Ascetic, "On Baptism." St Kallistos and St Ignatius Xanthopoulos, *The Philokalia*, Part II, chapters 1–6.

360. Ioanni Chrisostomi in Epistola II ad Cor. Homila 7, cap. 5.

361. This account is taken from Fleury's Ecclesiastical History. A similar story is also told in *The Lives of the Saints* (September 15), where a certain Porphyrius, who plunged himself in water to mock baptism, was transformed by the action into a Christian. This occurred before the gaze of Emperor Julian the Apostate. Porphyrius confessed Christ, accused the emperor of ungodliness, and was cruelly tortured and eventually martyred.

362. Oration 18. Translated by Charles Gordon Browne and James Edward Swallow. From Nicene and Post-Nicene Fathers, Second Series, vol. 7, ed. Philip Schaff and Henry Wace (Buffalo, NY: Christian Literature Publishing Co., 1894). Revised and edited for New Advent by Kevin Knight.

363. Oration 40. Translated by Charles Gordon Browne and James Edward Swallow. From Nicene and Post-Nicene Fathers, Second Series, vol. 7, ed. Philip Schaff and Henry Wace (Buffalo, NY: Christian Literature Publishing Co., 1894). Revised and edited for New Advent by Kevin Knight.

364. See *The Lives of the Saints*, January 1.

365. See John 7:38.

366. According to St John of the Ladder. *The Ladder*, Homily 4, "On Obedience."

367. See especially the works of St Gregory of Nazianzus, St Cyril of Jerusalem, and St John Chrysostom concerning catechization and baptism.

368. "The law of freedom," said St Mark the Ascetic, "is only understood by the true intellect. It is only understood by the doing of the commandments (of the Gospel)" ("On the Spiritual Law," chapter 32).

369. St Mark the Ascetic. The conclusion of his "On Baptism."

370. Homily 21 [St Isaac the Syrian].

371. St John of the Ladder. *The Ladder*. Homily 7.

372. Homily 5, "Advice Given by the Mind to the Heart" [St Mark the Ascetic].

373. Letter to Monk Nicholas.

374. For more on this topic, read *The Sunflower* by St John of Tobolsk (Maximovich) John of Tobolsk, The Sunflower—Conforming the Will of Man to the Will of God (Jordanville, NY: Holy Trinity Publications, 2018).

375. "On those who think to be justified by works," chapters 193, 197, 150–156.

376. Homily 36.

377. From the life of St Mary of Egypt by St Sophronius of Jerusalem. Interestingly, she said of herself: "I am a sinful woman, but I was guarded by holy baptism."

378. Homily 1, chapter 13.

379. St Peter Damascene. *The Philokalia*, Part III, Book 1, chapter 1.

380. St Isaiah the Solitary. Homily 11, "On the Mustard Seed."

381. According to the explanation of Theophylact of Bulgaria.

382. St Kallistos and St Ignatius Xanthopoulos, *The Philokalia*, Part II, chapter 92.

383. According to St Cyril of Jerusalem, in the first centuries of Christianity, pagans who saw the sacrament of baptism only saw the external rite and did not understand its essence, and so they mocked the insignificance, as they saw it, of the external aspect of the rite.

384. *Apophthegmata Patrum.*

385. St Symeon the New Theologian said, "A meticulous fulfillment of the commandments of the Gospel teaches a man how infirm he is" (*The Philokalia*, Part I). This means that by living by the commandments, man is led into the state of the first beatitude, "poverty of spirit," which gives rise to spiritual sorrow, which itself gives rise to meekness. The succession of beatitudes is especially well explained by St Peter Damascene in *The Philokalia*, Part III, Book 1.

386. Homily 48 [St Isaac the Syrian].

387. Homily 89 [St Isaac the Syrian].

388. Homily 89 [St Isaac the Syrian].

389. Homily 9 [St Macarius the Great].

390. Homily 55 [St Isaac the Syrian].

391. *The Ladder,* Homily 26.

392. *The Ladder,* Homily 27.

393. *The Philokalia*, Part III. "On the Seven Physical Labors."

394. *The Philokalia*, Part III. "On the Eight Visions of the Mind."

395. The prayer of St Ephraim the Syrian, read during Lent. Prayer Book (Jordanville, NY: Holy trinity Monastery, 2005), 171.

396. St Theoleptus, Metropolitan of Philadelphia. "Homily on the secret work of the soul." *The Philokalia*, Part IV, Book 2.

397. The beginning of our confidence, that is, the pledge of our covenant with God, is the grace of baptism, planted within us when we enter union with Christ, like the mustard seed. The preservation of this gift of grace is its development. As the Lord said, "He who does not gather with Me scatters" (Luke 11:23).

Subject Index

Note: In citations the letter "n" followed my a number refers to the note number on that page; for example p 357 n.291 refers to the text associated with note 291 on page 357.

Scripture Index

Note: In citations the letter "n" and a number refers to the note number on that page; for example p 357 n.291 refers to the text associated with note 291 on page 357.

Old Testament

Deuteronomy
    6:5, p 183
    32:9, p 62

Ecclesiasticus
    1:15, p 109
    3:1, p 215
    4:10, p 240
    10:4, p 126
    11:6, p 233
Exodus
    3:1, p 73
Ezekiel
    16:49, p 175

Genesis
    1:5, p 70
    1:25, p 107
    1:27, p 275
    1:31, p 107
    2:9, 17; 3:2, p 306
    2:17, p 322
    3:5, p 169
    3:19, p 269
    3:23–24, p 100
    5:3, p 275
    6:3, p 307
    22:12, p 54
    32, p 11
    32:10, p 12

33:4, p 12
37:5–8, p 13
37:10, p 14
37:21, p 15
37:25, p 16
37:26–27, p 16
37:9, p 14
39, p 17
41, p 20
42, p 23
43, p 26
45, p 30
46, p 31
47, p 31
48, p 34
50, p 37

Isaiah
    1:6, p 278
    1:10, p 62
    6:7, p 227
    8:12–13, p 251
    9:5–6, p 185
    9:6 (NKJV), p 281
    11:2–3, p 51
    21:3, p 234
    53:2–3, p 338
    53:12, p 338
    56:7, p 159
    57:15, p 136